IDW PUBLISHING
SAN DIEGO, CA

IDW PUBLISHING IS:
TED ADAMS, PUBLISHER
CHRIS RYALL, EDITOR-IN-CHIEF
ROBBIE ROBBINS, DESIGN DIRECTOR
KRIS OPRISKO, VICE PRESIDENT
ALEX GARNER, ART DIRECTOR
DAN TAYLOR, EDITOR
TOM B. LONG, DESIGNER
AARON MYERS, DISTRIBUTION MANAGER
CHANCE BOREN, EDITORIAL ASSISTANT
YUMIKO MIYANO, BUSINESS DEVELOPMENT
RICK PRIVMAN, BUSINESS DEVELOPMENT

ISBN: 1-932382-71-2
08 07 06 05   1 2 3 4 5
WWW.IDWPUBLISHING.COM

Special thanks to Kamaria Hill and Virginia King of 20th Century Fox for their invaluable assistance.

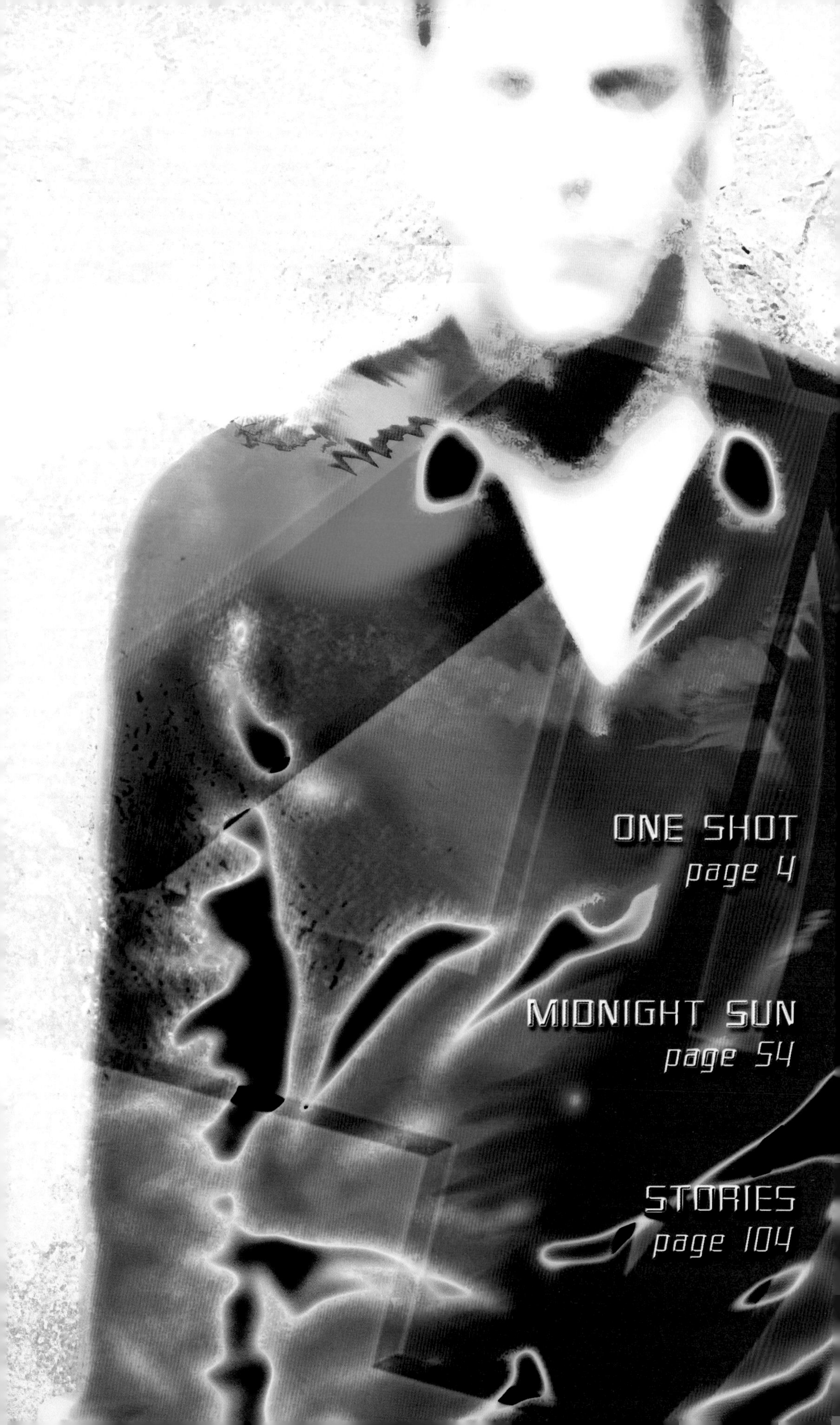

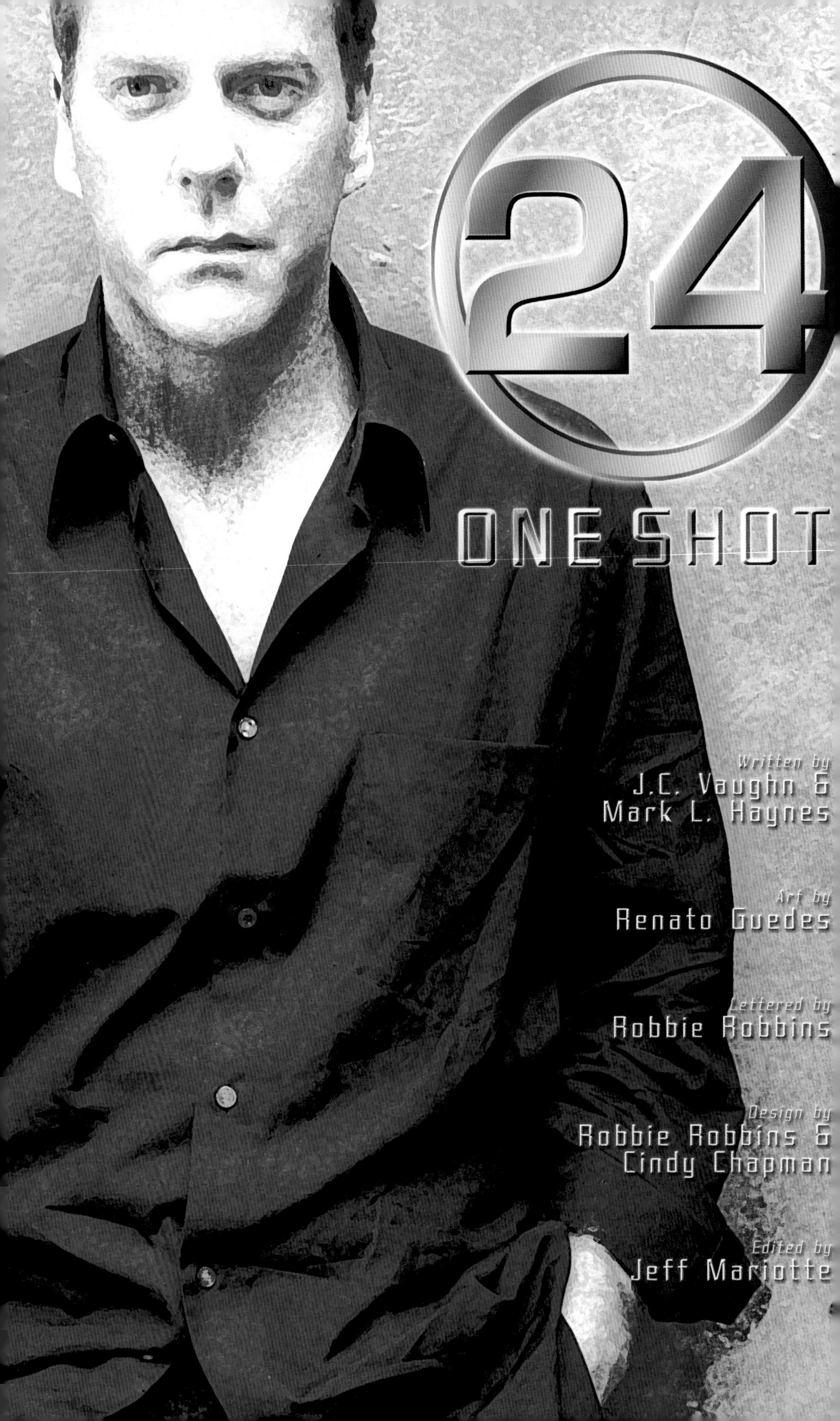

24
ONE SHOT

Written by
J.C. Vaughn &
Mark L. Haynes

Art by
Renato Guedes

Lettered by
Robbie Robbins

Design by
Robbie Robbins &
Cindy Chapman

Edited by
Jeff Mariotte

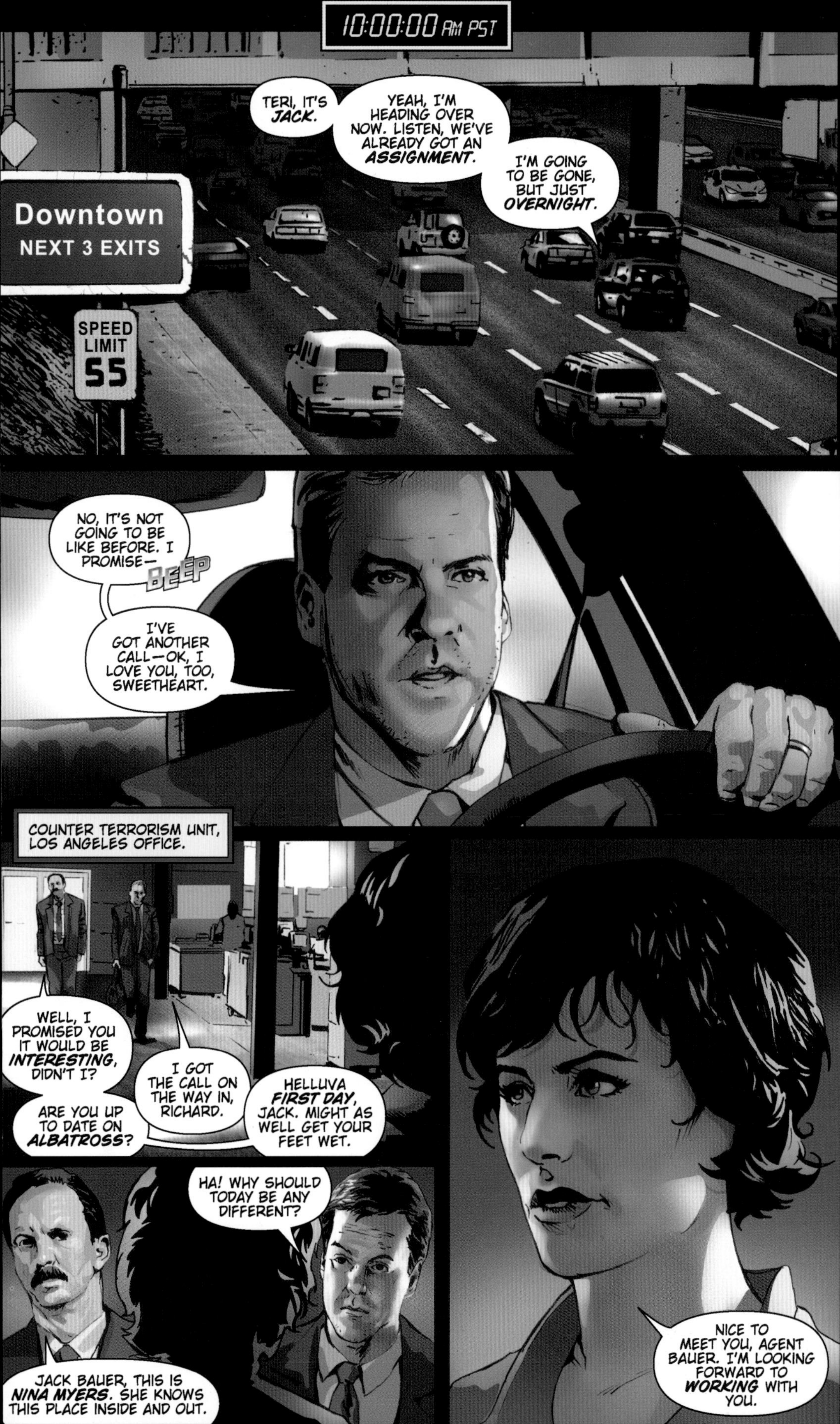
10:00:00 AM PST
Downtown
NEXT 3 EXITS
SPEED LIMIT 55
TERI, IT'S JACK.
YEAH, I'M HEADING OVER NOW. LISTEN, WE'VE ALREADY GOT AN ASSIGNMENT.
I'M GOING TO BE GONE, BUT JUST OVERNIGHT.
NO, IT'S NOT GOING TO BE LIKE BEFORE. I PROMISE—
BEEP
I'VE GOT ANOTHER CALL—OK, I LOVE YOU, TOO, SWEETHEART.
COUNTER TERRORISM UNIT, LOS ANGELES OFFICE.
WELL, I PROMISED YOU IT WOULD BE INTERESTING, DIDN'T I?
ARE YOU UP TO DATE ON ALBATROSS?
I GOT THE CALL ON THE WAY IN, RICHARD.
HELLUVA FIRST DAY, JACK. MIGHT AS WELL GET YOUR FEET WET.
HA! WHY SHOULD TODAY BE ANY DIFFERENT?
JACK BAUER, THIS IS NINA MYERS. SHE KNOWS THIS PLACE INSIDE AND OUT.
NICE TO MEET YOU, AGENT BAUER. I'M LOOKING FORWARD TO WORKING WITH YOU.

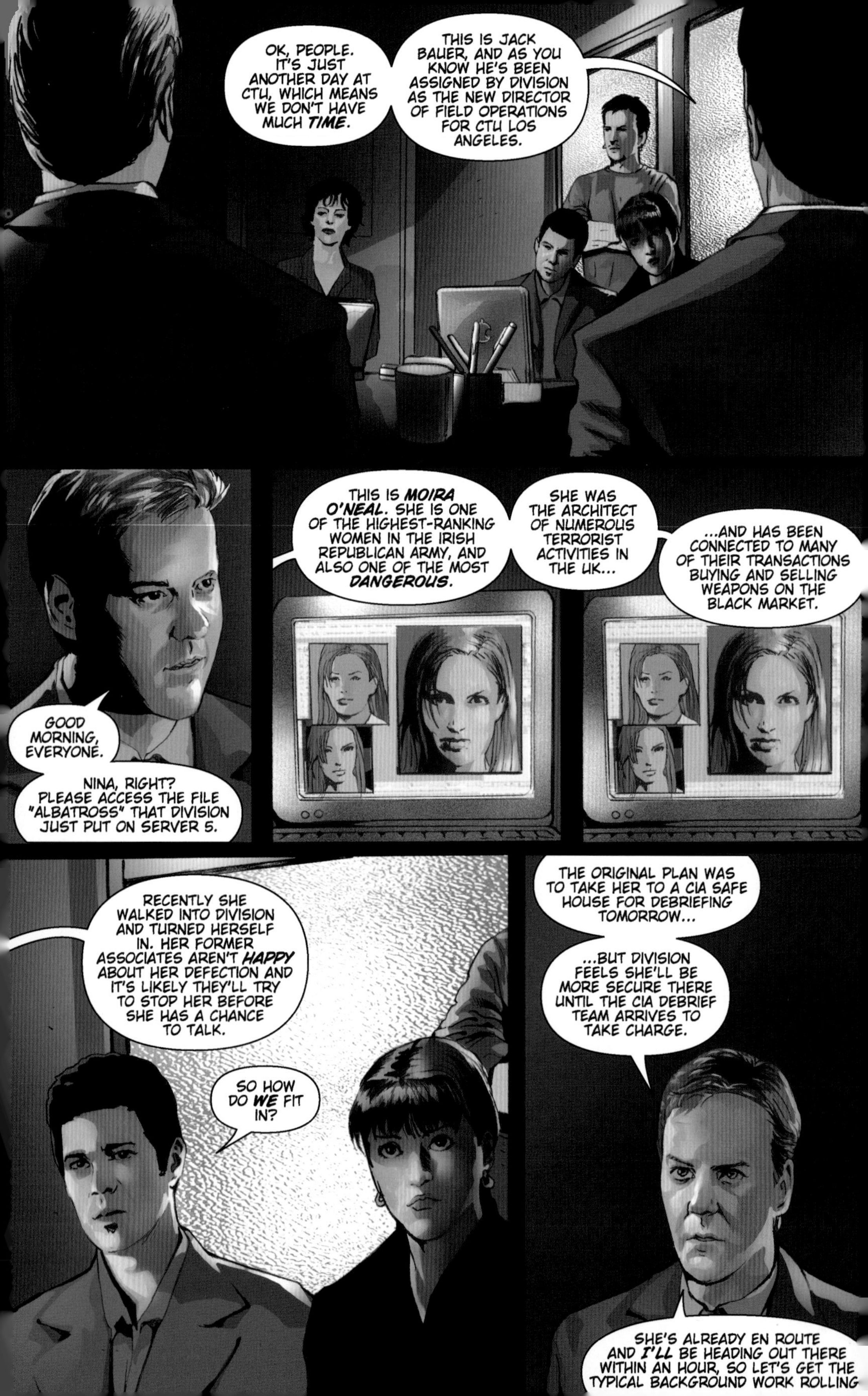
OK, PEOPLE. IT'S JUST ANOTHER DAY AT CTU, WHICH MEANS WE DON'T HAVE MUCH *TIME*.
THIS IS JACK BAUER, AND AS YOU KNOW HE'S BEEN ASSIGNED BY DIVISION AS THE NEW DIRECTOR OF FIELD OPERATIONS FOR CTU LOS ANGELES.
GOOD MORNING, EVERYONE.
NINA, RIGHT? PLEASE ACCESS THE FILE "ALBATROSS" THAT DIVISION JUST PUT ON SERVER 5.
THIS IS *MOIRA O'NEAL*. SHE IS ONE OF THE HIGHEST-RANKING WOMEN IN THE IRISH REPUBLICAN ARMY, AND ALSO ONE OF THE MOST *DANGEROUS*.
SHE WAS THE ARCHITECT OF NUMEROUS TERRORIST ACTIVITIES IN THE UK...
...AND HAS BEEN CONNECTED TO MANY OF THEIR TRANSACTIONS BUYING AND SELLING WEAPONS ON THE BLACK MARKET.
RECENTLY SHE WALKED INTO DIVISION AND TURNED HERSELF IN. HER FORMER ASSOCIATES AREN'T *HAPPY* ABOUT HER DEFECTION AND IT'S LIKELY THEY'LL TRY TO STOP HER BEFORE SHE HAS A CHANCE TO TALK.
SO HOW DO *WE* FIT IN?
THE ORIGINAL PLAN WAS TO TAKE HER TO A CIA SAFE HOUSE FOR DEBRIEFING TOMORROW...
...BUT DIVISION FEELS SHE'LL BE MORE SECURE THERE UNTIL THE CIA DEBRIEF TEAM ARRIVES TO TAKE CHARGE.
SHE'S ALREADY EN ROUTE AND *I'LL* BE HEADING OUT THERE WITHIN AN HOUR, SO LET'S GET THE TYPICAL BACKGROUND WORK ROLLING

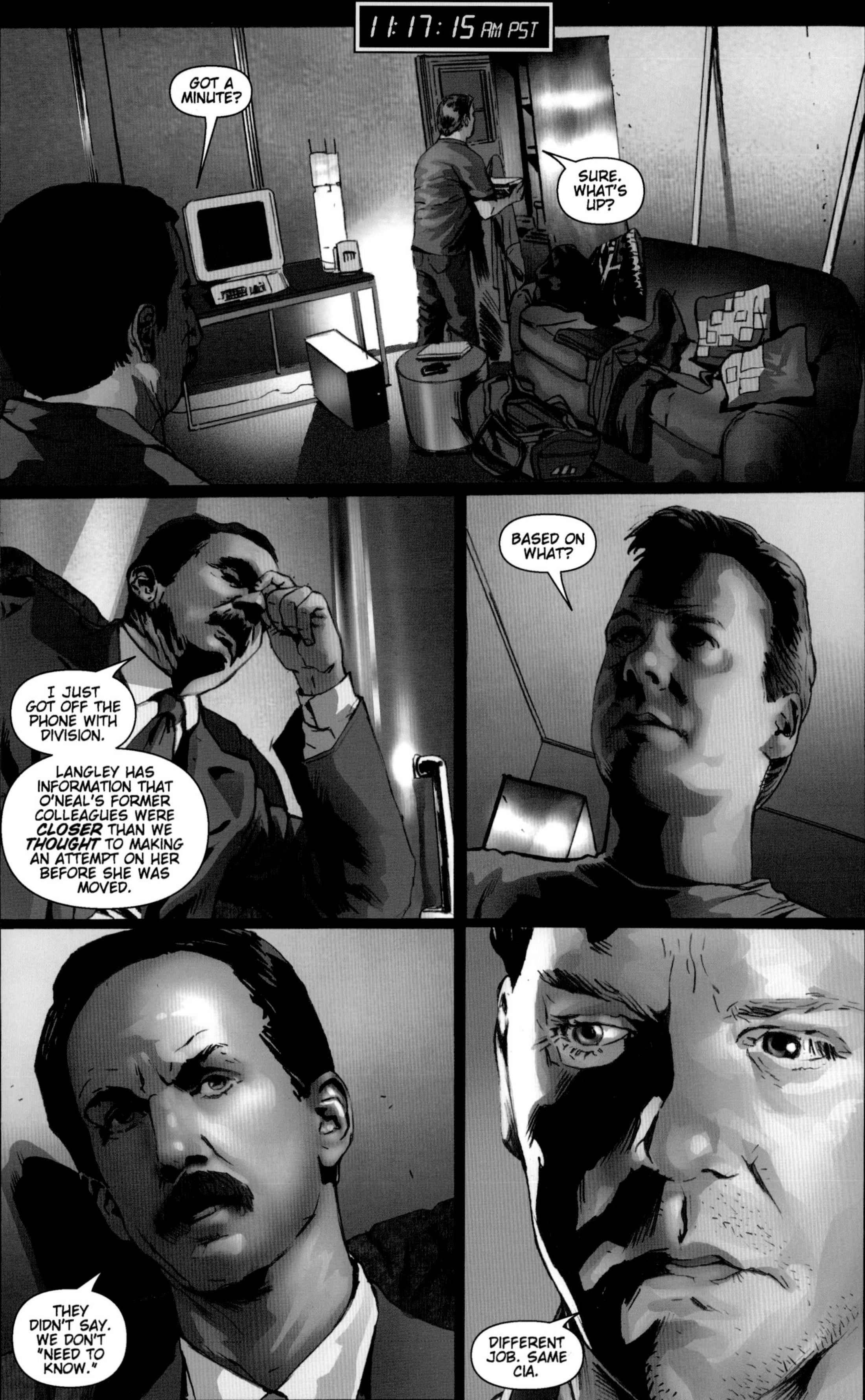
11:17:15 AM PST
GOT A MINUTE?
SURE. WHAT'S UP?
I JUST GOT OFF THE PHONE WITH DIVISION.
LANGLEY HAS INFORMATION THAT O'NEAL'S FORMER COLLEAGUES WERE CLOSER THAN WE THOUGHT TO MAKING AN ATTEMPT ON HER BEFORE SHE WAS MOVED.
BASED ON WHAT?
THEY DIDN'T SAY. WE DON'T "NEED TO KNOW."
DIFFERENT JOB. SAME CIA.

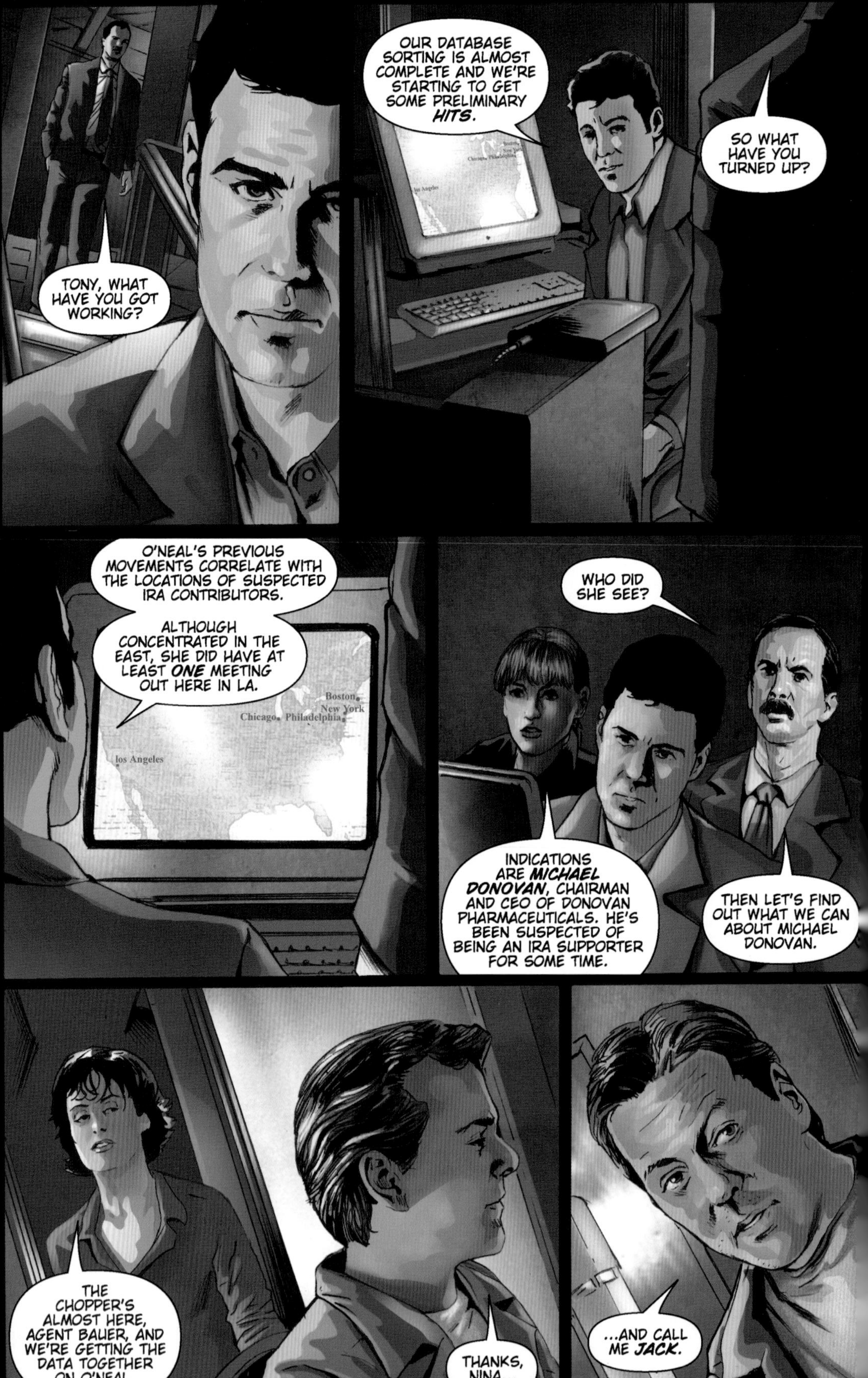
TONY, WHAT HAVE YOU GOT WORKING?
OUR DATABASE SORTING IS ALMOST COMPLETE AND WE'RE STARTING TO GET SOME PRELIMINARY HITS.
SO WHAT HAVE YOU TURNED UP?
O'NEAL'S PREVIOUS MOVEMENTS CORRELATE WITH THE LOCATIONS OF SUSPECTED IRA CONTRIBUTORS.
ALTHOUGH CONCENTRATED IN THE EAST, SHE DID HAVE AT LEAST ONE MEETING OUT HERE IN LA.
Boston
New York
Chicago
Philadelphia
los Angeles
WHO DID SHE SEE?
INDICATIONS ARE MICHAEL DONOVAN, CHAIRMAN AND CEO OF DONOVAN PHARMACEUTICALS. HE'S BEEN SUSPECTED OF BEING AN IRA SUPPORTER FOR SOME TIME.
THEN LET'S FIND OUT WHAT WE CAN ABOUT MICHAEL DONOVAN.
THE CHOPPER'S ALMOST HERE, AGENT BAUER, AND WE'RE GETTING THE DATA TOGETHER ON O'NEAL.
THANKS, NINA...
...AND CALL ME JACK.

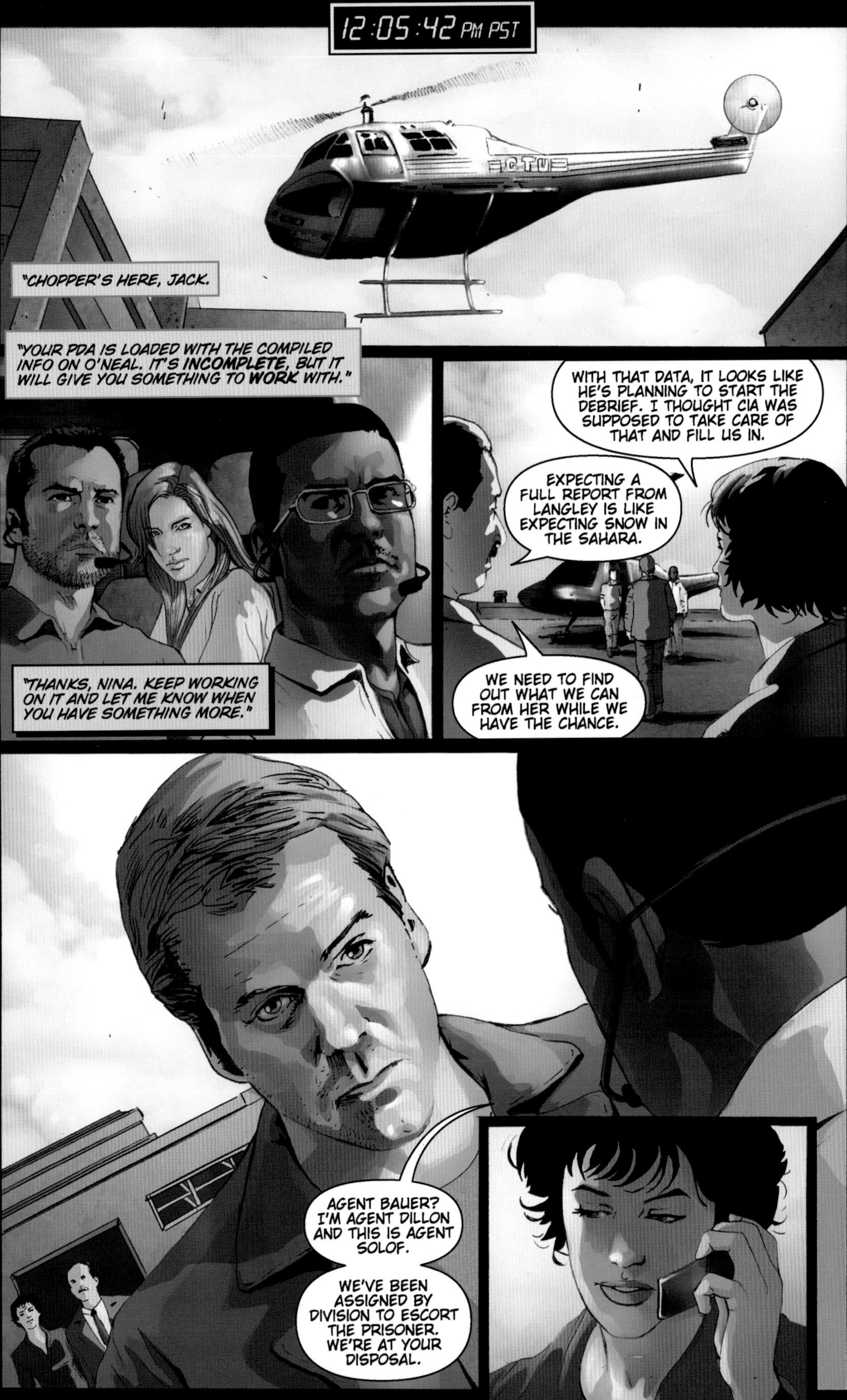
12:05:42 PM PST
"CHOPPER'S HERE, JACK.
"YOUR PDA IS LOADED WITH THE COMPILED INFO ON O'NEAL. IT'S INCOMPLETE, BUT IT WILL GIVE YOU SOMETHING TO WORK WITH."
"THANKS, NINA. KEEP WORKING ON IT AND LET ME KNOW WHEN YOU HAVE SOMETHING MORE."
WITH THAT DATA, IT LOOKS LIKE HE'S PLANNING TO START THE DEBRIEF. I THOUGHT CIA WAS SUPPOSED TO TAKE CARE OF THAT AND FILL US IN.
EXPECTING A FULL REPORT FROM LANGLEY IS LIKE EXPECTING SNOW IN THE SAHARA.
WE NEED TO FIND OUT WHAT WE CAN FROM HER WHILE WE HAVE THE CHANCE.
AGENT BAUER? I'M AGENT DILLON AND THIS IS AGENT SOLOF.
WE'VE BEEN ASSIGNED BY DIVISION TO ESCORT THE PRISONER. WE'RE AT YOUR DISPOSAL.

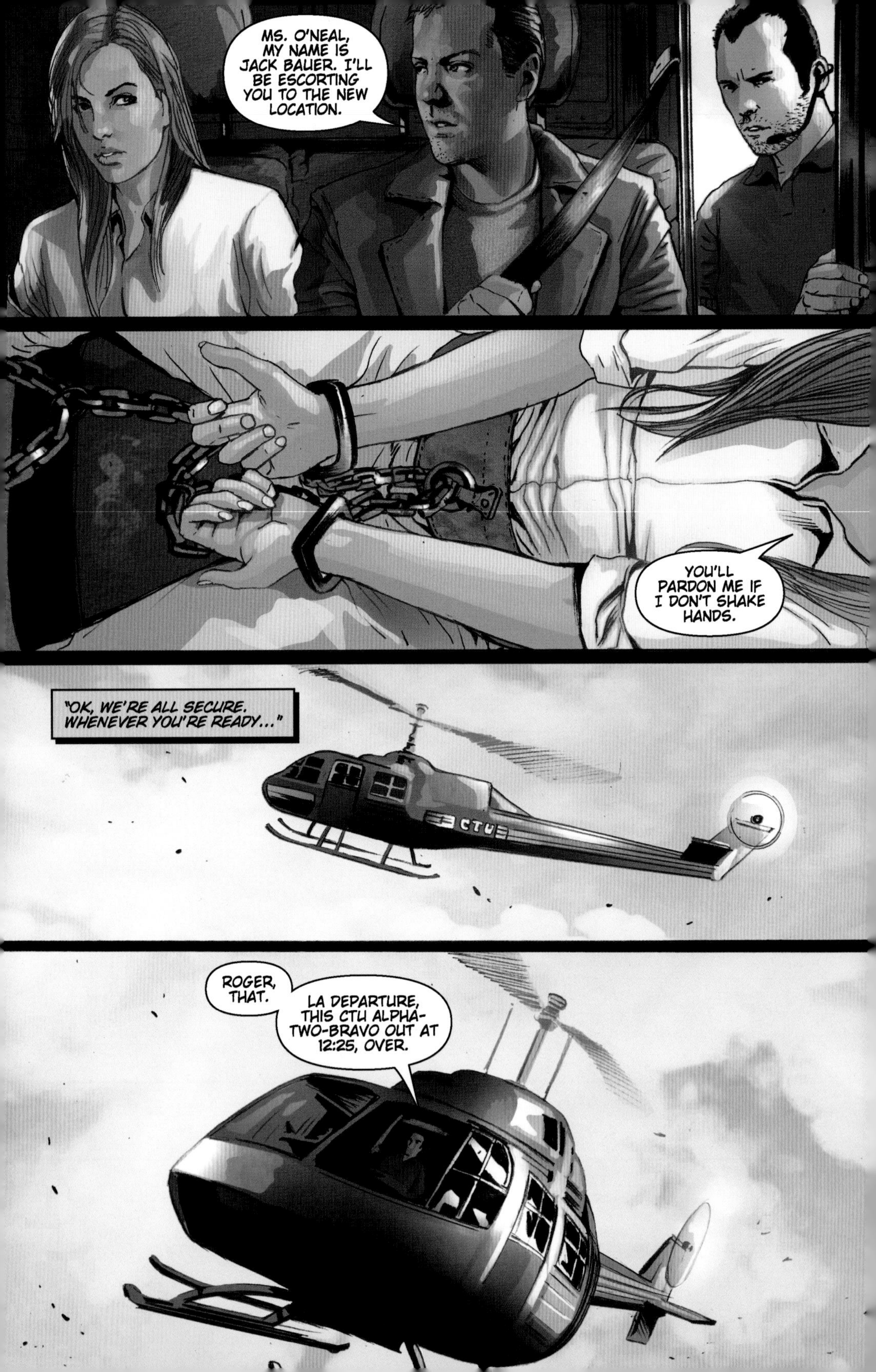
MS. O'NEAL, MY NAME IS JACK BAUER. I'LL BE ESCORTING YOU TO THE NEW LOCATION.
YOU'LL PARDON ME IF I DON'T SHAKE HANDS.
"OK, WE'RE ALL SECURE. WHENEVER YOU'RE READY..."
CTU
ROGER, THAT.
LA DEPARTURE, THIS CTU ALPHA-TWO-BRAVO OUT AT 12:25, OVER.

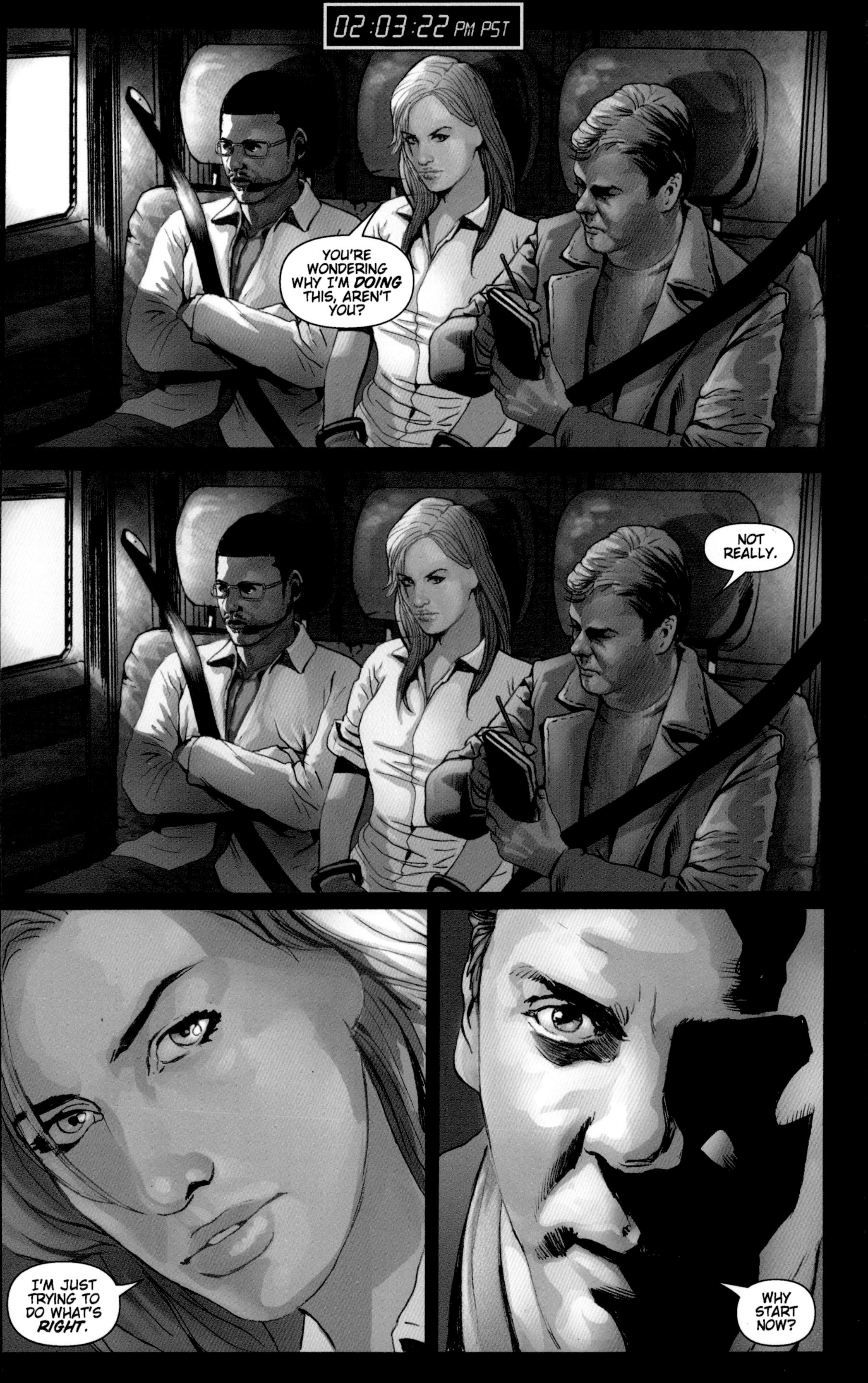
02:03:22 PM PST
YOU'RE WONDERING WHY I'M *DOING* THIS, AREN'T YOU?
NOT REALLY.
I'M JUST TRYING TO DO WHAT'S *RIGHT*.
WHY START NOW?

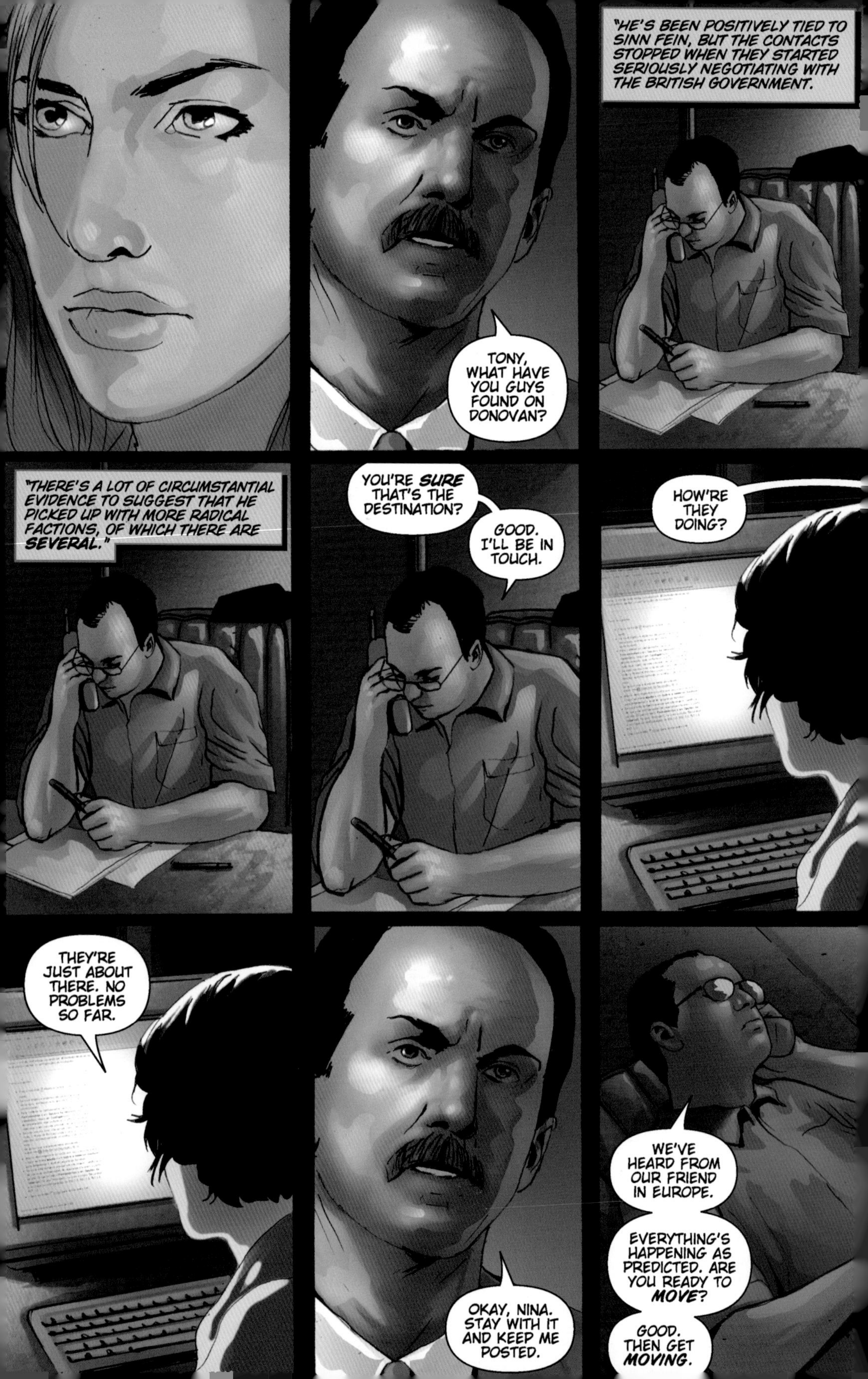
TONY, WHAT HAVE YOU GUYS FOUND ON DONOVAN?
"HE'S BEEN POSITIVELY TIED TO SINN FEIN, BUT THE CONTACTS STOPPED WHEN THEY STARTED SERIOUSLY NEGOTIATING WITH THE BRITISH GOVERNMENT.
"THERE'S A LOT OF CIRCUMSTANTIAL EVIDENCE TO SUGGEST THAT HE PICKED UP WITH MORE RADICAL FACTIONS, OF WHICH THERE ARE SEVERAL."
YOU'RE SURE THAT'S THE DESTINATION?
GOOD. I'LL BE IN TOUCH.
HOW'RE THEY DOING?
THEY'RE JUST ABOUT THERE. NO PROBLEMS SO FAR.
OKAY, NINA. STAY WITH IT AND KEEP ME POSTED.
WE'VE HEARD FROM OUR FRIEND IN EUROPE.
EVERYTHING'S HAPPENING AS PREDICTED. ARE YOU READY TO MOVE?
GOOD. THEN GET MOVING.

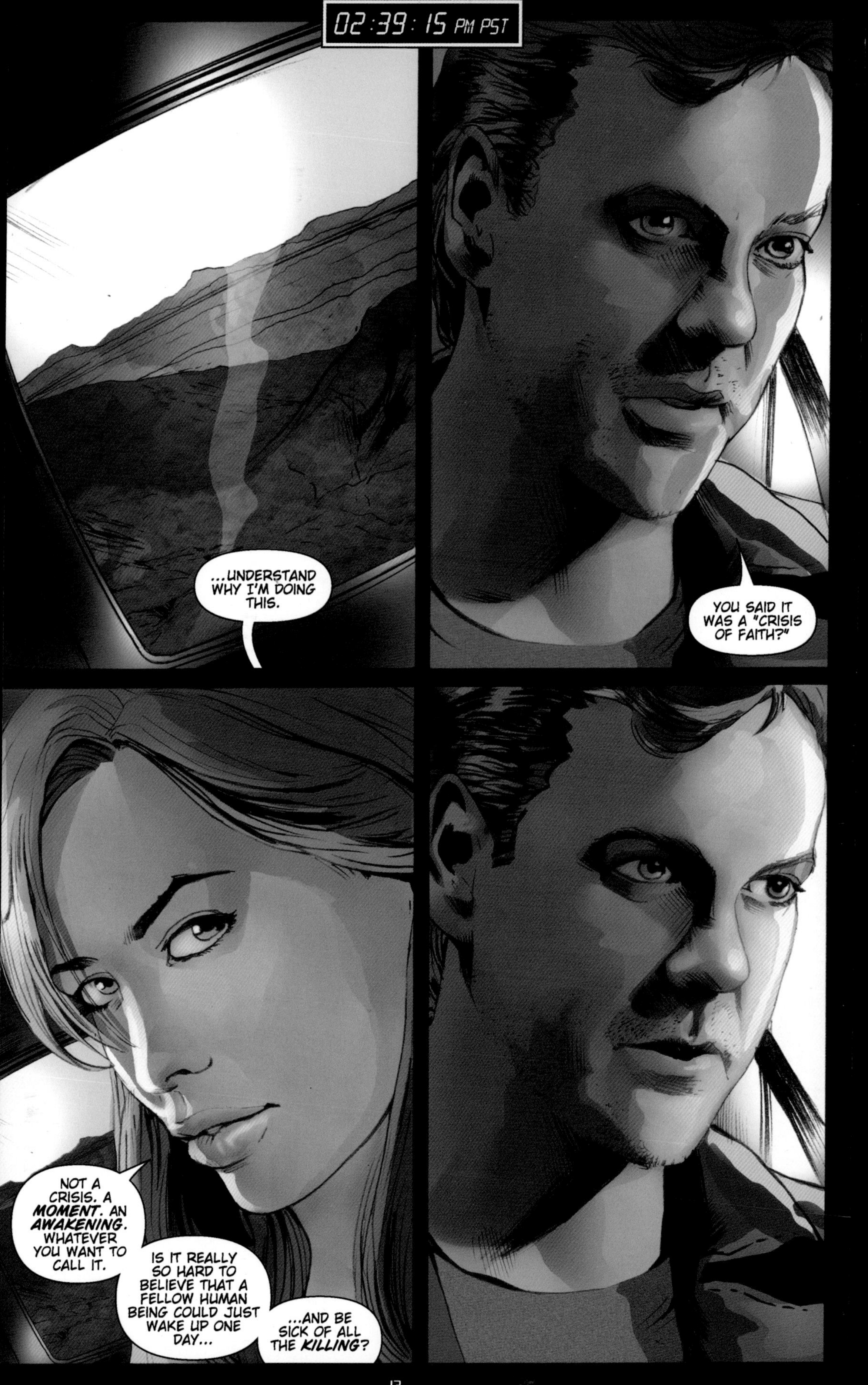

02:39:15 PM PST
...UNDERSTAND WHY I'M DOING THIS.
YOU SAID IT WAS A "CRISIS OF FAITH?"
NOT A CRISIS. A **MOMENT**. AN **AWAKENING**. WHATEVER YOU WANT TO CALL IT.
IS IT REALLY SO HARD TO BELIEVE THAT A FELLOW HUMAN BEING COULD JUST WAKE UP ONE DAY...
...AND BE SICK OF ALL THE **KILLING**?

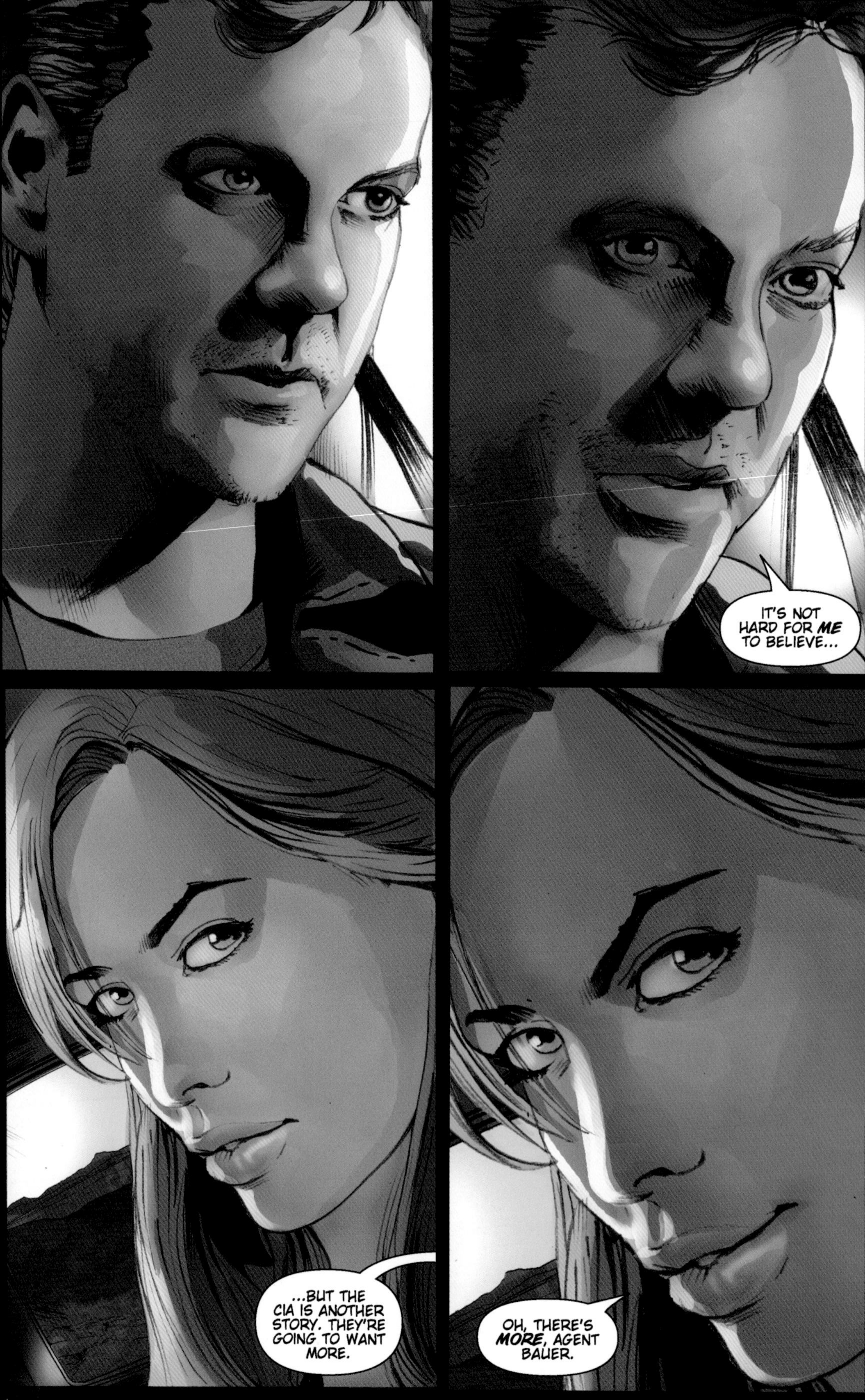
IT'S NOT HARD FOR ME TO BELIEVE...
...BUT THE CIA IS ANOTHER STORY. THEY'RE GOING TO WANT MORE.
OH, THERE'S MORE, AGENT BAUER.

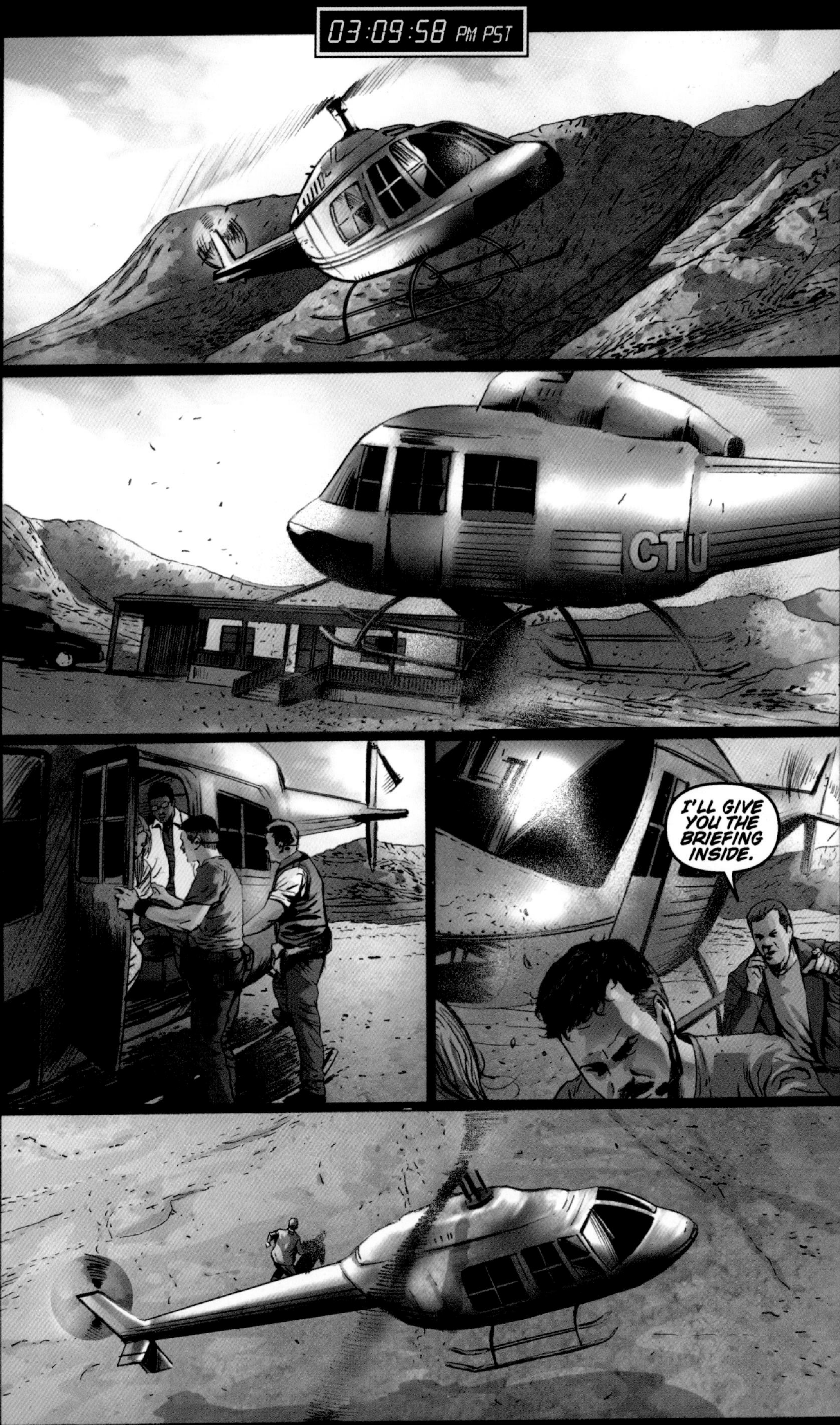
03:09:58 PM PST
CTU
I'LL GIVE YOU THE BRIEFING INSIDE.

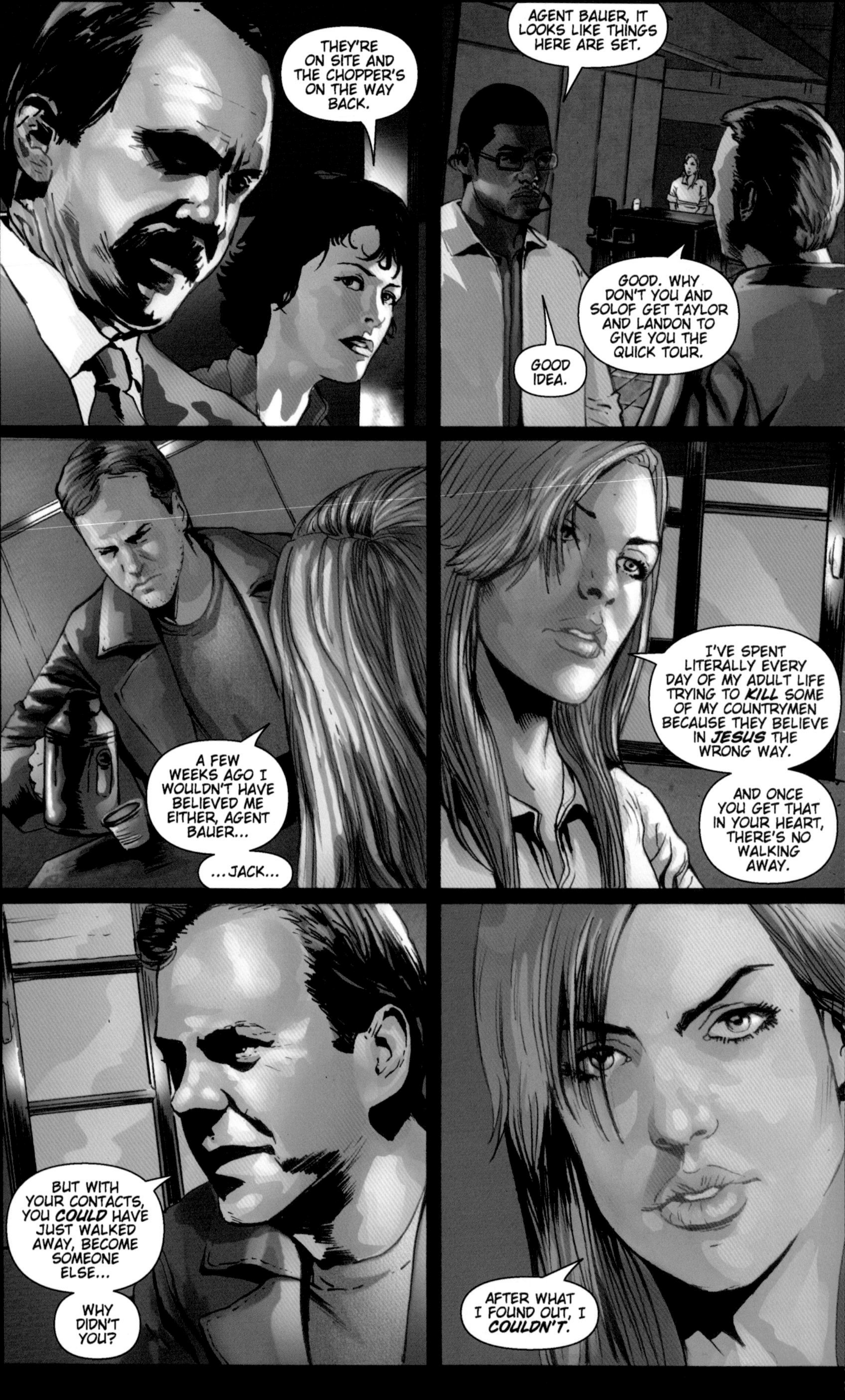
THEY'RE ON SITE AND THE CHOPPER'S ON THE WAY BACK.
AGENT BAUER, IT LOOKS LIKE THINGS HERE ARE SET.
GOOD. WHY DON'T YOU AND SOLOF GET TAYLOR AND LANDON TO GIVE YOU THE QUICK TOUR.
GOOD IDEA.
A FEW WEEKS AGO I WOULDN'T HAVE BELIEVED ME EITHER, AGENT BAUER...
...JACK...
I'VE SPENT LITERALLY EVERY DAY OF MY ADULT LIFE TRYING TO KILL SOME OF MY COUNTRYMEN BECAUSE THEY BELIEVE IN JESUS THE WRONG WAY.
AND ONCE YOU GET THAT IN YOUR HEART, THERE'S NO WALKING AWAY.
BUT WITH YOUR CONTACTS, YOU COULD HAVE JUST WALKED AWAY, BECOME SOMEONE ELSE...
WHY DIDN'T YOU?
AFTER WHAT I FOUND OUT, I COULDN'T.

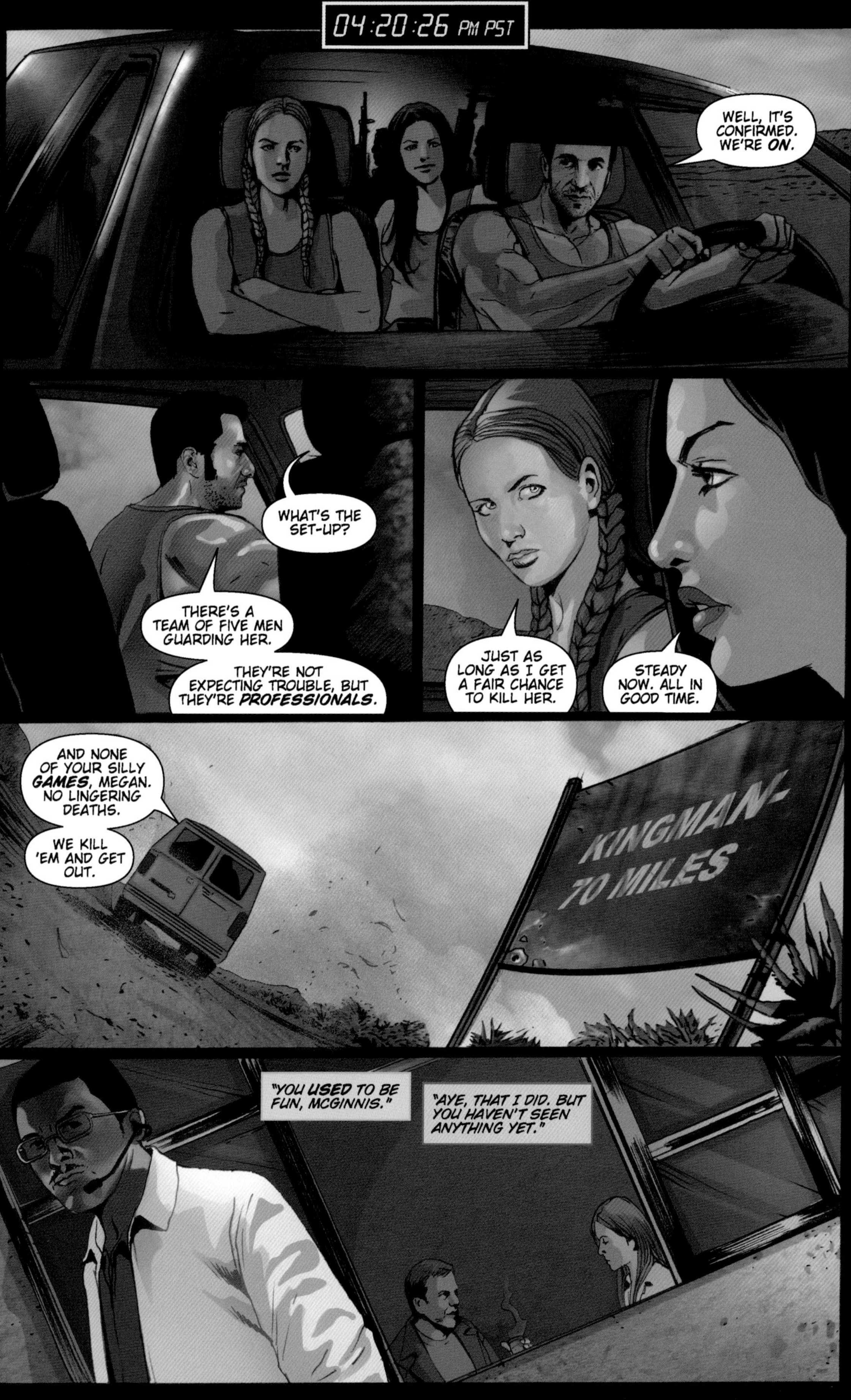
04:20:26 PM PST
WELL, IT'S CONFIRMED. WE'RE ON.
WHAT'S THE SET-UP?
THERE'S A TEAM OF FIVE MEN GUARDING HER.
THEY'RE NOT EXPECTING TROUBLE, BUT THEY'RE PROFESSIONALS.
JUST AS LONG AS I GET A FAIR CHANCE TO KILL HER.
STEADY NOW. ALL IN GOOD TIME.
AND NONE OF YOUR SILLY GAMES, MEGAN. NO LINGERING DEATHS.
WE KILL 'EM AND GET OUT.
KINGMAN- 70 MILES
"YOU USED TO BE FUN, MCGINNIS."
"AYE, THAT I DID. BUT YOU HAVEN'T SEEN ANYTHING YET."

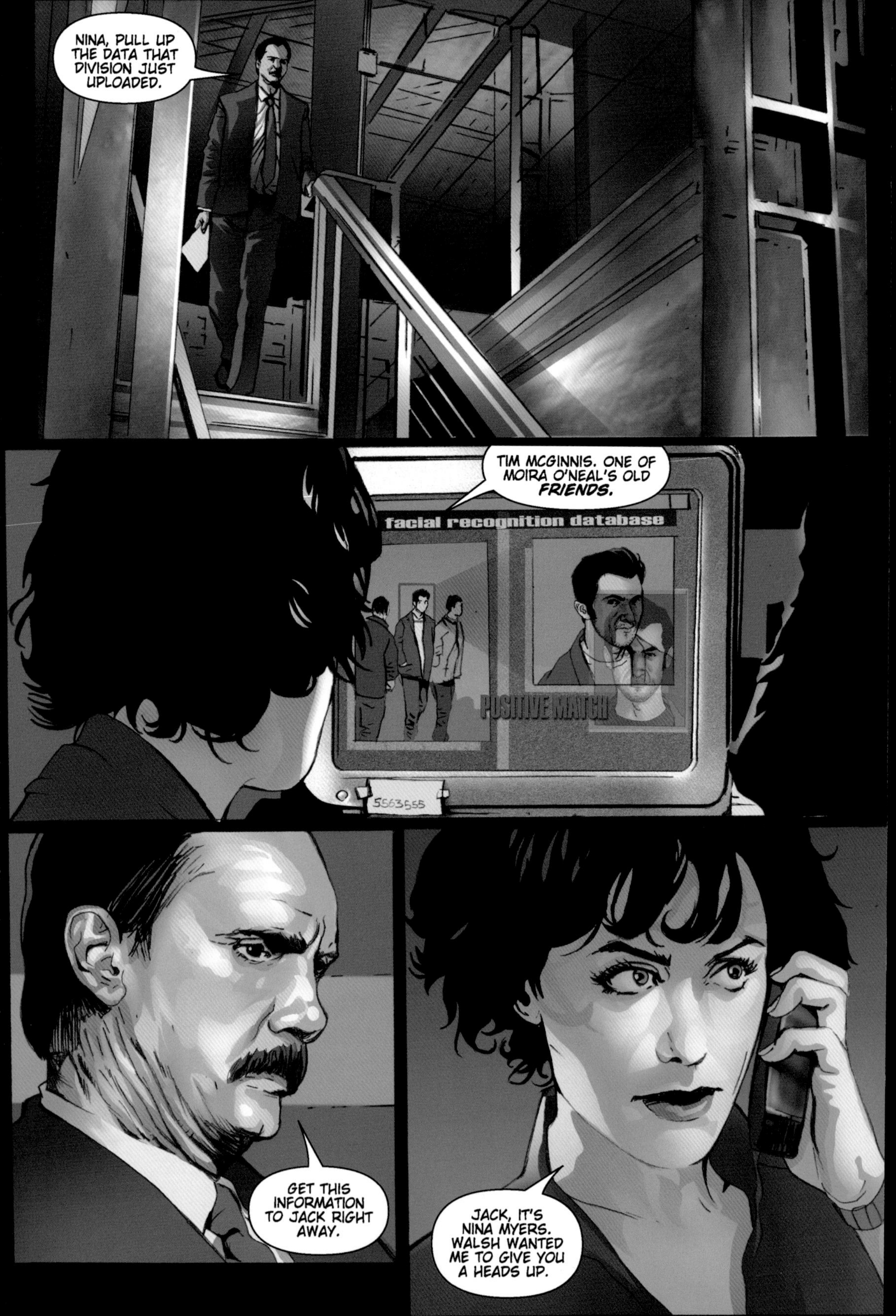
NINA, PULL UP THE DATA THAT DIVISION JUST UPLOADED.
TIM MCGINNIS. ONE OF MOIRA O'NEAL'S OLD FRIENDS.
facial recognition database
POSITIVE MATCH
5563555
GET THIS INFORMATION TO JACK RIGHT AWAY.
JACK, IT'S NINA MYERS. WALSH WANTED ME TO GIVE YOU A HEADS UP.

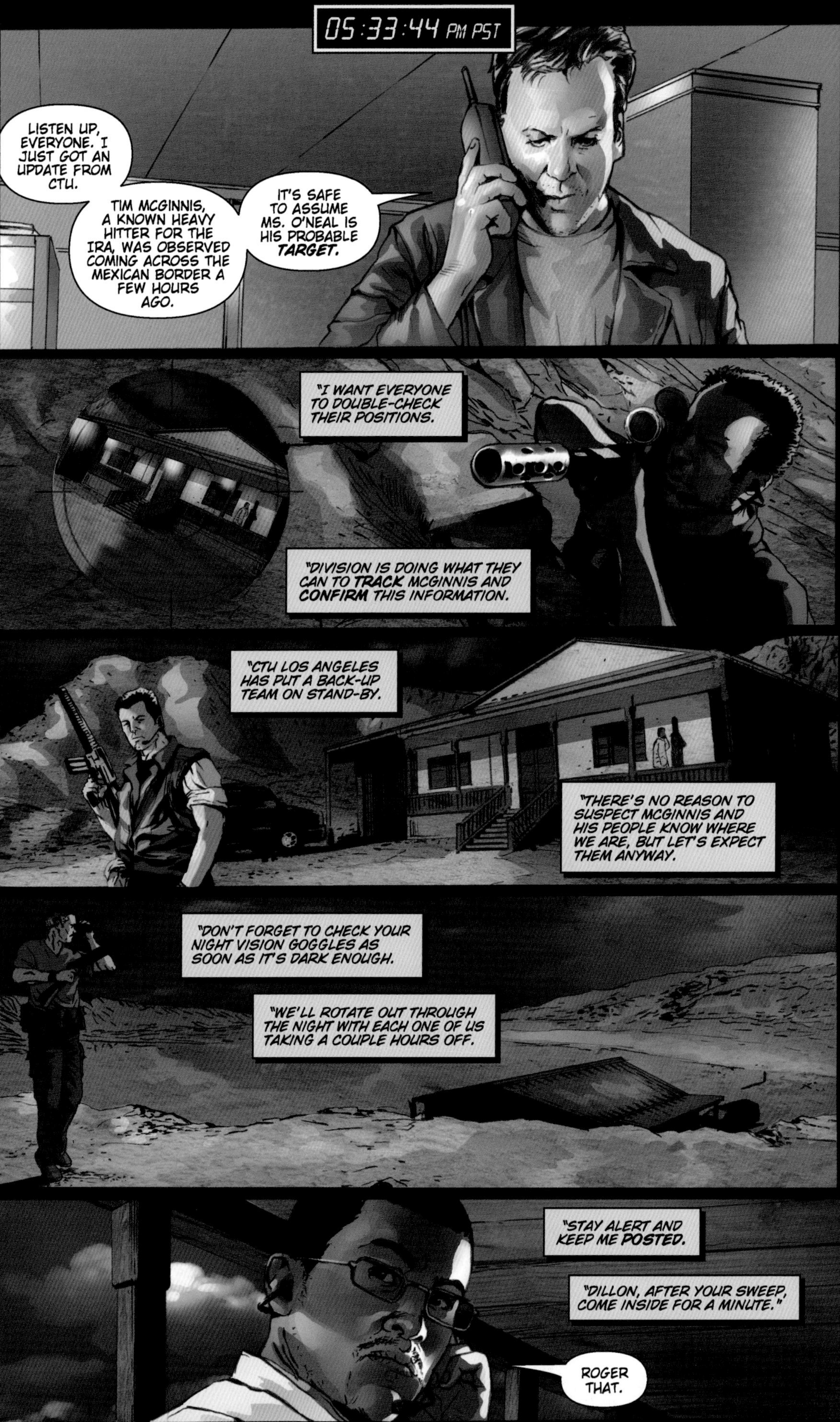
05:33:44 PM PST
LISTEN UP, EVERYONE. I JUST GOT AN UPDATE FROM CTU.
TIM MCGINNIS, A KNOWN HEAVY HITTER FOR THE IRA, WAS OBSERVED COMING ACROSS THE MEXICAN BORDER A FEW HOURS AGO.
IT'S SAFE TO ASSUME MS. O'NEAL IS HIS PROBABLE TARGET.
"I WANT EVERYONE TO DOUBLE-CHECK THEIR POSITIONS.
"DIVISION IS DOING WHAT THEY CAN TO TRACK MCGINNIS AND CONFIRM THIS INFORMATION.
"CTU LOS ANGELES HAS PUT A BACK-UP TEAM ON STAND-BY.
"THERE'S NO REASON TO SUSPECT MCGINNIS AND HIS PEOPLE KNOW WHERE WE ARE, BUT LET'S EXPECT THEM ANYWAY.
"DON'T FORGET TO CHECK YOUR NIGHT VISION GOGGLES AS SOON AS IT'S DARK ENOUGH.
"WE'LL ROTATE OUT THROUGH THE NIGHT WITH EACH ONE OF US TAKING A COUPLE HOURS OFF.
"STAY ALERT AND KEEP ME POSTED.
"DILLON, AFTER YOUR SWEEP, COME INSIDE FOR A MINUTE."
ROGER THAT.

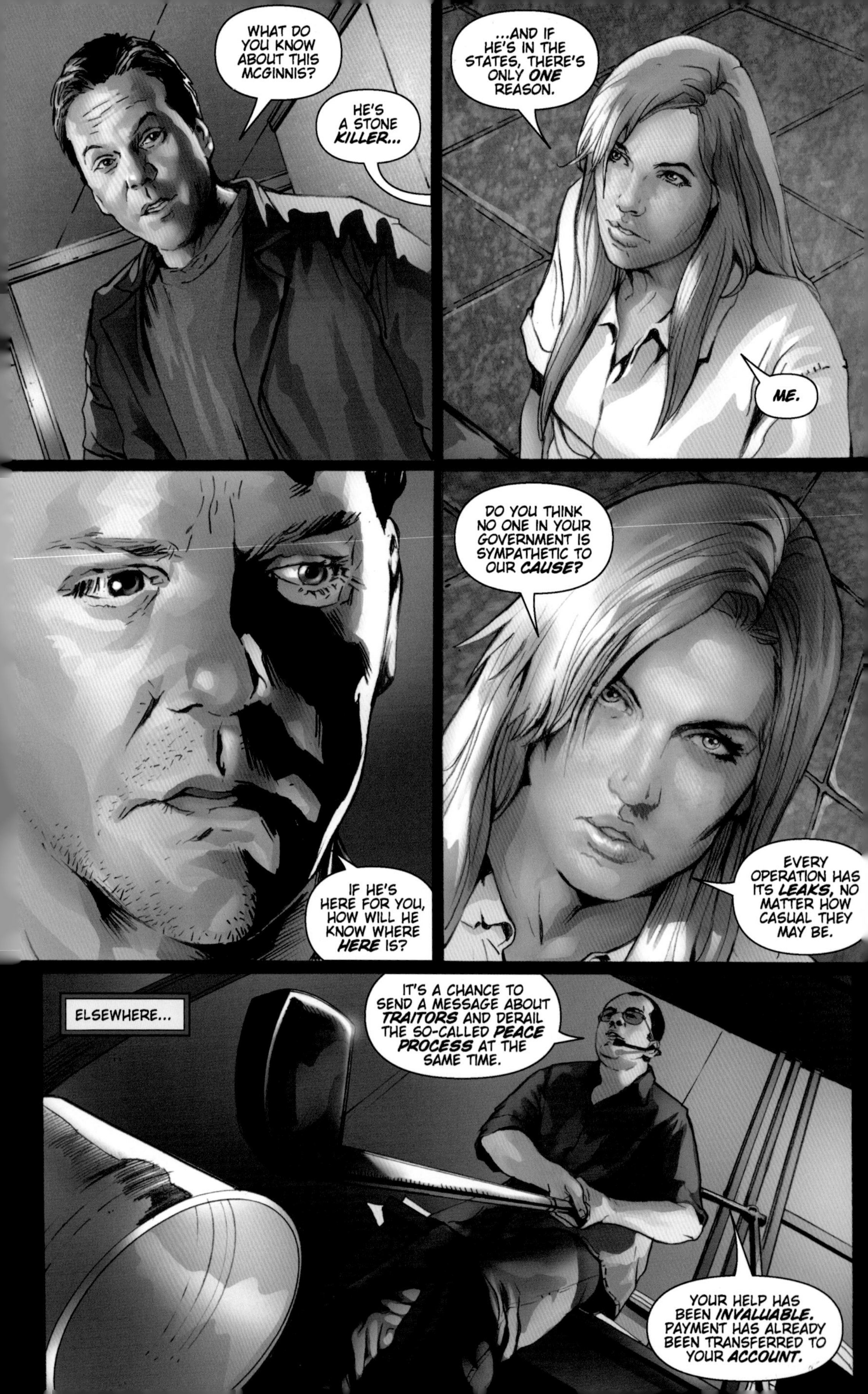
WHAT DO YOU KNOW ABOUT THIS MCGINNIS?
HE'S A STONE KILLER...
...AND IF HE'S IN THE STATES, THERE'S ONLY ONE REASON.
ME.
DO YOU THINK NO ONE IN YOUR GOVERNMENT IS SYMPATHETIC TO OUR CAUSE?
IF HE'S HERE FOR YOU, HOW WILL HE KNOW WHERE HERE IS?
EVERY OPERATION HAS ITS LEAKS, NO MATTER HOW CASUAL THEY MAY BE.
ELSEWHERE...
IT'S A CHANCE TO SEND A MESSAGE ABOUT TRAITORS AND DERAIL THE SO-CALLED PEACE PROCESS AT THE SAME TIME.
YOUR HELP HAS BEEN INVALUABLE. PAYMENT HAS ALREADY BEEN TRANSFERRED TO YOUR ACCOUNT.

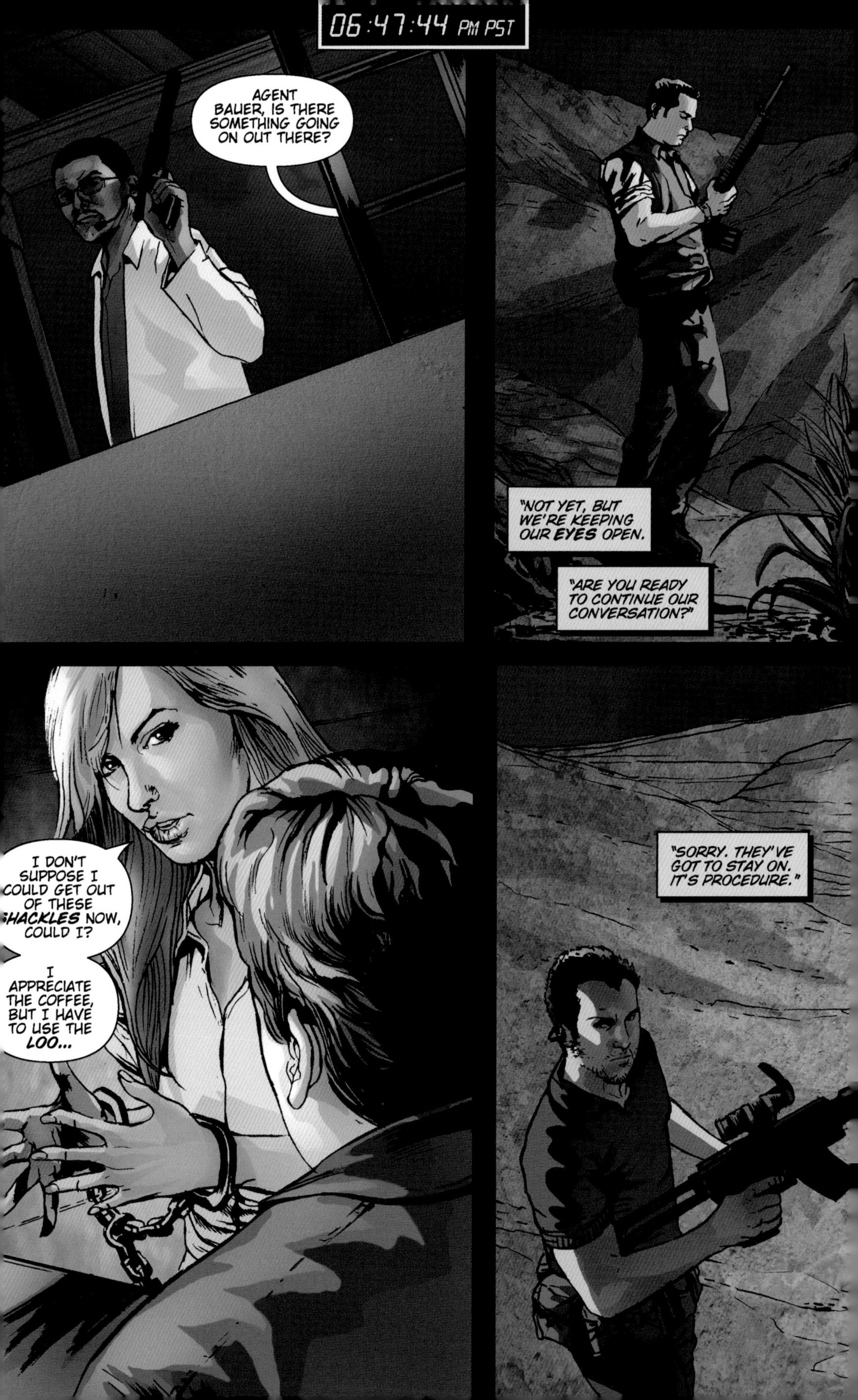
06:47:44 PM PST
AGENT BAUER, IS THERE SOMETHING GOING ON OUT THERE?
"NOT YET, BUT WE'RE KEEPING OUR EYES OPEN.
"ARE YOU READY TO CONTINUE OUR CONVERSATION?"
I DON'T SUPPOSE I COULD GET OUT OF THESE SHACKLES NOW, COULD I?
I APPRECIATE THE COFFEE, BUT I HAVE TO USE THE LOO...
"SORRY. THEY'VE GOT TO STAY ON. IT'S PROCEDURE."

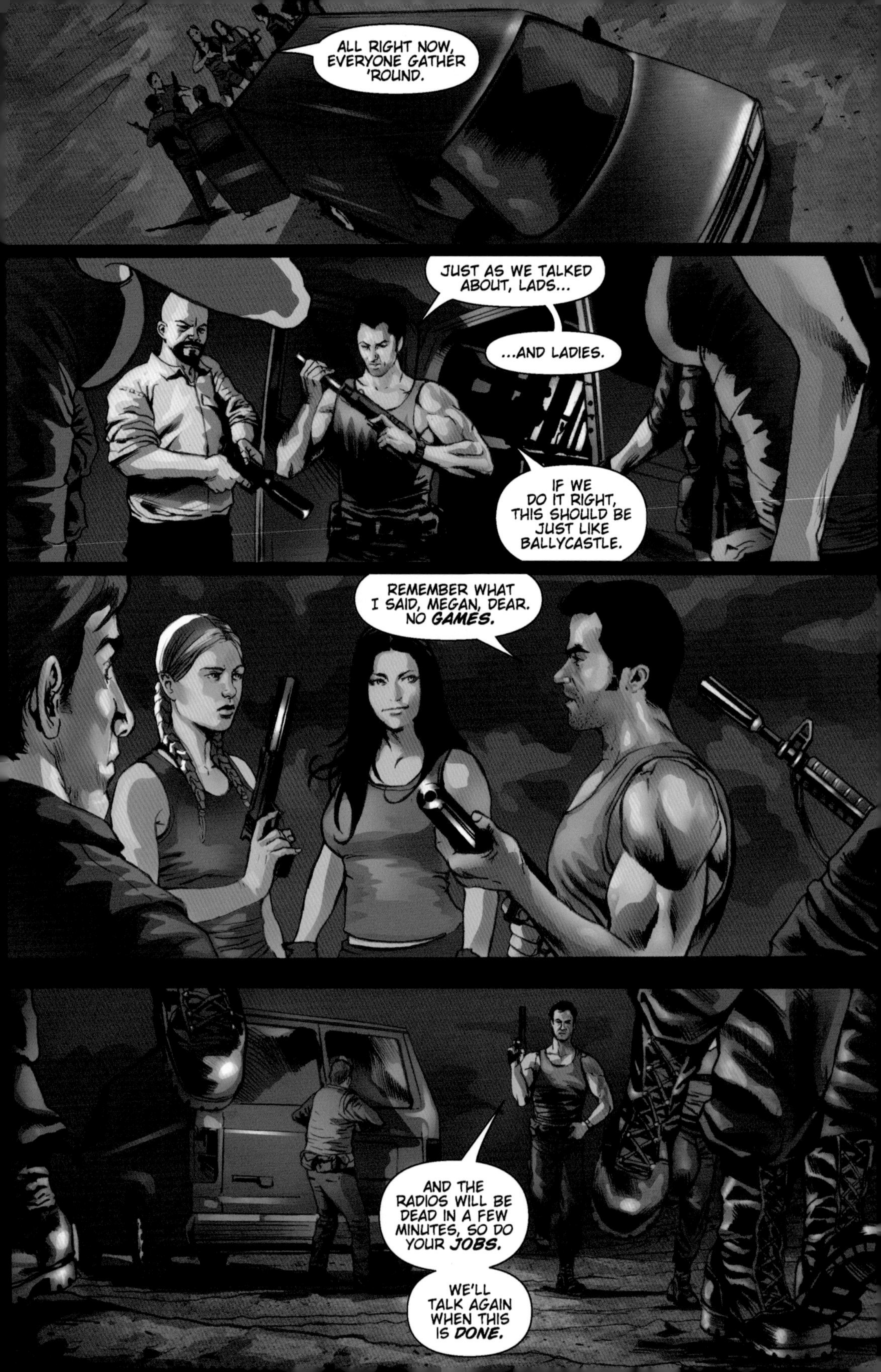
ALL RIGHT NOW, EVERYONE GATHER 'ROUND.
JUST AS WE TALKED ABOUT, LADS...
...AND LADIES.
IF WE DO IT RIGHT, THIS SHOULD BE JUST LIKE BALLYCASTLE.
REMEMBER WHAT I SAID, MEGAN, DEAR. NO *GAMES.*
AND THE RADIOS WILL BE DEAD IN A FEW MINUTES, SO DO YOUR *JOBS.*
WE'LL TALK AGAIN WHEN THIS IS *DONE.*

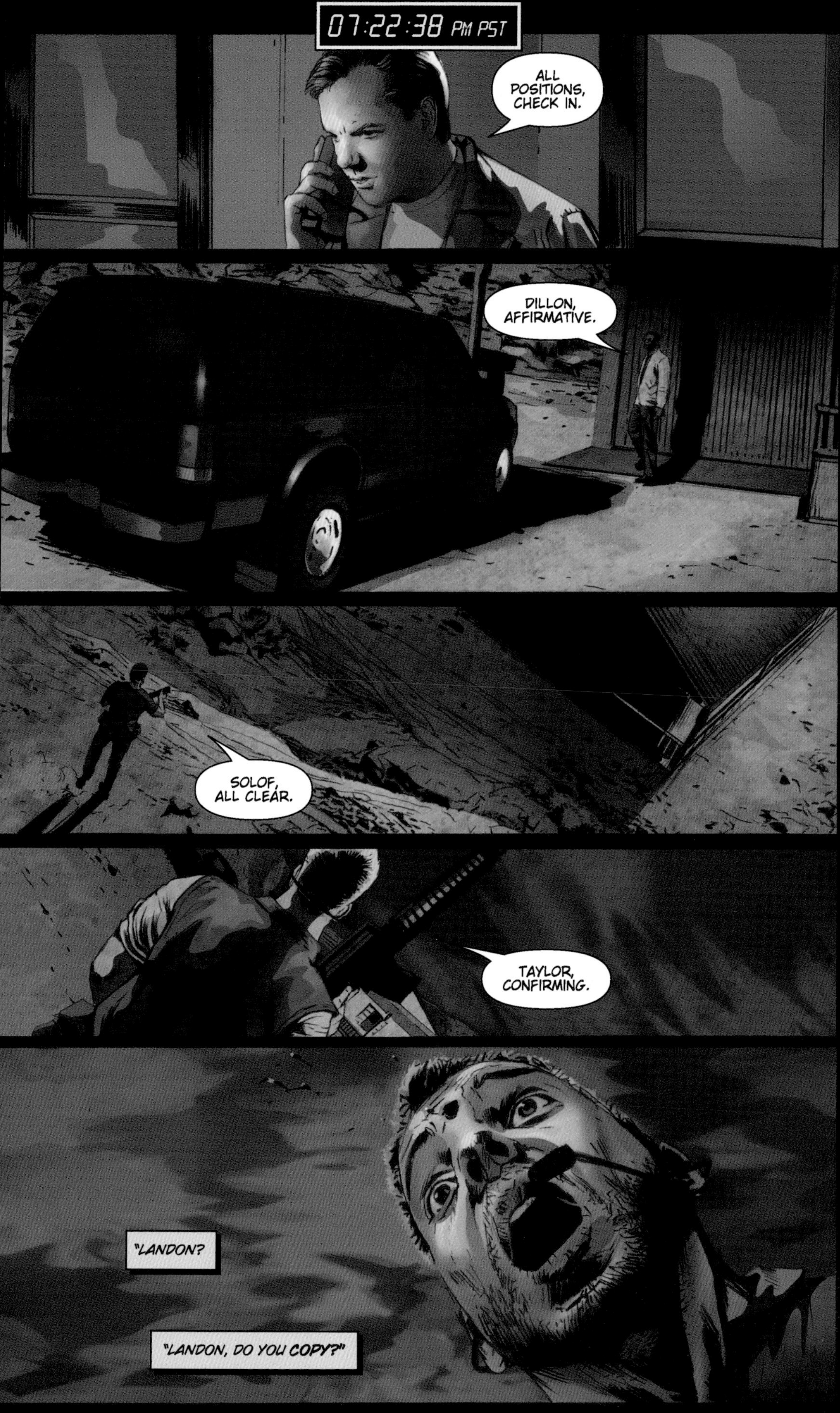
07:22:38 PM PST
ALL POSITIONS, CHECK IN.
DILLON, AFFIRMATIVE.
SOLOF, ALL CLEAR.
TAYLOR, CONFIRMING.
"LANDON?
"LANDON, DO YOU COPY?"

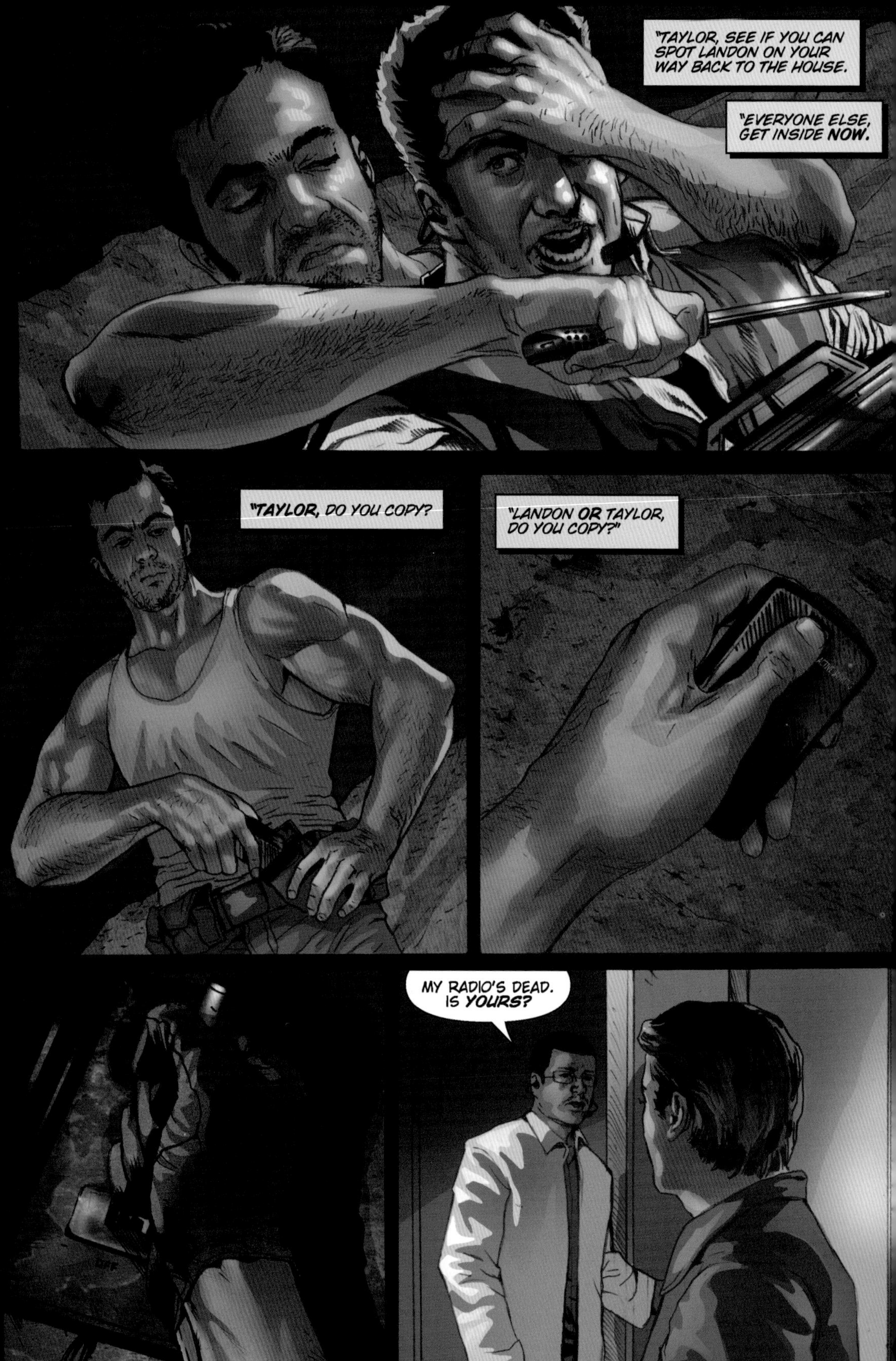
"TAYLOR, SEE IF YOU CAN SPOT LANDON ON YOUR WAY BACK TO THE HOUSE.
"EVERYONE ELSE, GET INSIDE NOW.
"TAYLOR, DO YOU COPY?
"LANDON OR TAYLOR, DO YOU COPY?"
MY RADIO'S DEAD. IS YOURS?

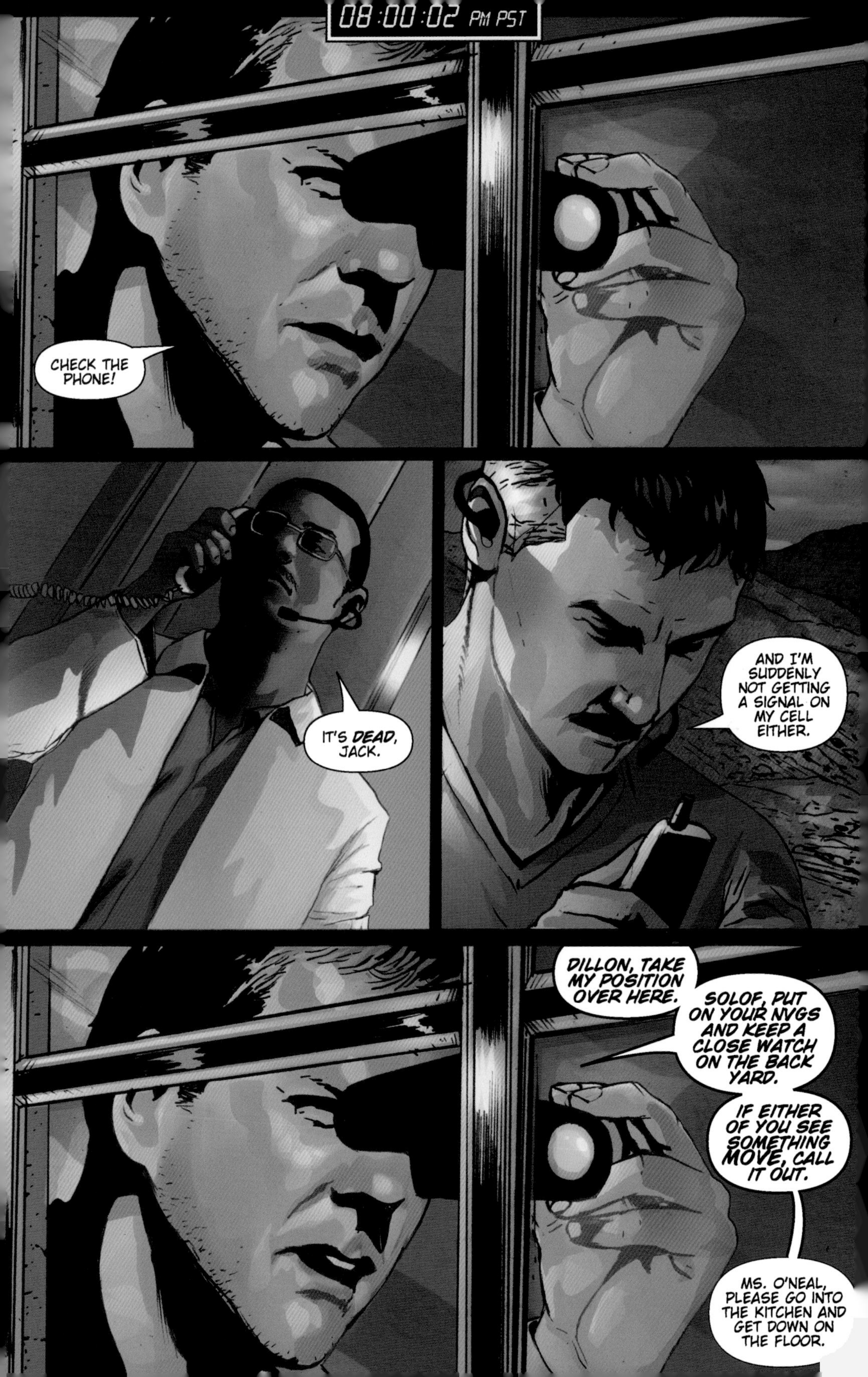
08:00:02 PM PST
CHECK THE PHONE!
IT'S DEAD, JACK.
AND I'M SUDDENLY NOT GETTING A SIGNAL ON MY CELL EITHER.
DILLON, TAKE MY POSITION OVER HERE.
SOLOF, PUT ON YOUR NVGS AND KEEP A CLOSE WATCH ON THE BACK YARD.
IF EITHER OF YOU SEE SOMETHING MOVE, CALL IT OUT.
MS. O'NEAL, PLEASE GO INTO THE KITCHEN AND GET DOWN ON THE FLOOR.

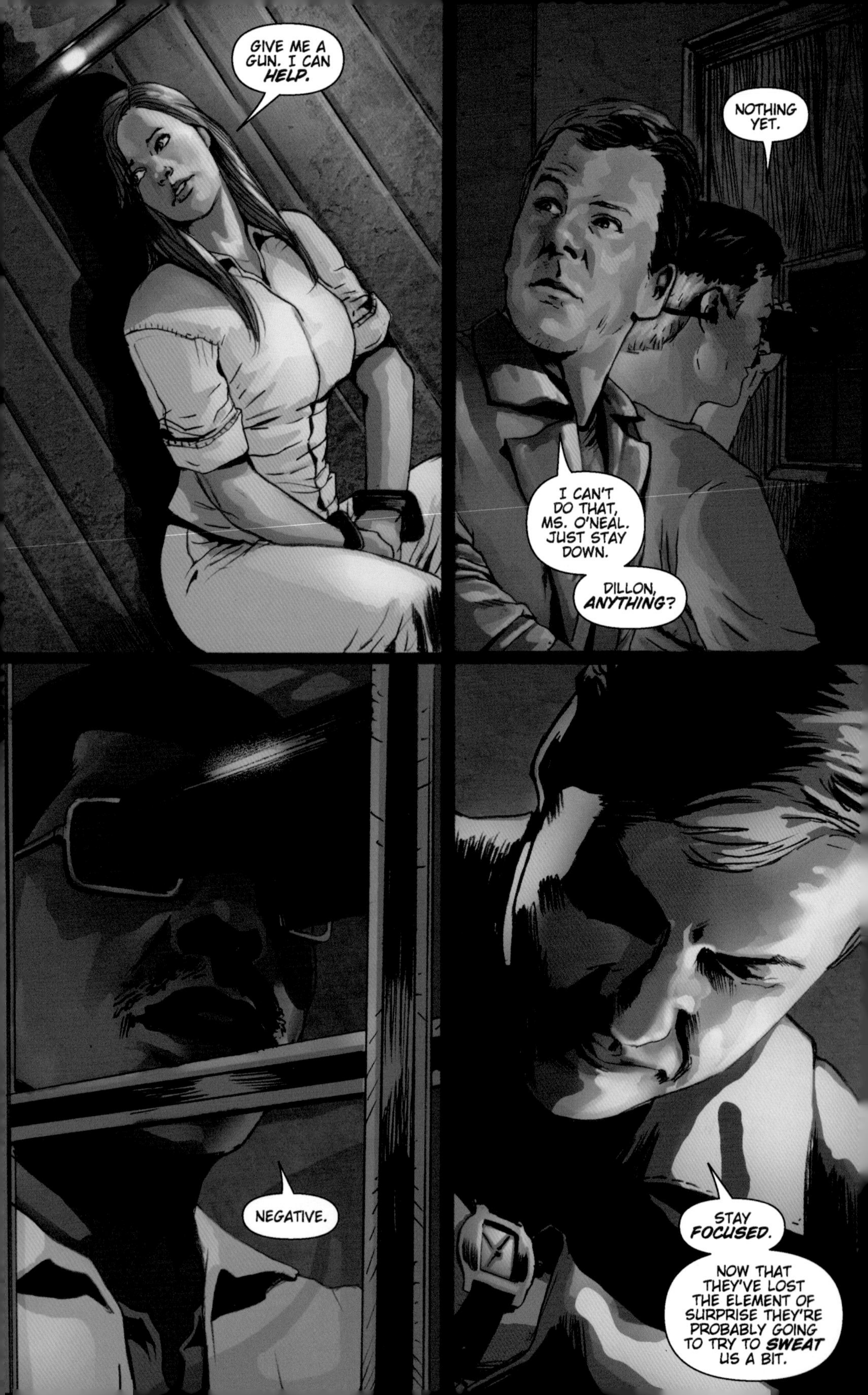
GIVE ME A GUN. I CAN HELP.
NOTHING YET.
I CAN'T DO THAT, MS. O'NEAL. JUST STAY DOWN.
DILLON, ANYTHING?
NEGATIVE.
STAY FOCUSED.
NOW THAT THEY'VE LOST THE ELEMENT OF SURPRISE THEY'RE PROBABLY GOING TO TRY TO SWEAT US A BIT.

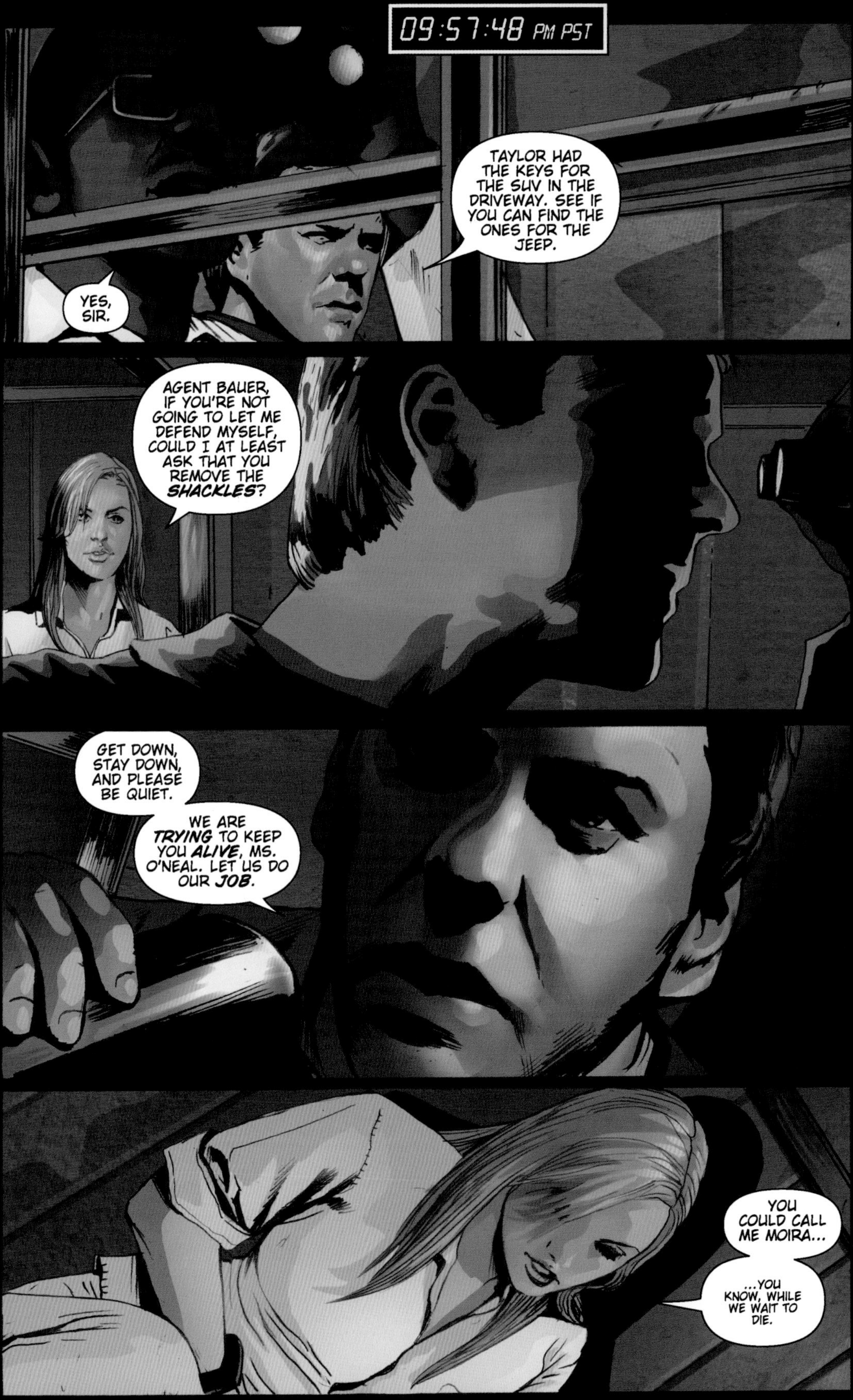
09:57:48 PM PST
TAYLOR HAD THE KEYS FOR THE SUV IN THE DRIVEWAY. SEE IF YOU CAN FIND THE ONES FOR THE JEEP.
YES, SIR.
AGENT BAUER, IF YOU'RE NOT GOING TO LET ME DEFEND MYSELF, COULD I AT LEAST ASK THAT YOU REMOVE THE ***SHACKLES***?
GET DOWN, STAY DOWN, AND PLEASE BE QUIET.
WE ARE ***TRYING*** TO KEEP YOU ***ALIVE***, MS. O'NEAL. LET US DO OUR ***JOB***.
YOU COULD CALL ME MOIRA...
...YOU KNOW, WHILE WE WAIT TO DIE.

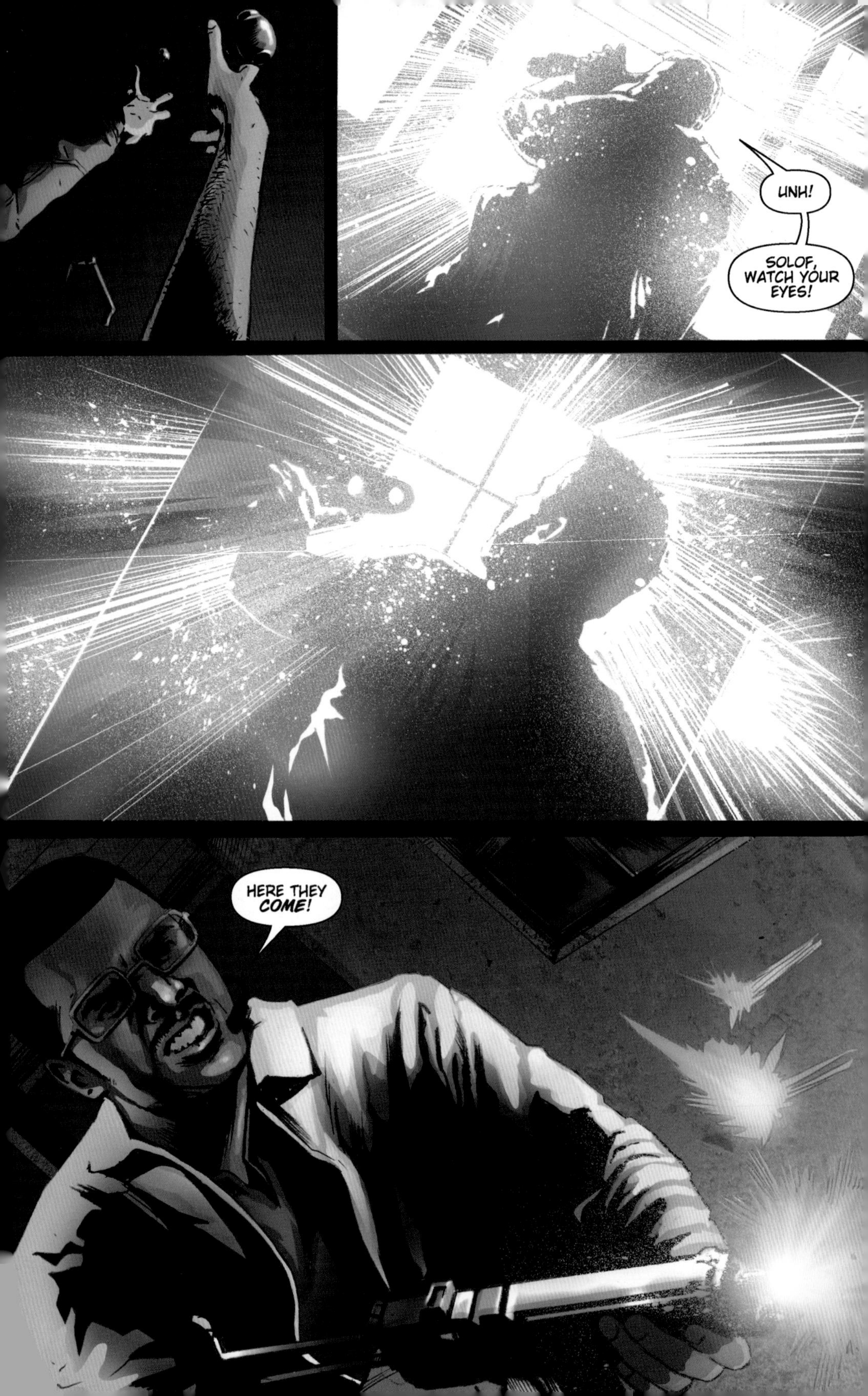
UNH!
SOLOF, WATCH YOUR EYES!
HERE THEY COME!

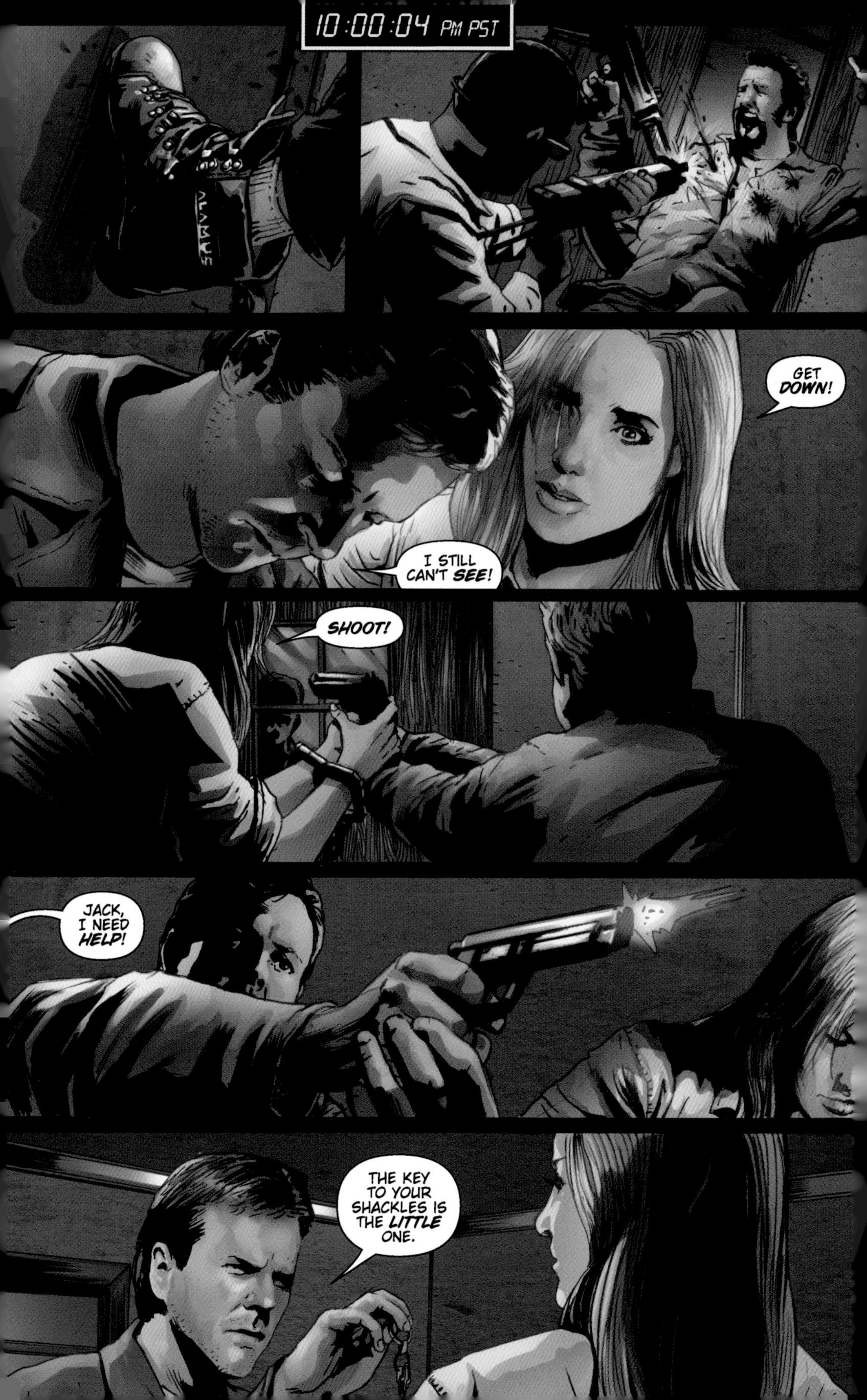

10:00:04 PM PST
GET DOWN!
I STILL CAN'T SEE!
SHOOT!
JACK, I NEED HELP!
THE KEY TO YOUR SHACKLES IS THE LITTLE ONE.

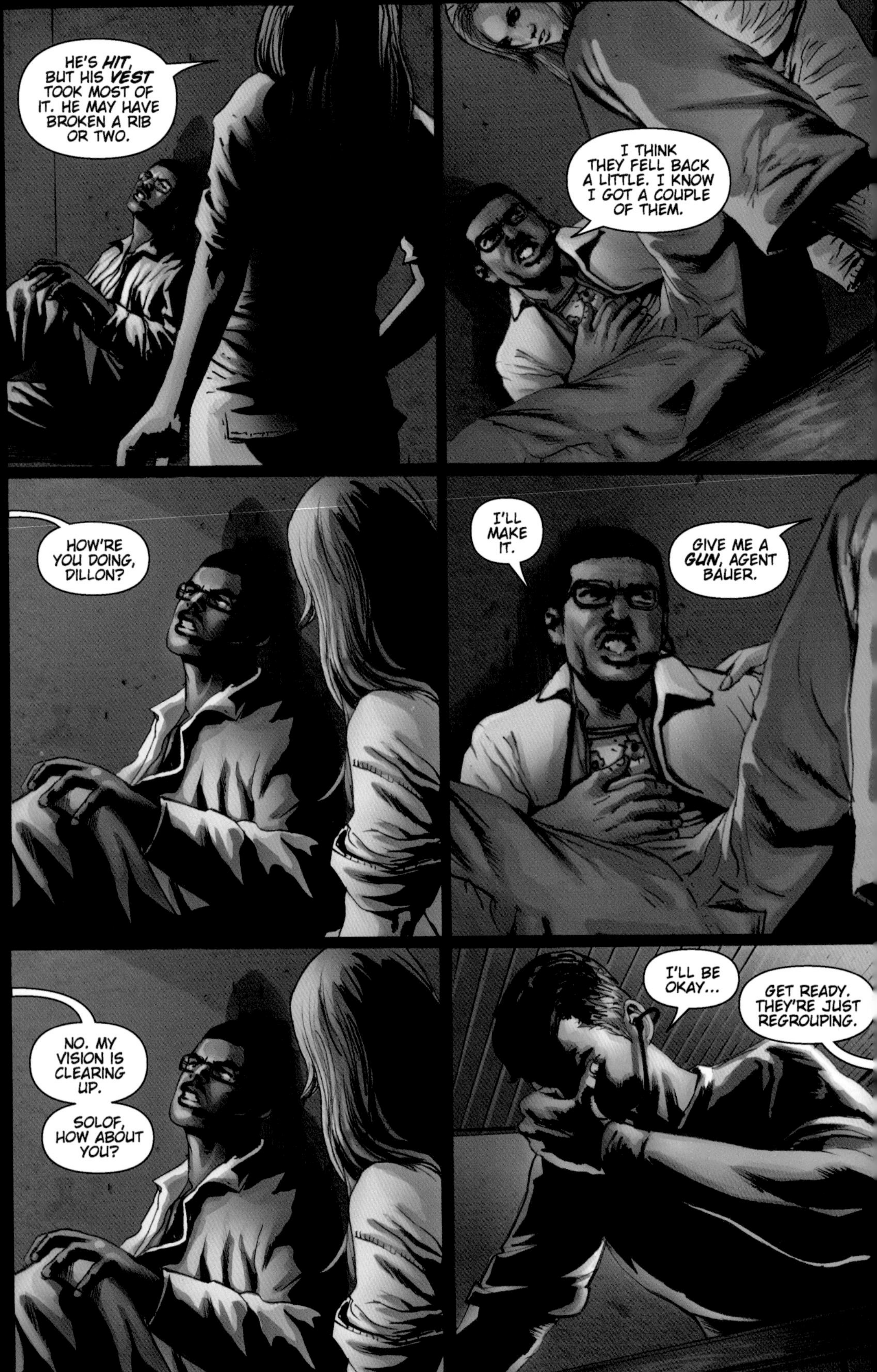
HE'S HIT, BUT HIS VEST TOOK MOST OF IT. HE MAY HAVE BROKEN A RIB OR TWO.
I THINK THEY FELL BACK A LITTLE. I KNOW I GOT A COUPLE OF THEM.
HOW'RE YOU DOING, DILLON?
I'LL MAKE IT.
GIVE ME A GUN, AGENT BAUER.
NO. MY VISION IS CLEARING UP.
SOLOF, HOW ABOUT YOU?
I'LL BE OKAY...
GET READY. THEY'RE JUST REGROUPING.

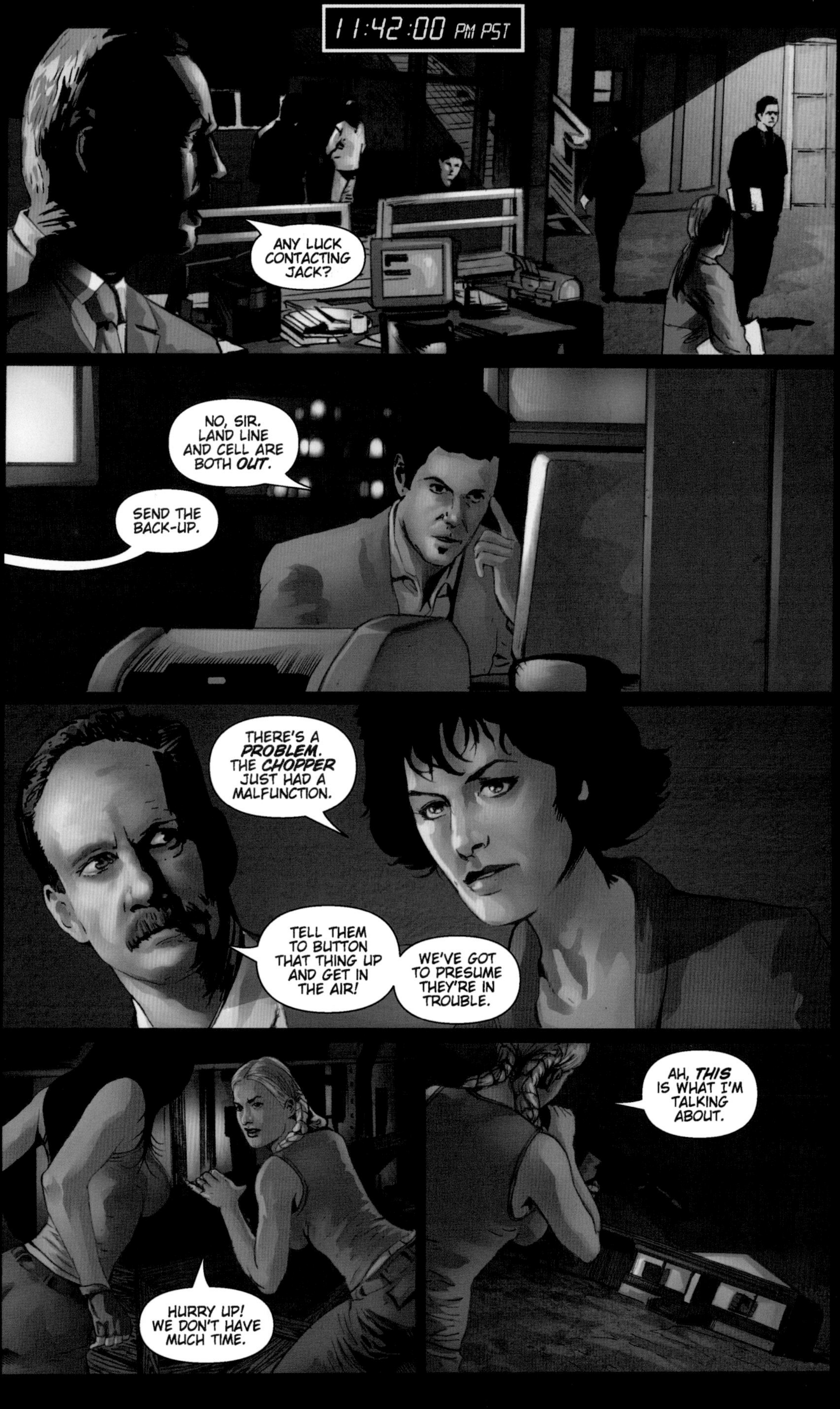
11:42:00 PM PST
ANY LUCK CONTACTING JACK?
NO, SIR. LAND LINE AND CELL ARE BOTH OUT.
SEND THE BACK-UP.
THERE'S A PROBLEM. THE CHOPPER JUST HAD A MALFUNCTION.
TELL THEM TO BUTTON THAT THING UP AND GET IN THE AIR!
WE'VE GOT TO PRESUME THEY'RE IN TROUBLE.
HURRY UP! WE DON'T HAVE MUCH TIME.
AH, THIS IS WHAT I'M TALKING ABOUT.

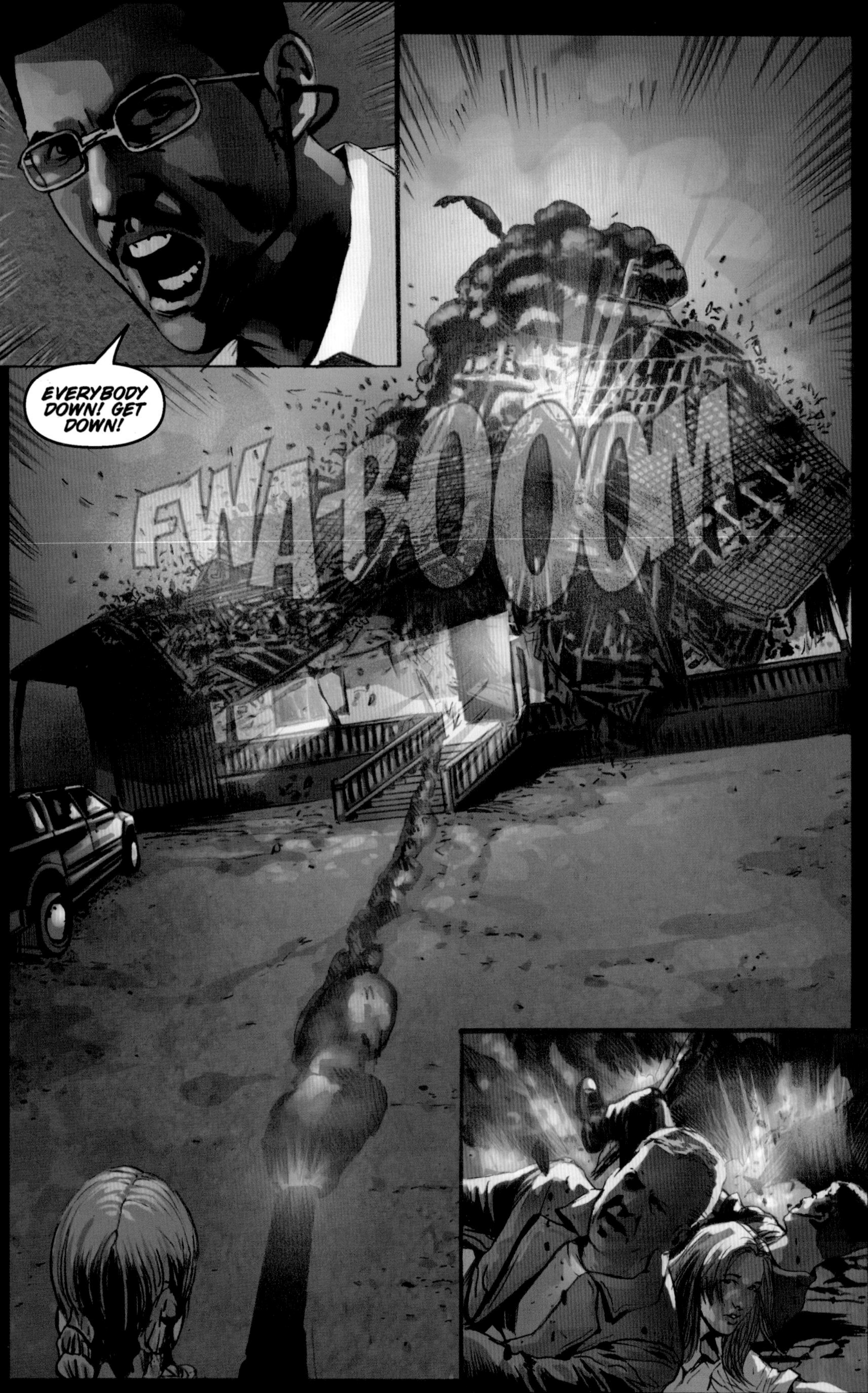
EVERYBODY DOWN! GET DOWN!
FWABOOOM

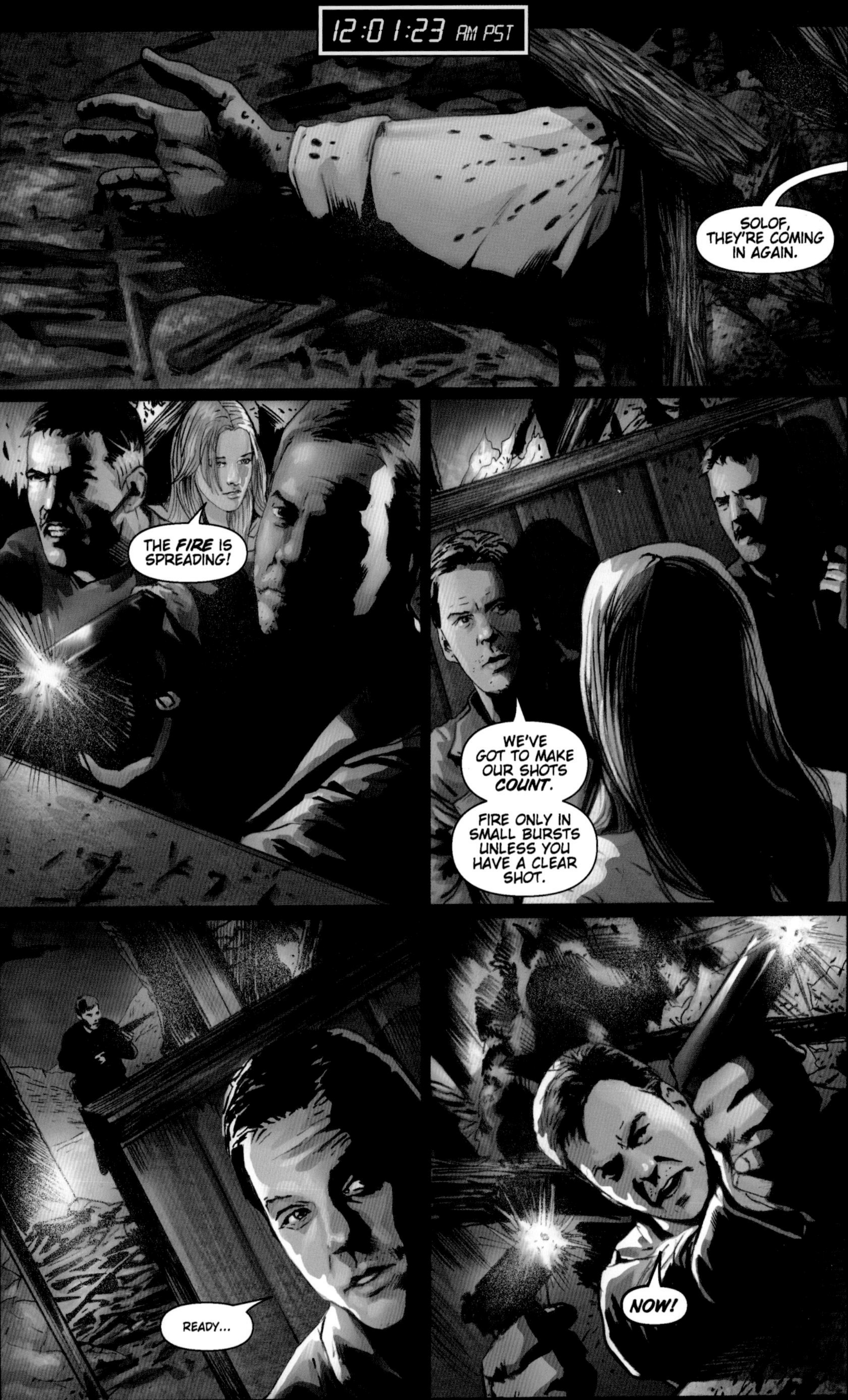
12:01:23 AM PST
SOLOF, THEY'RE COMING IN AGAIN.
THE *FIRE* IS SPREADING!
WE'VE GOT TO MAKE OUR SHOTS *COUNT*.
FIRE ONLY IN SMALL BURSTS UNLESS YOU HAVE A CLEAR SHOT.
READY...
NOW!

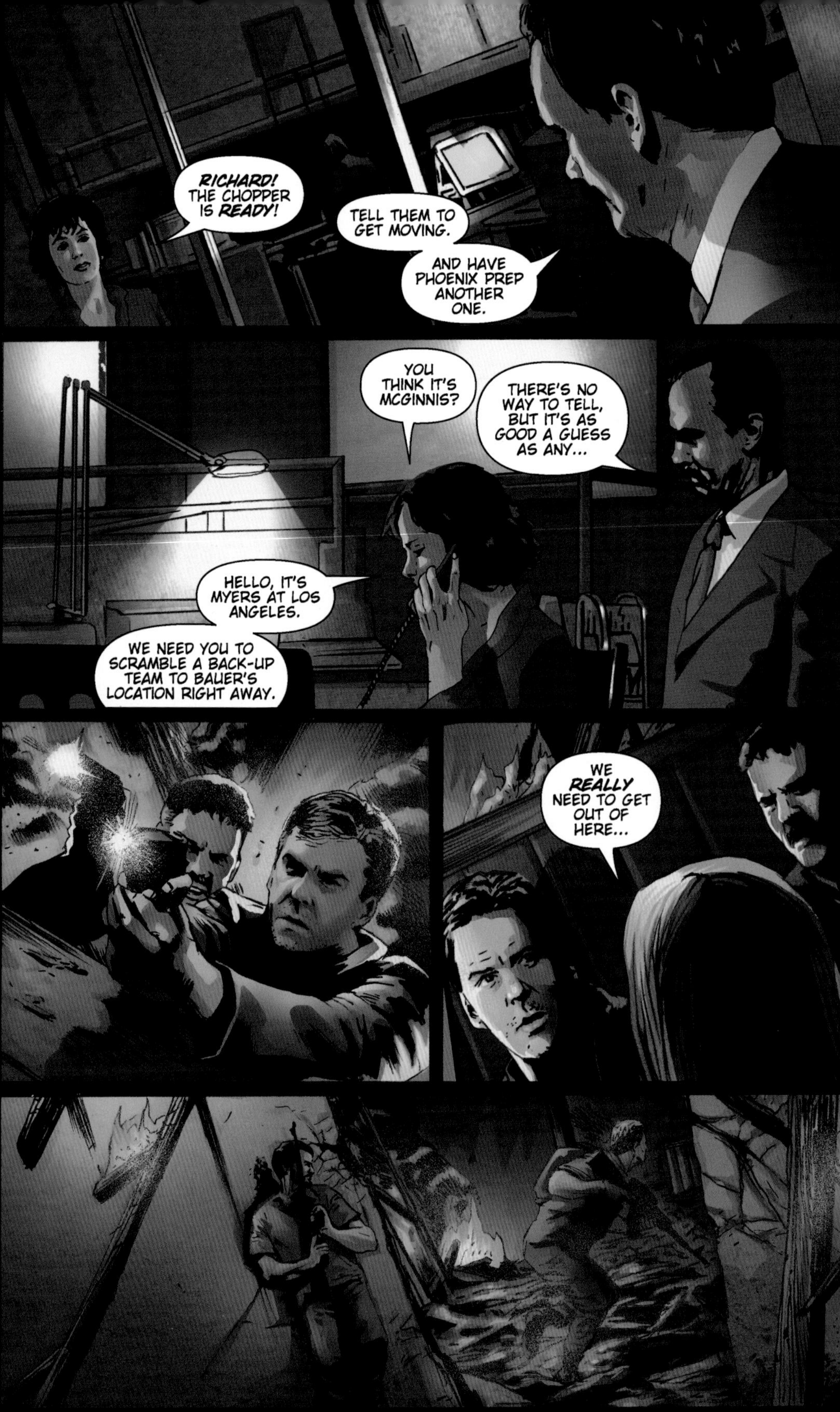
RICHARD! THE CHOPPER IS READY!
TELL THEM TO GET MOVING.
AND HAVE PHOENIX PREP ANOTHER ONE.
YOU THINK IT'S MCGINNIS?
THERE'S NO WAY TO TELL, BUT IT'S AS GOOD A GUESS AS ANY...
HELLO, IT'S MYERS AT LOS ANGELES.
WE NEED YOU TO SCRAMBLE A BACK-UP TEAM TO BAUER'S LOCATION RIGHT AWAY.
WE REALLY NEED TO GET OUT OF HERE...

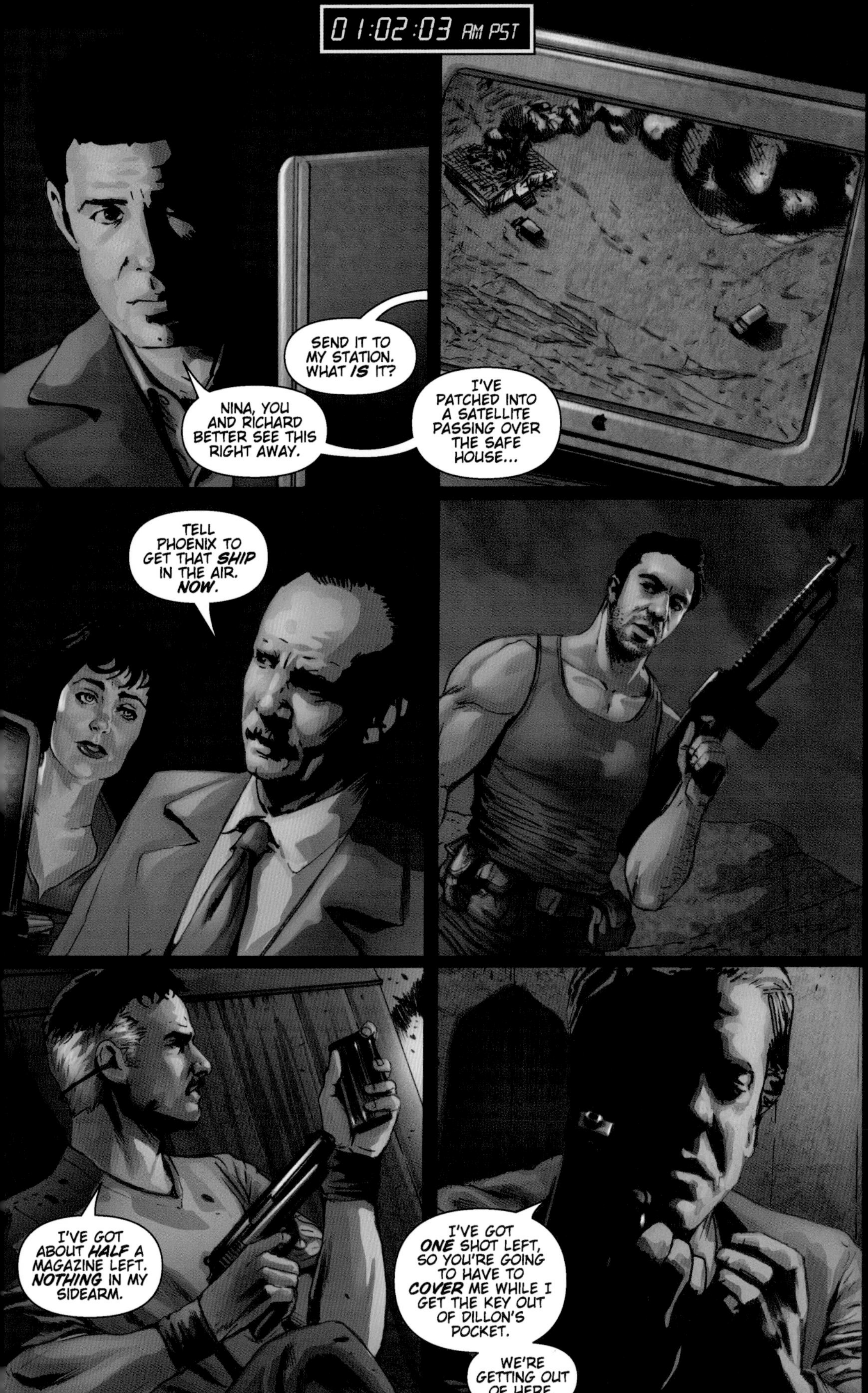
01:02:03 AM PST
NINA, YOU AND RICHARD BETTER SEE THIS RIGHT AWAY.
SEND IT TO MY STATION. WHAT IS IT?
I'VE PATCHED INTO A SATELLITE PASSING OVER THE SAFE HOUSE...
TELL PHOENIX TO GET THAT SHIP IN THE AIR. NOW.
I'VE GOT ABOUT HALF A MAGAZINE LEFT. NOTHING IN MY SIDEARM.
I'VE GOT ONE SHOT LEFT, SO YOU'RE GOING TO HAVE TO COVER ME WHILE I GET THE KEY OUT OF DILLON'S POCKET.
WE'RE GETTING OUT OF HERE.

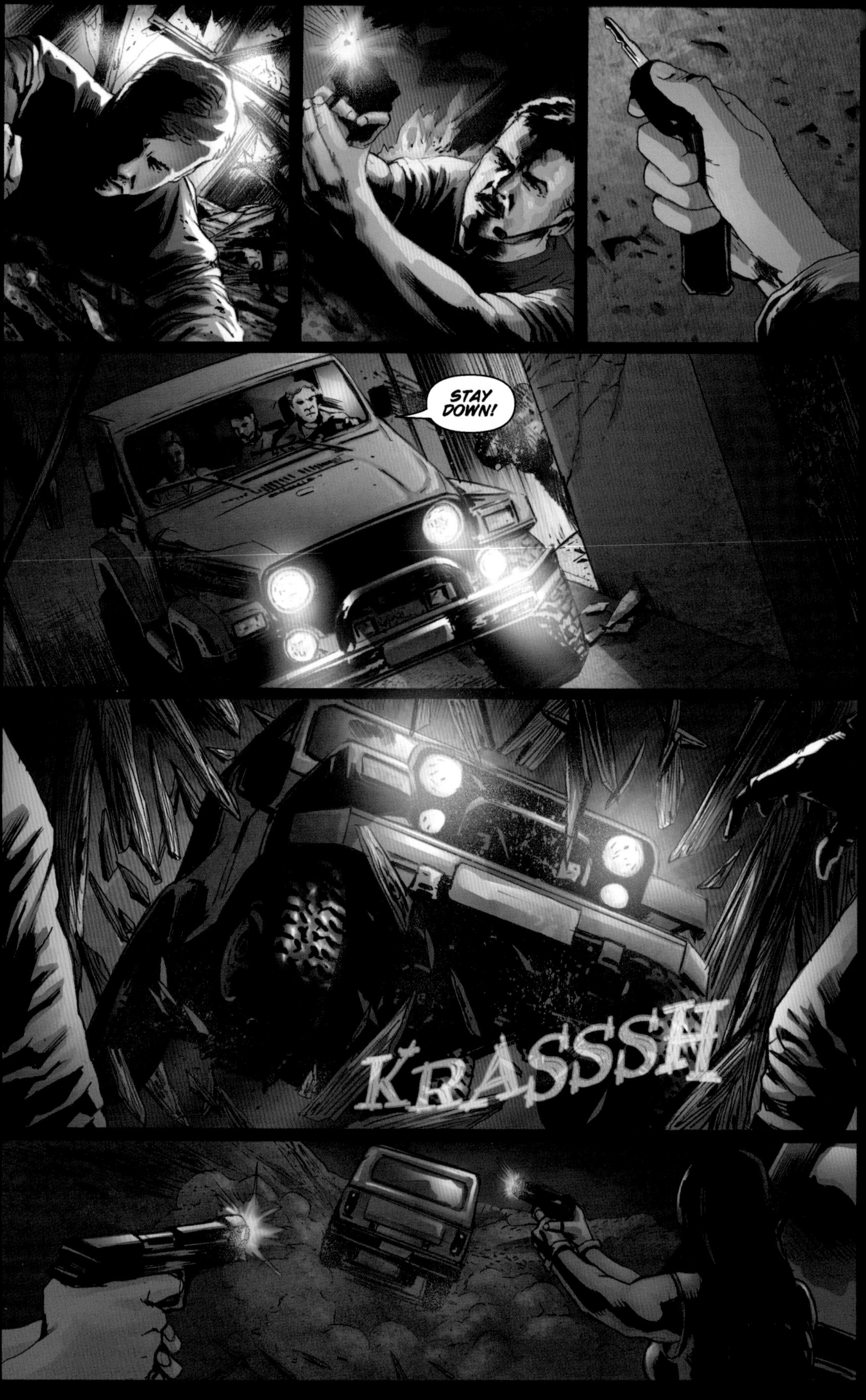
STAY DOWN!
KRASSSH

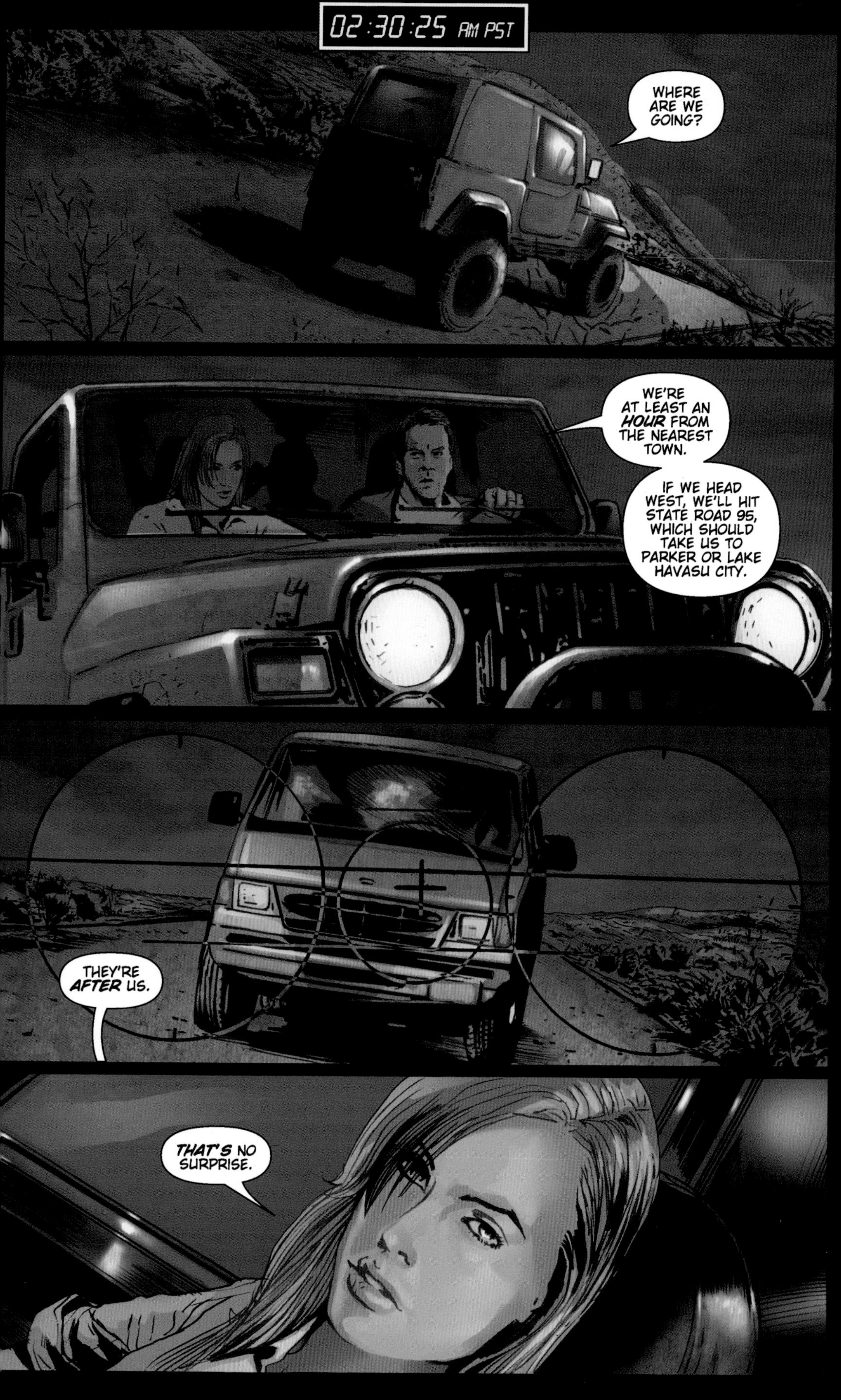
02:30:25 AM PST
WHERE ARE WE GOING?
WE'RE AT LEAST AN HOUR FROM THE NEAREST TOWN.
IF WE HEAD WEST, WE'LL HIT STATE ROAD 95, WHICH SHOULD TAKE US TO PARKER OR LAKE HAVASU CITY.
THEY'RE AFTER US.
THAT'S NO SURPRISE.

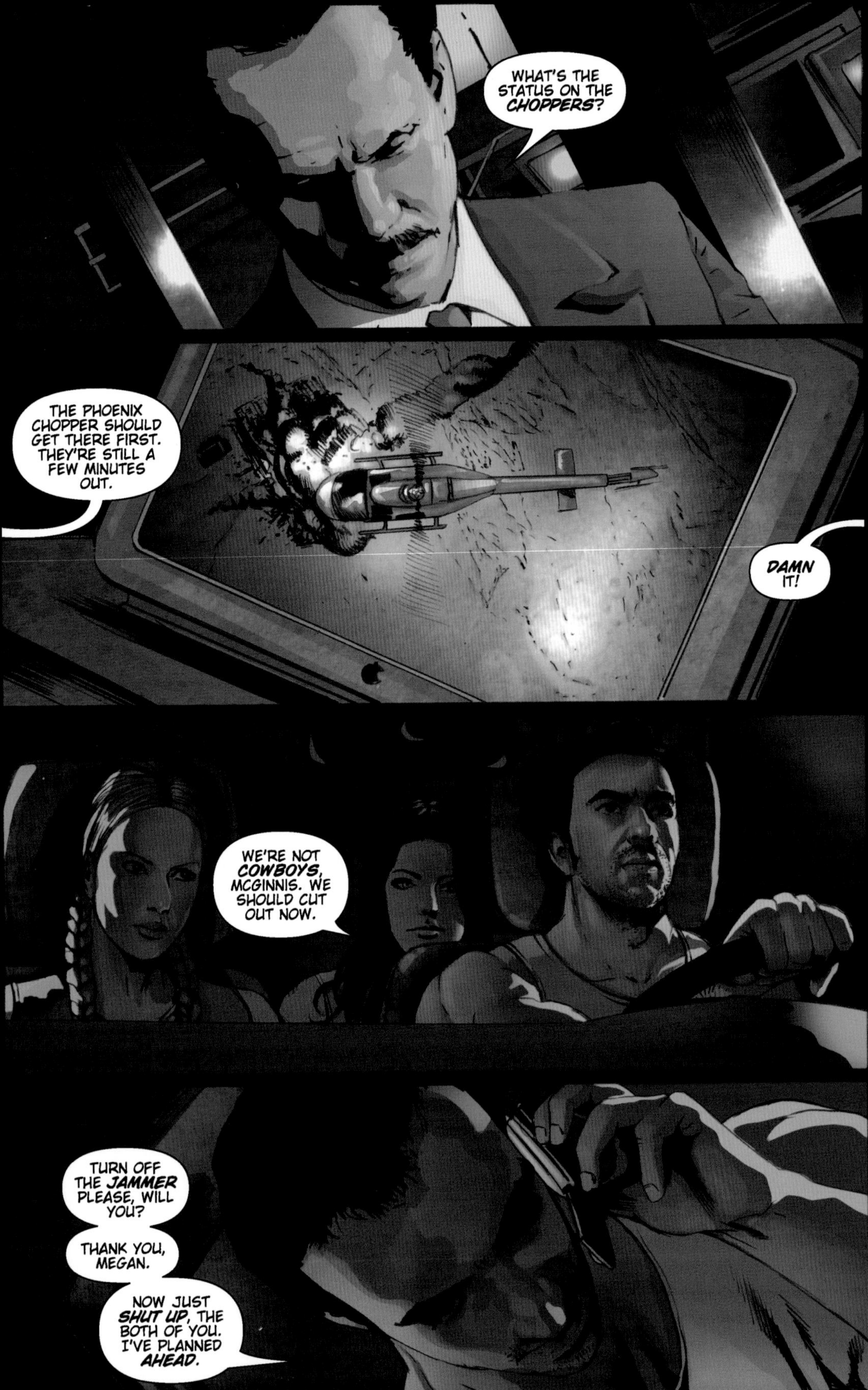
WHAT'S THE STATUS ON THE CHOPPERS?
THE PHOENIX CHOPPER SHOULD GET THERE FIRST. THEY'RE STILL A FEW MINUTES OUT.
DAMN IT!
WE'RE NOT COWBOYS, MCGINNIS. WE SHOULD CUT OUT NOW.
TURN OFF THE JAMMER PLEASE, WILL YOU?
THANK YOU, MEGAN.
NOW JUST SHUT UP, THE BOTH OF YOU. I'VE PLANNED AHEAD.

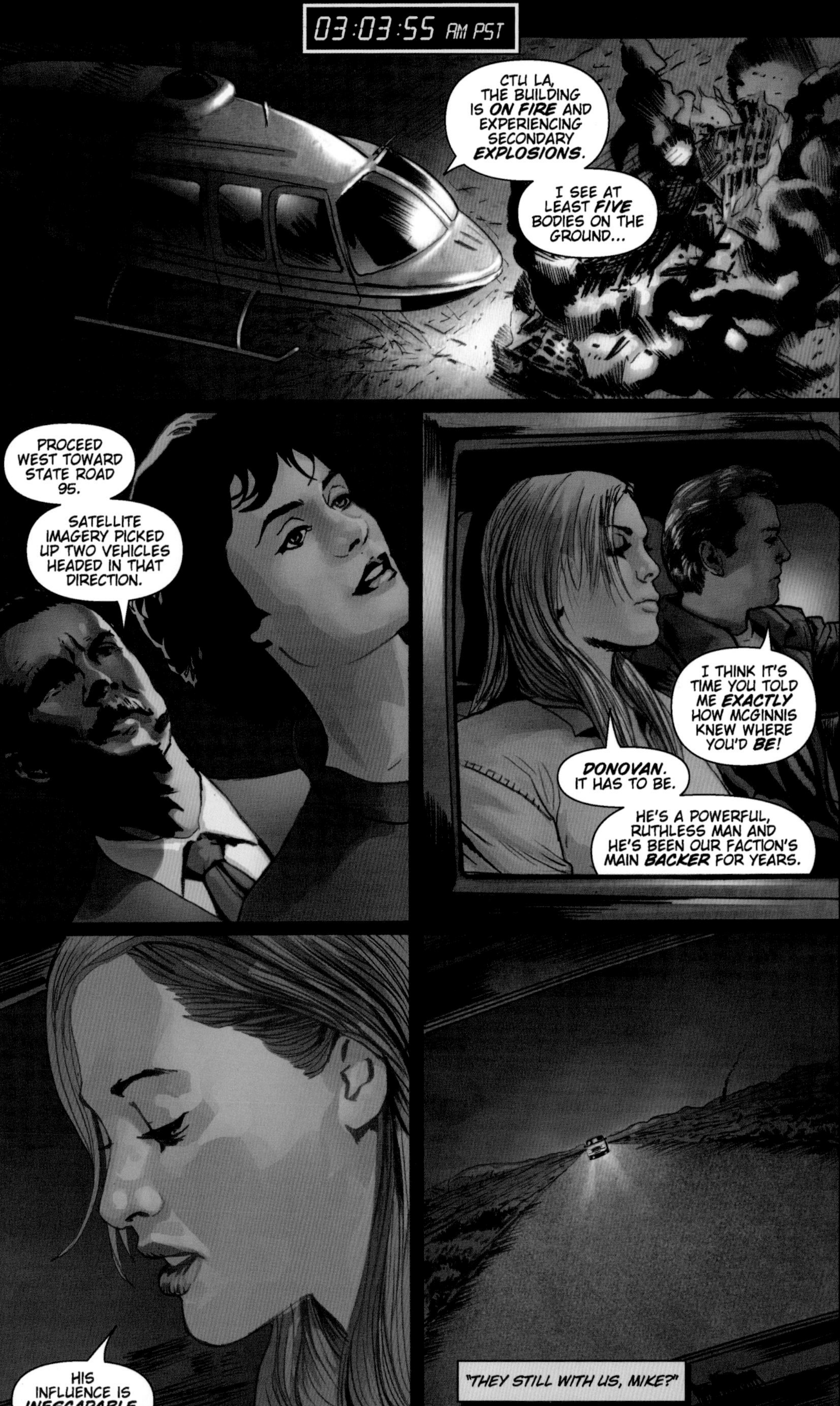
03:03:55 AM PST
CTU LA, THE BUILDING IS ON FIRE AND EXPERIENCING SECONDARY EXPLOSIONS.
I SEE AT LEAST FIVE BODIES ON THE GROUND...
PROCEED WEST TOWARD STATE ROAD 95.
SATELLITE IMAGERY PICKED UP TWO VEHICLES HEADED IN THAT DIRECTION.
I THINK IT'S TIME YOU TOLD ME EXACTLY HOW MCGINNIS KNEW WHERE YOU'D BE!
DONOVAN. IT HAS TO BE.
HE'S A POWERFUL, RUTHLESS MAN AND HE'S BEEN OUR FACTION'S MAIN BACKER FOR YEARS.
HIS INFLUENCE IS
"THEY STILL WITH US, MIKE?"

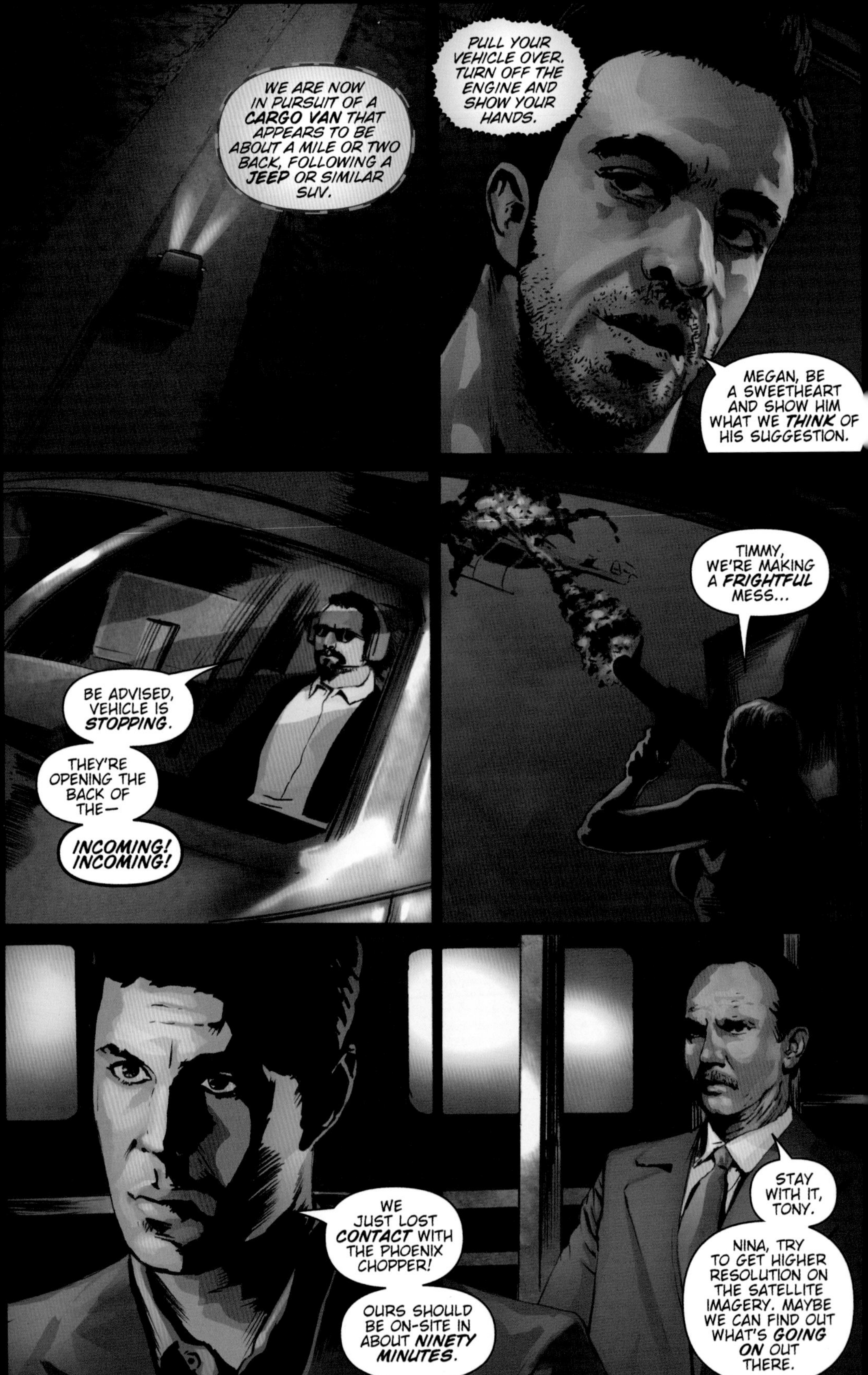

WE ARE NOW IN PURSUIT OF A CARGO VAN THAT APPEARS TO BE ABOUT A MILE OR TWO BACK, FOLLOWING A JEEP OR SIMILAR SUV.
PULL YOUR VEHICLE OVER. TURN OFF THE ENGINE AND SHOW YOUR HANDS.
MEGAN, BE A SWEETHEART AND SHOW HIM WHAT WE THINK OF HIS SUGGESTION.
BE ADVISED, VEHICLE IS STOPPING.
THEY'RE OPENING THE BACK OF THE—
INCOMING! INCOMING!
TIMMY, WE'RE MAKING A FRIGHTFUL MESS...
WE JUST LOST CONTACT WITH THE PHOENIX CHOPPER!
OURS SHOULD BE ON-SITE IN ABOUT NINETY MINUTES.
STAY WITH IT, TONY.
NINA, TRY TO GET HIGHER RESOLUTION ON THE SATELLITE IMAGERY. MAYBE WE CAN FIND OUT WHAT'S GOING ON OUT THERE.

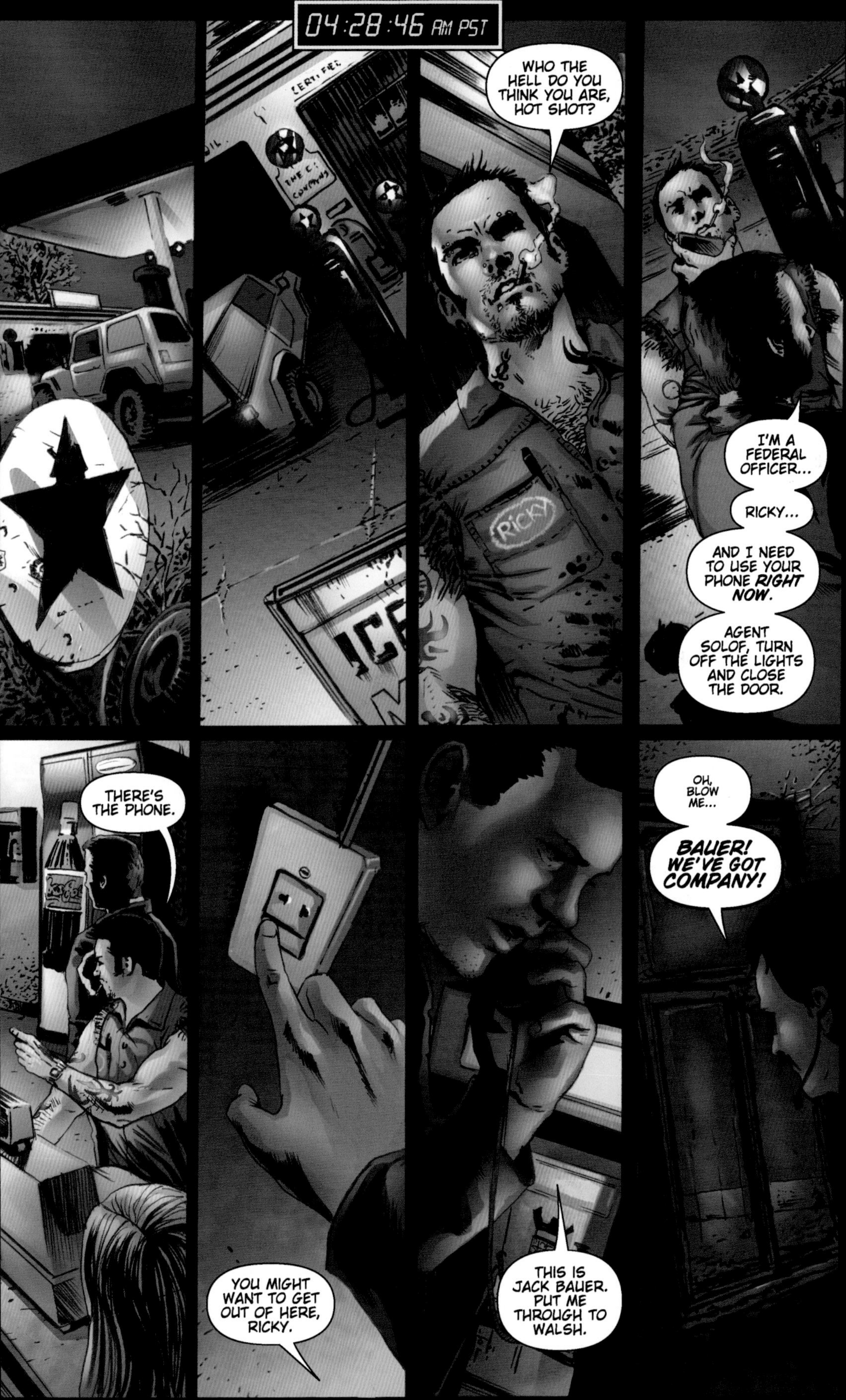
04:28:46 AM PST
WHO THE HELL DO YOU THINK YOU ARE, HOT SHOT?
RICKY
ICE
I'M A FEDERAL OFFICER...
RICKY...
AND I NEED TO USE YOUR PHONE *RIGHT NOW*.
AGENT SOLOF, TURN OFF THE LIGHTS AND CLOSE THE DOOR.
THERE'S THE PHONE.
YOU MIGHT WANT TO GET OUT OF HERE, RICKY.
THIS IS JACK BAUER. PUT ME THROUGH TO WALSH.
OH, BLOW ME...
BAUER! WE'VE GOT COMPANY!

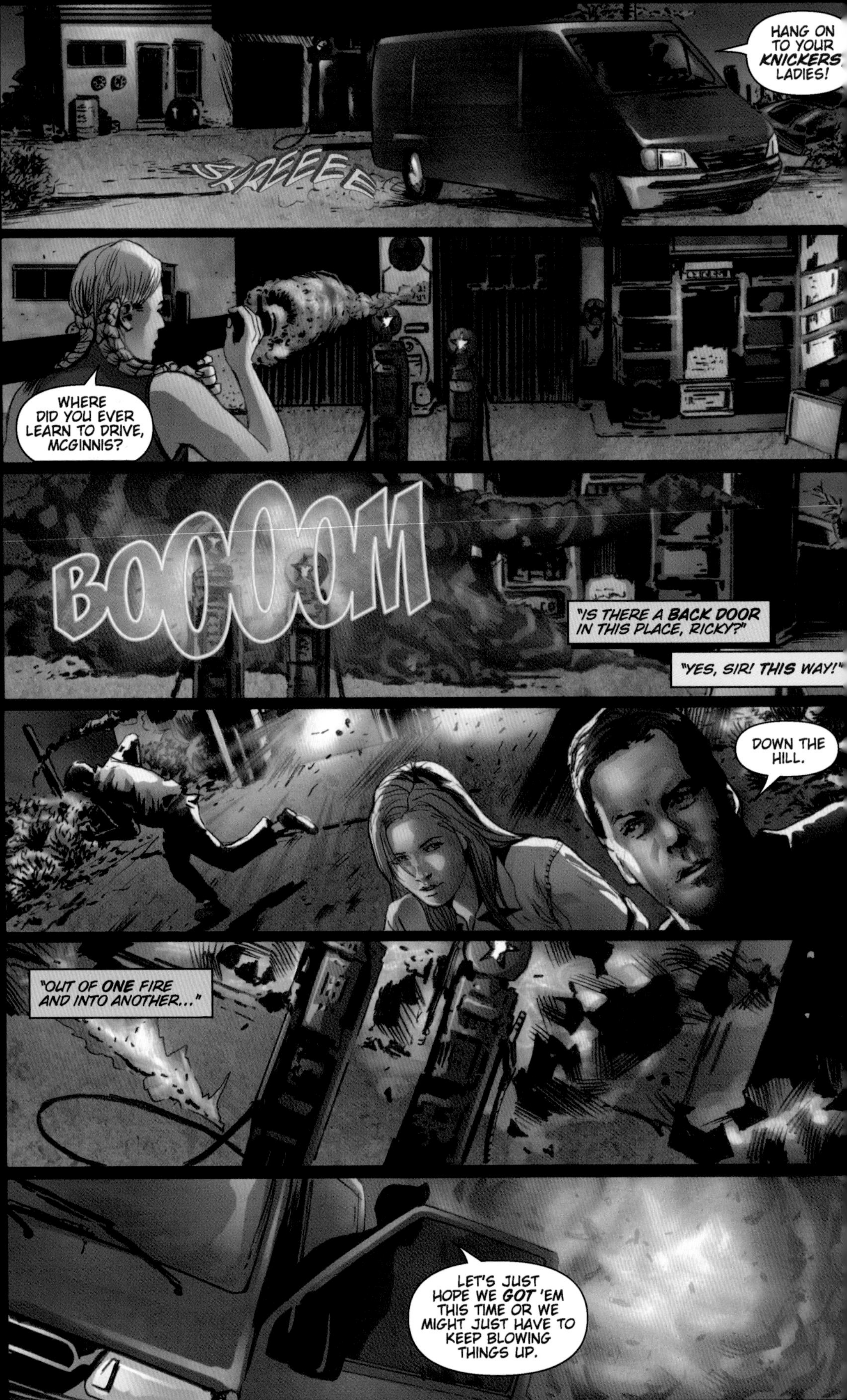
HANG ON TO YOUR KNICKERS, LADIES!
SKREEEEE
WHERE DID YOU EVER LEARN TO DRIVE, MCGINNIS?
BOOOOM
"IS THERE A BACK DOOR IN THIS PLACE, RICKY?"
"YES, SIR! THIS WAY!"
DOWN THE HILL.
"OUT OF ONE FIRE AND INTO ANOTHER..."
LET'S JUST HOPE WE GOT 'EM THIS TIME OR WE MIGHT JUST HAVE TO KEEP BLOWING THINGS UP.

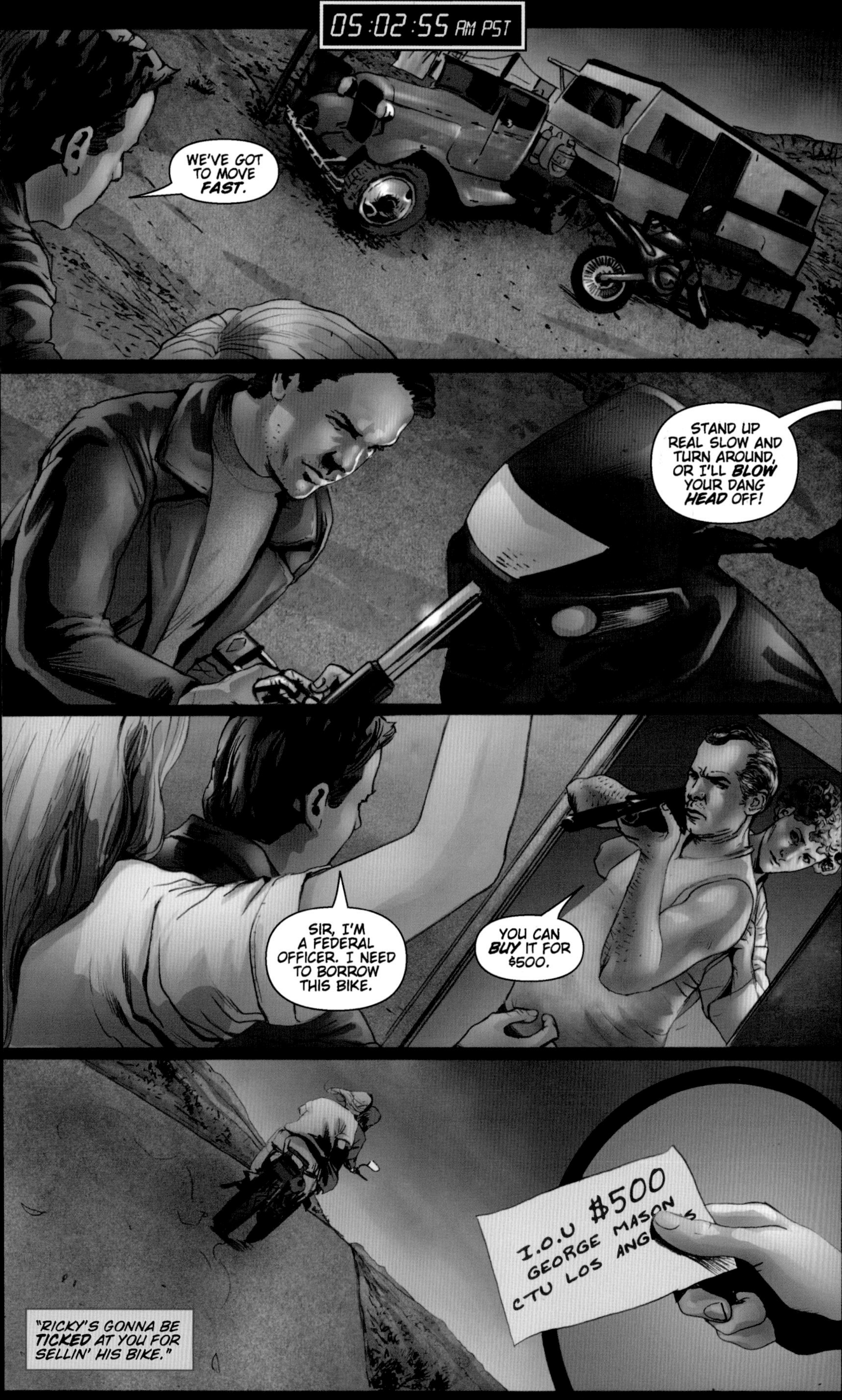
05:02:55 AM PST
WE'VE GOT TO MOVE **FAST**.
STAND UP REAL SLOW AND TURN AROUND, OR I'LL **BLOW** YOUR DANG **HEAD** OFF!
SIR, I'M A FEDERAL OFFICER. I NEED TO BORROW THIS BIKE.
YOU CAN **BUY** IT FOR $500.
"RICKY'S GONNA BE **TICKED** AT YOU FOR SELLIN' HIS BIKE."
I.O.U $500
GEORGE MASON
CTU LOS ANG

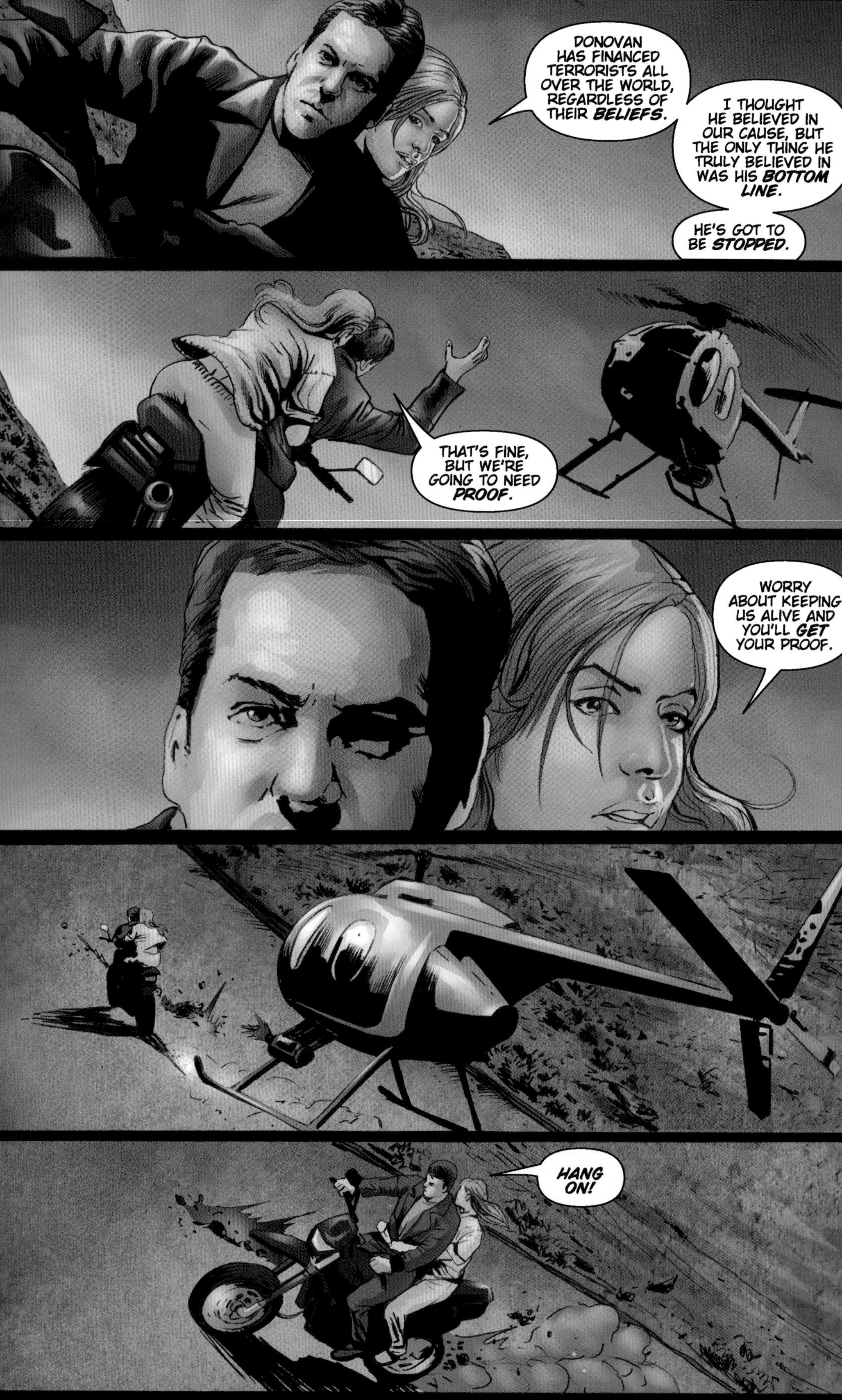
DONOVAN HAS FINANCED TERRORISTS ALL OVER THE WORLD, REGARDLESS OF THEIR BELIEFS.
I THOUGHT HE BELIEVED IN OUR CAUSE, BUT THE ONLY THING HE TRULY BELIEVED IN WAS HIS BOTTOM LINE.
HE'S GOT TO BE STOPPED.
THAT'S FINE, BUT WE'RE GOING TO NEED PROOF.
WORRY ABOUT KEEPING US ALIVE AND YOU'LL GET YOUR PROOF.
HANG ON!

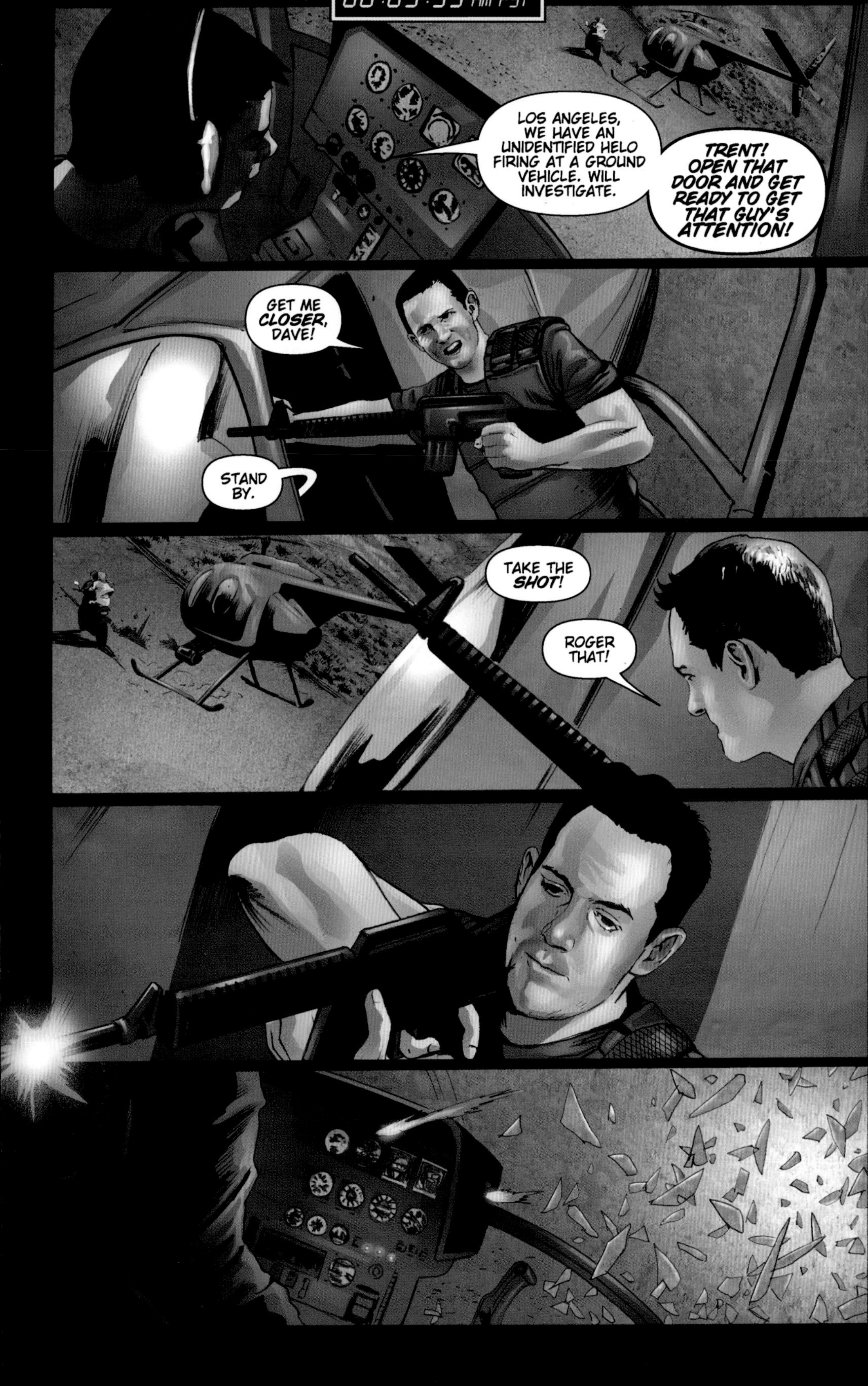
LOS ANGELES, WE HAVE AN UNIDENTIFIED HELO FIRING AT A GROUND VEHICLE. WILL INVESTIGATE.
TRENT! OPEN THAT DOOR AND GET READY TO GET THAT GUY'S ATTENTION!
GET ME CLOSER, DAVE!
STAND BY.
TAKE THE SHOT!
ROGER THAT!

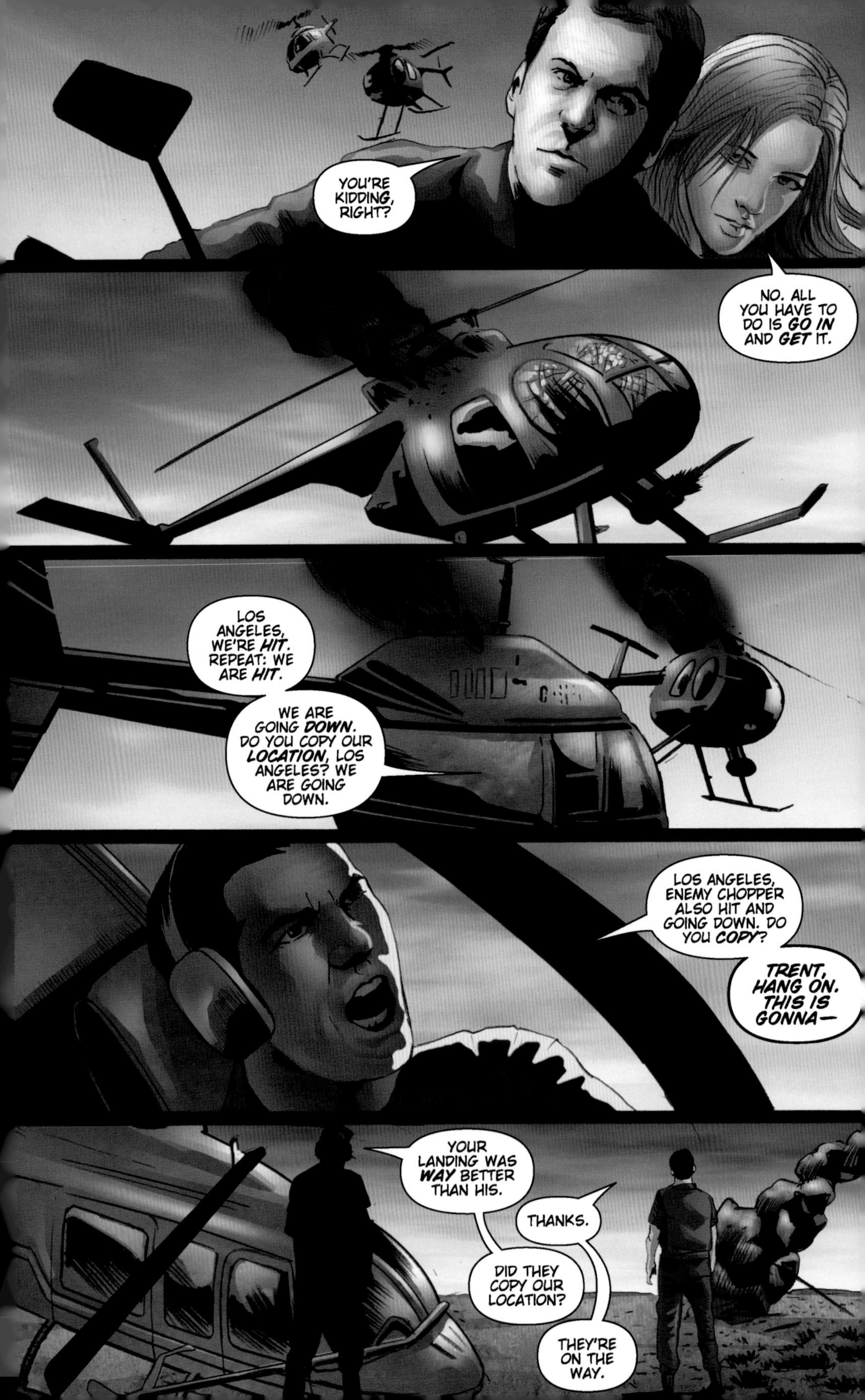

YOU'RE KIDDING, RIGHT?
NO. ALL YOU HAVE TO DO IS GO IN AND GET IT.
LOS ANGELES, WE'RE HIT. REPEAT: WE ARE HIT.
WE ARE GOING DOWN. DO YOU COPY OUR LOCATION, LOS ANGELES? WE ARE GOING DOWN.
LOS ANGELES, ENEMY CHOPPER ALSO HIT AND GOING DOWN. DO YOU COPY?
TRENT, HANG ON. THIS IS GONNA—
YOUR LANDING WAS WAY BETTER THAN HIS.
THANKS.
DID THEY COPY OUR LOCATION?
THEY'RE ON THE WAY.

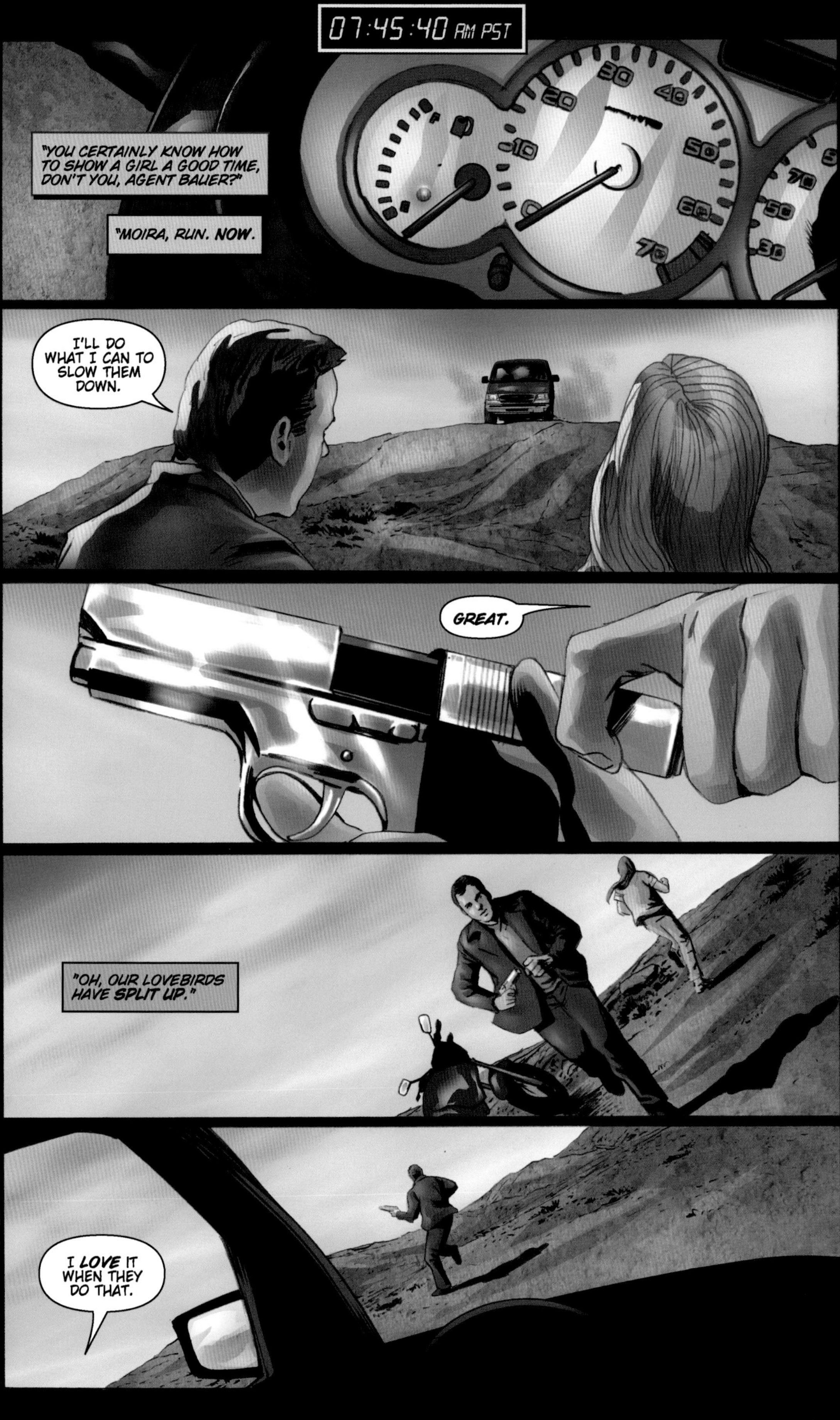
07:45:40 AM PST
"YOU CERTAINLY KNOW HOW TO SHOW A GIRL A GOOD TIME, DON'T YOU, AGENT BAUER?"
"MOIRA, RUN. NOW.
I'LL DO WHAT I CAN TO SLOW THEM DOWN.
GREAT.
"OH, OUR LOVEBIRDS HAVE SPLIT UP."
I LOVE IT WHEN THEY DO THAT.

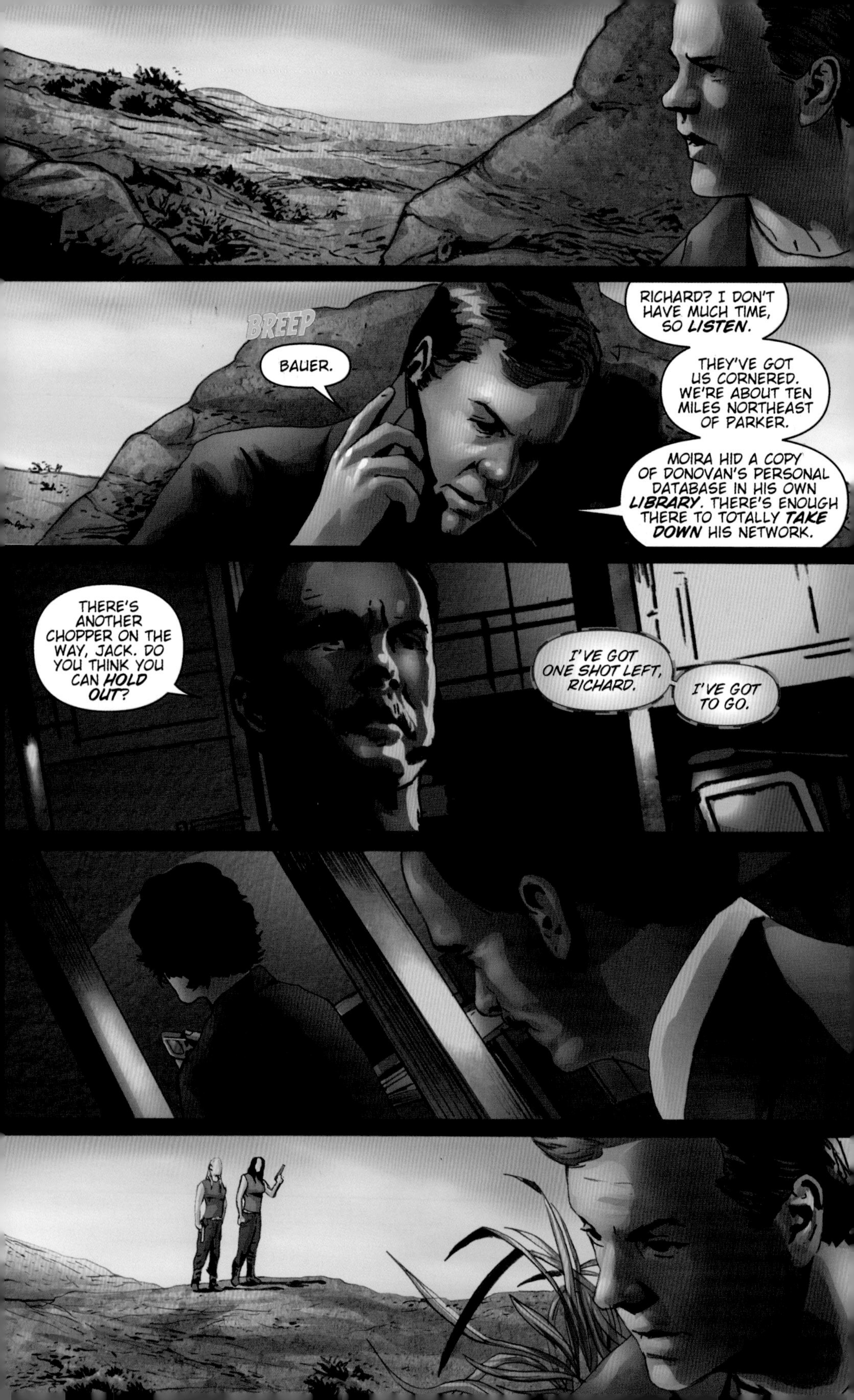
BREEP
BAUER.
RICHARD? I DON'T HAVE MUCH TIME, SO LISTEN.
THEY'VE GOT US CORNERED. WE'RE ABOUT TEN MILES NORTHEAST OF PARKER.
MOIRA HID A COPY OF DONOVAN'S PERSONAL DATABASE IN HIS OWN LIBRARY. THERE'S ENOUGH THERE TO TOTALLY TAKE DOWN HIS NETWORK.
THERE'S ANOTHER CHOPPER ON THE WAY, JACK. DO YOU THINK YOU CAN HOLD OUT?
I'VE GOT ONE SHOT LEFT, RICHARD.
I'VE GOT TO GO.

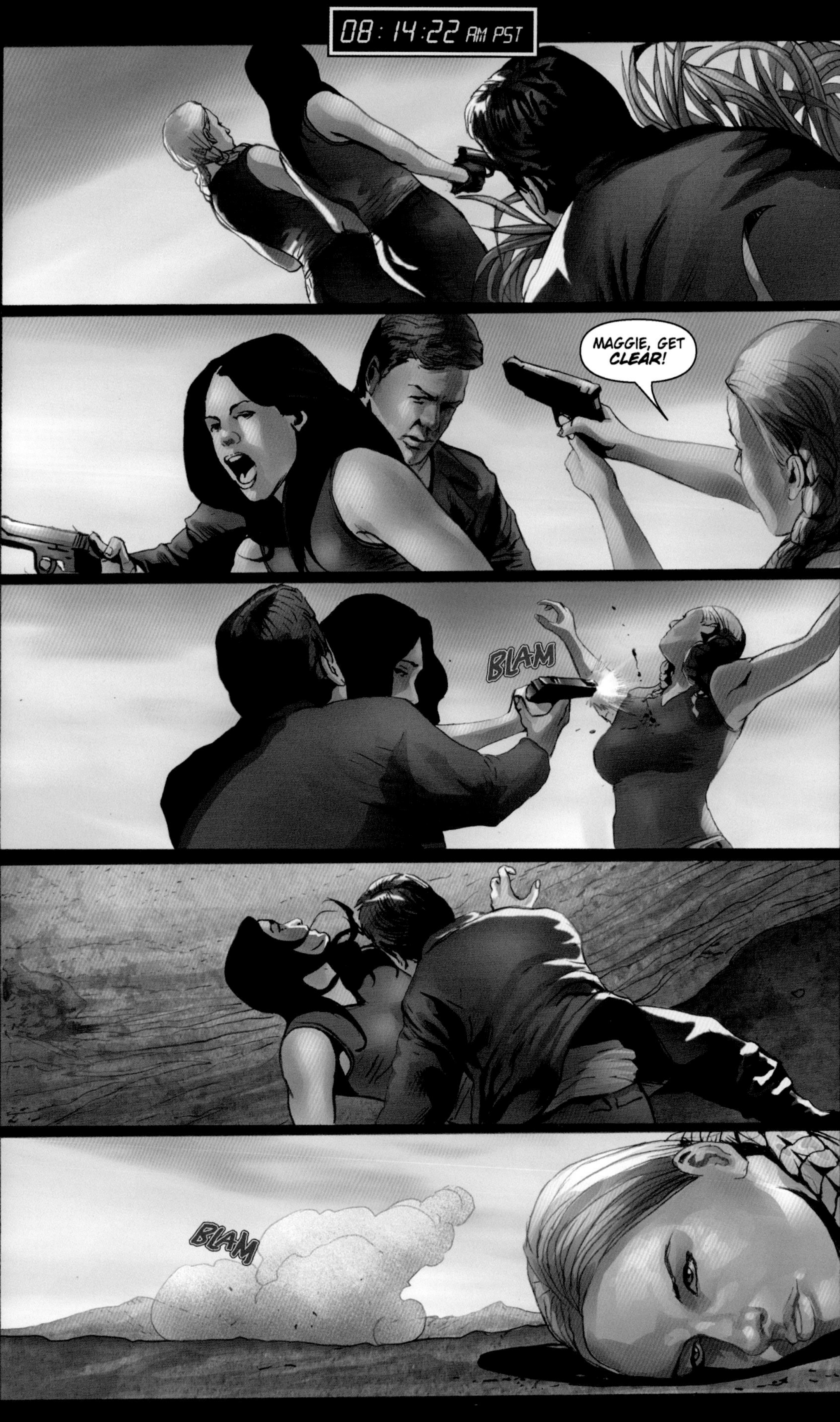
08 : 14 : 22 AM PST
MAGGIE, GET CLEAR!
BLAM
BLAM

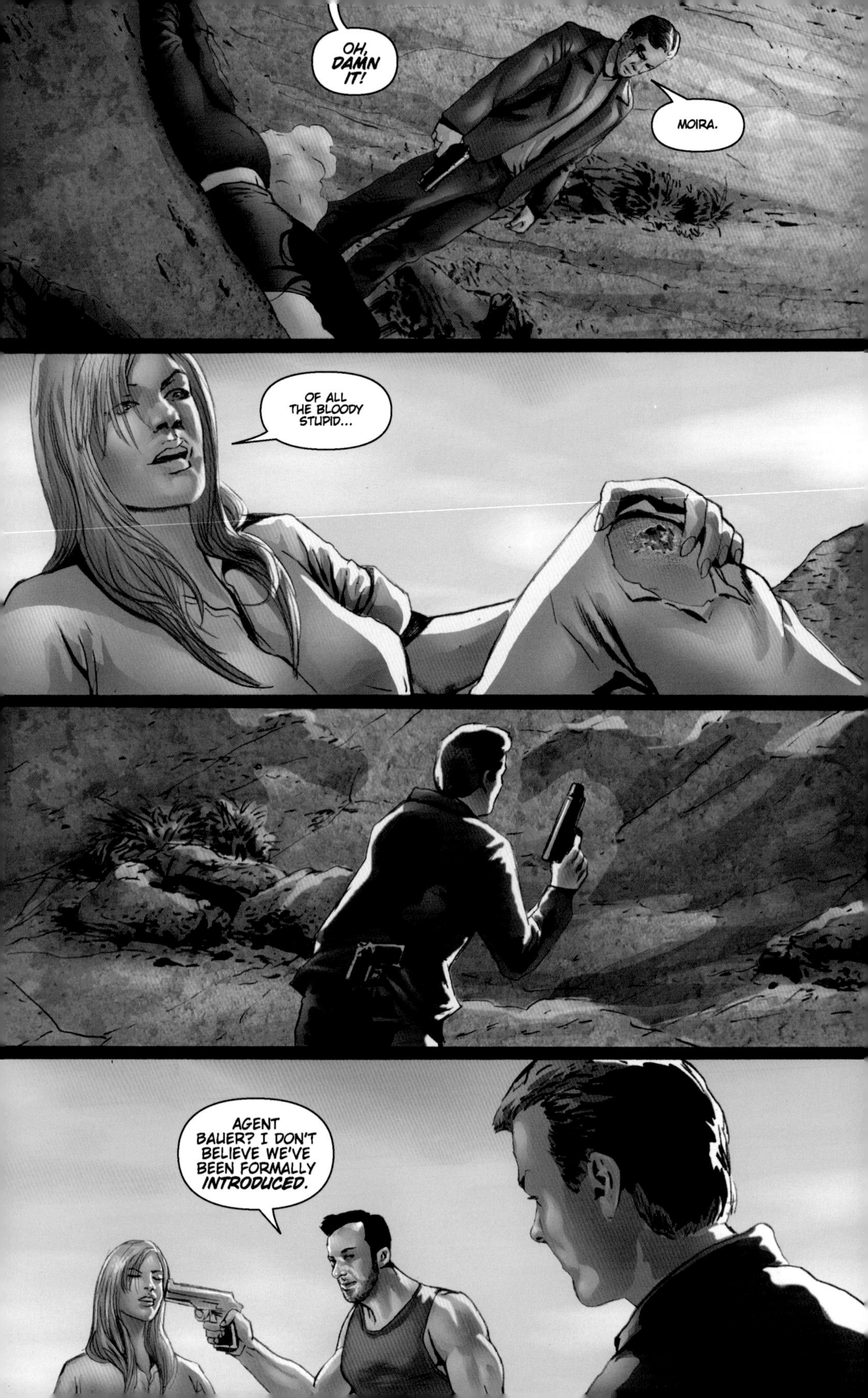
OH, DAMN IT!
MOIRA.
OF ALL THE BLOODY STUPID...
AGENT BAUER? I DON'T BELIEVE WE'VE BEEN FORMALLY INTRODUCED.

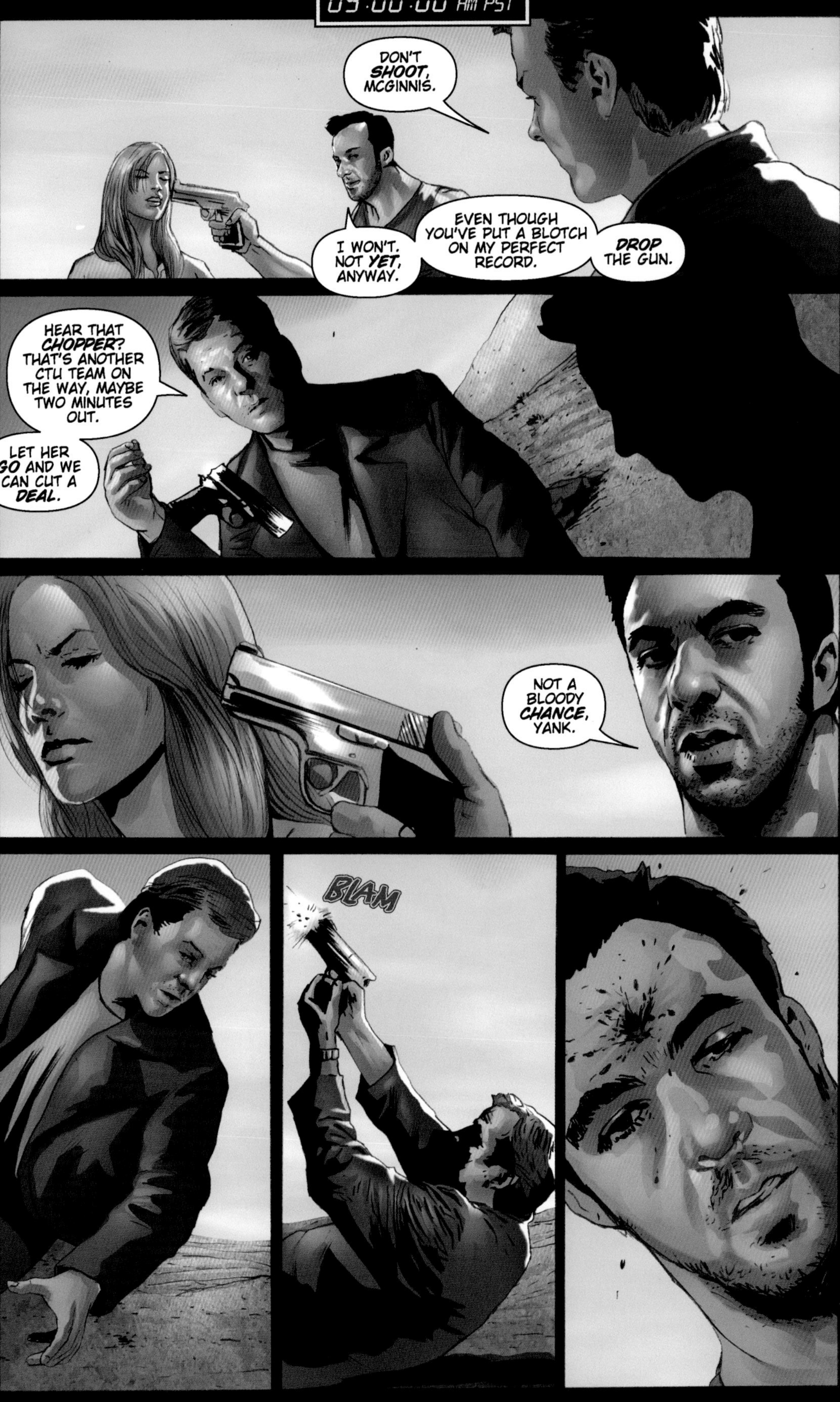
DON'T SHOOT, MCGINNIS.
I WON'T. NOT YET, ANYWAY.
EVEN THOUGH YOU'VE PUT A BLOTCH ON MY PERFECT RECORD.
DROP THE GUN.
HEAR THAT CHOPPER? THAT'S ANOTHER CTU TEAM ON THE WAY, MAYBE TWO MINUTES OUT.
LET HER GO AND WE CAN CUT A DEAL.
NOT A BLOODY CHANCE, YANK.
BLAM

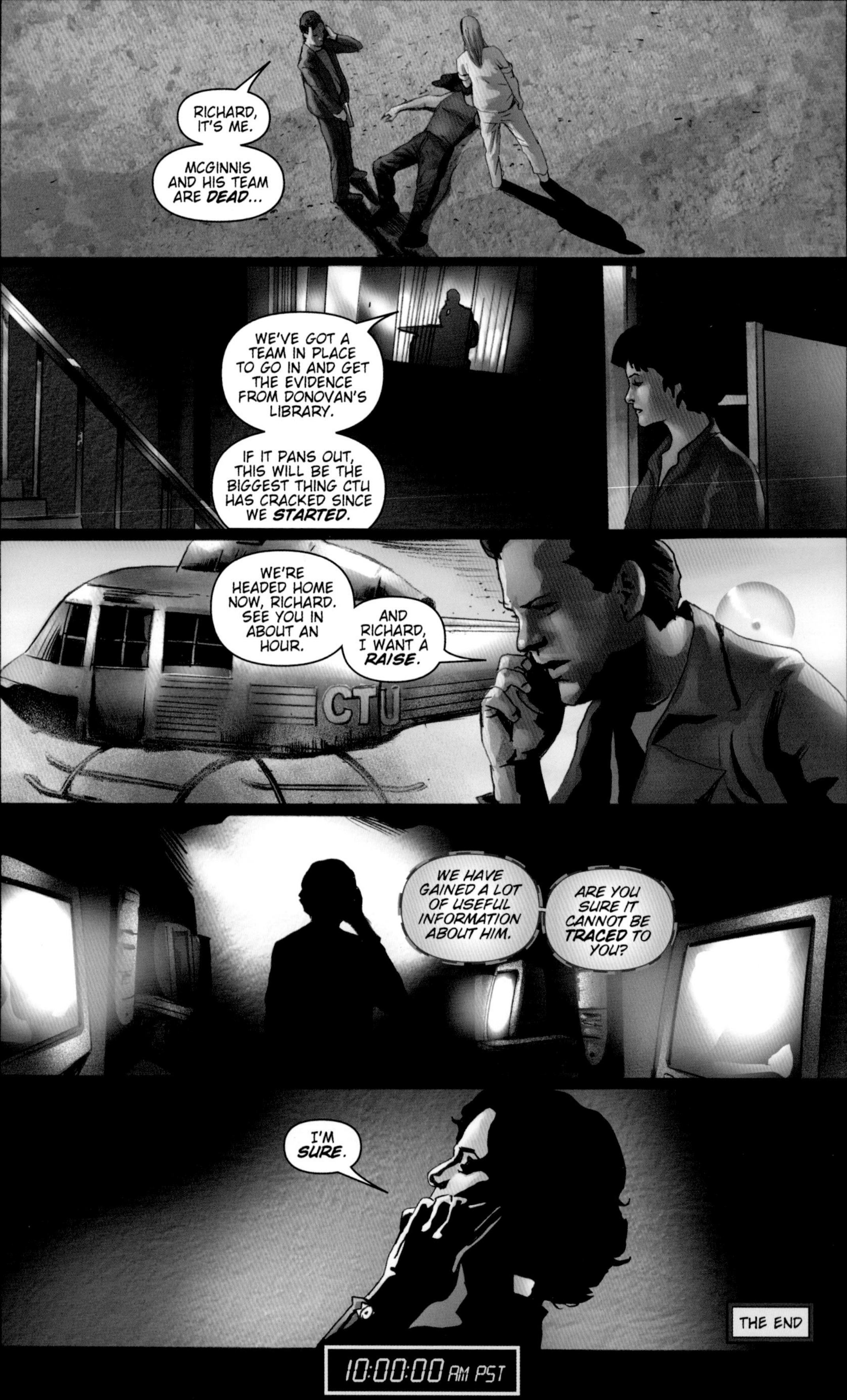
RICHARD, IT'S ME.
MCGINNIS AND HIS TEAM ARE DEAD...
WE'VE GOT A TEAM IN PLACE TO GO IN AND GET THE EVIDENCE FROM DONOVAN'S LIBRARY.
IF IT PANS OUT, THIS WILL BE THE BIGGEST THING CTU HAS CRACKED SINCE WE STARTED.
WE'RE HEADED HOME NOW, RICHARD. SEE YOU IN ABOUT AN HOUR.
AND RICHARD, I WANT A RAISE.
CTU
WE HAVE GAINED A LOT OF USEFUL INFORMATION ABOUT HIM.
ARE YOU SURE IT CANNOT BE TRACED TO YOU?
I'M SURE.
THE END
10:00:00 AM PST

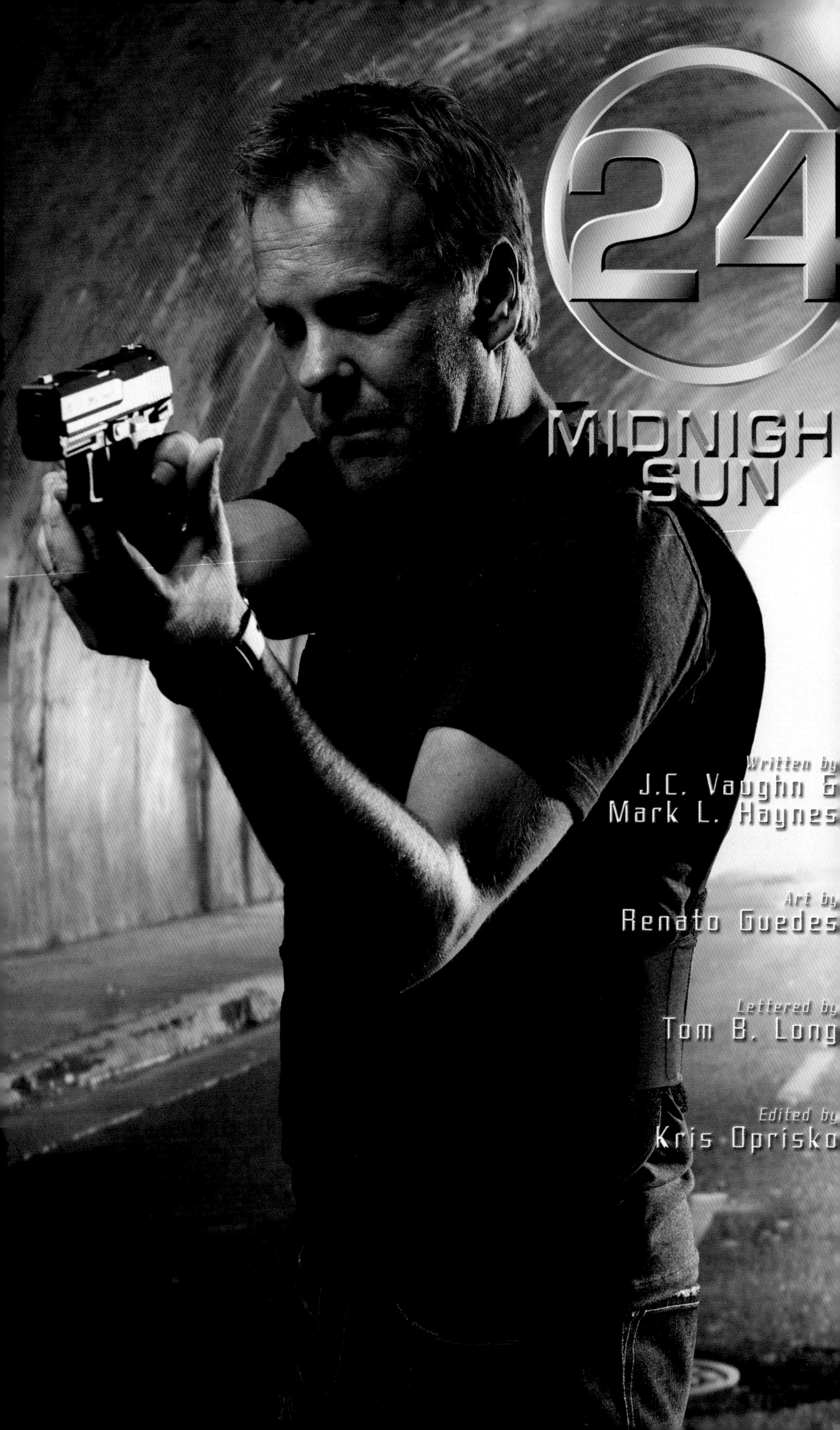
24
MIDNIGH
SUN
Written by
J.C. Vaughn &
Mark L. Haynes
Art by
Renato Guedes
Lettered by
Tom B. Long
Edited by
Kris Oprisko

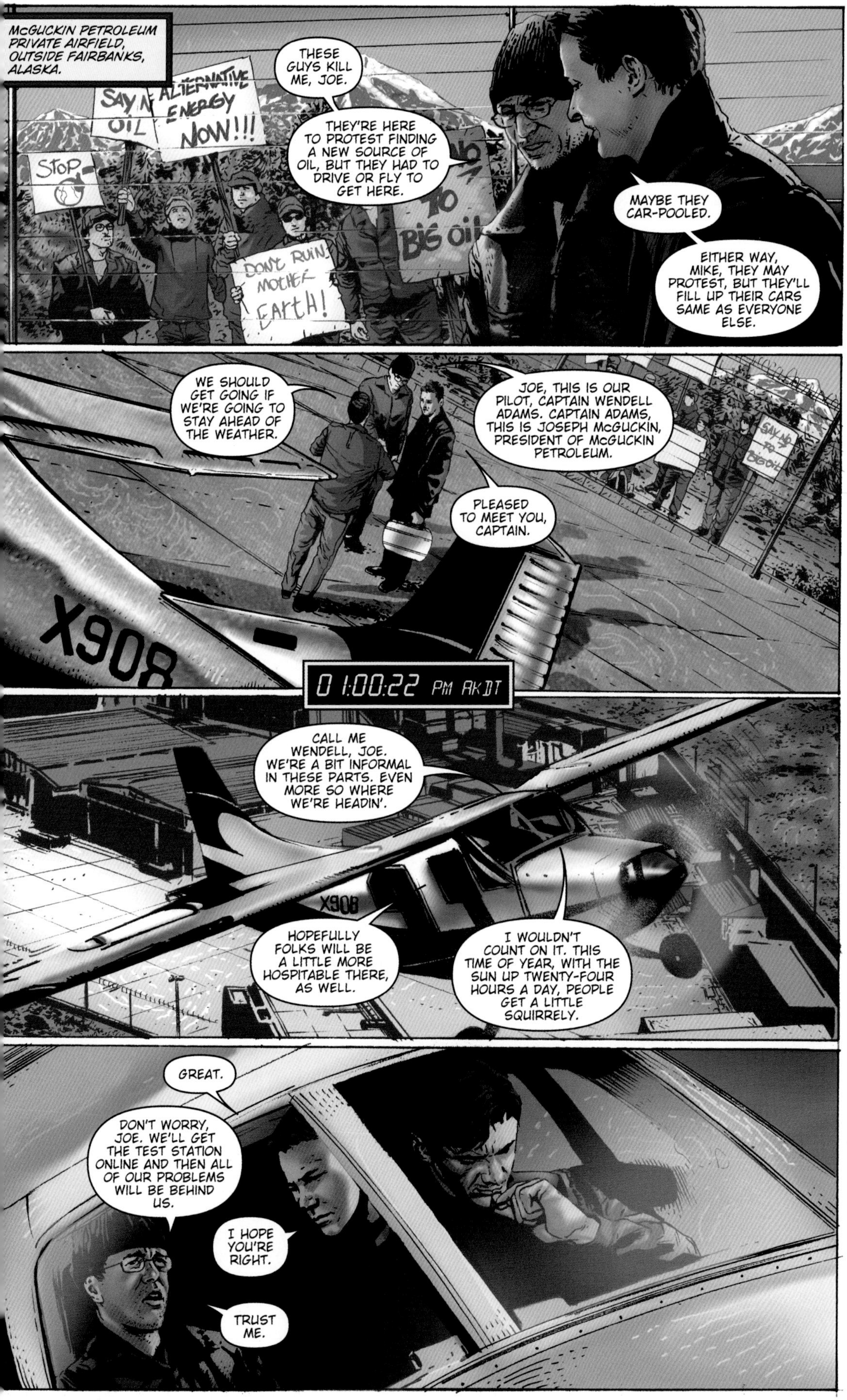
McGUCKIN PETROLEUM PRIVATE AIRFIELD, OUTSIDE FAIRBANKS, ALASKA.
THESE GUYS KILL ME, JOE.
THEY'RE HERE TO PROTEST FINDING A NEW SOURCE OF OIL, BUT THEY HAD TO DRIVE OR FLY TO GET HERE.
MAYBE THEY CAR-POOLED.
EITHER WAY, MIKE, THEY MAY PROTEST, BUT THEY'LL FILL UP THEIR CARS SAME AS EVERYONE ELSE.
ALTERNATIVE ENERGY NOW!!!
STOP
NO TO BIG OIL
DON'T RUIN MOTHER EARTH!
WE SHOULD GET GOING IF WE'RE GOING TO STAY AHEAD OF THE WEATHER.
JOE, THIS IS OUR PILOT, CAPTAIN WENDELL ADAMS. CAPTAIN ADAMS, THIS IS JOSEPH McGUCKIN, PRESIDENT OF McGUCKIN PETROLEUM.
PLEASED TO MEET YOU, CAPTAIN.
X908
01:00:22 PM AKDT
CALL ME WENDELL, JOE. WE'RE A BIT INFORMAL IN THESE PARTS. EVEN MORE SO WHERE WE'RE HEADIN'.
HOPEFULLY FOLKS WILL BE A LITTLE MORE HOSPITABLE THERE, AS WELL.
I WOULDN'T COUNT ON IT. THIS TIME OF YEAR, WITH THE SUN UP TWENTY-FOUR HOURS A DAY, PEOPLE GET A LITTLE SQUIRRELY.
GREAT.
DON'T WORRY, JOE. WE'LL GET THE TEST STATION ONLINE AND THEN ALL OF OUR PROBLEMS WILL BE BEHIND US.
I HOPE YOU'RE RIGHT.
TRUST ME.

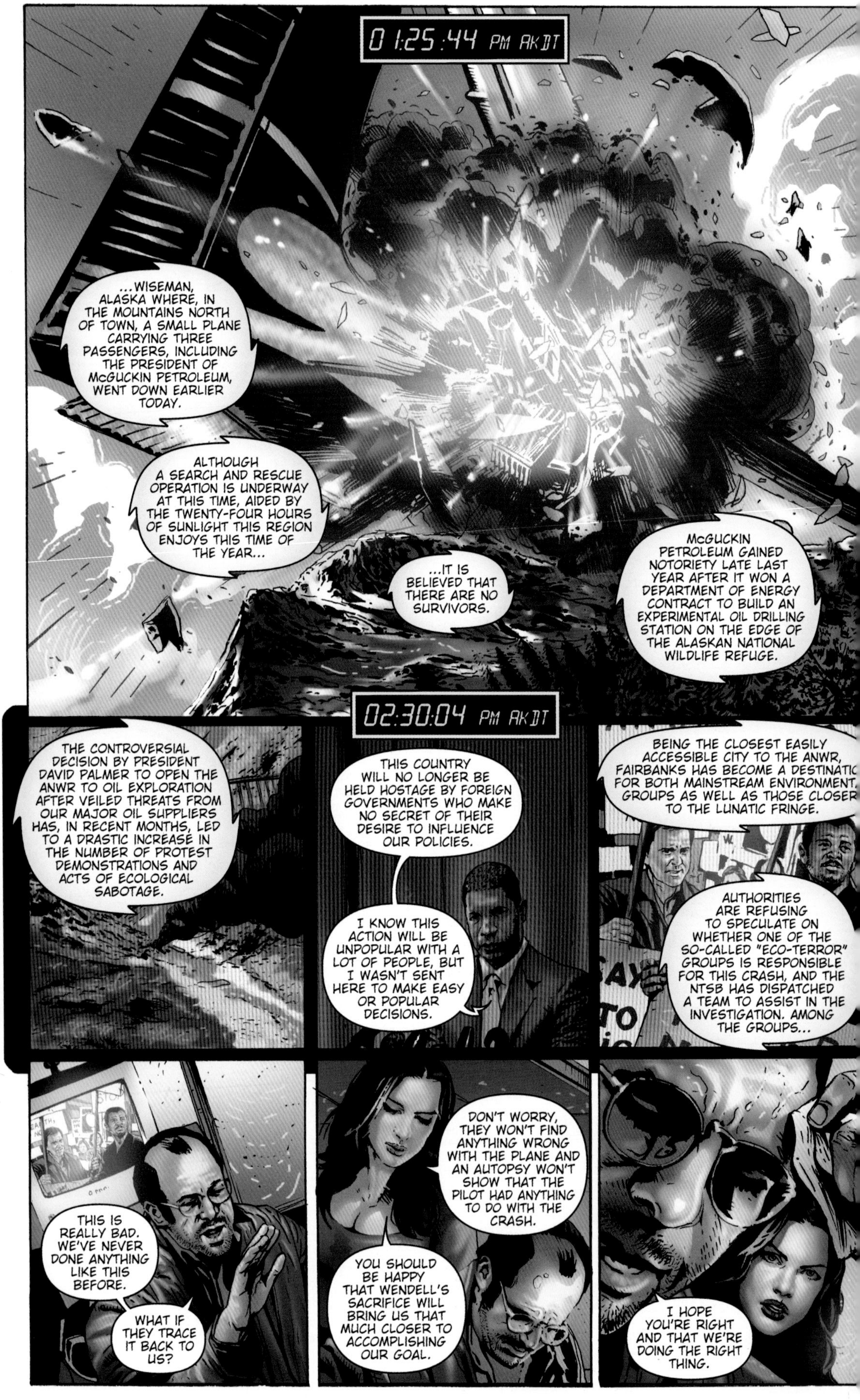
01:25:44 PM AKDT
...WISEMAN, ALASKA WHERE, IN THE MOUNTAINS NORTH OF TOWN, A SMALL PLANE CARRYING THREE PASSENGERS, INCLUDING THE PRESIDENT OF McGUCKIN PETROLEUM, WENT DOWN EARLIER TODAY.
ALTHOUGH A SEARCH AND RESCUE OPERATION IS UNDERWAY AT THIS TIME, AIDED BY THE TWENTY-FOUR HOURS OF SUNLIGHT THIS REGION ENJOYS THIS TIME OF THE YEAR...
...IT IS BELIEVED THAT THERE ARE NO SURVIVORS.
McGUCKIN PETROLEUM GAINED NOTORIETY LATE LAST YEAR AFTER IT WON A DEPARTMENT OF ENERGY CONTRACT TO BUILD AN EXPERIMENTAL OIL DRILLING STATION ON THE EDGE OF THE ALASKAN NATIONAL WILDLIFE REFUGE.
02:30:04 PM AKDT
THE CONTROVERSIAL DECISION BY PRESIDENT DAVID PALMER TO OPEN THE ANWR TO OIL EXPLORATION AFTER VEILED THREATS FROM OUR MAJOR OIL SUPPLIERS HAS, IN RECENT MONTHS, LED TO A DRASTIC INCREASE IN THE NUMBER OF PROTEST DEMONSTRATIONS AND ACTS OF ECOLOGICAL SABOTAGE.
THIS COUNTRY WILL NO LONGER BE HELD HOSTAGE BY FOREIGN GOVERNMENTS WHO MAKE NO SECRET OF THEIR DESIRE TO INFLUENCE OUR POLICIES.
I KNOW THIS ACTION WILL BE UNPOPULAR WITH A LOT OF PEOPLE, BUT I WASN'T SENT HERE TO MAKE EASY OR POPULAR DECISIONS.
BEING THE CLOSEST EASILY ACCESSIBLE CITY TO THE ANWR, FAIRBANKS HAS BECOME A DESTINATIC FOR BOTH MAINSTREAM ENVIRONMENT GROUPS AS WELL AS THOSE CLOSER TO THE LUNATIC FRINGE.
AUTHORITIES ARE REFUSING TO SPECULATE ON WHETHER ONE OF THE SO-CALLED "ECO-TERROR" GROUPS IS RESPONSIBLE FOR THIS CRASH, AND THE NTSB HAS DISPATCHED A TEAM TO ASSIST IN THE INVESTIGATION. AMONG THE GROUPS...
THIS IS REALLY BAD. WE'VE NEVER DONE ANYTHING LIKE THIS BEFORE.
WHAT IF THEY TRACE IT BACK TO US?
DON'T WORRY, THEY WON'T FIND ANYTHING WRONG WITH THE PLANE AND AN AUTOPSY WON'T SHOW THAT THE PILOT HAD ANYTHING TO DO WITH THE CRASH.
YOU SHOULD BE HAPPY THAT WENDELL'S SACRIFICE WILL BRING US THAT MUCH CLOSER TO ACCOMPLISHING OUR GOAL.
I HOPE YOU'RE RIGHT AND THAT WE'RE DOING THE RIGHT THING.

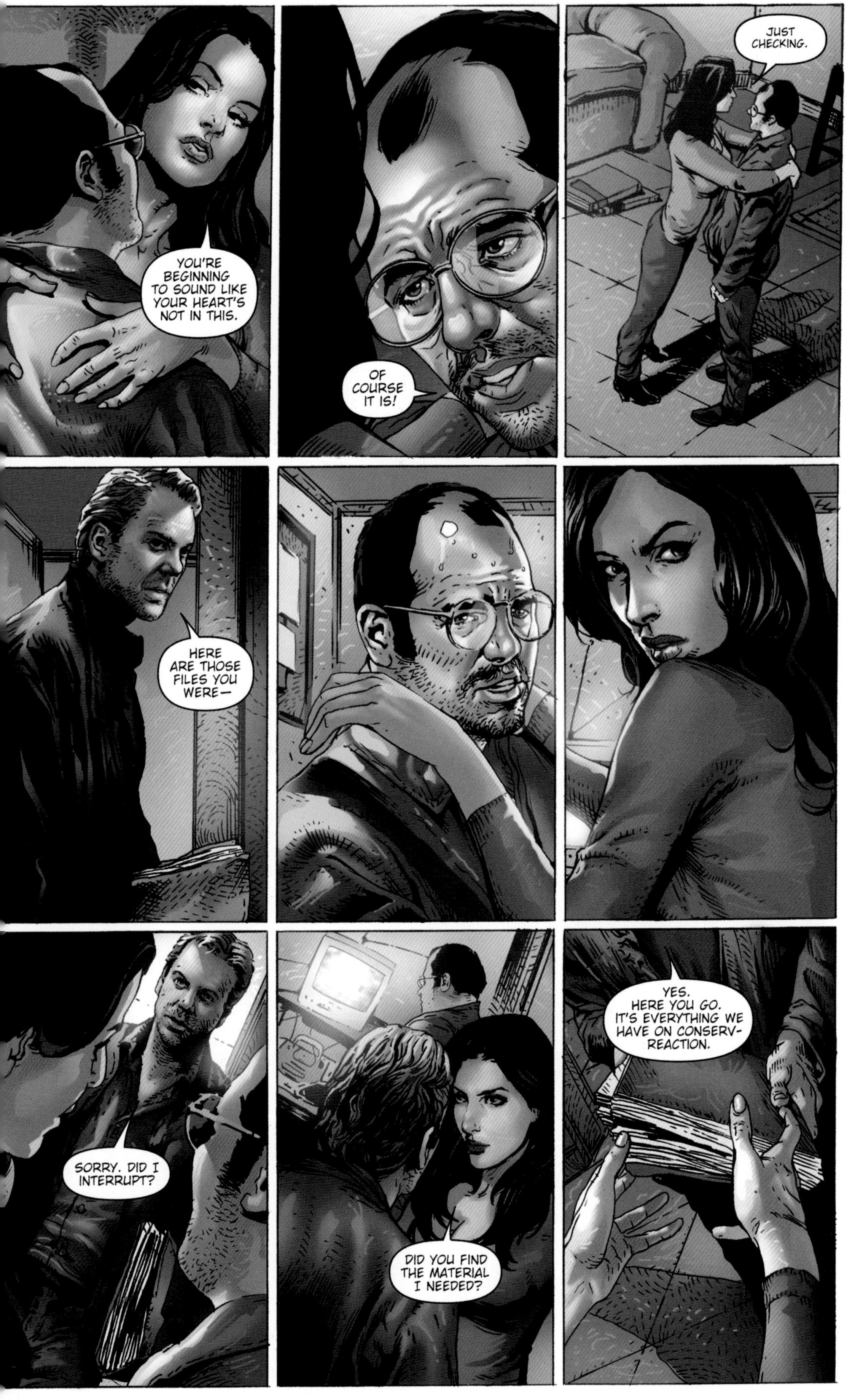
YOU'RE BEGINNING TO SOUND LIKE YOUR HEART'S NOT IN THIS.
OF COURSE IT IS!
JUST CHECKING.
HERE ARE THOSE FILES YOU WERE—
SORRY. DID I INTERRUPT?
DID YOU FIND THE MATERIAL I NEEDED?
YES. HERE YOU GO. IT'S EVERYTHING WE HAVE ON CONSERV-REACTION.

GOOD WORK, JACK. KEEP IT UP.

THANKS.

IF, HOWEVER, THE CRASH IS THE RESULT OF FOUL PLAY, ONE THING WILL HAVE BECOME CLEAR: THE LENGTHS TO WHICH THESE GROUPS WILL GO TO MAKE THEIR POINT MAY HAVE JUST BEEN TAKEN TO THE NEXT LEVEL.

CTU FIELD OFFICE, FAIRBANKS, ALASKA.

ALRIGHT, PEOPLE, LISTEN UP.

THIS IS CHASE EDMUNDS FROM THE L.A. OFFICE. HE'S HERE TO BRIEF US ON AN ONGOING OPERATION THAT HAS BROUGHT THEM TO OUR NEIGHBORHOOD. CHASE?

THANKS, MIKE. SEVERAL MONTHS AGO, AGENT JACK BAUER WAS SENT UNDERCOVER WITH GLOBAL PEACE FOR A CLEANER ENVIRONMENT, OR G-PACE.

`03:00:58 PM AKDT`

THE MISSION WAS UNDERTAKEN AFTER ECHELON INTERCEPTS LED HOMELAND SECURITY TO SUSPECT THAT ONCE-PEACEFUL GROUPS WERE LOOKING TO ALLY THEMSELVES WITH MORE EXTREME ELEMENTS.

SO FAR, JACK HAS BEEN ABLE TO ESTABLISH THAT THERE ARE INDEED CONNECTIONS BETWEEN G-PACE AND THE MORNINGSIDE DAWN, AN ENVIRONMENTAL TERRORIST GROUP RESPONSIBLE FOR NUMEROUS ACTS OF VANDALISM AGAINST EVERYONE FROM CAR DEALERS TO LARGE LUMBER COMPANIES. WHAT WE NEED TO—

BREPEPEPEP

EXCUSE ME.

WHILE PRESIDENT PALMER OPENED THE ANWR VERY CAUTIOUSLY AND HE REMAINS COMMITTED TO ENVIRONMENTALISM, THERE ARE ELEMENTS THAT WOULD STOP AT NOTHING TO MAKE SURE THE ANWR IS PRESERVED AT ANY COST.

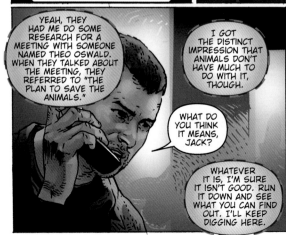

YEAH, THEY HAD ME DO SOME RESEARCH FOR A MEETING WITH SOMEONE NAMED THEO OSWALD. WHEN THEY TALKED ABOUT THE MEETING, THEY REFERRED TO "THE PLAN TO SAVE THE ANIMALS."

I GOT THE DISTINCT IMPRESSION THAT ANIMALS DON'T HAVE MUCH TO DO WITH IT, THOUGH.

WHAT DO YOU THINK IT MEANS, JACK?

WHATEVER IT IS, I'M SURE IT ISN'T GOOD. RUN IT DOWN AND SEE WHAT YOU CAN FIND OUT. I'LL KEEP DIGGING HERE.

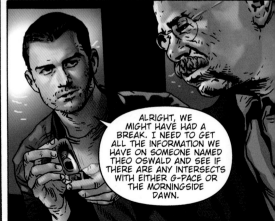

ALRIGHT, WE MIGHT HAVE HAD A BREAK. I NEED TO GET ALL THE INFORMATION WE HAVE ON SOMEONE NAMED THEO OSWALD AND SEE IF THERE ARE ANY INTERSECTS WITH EITHER G-PACE OR THE MORNINGSIDE DAWN.

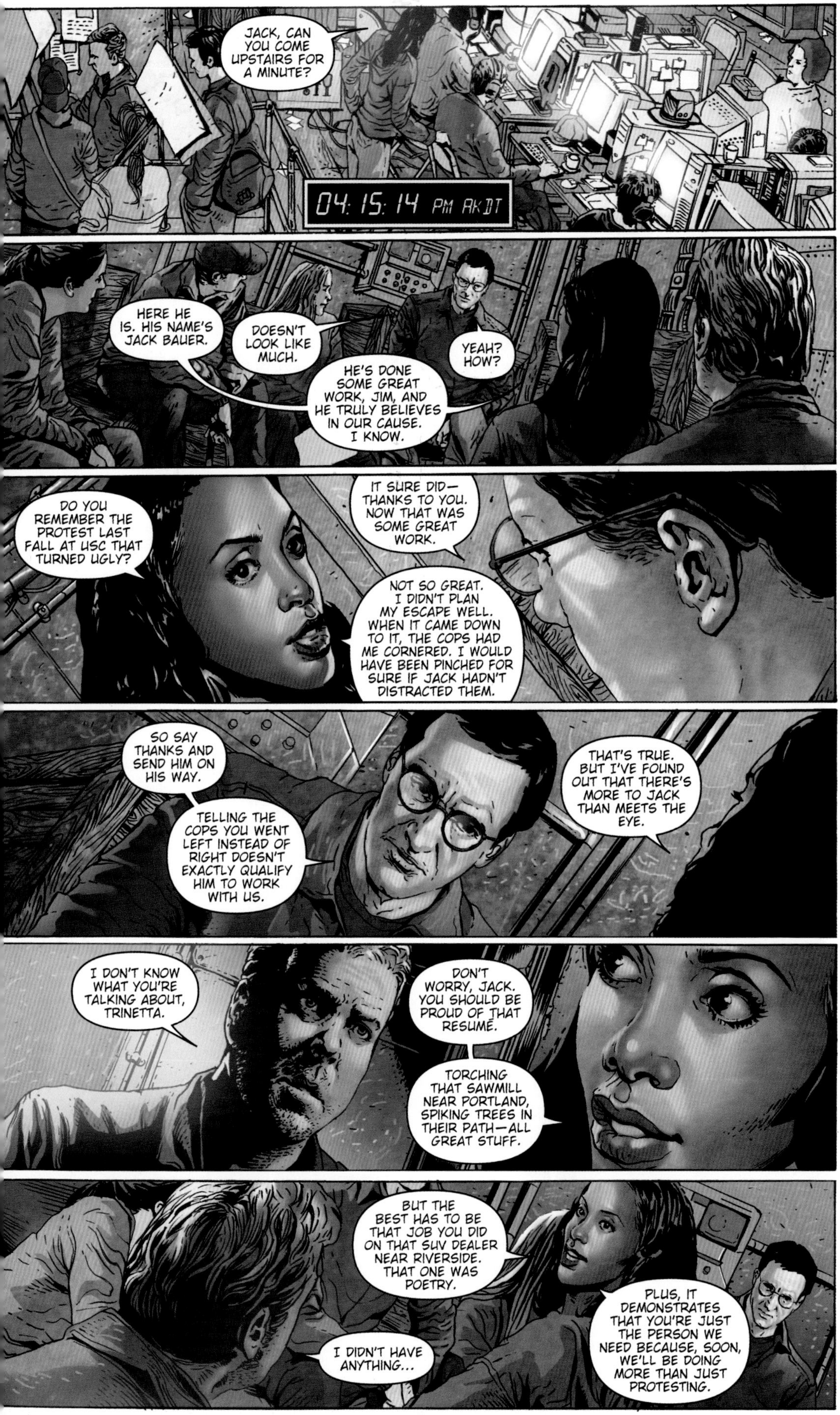
JACK, CAN YOU COME UPSTAIRS FOR A MINUTE?
04:15:14 PM AKDT
HERE HE IS. HIS NAME'S JACK BAUER.
DOESN'T LOOK LIKE MUCH.
YEAH? HOW?
HE'S DONE SOME GREAT WORK, JIM, AND HE TRULY BELIEVES IN OUR CAUSE. I KNOW.
DO YOU REMEMBER THE PROTEST LAST FALL AT USC THAT TURNED UGLY?
IT SURE DID—THANKS TO YOU. NOW THAT WAS SOME GREAT WORK.
NOT SO GREAT. I DIDN'T PLAN MY ESCAPE WELL. WHEN IT CAME DOWN TO IT, THE COPS HAD ME CORNERED. I WOULD HAVE BEEN PINCHED FOR SURE IF JACK HADN'T DISTRACTED THEM.
SO SAY THANKS AND SEND HIM ON HIS WAY.
TELLING THE COPS YOU WENT LEFT INSTEAD OF RIGHT DOESN'T EXACTLY QUALIFY HIM TO WORK WITH US.
THAT'S TRUE. BUT I'VE FOUND OUT THAT THERE'S MORE TO JACK THAN MEETS THE EYE.
I DON'T KNOW WHAT YOU'RE TALKING ABOUT, TRINETTA.
DON'T WORRY, JACK. YOU SHOULD BE PROUD OF THAT RESUMÉ.
TORCHING THAT SAWMILL NEAR PORTLAND, SPIKING TREES IN THEIR PATH—ALL GREAT STUFF.
BUT THE BEST HAS TO BE THAT JOB YOU DID ON THAT SUV DEALER NEAR RIVERSIDE. THAT ONE WAS POETRY.
I DIDN'T HAVE ANYTHING...
PLUS, IT DEMONSTRATES THAT YOU'RE JUST THE PERSON WE NEED BECAUSE, SOON, WE'LL BE DOING MORE THAN JUST PROTESTING.

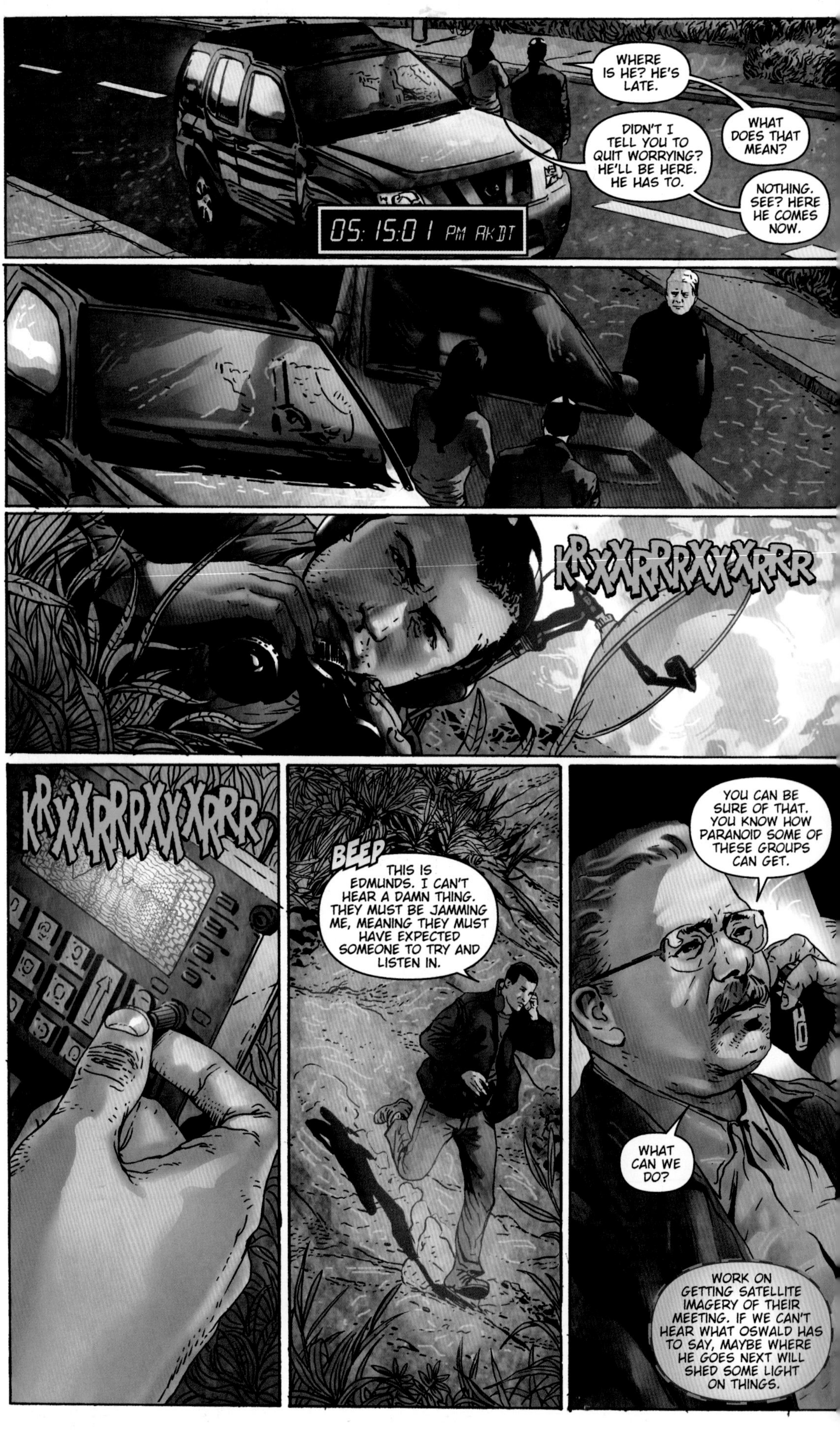
WHERE IS HE? HE'S LATE.
DIDN'T I TELL YOU TO QUIT WORRYING? HE'LL BE HERE. HE HAS TO.
WHAT DOES THAT MEAN?
NOTHING. SEE? HERE HE COMES NOW.
05:15:01 PM AKDT
KRXXRRRXXXRRR
KRXXRRRXXXRRR
BEEP
THIS IS EDMUNDS. I CAN'T HEAR A DAMN THING. THEY MUST BE JAMMING ME, MEANING THEY MUST HAVE EXPECTED SOMEONE TO TRY AND LISTEN IN.
YOU CAN BE SURE OF THAT. YOU KNOW HOW PARANOID SOME OF THESE GROUPS CAN GET.
WHAT CAN WE DO?
WORK ON GETTING SATELLITE IMAGERY OF THEIR MEETING. IF WE CAN'T HEAR WHAT OSWALD HAS TO SAY, MAYBE WHERE HE GOES NEXT WILL SHED SOME LIGHT ON THINGS.

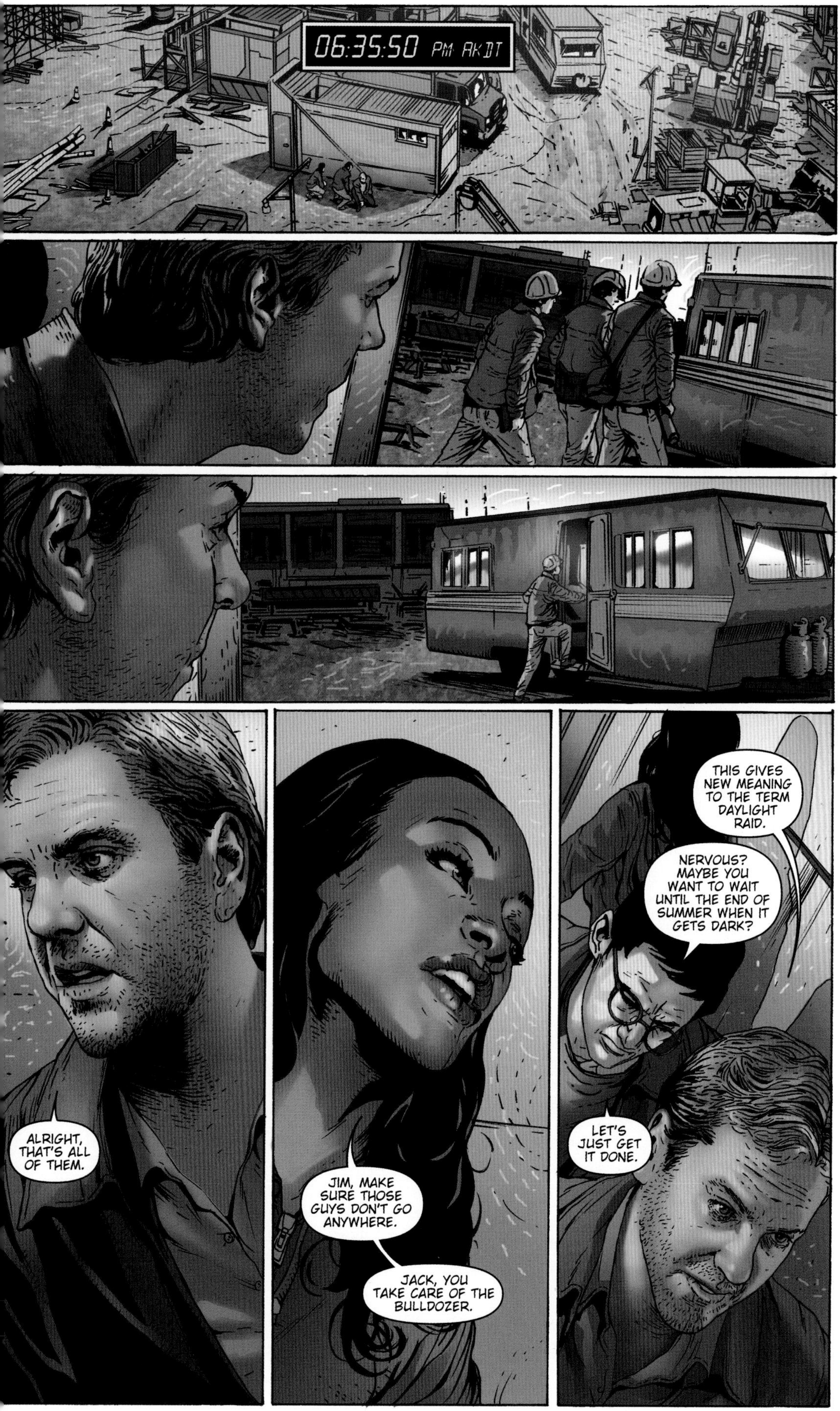
06:35:50 PM AKDT
ALRIGHT, THAT'S ALL OF THEM.
JIM, MAKE SURE THOSE GUYS DON'T GO ANYWHERE.
JACK, YOU TAKE CARE OF THE BULLDOZER.
THIS GIVES NEW MEANING TO THE TERM DAYLIGHT RAID.
NERVOUS? MAYBE YOU WANT TO WAIT UNTIL THE END OF SUMMER WHEN IT GETS DARK?
LET'S JUST GET IT DONE.

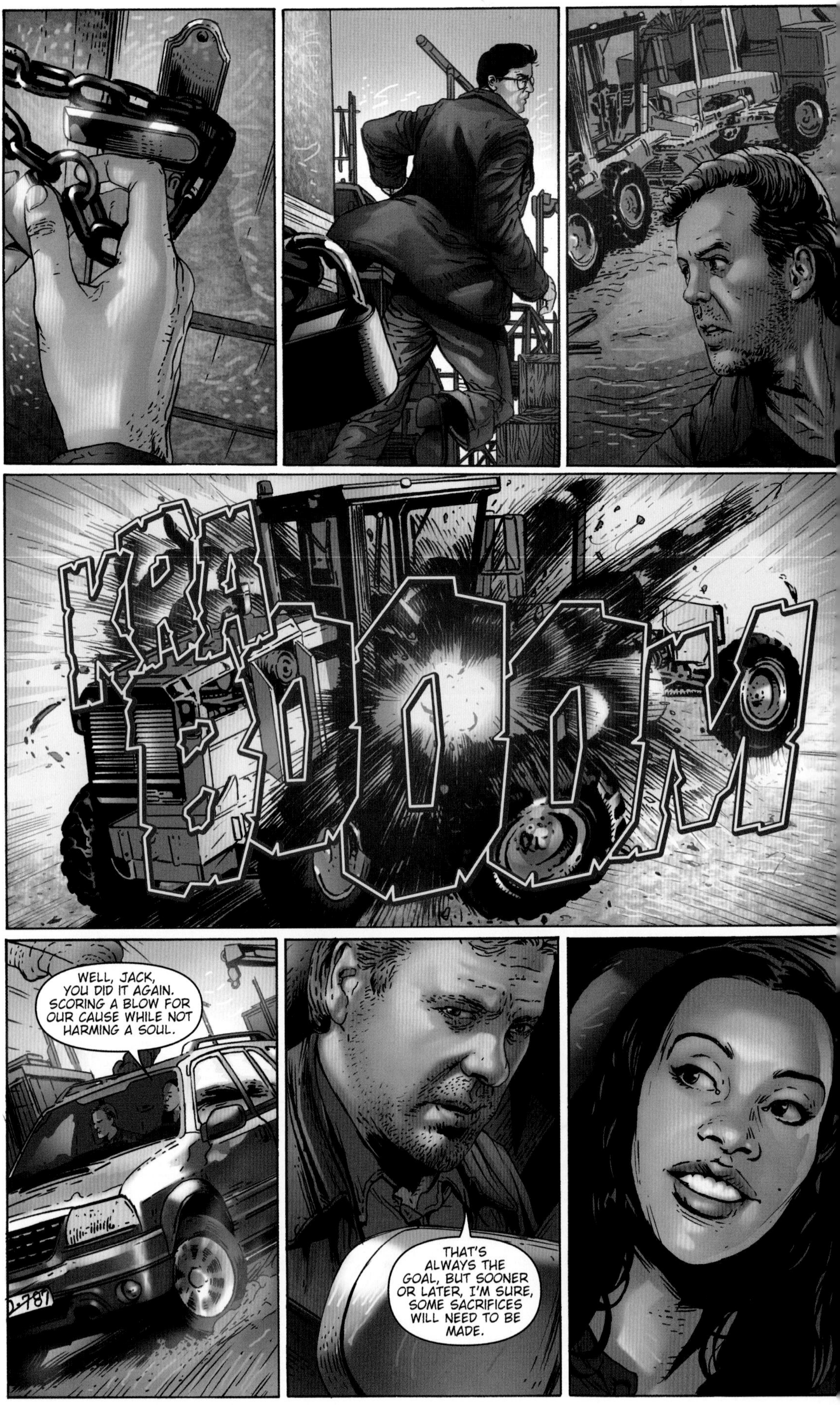
KRA-BOOOM
WELL, JACK, YOU DID IT AGAIN. SCORING A BLOW FOR OUR CAUSE WHILE NOT HARMING A SOUL.
THAT'S ALWAYS THE GOAL, BUT SOONER OR LATER, I'M SURE, SOME SACRIFICES WILL NEED TO BE MADE.

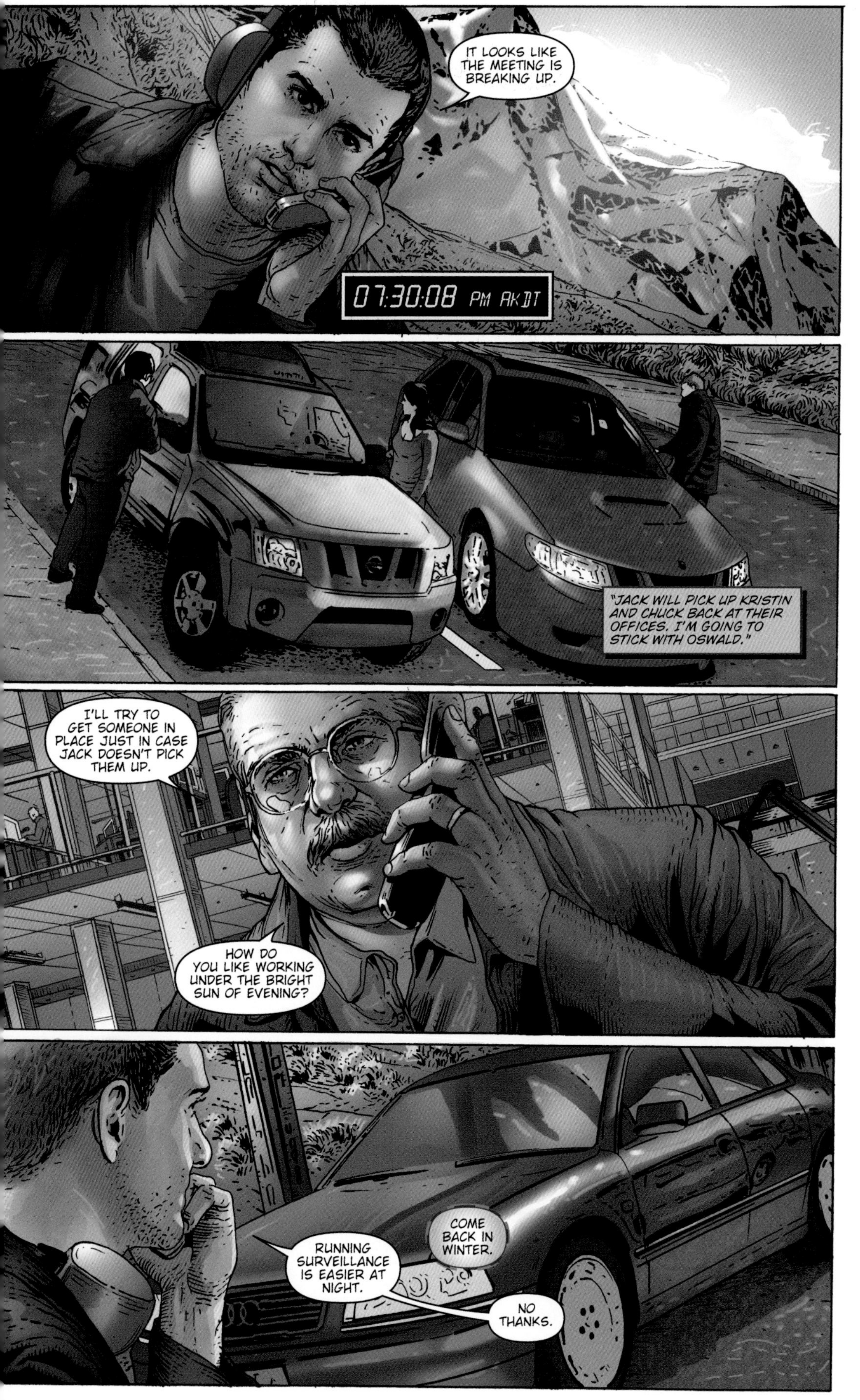
IT LOOKS LIKE THE MEETING IS BREAKING UP.
07:30:08 PM AKDT
"JACK WILL PICK UP KRISTIN AND CHUCK BACK AT THEIR OFFICES. I'M GOING TO STICK WITH OSWALD."
I'LL TRY TO GET SOMEONE IN PLACE JUST IN CASE JACK DOESN'T PICK THEM UP.
HOW DO YOU LIKE WORKING UNDER THE BRIGHT SUN OF EVENING?
RUNNING SURVEILLANCE IS EASIER AT NIGHT.
COME BACK IN WINTER.
NO THANKS.

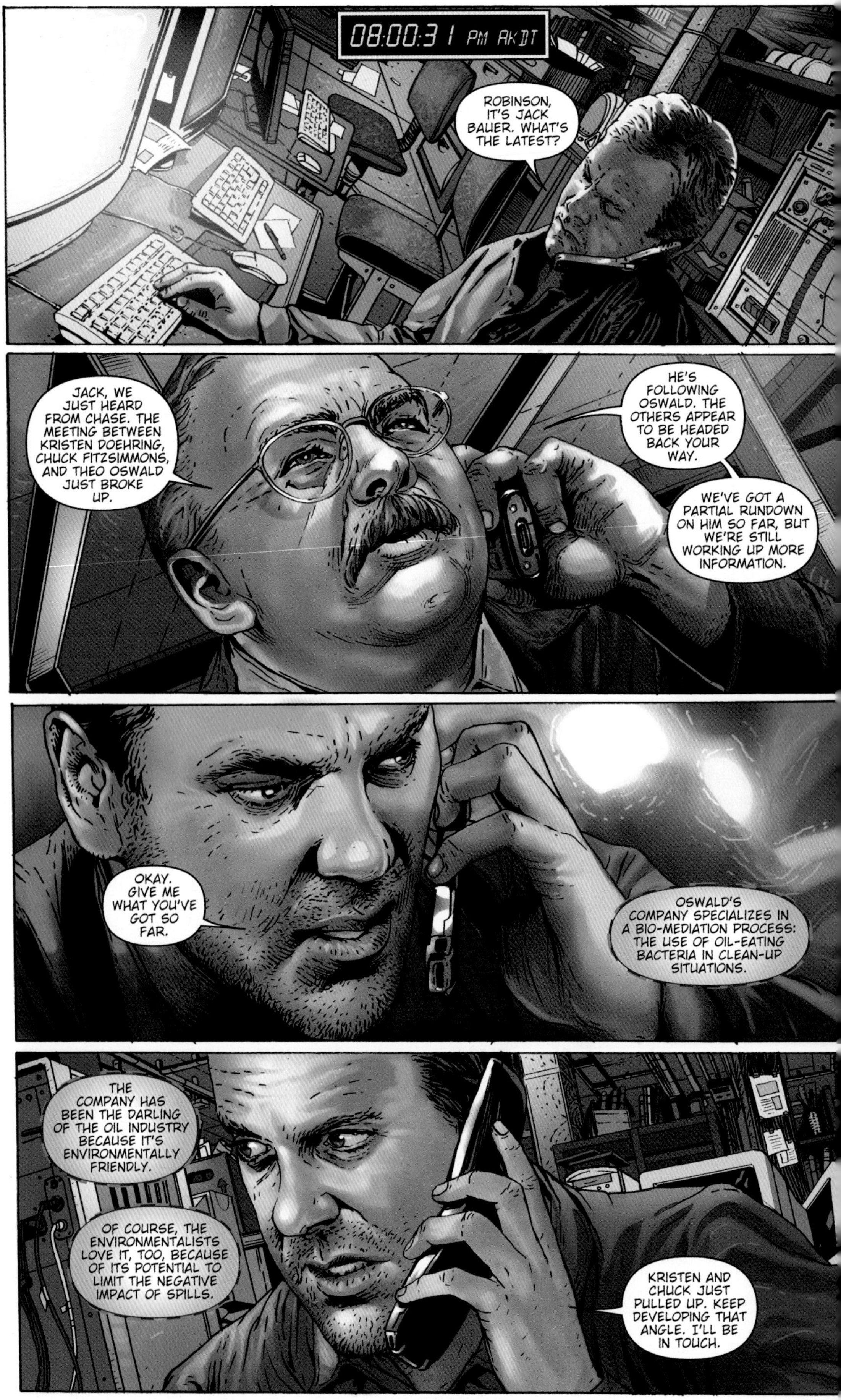
08:00:31 PM AKDT
ROBINSON, IT'S JACK BAUER. WHAT'S THE LATEST?
JACK, WE JUST HEARD FROM CHASE. THE MEETING BETWEEN KRISTEN DOEHRING, CHUCK FITZSIMMONS, AND THEO OSWALD JUST BROKE UP.
HE'S FOLLOWING OSWALD. THE OTHERS APPEAR TO BE HEADED BACK YOUR WAY.
WE'VE GOT A PARTIAL RUNDOWN ON HIM SO FAR, BUT WE'RE STILL WORKING UP MORE INFORMATION.
OKAY. GIVE ME WHAT YOU'VE GOT SO FAR.
OSWALD'S COMPANY SPECIALIZES IN A BIO-MEDIATION PROCESS: THE USE OF OIL-EATING BACTERIA IN CLEAN-UP SITUATIONS.
THE COMPANY HAS BEEN THE DARLING OF THE OIL INDUSTRY BECAUSE IT'S ENVIRONMENTALLY FRIENDLY.
OF COURSE, THE ENVIRONMENTALISTS LOVE IT, TOO, BECAUSE OF ITS POTENTIAL TO LIMIT THE NEGATIVE IMPACT OF SPILLS.
KRISTEN AND CHUCK JUST PULLED UP. KEEP DEVELOPING THAT ANGLE. I'LL BE IN TOUCH.

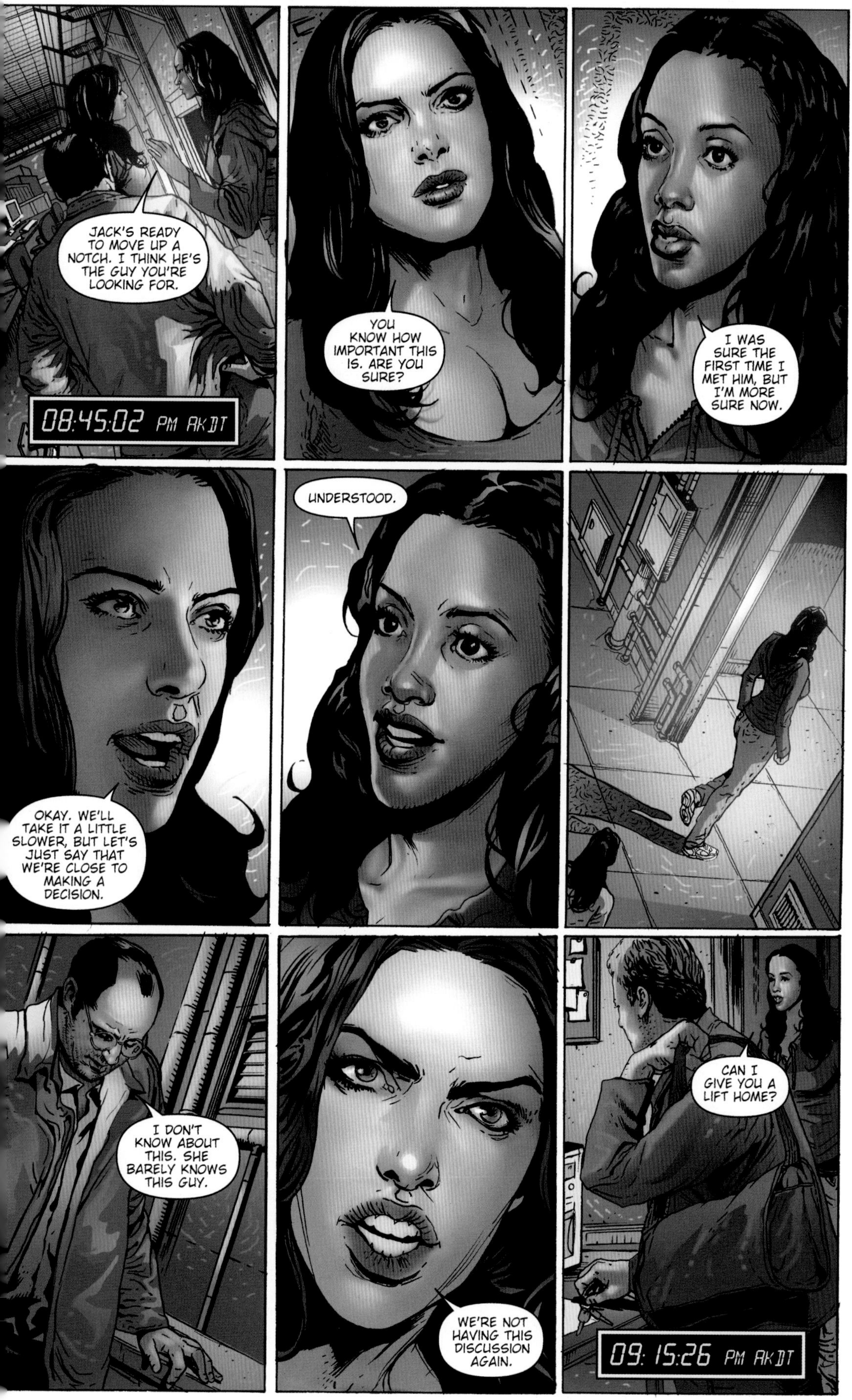
JACK'S READY TO MOVE UP A NOTCH. I THINK HE'S THE GUY YOU'RE LOOKING FOR.
08:45:02 PM AKDT
YOU KNOW HOW IMPORTANT THIS IS. ARE YOU SURE?
I WAS SURE THE FIRST TIME I MET HIM, BUT I'M MORE SURE NOW.
OKAY. WE'LL TAKE IT A LITTLE SLOWER, BUT LET'S JUST SAY THAT WE'RE CLOSE TO MAKING A DECISION.
UNDERSTOOD.
I DON'T KNOW ABOUT THIS. SHE BARELY KNOWS THIS GUY.
WE'RE NOT HAVING THIS DISCUSSION AGAIN.
CAN I GIVE YOU A LIFT HOME?
09: 15:26 PM AKDT

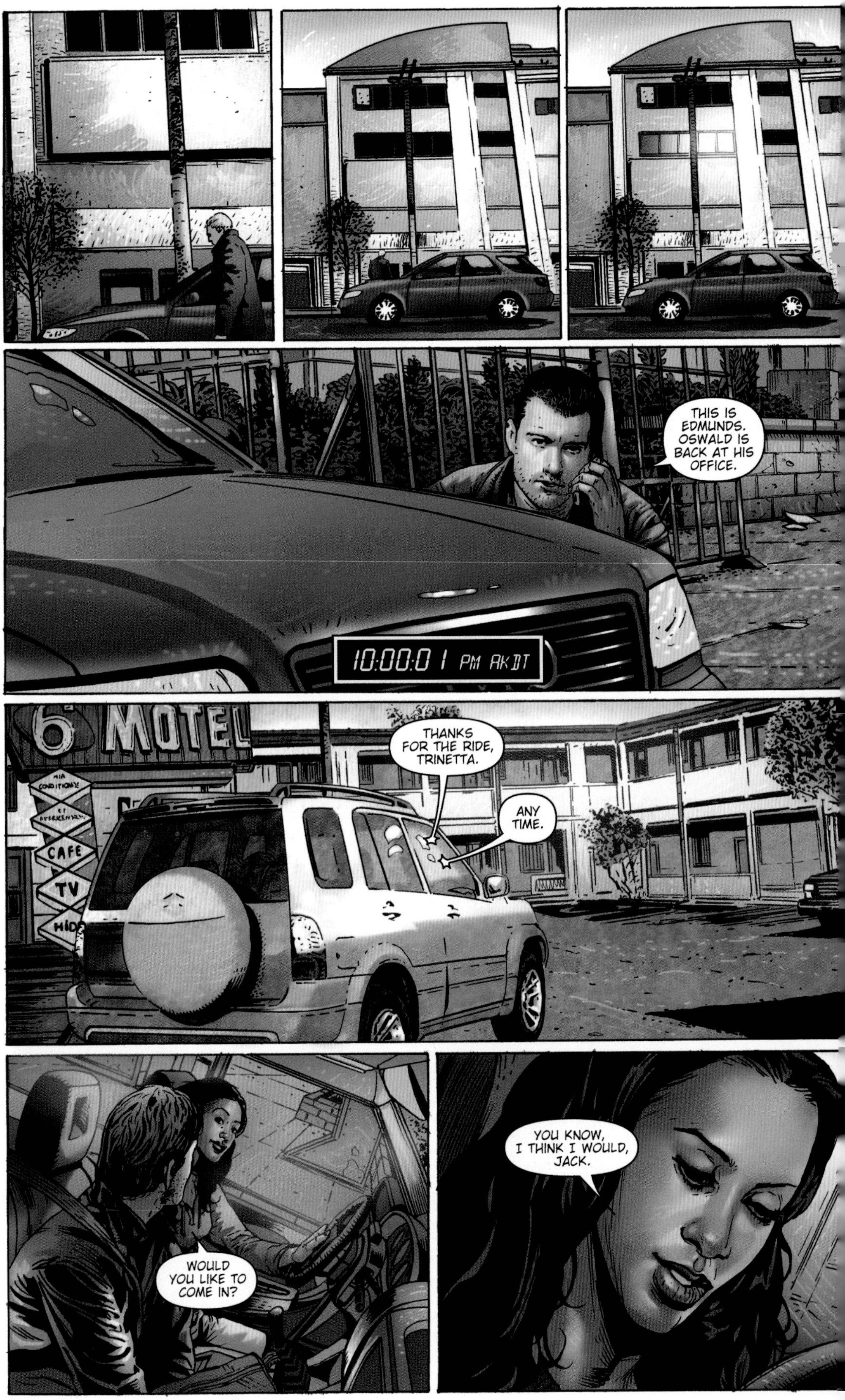
THIS IS EDMUNDS. OSWALD IS BACK AT HIS OFFICE.
10:00:01 PM AKDT
MOTEL
CAFE
TV
THANKS FOR THE RIDE, TRINETTA.
ANY TIME.
WOULD YOU LIKE TO COME IN?
YOU KNOW, I THINK I WOULD, JACK.

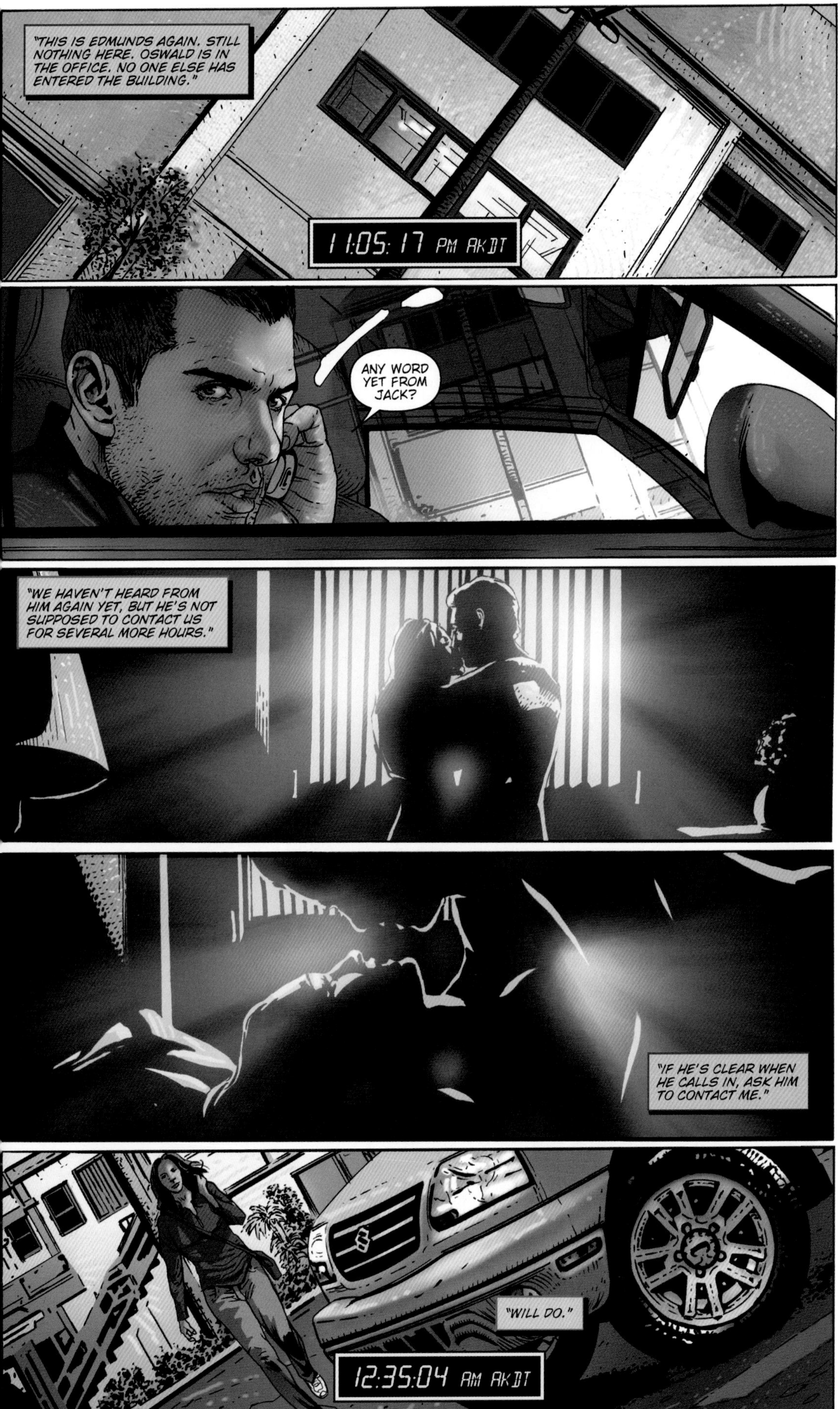
"THIS IS EDMUNDS AGAIN. STILL NOTHING HERE. OSWALD IS IN THE OFFICE. NO ONE ELSE HAS ENTERED THE BUILDING."
11:05:17 PM AKDT
ANY WORD YET FROM JACK?
"WE HAVEN'T HEARD FROM HIM AGAIN YET, BUT HE'S NOT SUPPOSED TO CONTACT US FOR SEVERAL MORE HOURS."
"IF HE'S CLEAR WHEN HE CALLS IN, ASK HIM TO CONTACT ME."
"WILL DO."
12:35:04 AM AKDT

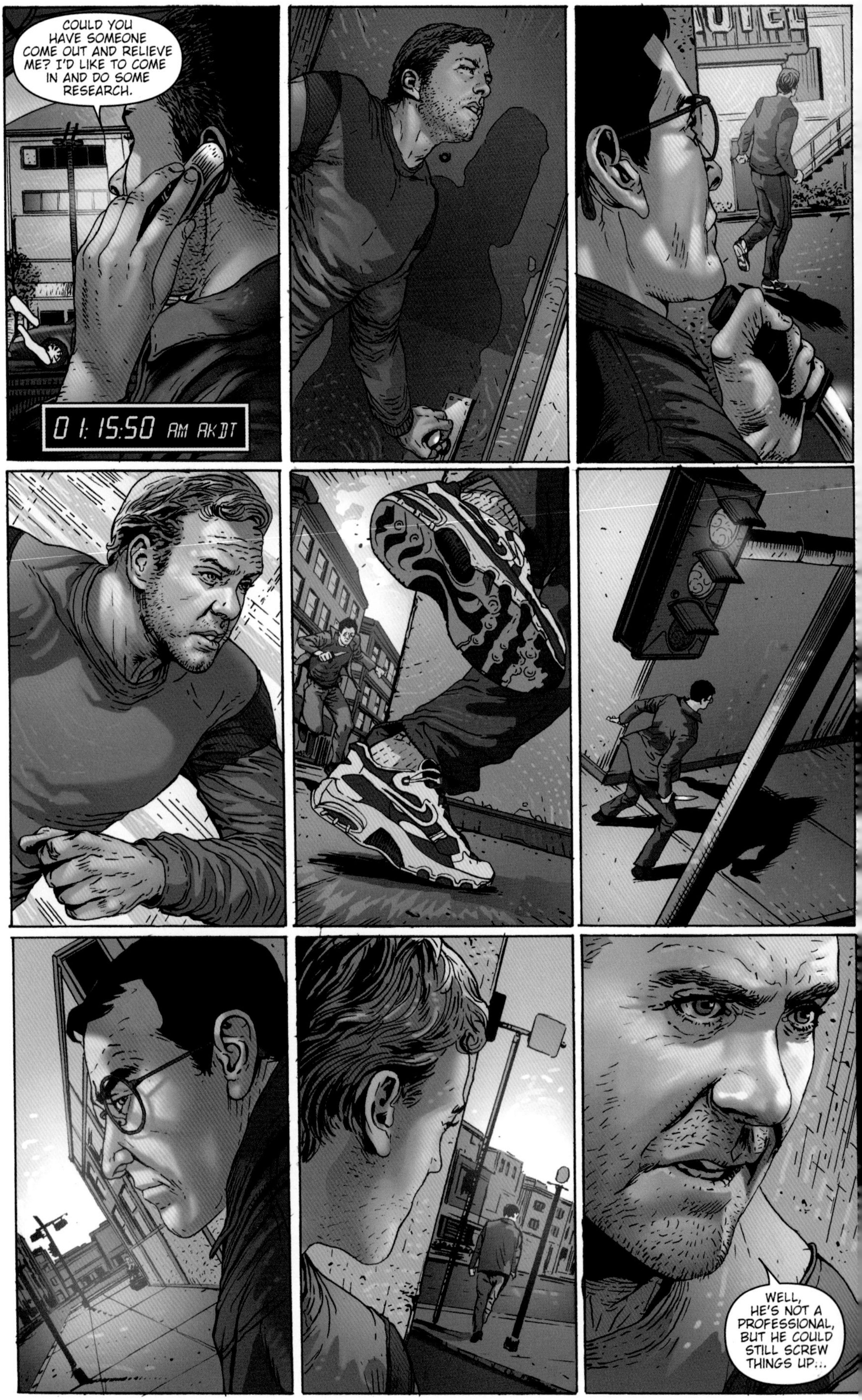
COULD YOU HAVE SOMEONE COME OUT AND RELIEVE ME? I'D LIKE TO COME IN AND DO SOME RESEARCH.
01:15:50 AM AKDT
WELL, HE'S NOT A PROFESSIONAL, BUT HE COULD STILL SCREW THINGS UP...

MIKE, COULD YOU HAVE ONE OF YOUR PEOPLE DO A FULL WORK-UP ON HIM?

LIKE I SAID, HE'S NO PRO, BUT I'D LIKE TO KNOW WHAT HE'S ABOUT.

01:35:56 AM AkDT

NO PROBLEM. CAREY'S ALREADY ON IT. HAVE YOU TWO HAD A CHANCE TO TALK ABOUT OSWALD YET?

NOT YET.

LET'S USE THE CONFERENCE ROOM.

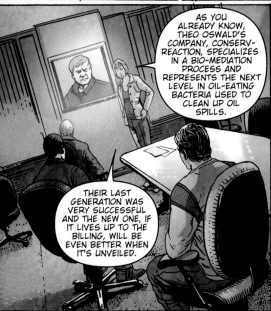

AS YOU ALREADY KNOW, THEO OSWALD'S COMPANY, CONSERV-REACTION, SPECIALIZES IN A BIO-MEDIATION PROCESS AND REPRESENTS THE NEXT LEVEL IN OIL-EATING BACTERIA USED TO CLEAN UP OIL SPILLS.

THEIR LAST GENERATION WAS VERY SUCCESSFUL AND THE NEW ONE, IF IT LIVES UP TO THE BILLING, WILL BE EVEN BETTER WHEN IT'S UNVEILED.

WHILE HE CERTAINLY HAS BEEN A FAVORITE OF MANY ENVIRONMENTALISTS, HE HAS NEVER DONE ANYTHING PUBLICLY TO ALIGN HIMSELF WITH EXTREMISTS OR ECO-TERRORISM.

IF HE'S WITH THEM, HE'S EITHER BEEN VERY THOROUGH IN COVERING IT UP OR IT'S SOMETHING THAT HAPPENED RECENTLY.

THANKS, CAREY. KEEP RUNNING IT AND KEEP ME POSTED.

MIKE, MAKE SURE ALL YOUR FIELD OPERATIVES HAVE THE FULL WORK-UP ON TRINETTA ANDERSON, TOO. SHE SEEMS TO BE MORE INVOLVED IN THIS THAN I THOUGHT.

I ALSO THINK THAT WHATEVER IS GOING TO HAPPEN IS GOING TO HAPPEN SOON, SO BE READY.

69

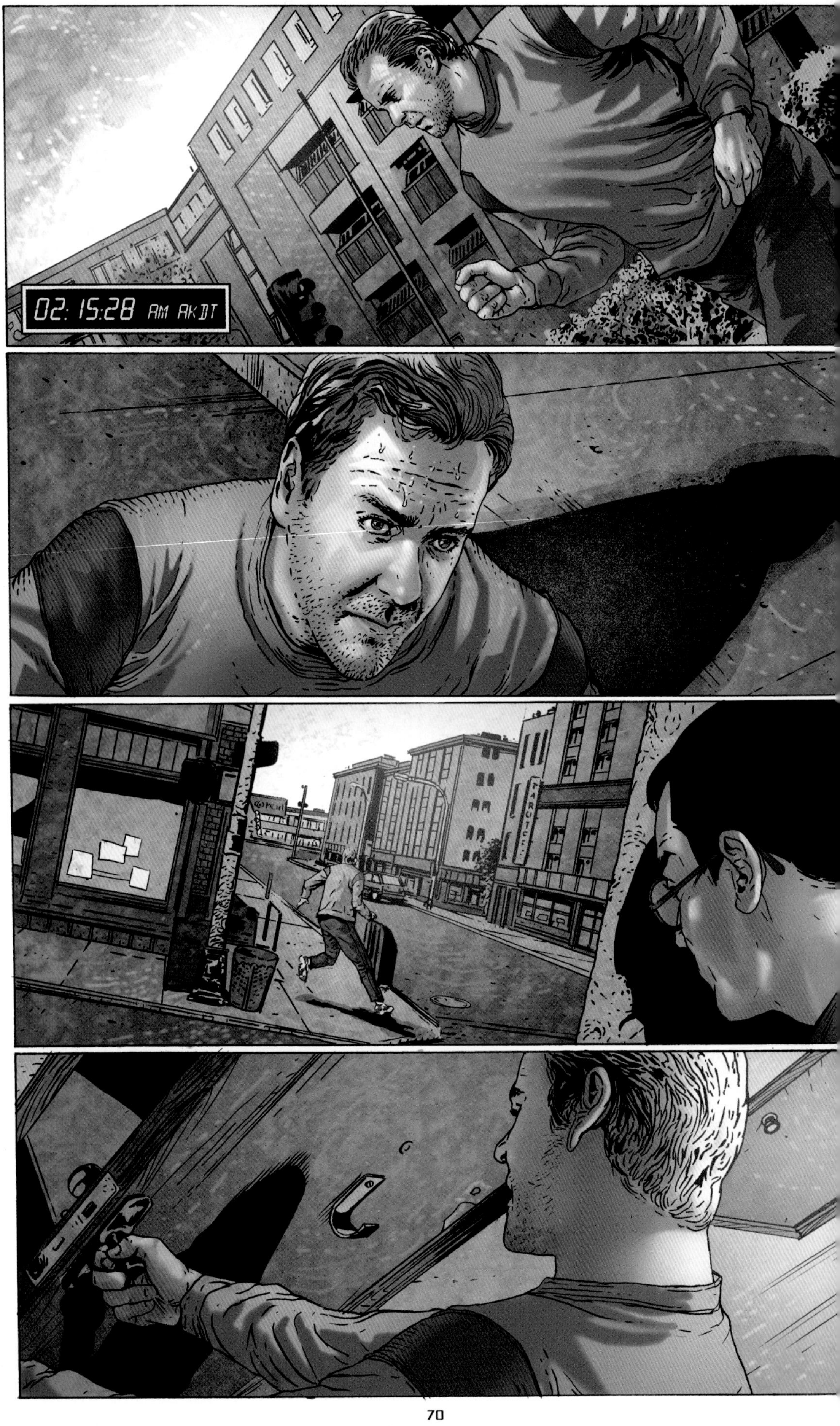
02: 15:28 AM AKDT

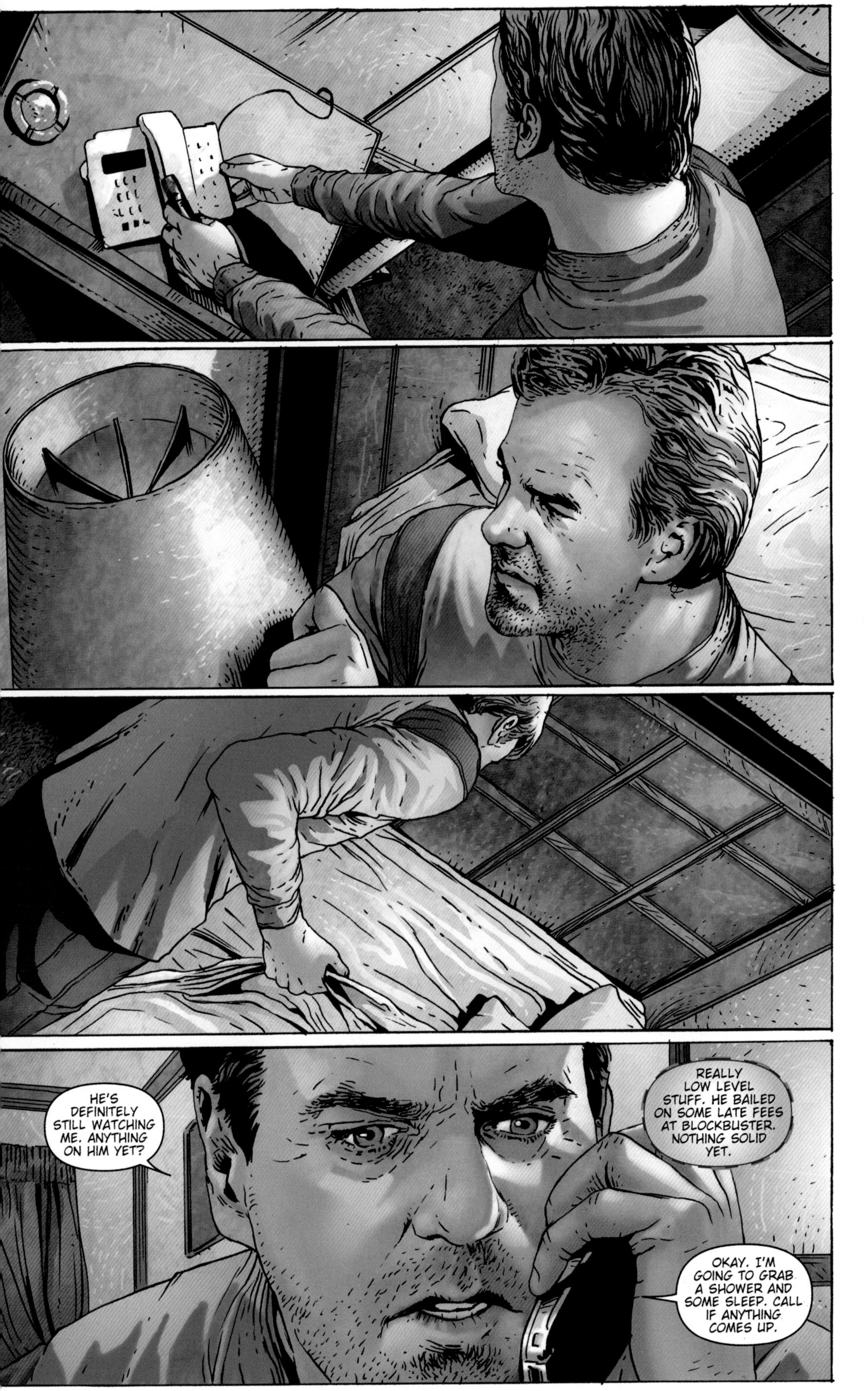
HE'S DEFINITELY STILL WATCHING ME. ANYTHING ON HIM YET?
REALLY LOW LEVEL STUFF. HE BAILED ON SOME LATE FEES AT BLOCKBUSTER. NOTHING SOLID YET.
OKAY. I'M GOING TO GRAB A SHOWER AND SOME SLEEP. CALL IF ANYTHING COMES UP.

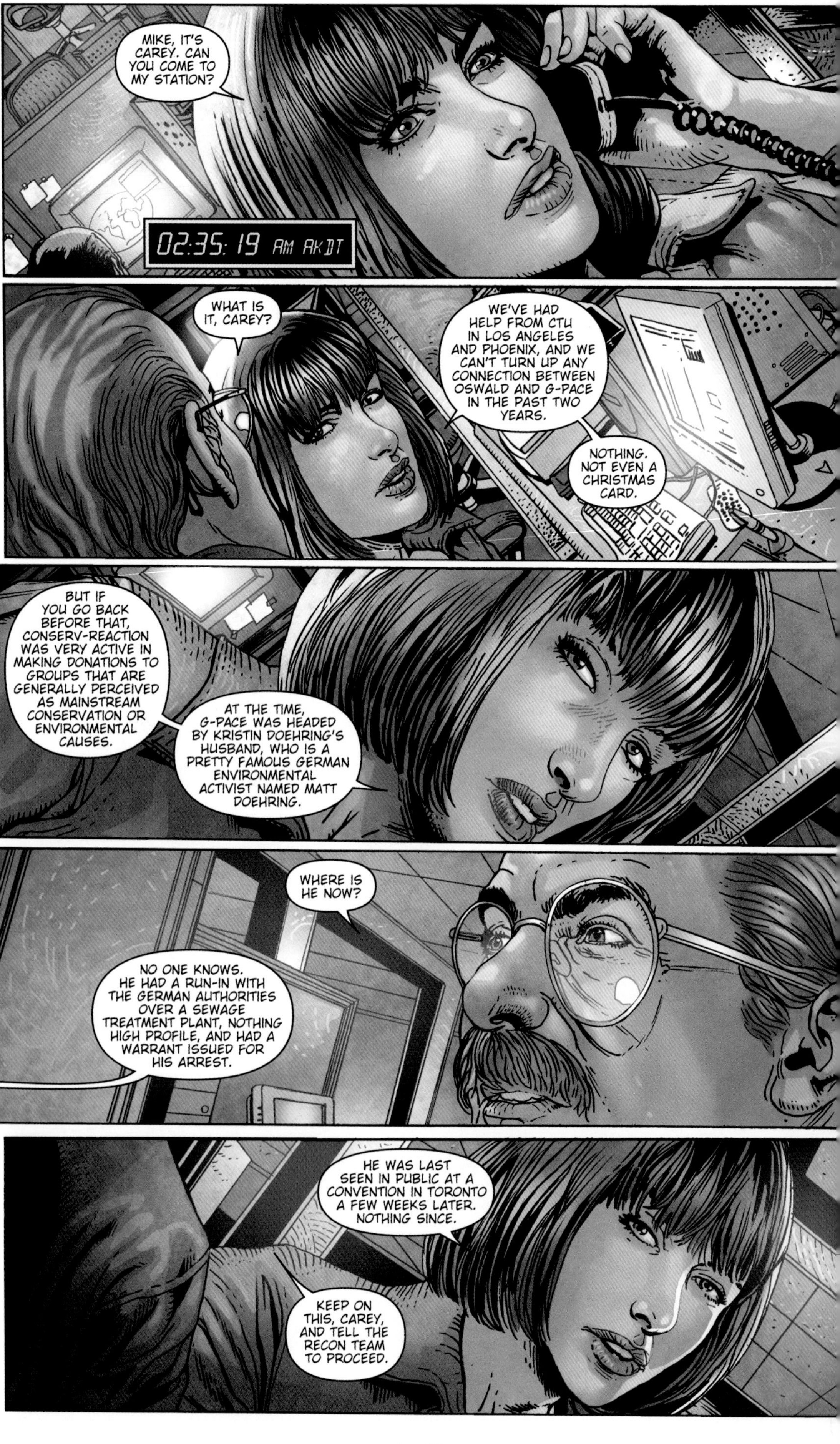
MIKE, IT'S CAREY. CAN YOU COME TO MY STATION?
02:35:19 AM AKDT
WHAT IS IT, CAREY?
WE'VE HAD HELP FROM CTU IN LOS ANGELES AND PHOENIX, AND WE CAN'T TURN UP ANY CONNECTION BETWEEN OSWALD AND G-PACE IN THE PAST TWO YEARS.
NOTHING. NOT EVEN A CHRISTMAS CARD.
BUT IF YOU GO BACK BEFORE THAT, CONSERV-REACTION WAS VERY ACTIVE IN MAKING DONATIONS TO GROUPS THAT ARE GENERALLY PERCEIVED AS MAINSTREAM CONSERVATION OR ENVIRONMENTAL CAUSES.
AT THE TIME, G-PACE WAS HEADED BY KRISTIN DOEHRING'S HUSBAND, WHO IS A PRETTY FAMOUS GERMAN ENVIRONMENTAL ACTIVIST NAMED MATT DOEHRING.
WHERE IS HE NOW?
NO ONE KNOWS. HE HAD A RUN-IN WITH THE GERMAN AUTHORITIES OVER A SEWAGE TREATMENT PLANT, NOTHING HIGH PROFILE, AND HAD A WARRANT ISSUED FOR HIS ARREST.
HE WAS LAST SEEN IN PUBLIC AT A CONVENTION IN TORONTO A FEW WEEKS LATER. NOTHING SINCE.
KEEP ON THIS, CAREY, AND TELL THE RECON TEAM TO PROCEED.

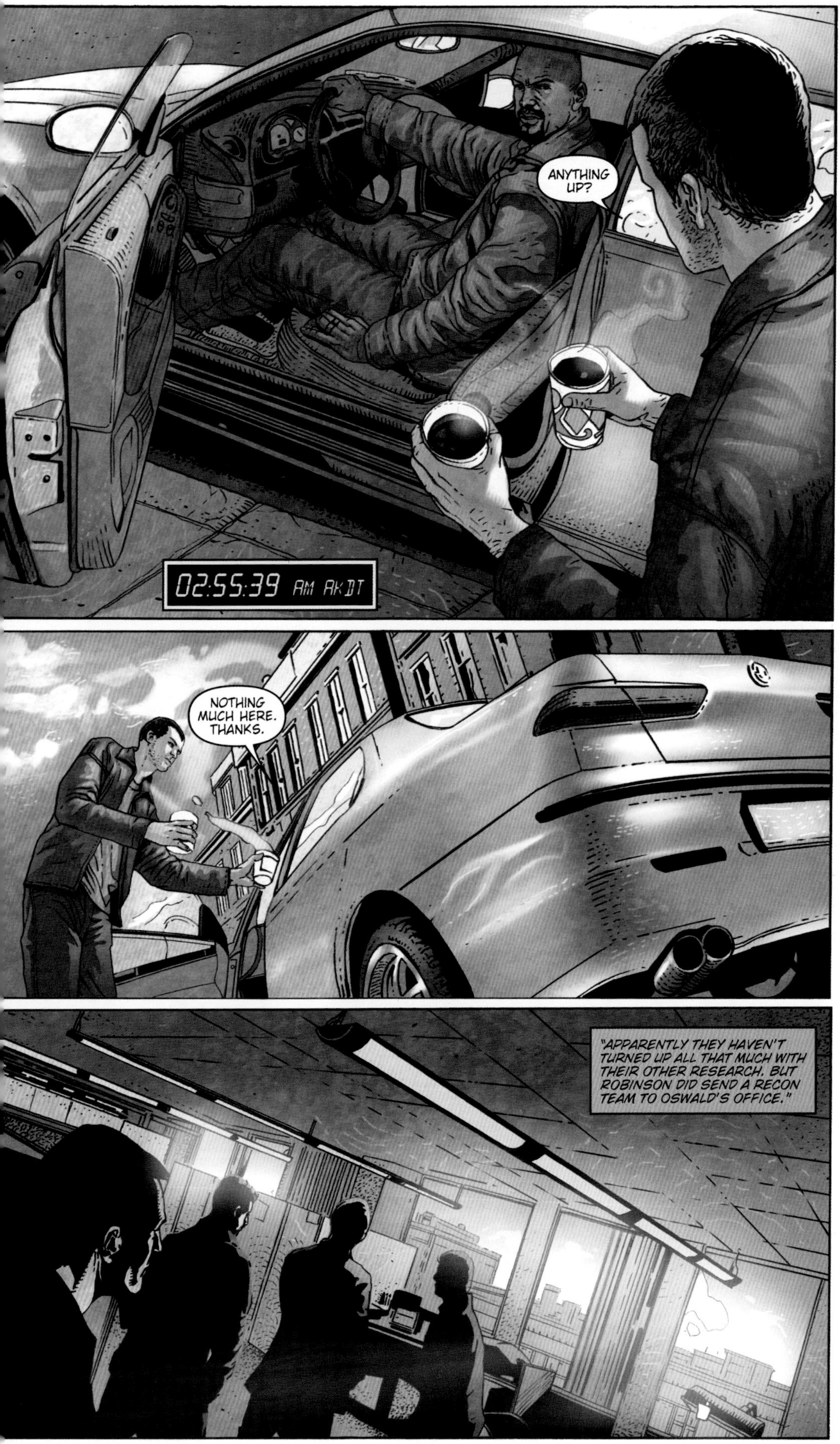
ANYTHING UP?
02:55:39 AM AKDT
NOTHING MUCH HERE. THANKS.
"APPARENTLY THEY HAVEN'T TURNED UP ALL THAT MUCH WITH THEIR OTHER RESEARCH. BUT ROBINSON DID SEND A RECON TEAM TO OSWALD'S OFFICE."

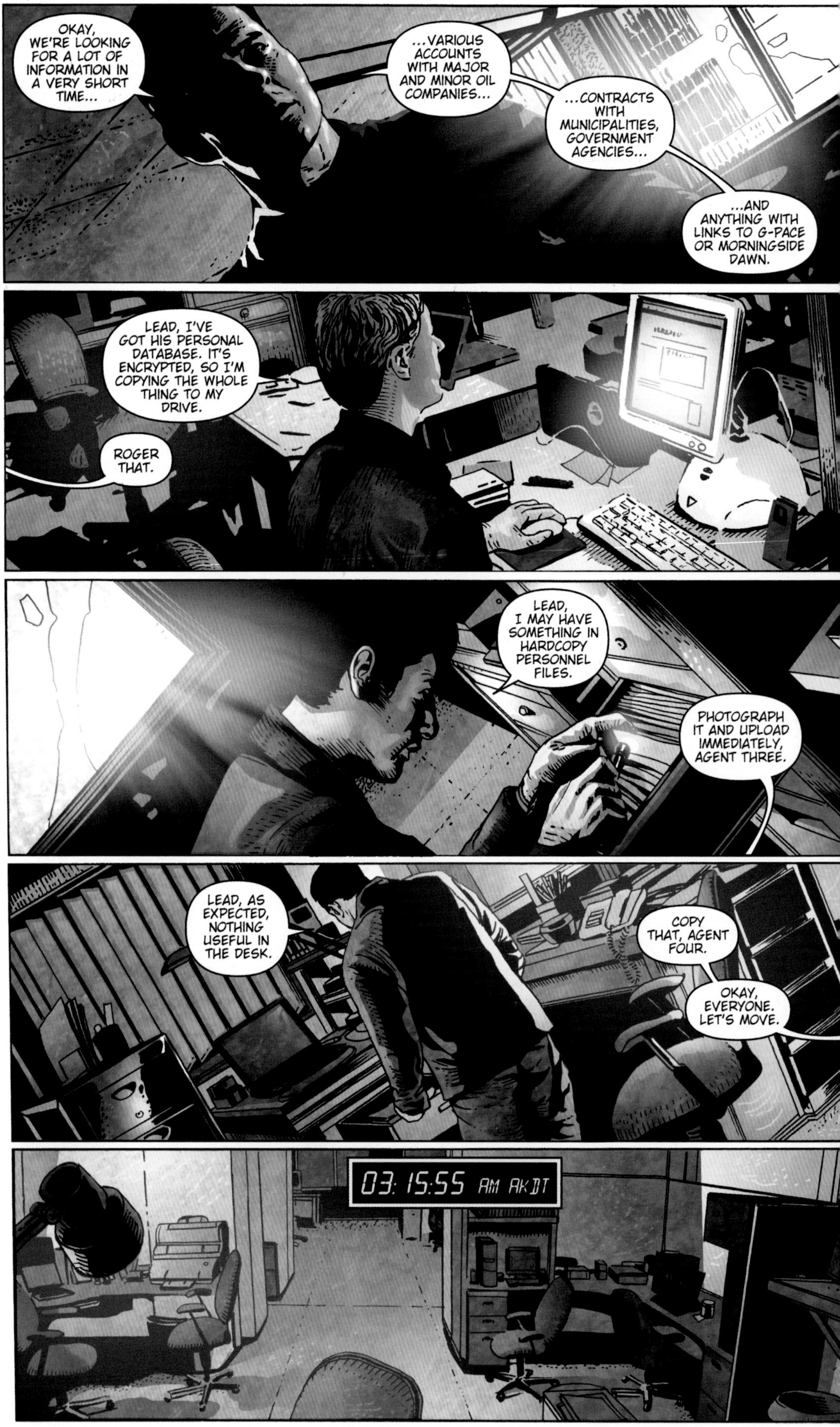
OKAY, WE'RE LOOKING FOR A LOT OF INFORMATION IN A VERY SHORT TIME...
...VARIOUS ACCOUNTS WITH MAJOR AND MINOR OIL COMPANIES...
...CONTRACTS WITH MUNICIPALITIES, GOVERNMENT AGENCIES...
...AND ANYTHING WITH LINKS TO G-PACE OR MORNINGSIDE DAWN.
LEAD, I'VE GOT HIS PERSONAL DATABASE. IT'S ENCRYPTED, SO I'M COPYING THE WHOLE THING TO MY DRIVE.
ROGER THAT.
LEAD, I MAY HAVE SOMETHING IN HARDCOPY PERSONNEL FILES.
PHOTOGRAPH IT AND UPLOAD IMMEDIATELY, AGENT THREE.
LEAD, AS EXPECTED, NOTHING USEFUL IN THE DESK.
COPY THAT, AGENT FOUR.
OKAY, EVERYONE. LET'S MOVE.
03:15:55 AM AKDT

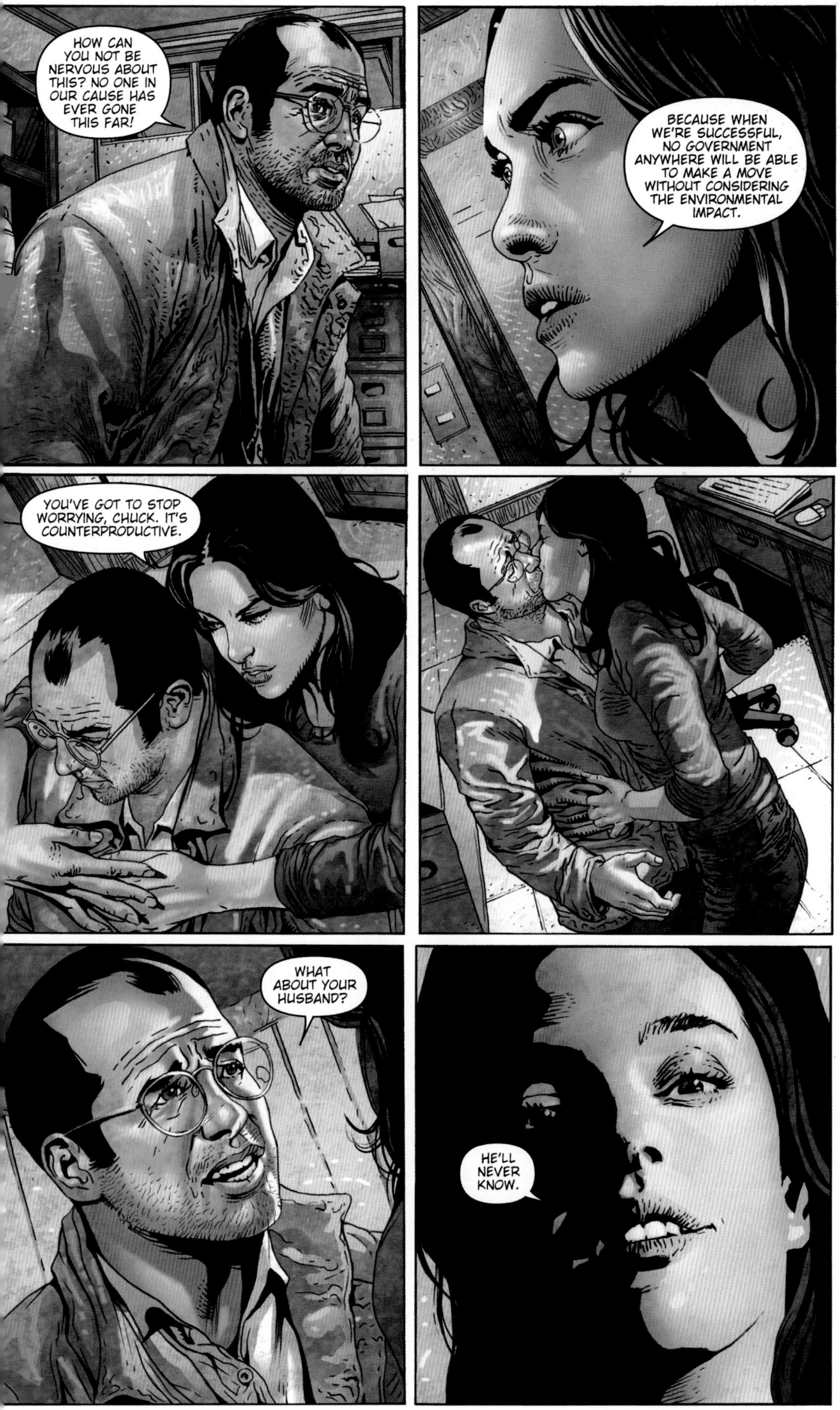
HOW CAN YOU NOT BE NERVOUS ABOUT THIS? NO ONE IN OUR CAUSE HAS EVER GONE THIS FAR!
BECAUSE WHEN WE'RE SUCCESSFUL, NO GOVERNMENT ANYWHERE WILL BE ABLE TO MAKE A MOVE WITHOUT CONSIDERING THE ENVIRONMENTAL IMPACT.
YOU'VE GOT TO STOP WORRYING, CHUCK. IT'S COUNTERPRODUCTIVE.
WHAT ABOUT YOUR HUSBAND?
HE'LL NEVER KNOW.

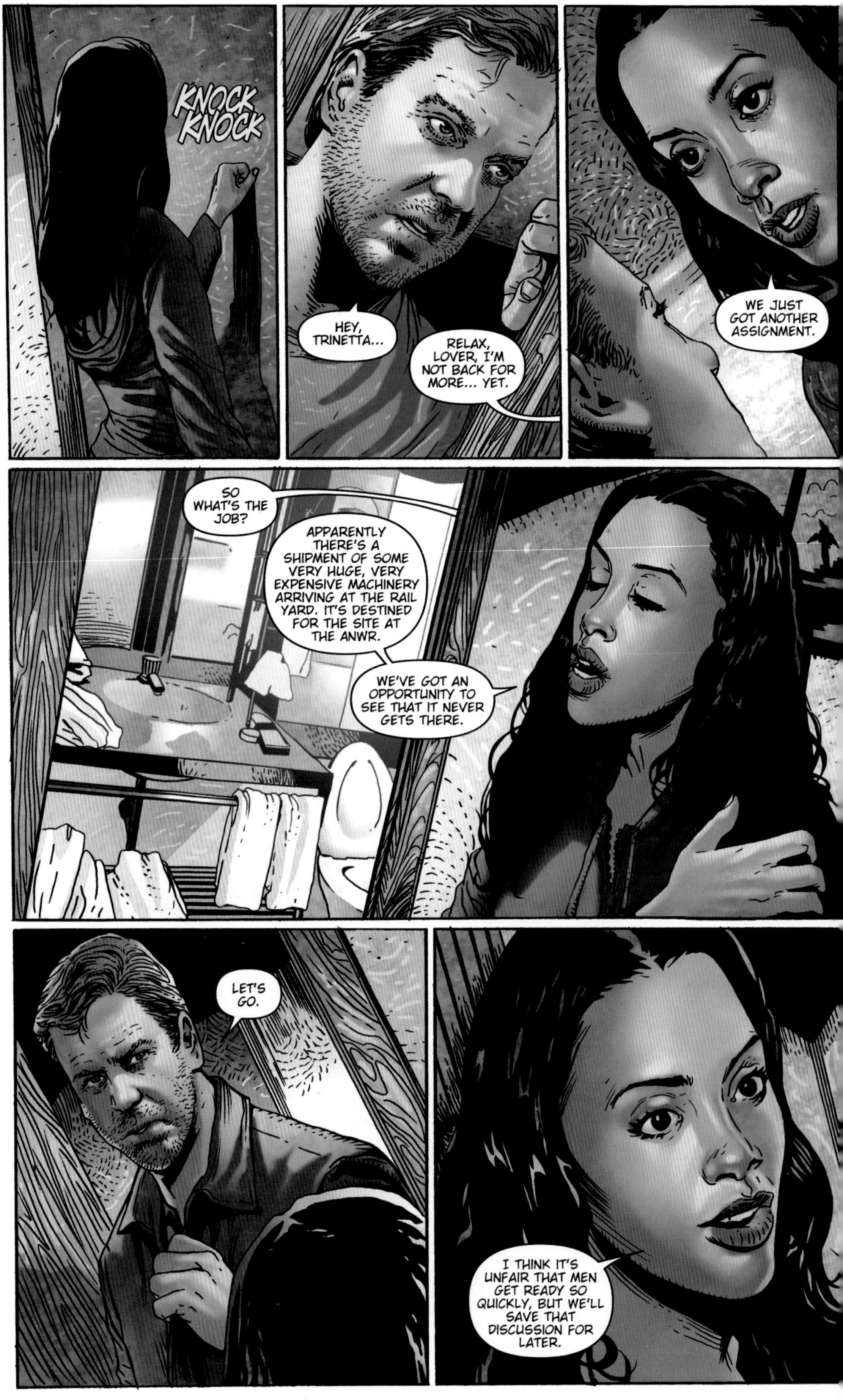
KNOCK KNOCK
HEY, TRINETTA...
RELAX, LOVER, I'M NOT BACK FOR MORE... YET.
WE JUST GOT ANOTHER ASSIGNMENT.
SO WHAT'S THE JOB?
APPARENTLY THERE'S A SHIPMENT OF SOME VERY HUGE, VERY EXPENSIVE MACHINERY ARRIVING AT THE RAIL YARD. IT'S DESTINED FOR THE SITE AT THE ANWR.
WE'VE GOT AN OPPORTUNITY TO SEE THAT IT NEVER GETS THERE.
LET'S GO.
I THINK IT'S UNFAIR THAT MEN GET READY SO QUICKLY, BUT WE'LL SAVE THAT DISCUSSION FOR LATER.

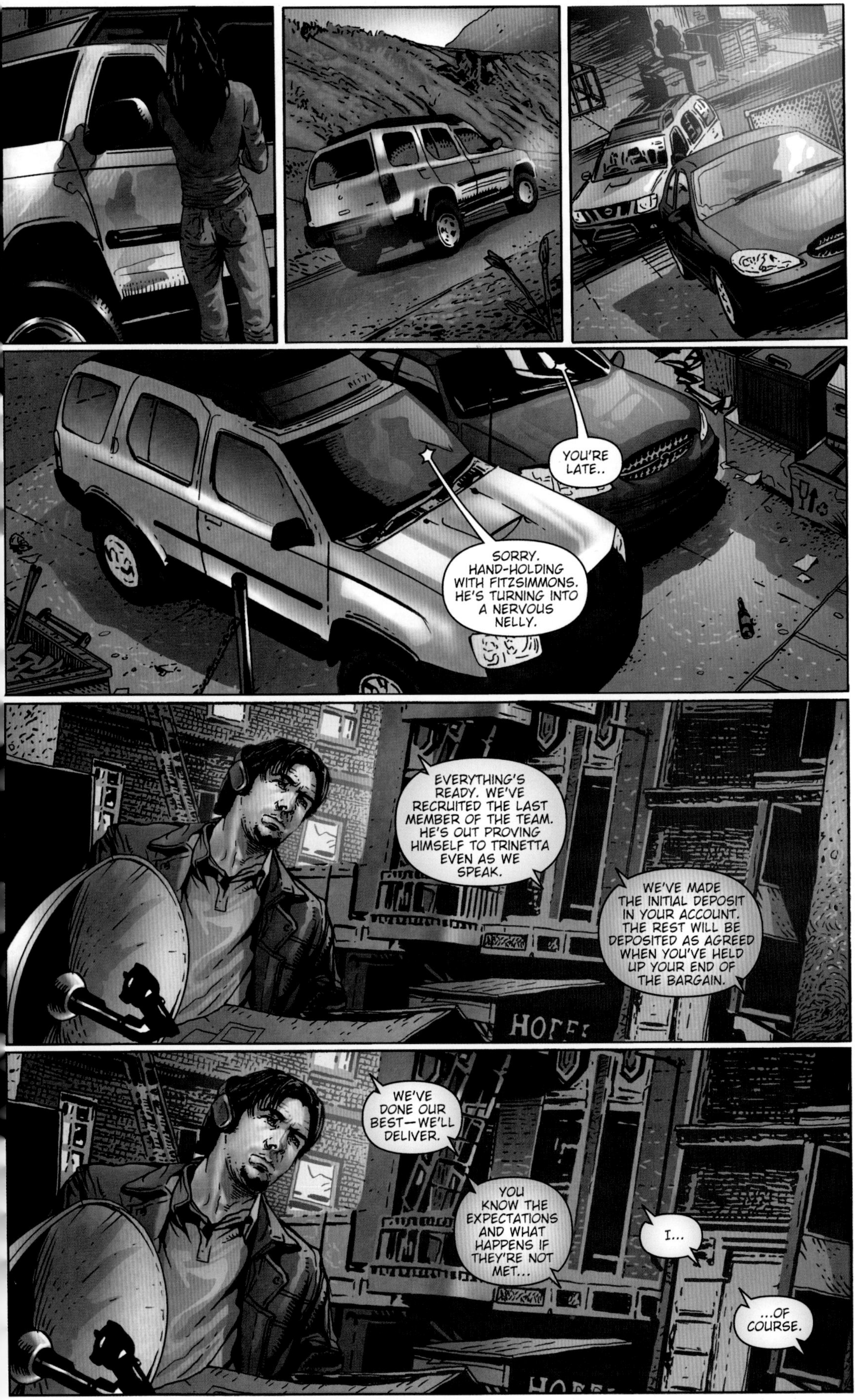
YOU'RE LATE..
SORRY. HAND-HOLDING WITH FITZSIMMONS. HE'S TURNING INTO A NERVOUS NELLY.
EVERYTHING'S READY. WE'VE RECRUITED THE LAST MEMBER OF THE TEAM. HE'S OUT PROVING HIMSELF TO TRINETTA EVEN AS WE SPEAK.
WE'VE MADE THE INITIAL DEPOSIT IN YOUR ACCOUNT. THE REST WILL BE DEPOSITED AS AGREED WHEN YOU'VE HELD UP YOUR END OF THE BARGAIN.
WE'VE DONE OUR BEST—WE'LL DELIVER.
YOU KNOW THE EXPECTATIONS AND WHAT HAPPENS IF THEY'RE NOT MET...
I...
...OF COURSE.

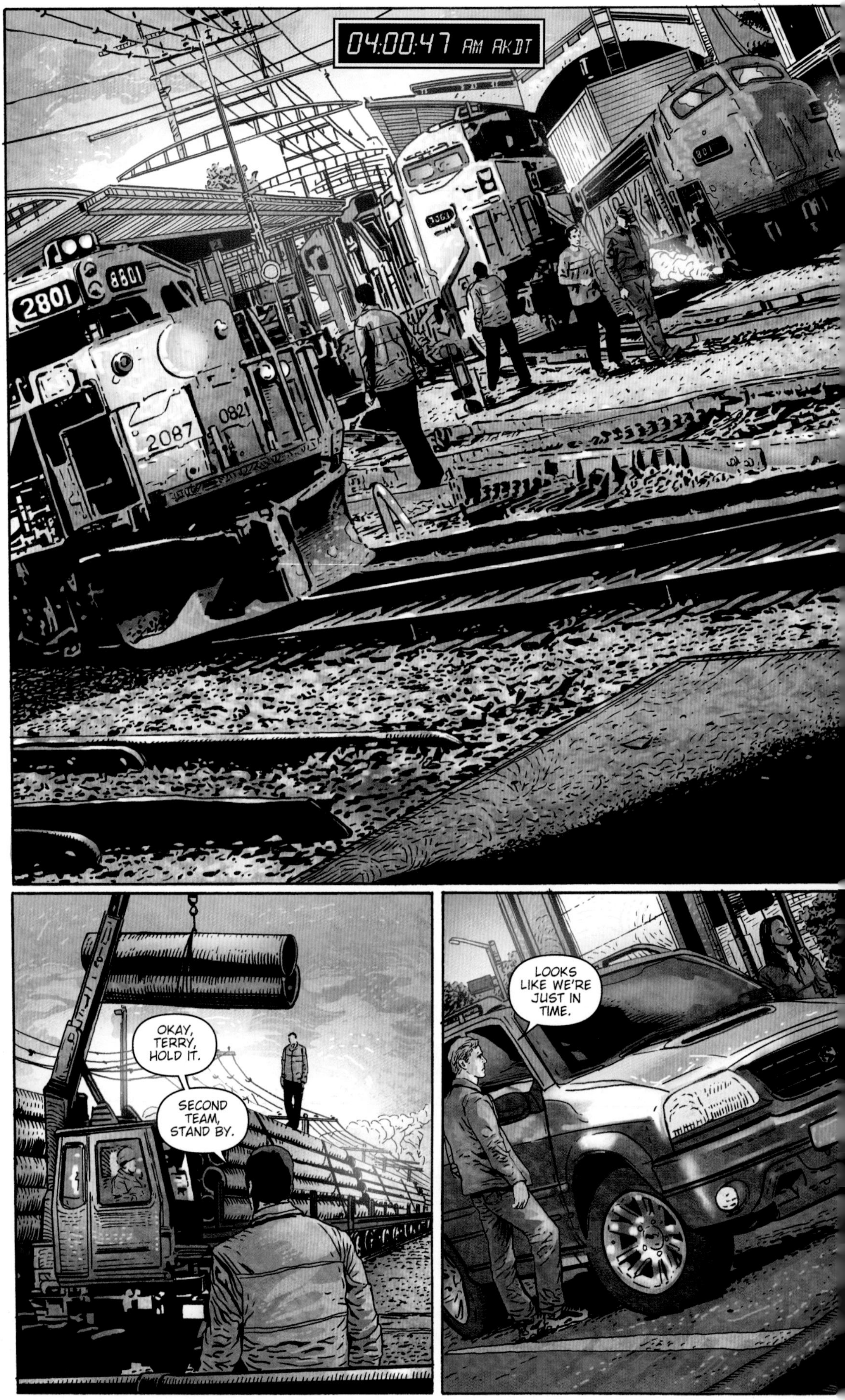
04:00:47 AM AKDT
OKAY, TERRY, HOLD IT.
SECOND TEAM, STAND BY.
LOOKS LIKE WE'RE JUST IN TIME.

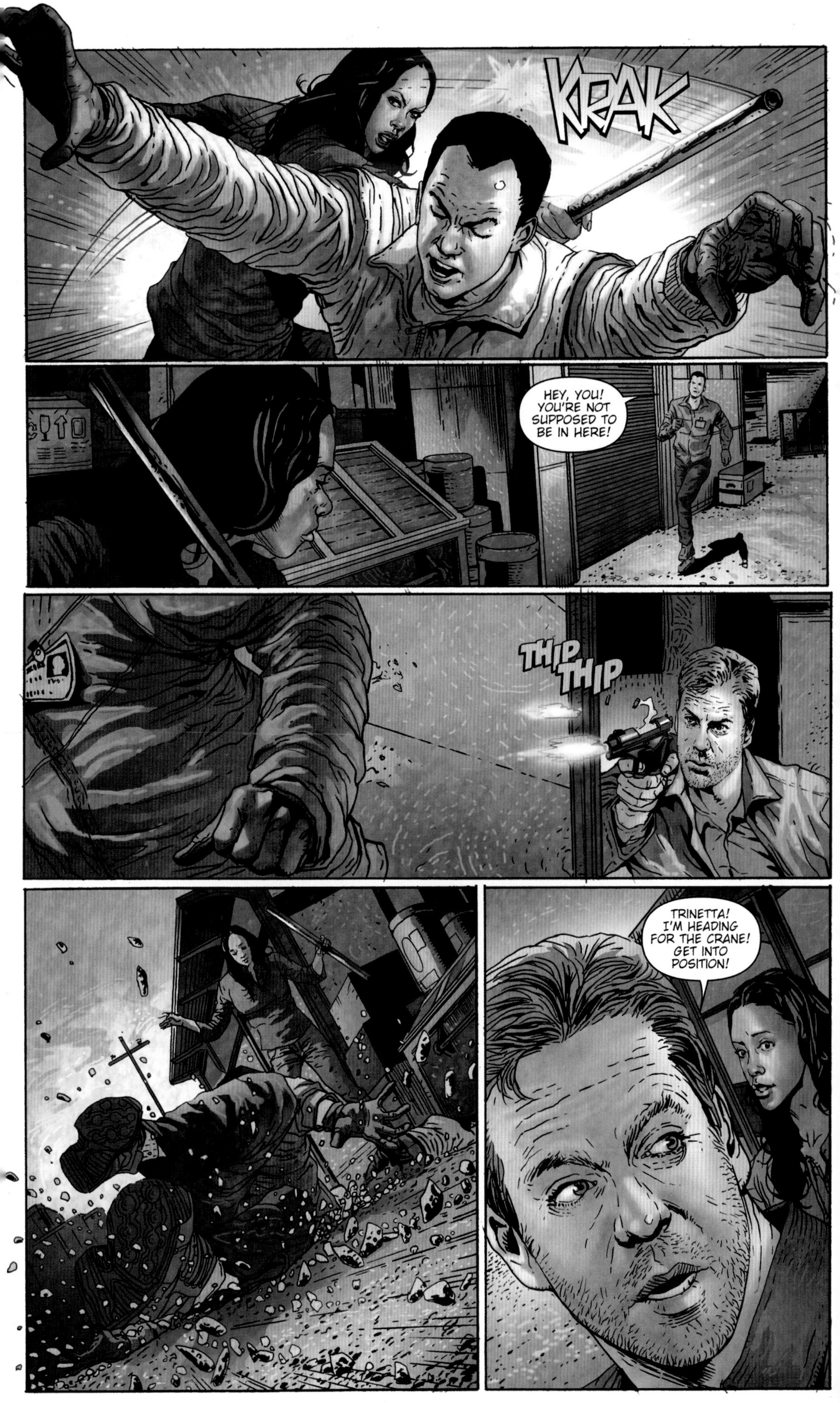
KRAK
HEY, YOU! YOU'RE NOT SUPPOSED TO BE IN HERE!
THIP THIP
TRINETTA! I'M HEADING FOR THE CRANE! GET INTO POSITION!

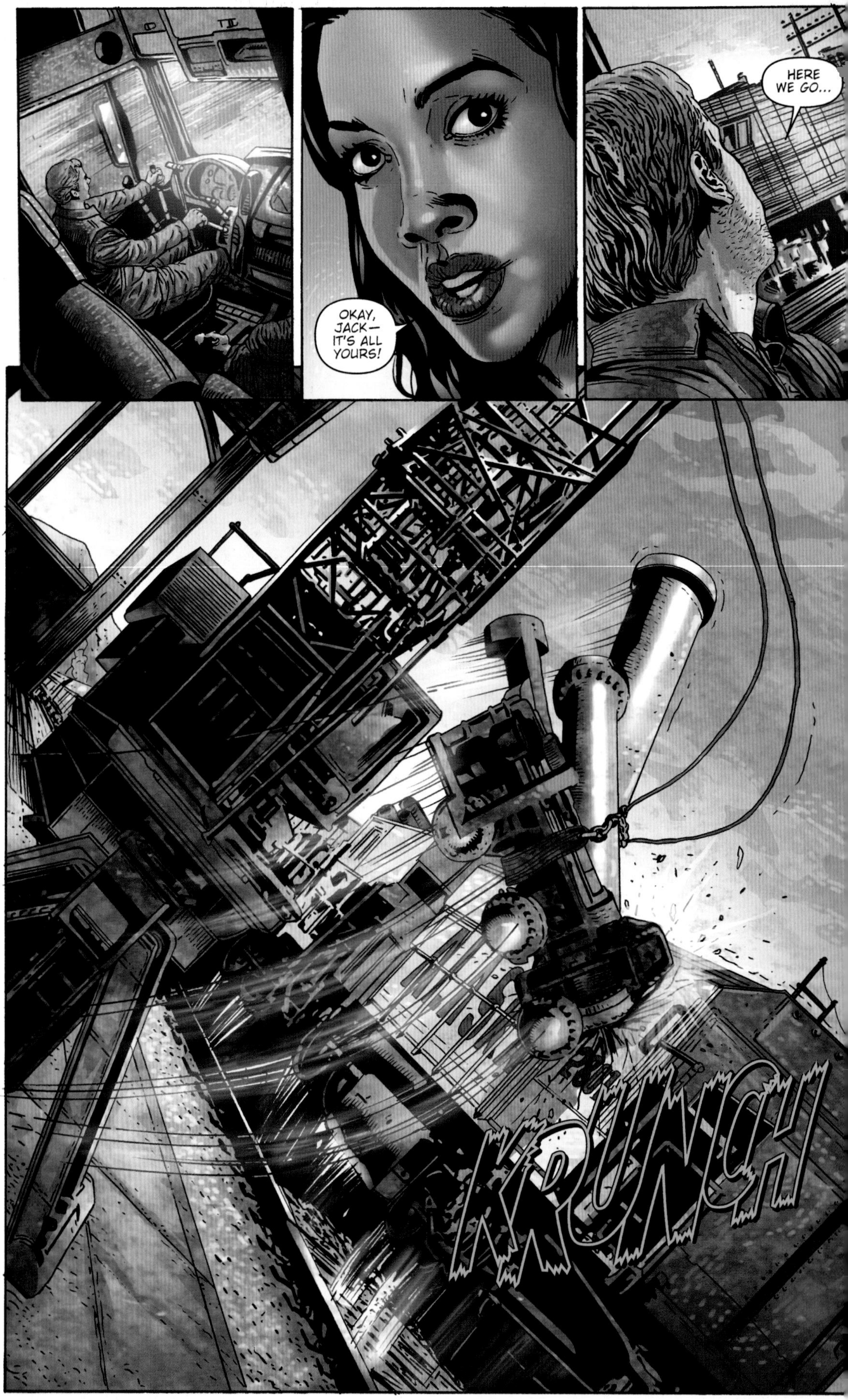
OKAY, JACK— IT'S ALL YOURS!
HERE WE GO...
KRUNCH

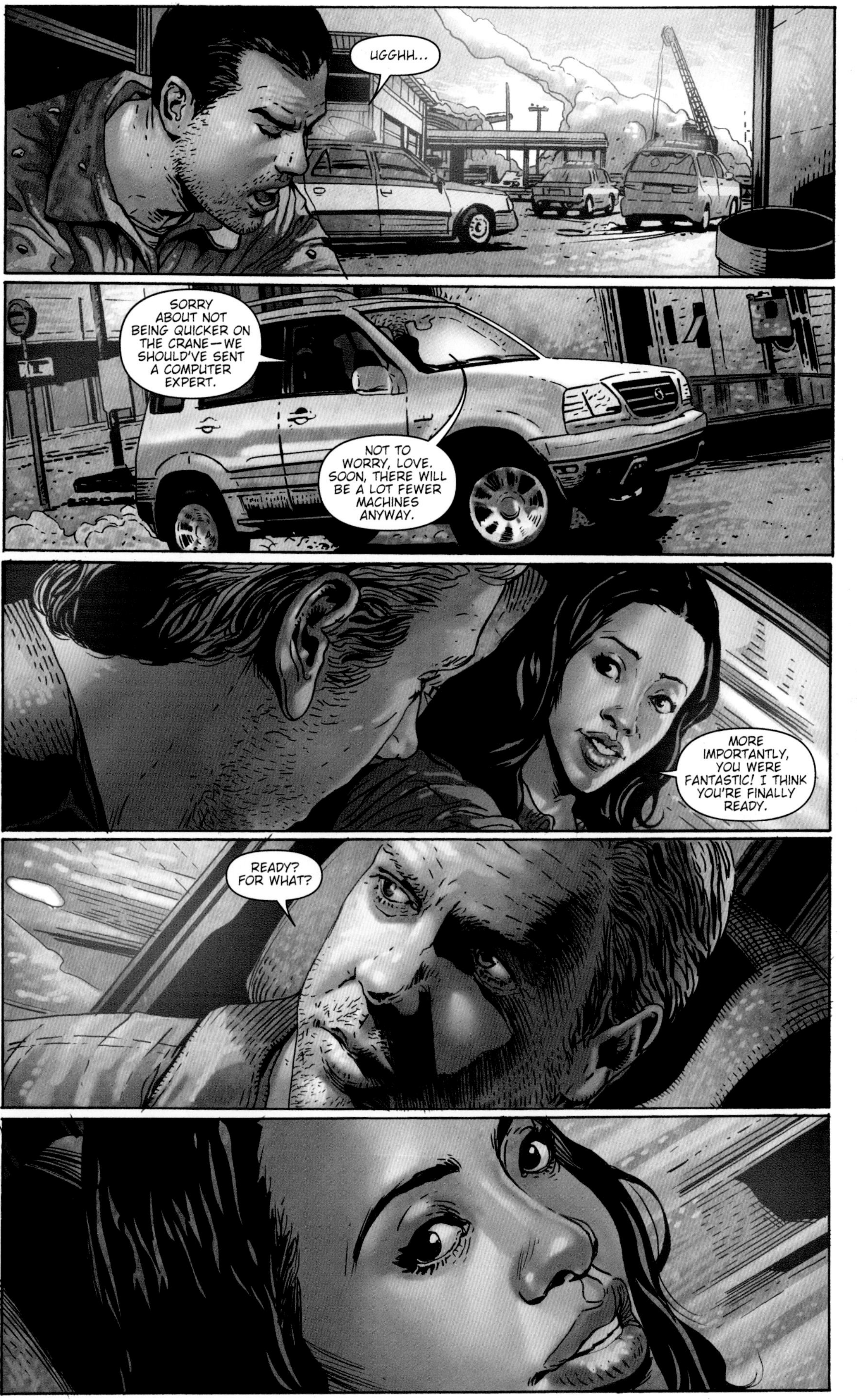
UGGHH...
SORRY ABOUT NOT BEING QUICKER ON THE CRANE—WE SHOULD'VE SENT A COMPUTER EXPERT.
NOT TO WORRY, LOVE. SOON, THERE WILL BE A LOT FEWER MACHINES ANYWAY.
MORE IMPORTANTLY, YOU WERE FANTASTIC! I THINK YOU'RE FINALLY READY.
READY? FOR WHAT?

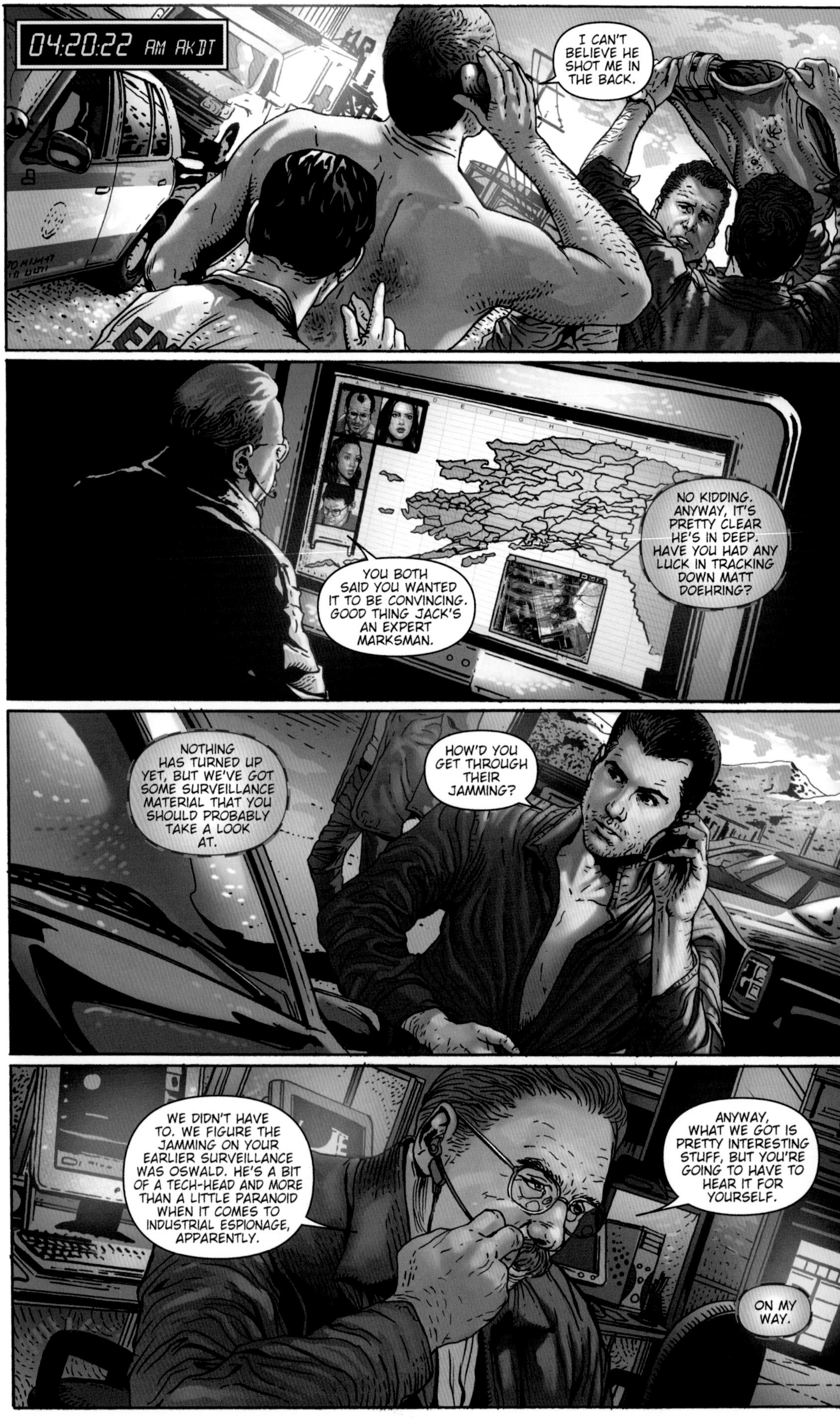
04:20:22 AM AKDT
I CAN'T BELIEVE HE SHOT ME IN THE BACK.
YOU BOTH SAID YOU WANTED IT TO BE CONVINCING. GOOD THING JACK'S AN EXPERT MARKSMAN.
NO KIDDING. ANYWAY, IT'S PRETTY CLEAR HE'S IN DEEP. HAVE YOU HAD ANY LUCK IN TRACKING DOWN MATT DOEHRING?
NOTHING HAS TURNED UP YET, BUT WE'VE GOT SOME SURVEILLANCE MATERIAL THAT YOU SHOULD PROBABLY TAKE A LOOK AT.
HOW'D YOU GET THROUGH THEIR JAMMING?
WE DIDN'T HAVE TO. WE FIGURE THE JAMMING ON YOUR EARLIER SURVEILLANCE WAS OSWALD. HE'S A BIT OF A TECH-HEAD AND MORE THAN A LITTLE PARANOID WHEN IT COMES TO INDUSTRIAL ESPIONAGE, APPARENTLY.
ANYWAY, WHAT WE GOT IS PRETTY INTERESTING STUFF, BUT YOU'RE GOING TO HAVE TO HEAR IT FOR YOURSELF.
ON MY WAY.

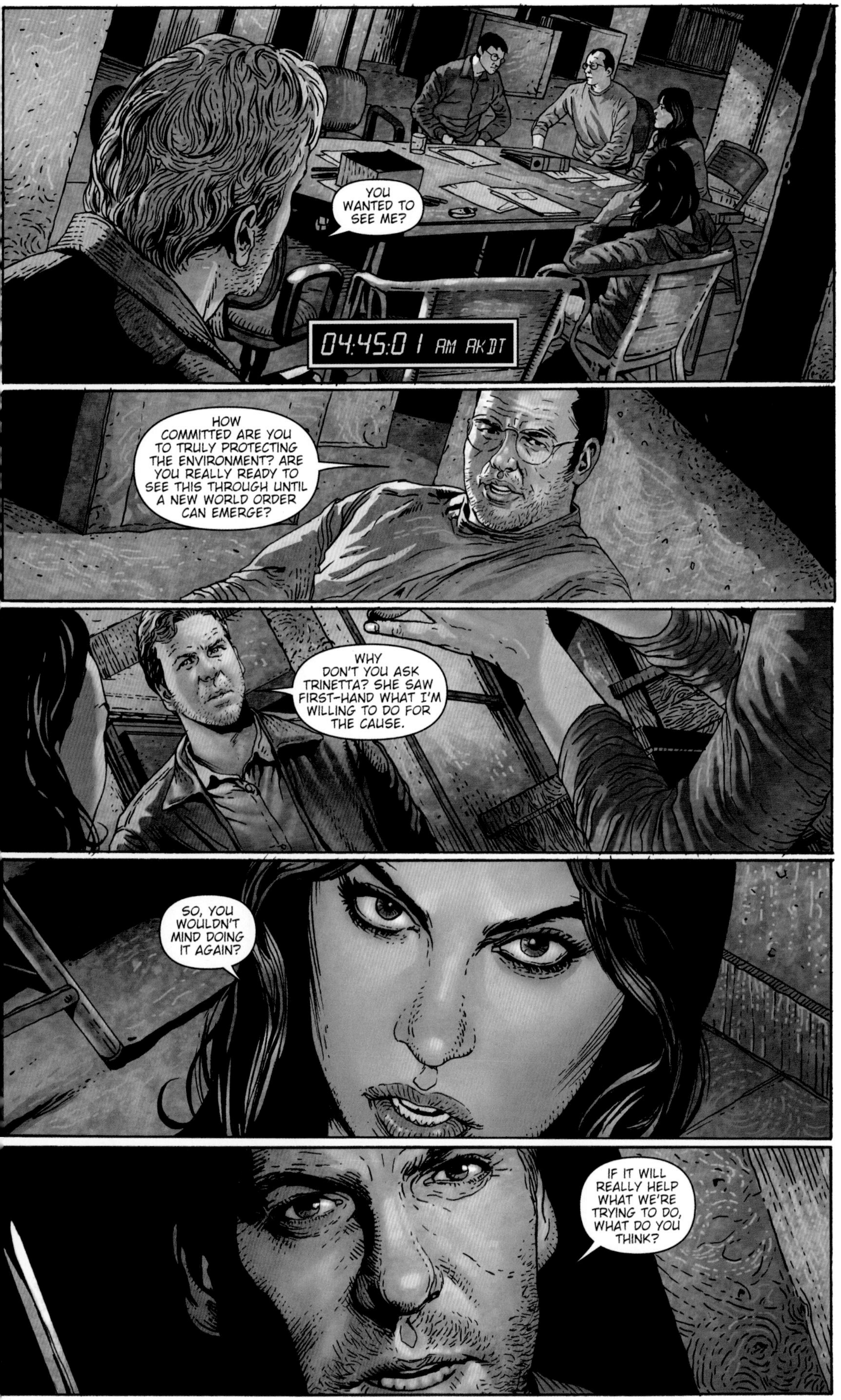
YOU WANTED TO SEE ME?
04:45:01 AM AKDT
HOW COMMITTED ARE YOU TO TRULY PROTECTING THE ENVIRONMENT? ARE YOU REALLY READY TO SEE THIS THROUGH UNTIL A NEW WORLD ORDER CAN EMERGE?
WHY DON'T YOU ASK TRINETTA? SHE SAW FIRST-HAND WHAT I'M WILLING TO DO FOR THE CAUSE.
SO, YOU WOULDN'T MIND DOING IT AGAIN?
IF IT WILL REALLY HELP WHAT WE'RE TRYING TO DO, WHAT DO YOU THINK?

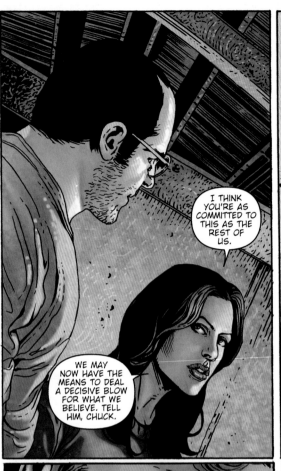

I THINK YOU'RE AS COMMITTED TO THIS AS THE REST OF US.

WE MAY NOW HAVE THE MEANS TO DEAL A DECISIVE BLOW FOR WHAT WE BELIEVE. TELL HIM, CHUCK.

DO YOU KNOW ANYTHING ABOUT A COMPANY CALLED CONSERV-REACTION?

I PULLED SOME RESEARCH FOR YOU THE OTHER DAY. THEY'RE AN OIL SPILL CLEAN-UP COMPANY.

WE'RE ABOUT TO TAKE ONE OF THEIR PRODUCTS AND MAKE IT A WEAPON FOR OUR CAUSE.

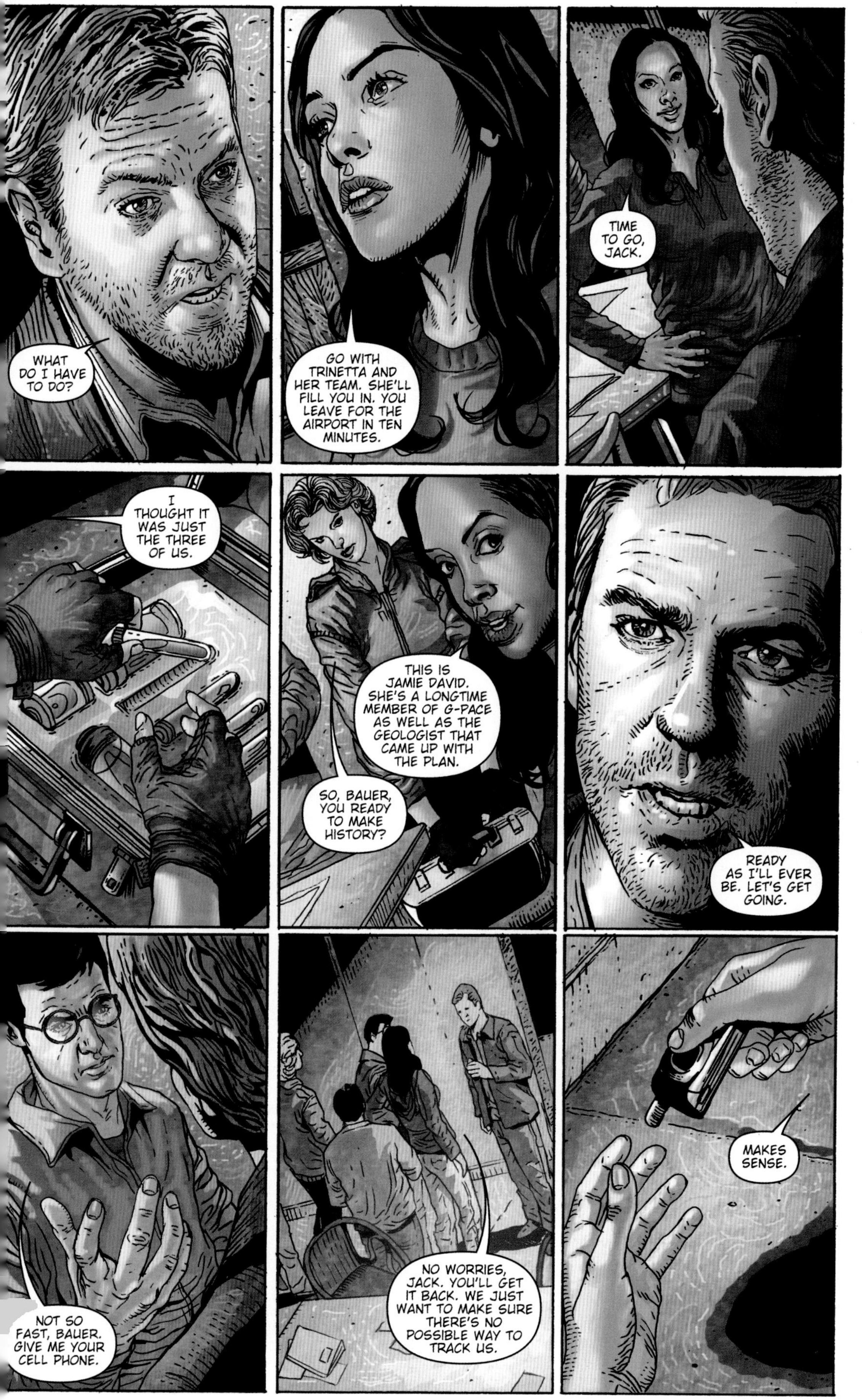
WHAT DO I HAVE TO DO?
GO WITH TRINETTA AND HER TEAM. SHE'LL FILL YOU IN. YOU LEAVE FOR THE AIRPORT IN TEN MINUTES.
TIME TO GO, JACK.
I THOUGHT IT WAS JUST THE THREE OF US.
THIS IS JAMIE DAVID. SHE'S A LONGTIME MEMBER OF G-PACE AS WELL AS THE GEOLOGIST THAT CAME UP WITH THE PLAN.
SO, BAUER, YOU READY TO MAKE HISTORY?
READY AS I'LL EVER BE. LET'S GET GOING.
NOT SO FAST, BAUER. GIVE ME YOUR CELL PHONE.
NO WORRIES, JACK. YOU'LL GET IT BACK. WE JUST WANT TO MAKE SURE THERE'S NO POSSIBLE WAY TO TRACK US.
MAKES SENSE.

JUST SIT BACK AND ENJOY THE VIEW, BAUER. WE'VE GOT A LONG TRIP AHEAD OF US.

05:35:12 AM AKDT

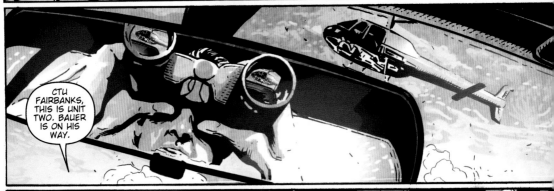

CTU FAIRBANKS, THIS IS UNIT TWO. BAUER IS ON HIS WAY.

GETTING ANY INSIGHT?

NO. WHAT HAVE YOUR PEOPLE TURNED UP?

THE CAR IS A RENTAL. NO SURPRISE.

RENTED WITH A FAKE CARD. NO SURPRISE THERE, EITHER.

WHO IS THIS GUY? HE'S TALKING SERIOUS MONEY, SWISS BANK ACCOUNTS— THE WORKS.

WE'RE STILL WORKING ON MATCHING HIM TO THE FACIAL DATABASE BUT COMING UP DRY.

THE PROFILERS HAVE LOOKED AT THE TAPE AND THEY TELL ME THAT, BASED ON THEIR BODY POSTURES, THE MYSTERY MAN IS DEFINITELY IN THE POWER POSITION.

FURTHER, THEY SAY THAT KRISTIN DOESN'T LIKE IT VERY MUCH SO, OBVIOUSLY, SHE'S GOT TO GO ALONG WITH HIM. WHY? WE STILL DON'T KNOW.

WELL, WE'D BETTER FIND OUT FAST OR...

GUYS, WE'VE GOT A REPORT. JACK AND SOME PEOPLE FROM G-PACE JUST TOOK OFF IN A CHOPPER AND HEADED NORTH.

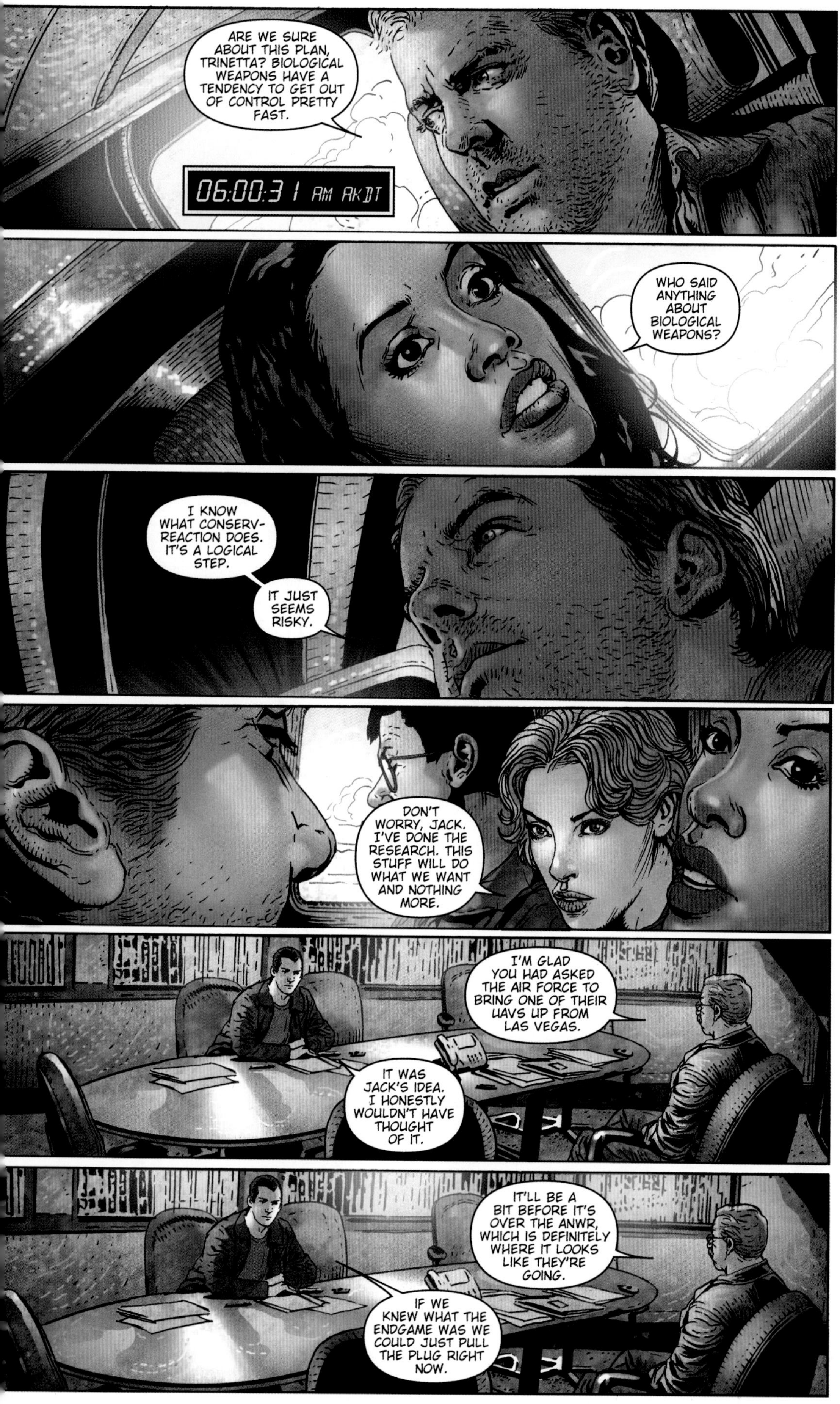
ARE WE SURE ABOUT THIS PLAN, TRINETTA? BIOLOGICAL WEAPONS HAVE A TENDENCY TO GET OUT OF CONTROL PRETTY FAST.
06:00:31 AM AKDT
WHO SAID ANYTHING ABOUT BIOLOGICAL WEAPONS?
I KNOW WHAT CONSERV-REACTION DOES. IT'S A LOGICAL STEP.
IT JUST SEEMS RISKY.
DON'T WORRY, JACK. I'VE DONE THE RESEARCH. THIS STUFF WILL DO WHAT WE WANT AND NOTHING MORE.
I'M GLAD YOU HAD ASKED THE AIR FORCE TO BRING ONE OF THEIR UAVS UP FROM LAS VEGAS.
IT WAS JACK'S IDEA. I HONESTLY WOULDN'T HAVE THOUGHT OF IT.
IT'LL BE A BIT BEFORE IT'S OVER THE ANWR, WHICH IS DEFINITELY WHERE IT LOOKS LIKE THEY'RE GOING.
IF WE KNEW WHAT THE ENDGAME WAS WE COULD JUST PULL THE PLUG RIGHT NOW.

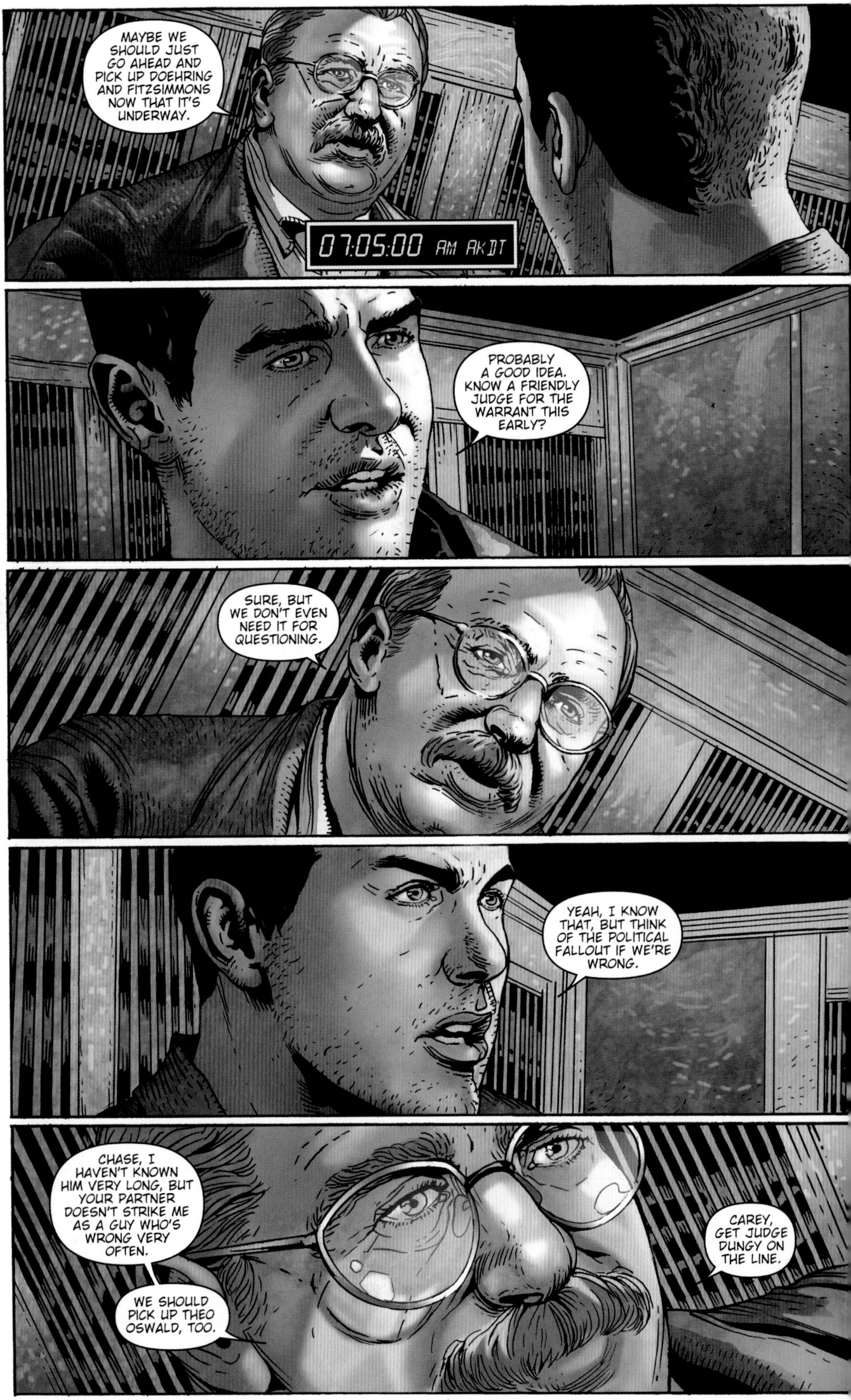
MAYBE WE SHOULD JUST GO AHEAD AND PICK UP DOEHRING AND FITZSIMMONS NOW THAT IT'S UNDERWAY.
07:05:00 AM AKDT
PROBABLY A GOOD IDEA. KNOW A FRIENDLY JUDGE FOR THE WARRANT THIS EARLY?
SURE, BUT WE DON'T EVEN NEED IT FOR QUESTIONING.
YEAH, I KNOW THAT, BUT THINK OF THE POLITICAL FALLOUT IF WE'RE WRONG.
CHASE, I HAVEN'T KNOWN HIM VERY LONG, BUT YOUR PARTNER DOESN'T STRIKE ME AS A GUY WHO'S WRONG VERY OFTEN.
WE SHOULD PICK UP THEO OSWALD, TOO.
CAREY, GET JUDGE DUNGY ON THE LINE.

WHAT THE HELL IS THIS?

WHAT THE HELL IS WHAT?

08:20:43 AM AKDT

YOU'VE BEEN TRANSFERRING G-PACE FUNDS TO OVERSEAS ACCOUNTS. WHAT THE HELL WERE YOU THINKING? THAT I WOULDN'T FIND OUT?

I ALWAYS ASSUMED YOU WOULD FIND OUT AT SOME POINT, CHUCK. I'M JUST SORRY IT WAS LIKE THIS.

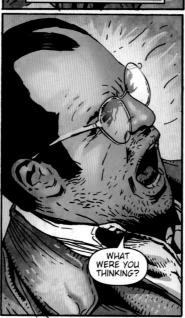

WHAT WERE YOU THINKING?

I WAS THINKING THAT AFTER THE ANWR IS RENDERED INERT, I'M GOING TO BE A VERY WEALTHY WOMAN...

...BUT I WOULDN'T MIND BEING A LITTLE MORE WEALTHY.

AND AFTER ALL, IT'S NOT LIKE G-PACE OR MORNINGSIDE DAWN WILL BE AROUND TO USE IT.

BUT THE CAUSE...

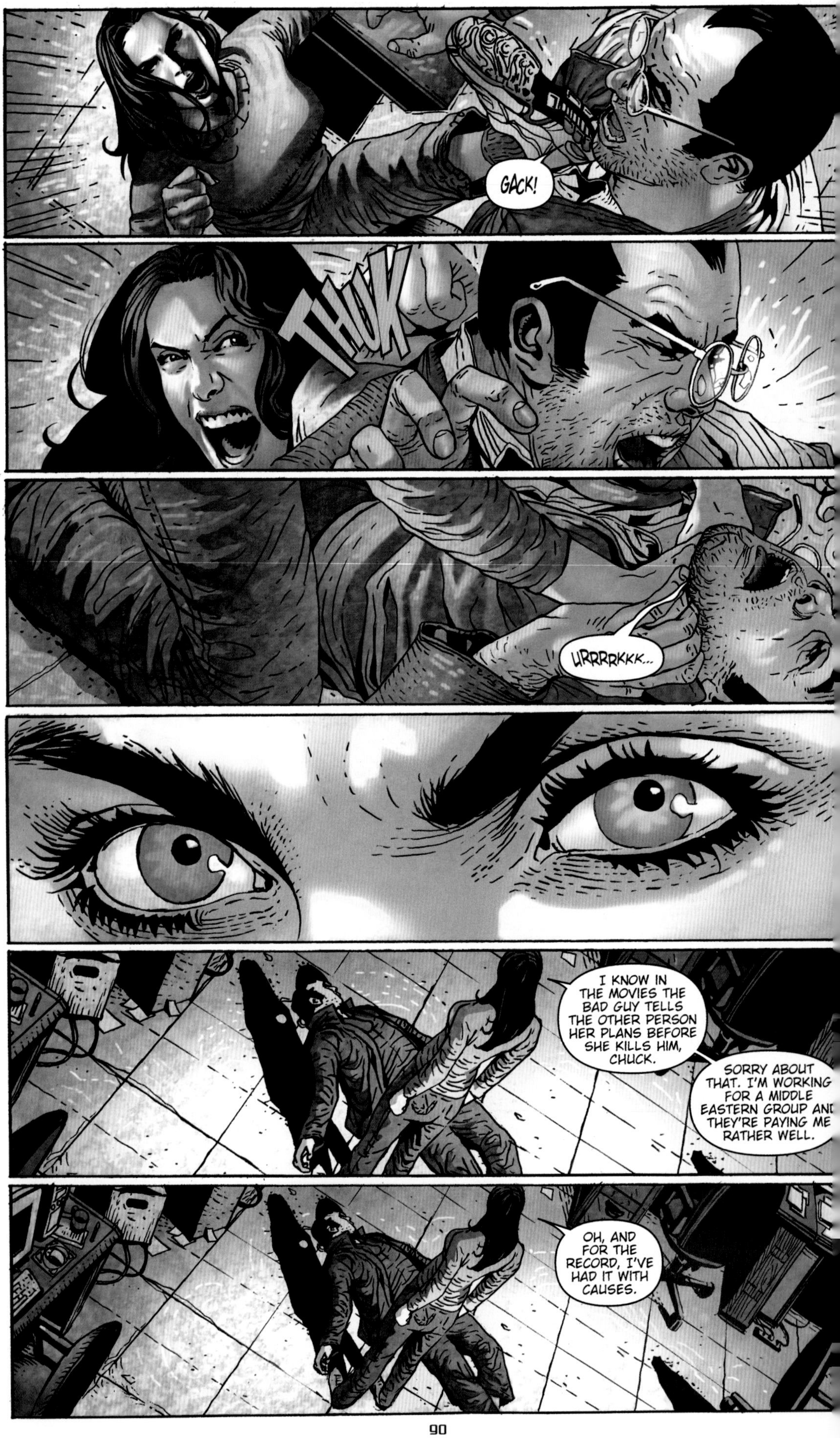
GACK!
THUK
URRRRKKK...
I KNOW IN THE MOVIES THE BAD GUY TELLS THE OTHER PERSON HER PLANS BEFORE SHE KILLS HIM, CHUCK.
SORRY ABOUT THAT. I'M WORKING FOR A MIDDLE EASTERN GROUP AND THEY'RE PAYING ME RATHER WELL.
OH, AND FOR THE RECORD, I'VE HAD IT WITH CAUSES.

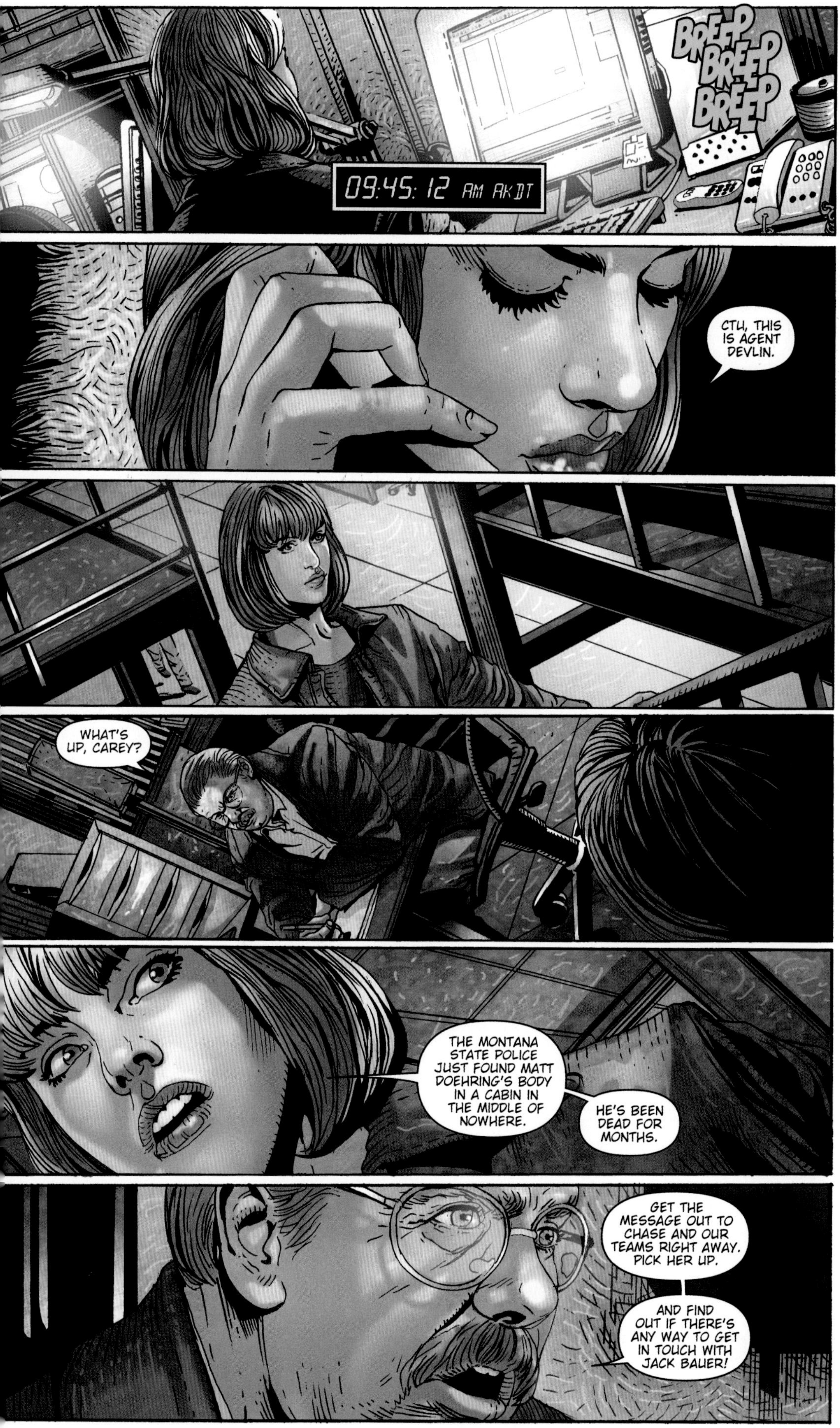
BREEP BREEP BREEP
09:45:12 AM AKDT
CTU, THIS IS AGENT DEVLIN.
WHAT'S UP, CAREY?
THE MONTANA STATE POLICE JUST FOUND MATT DOEHRING'S BODY IN A CABIN IN THE MIDDLE OF NOWHERE.
HE'S BEEN DEAD FOR MONTHS.
GET THE MESSAGE OUT TO CHASE AND OUR TEAMS RIGHT AWAY. PICK HER UP.
AND FIND OUT IF THERE'S ANY WAY TO GET IN TOUCH WITH JACK BAUER!

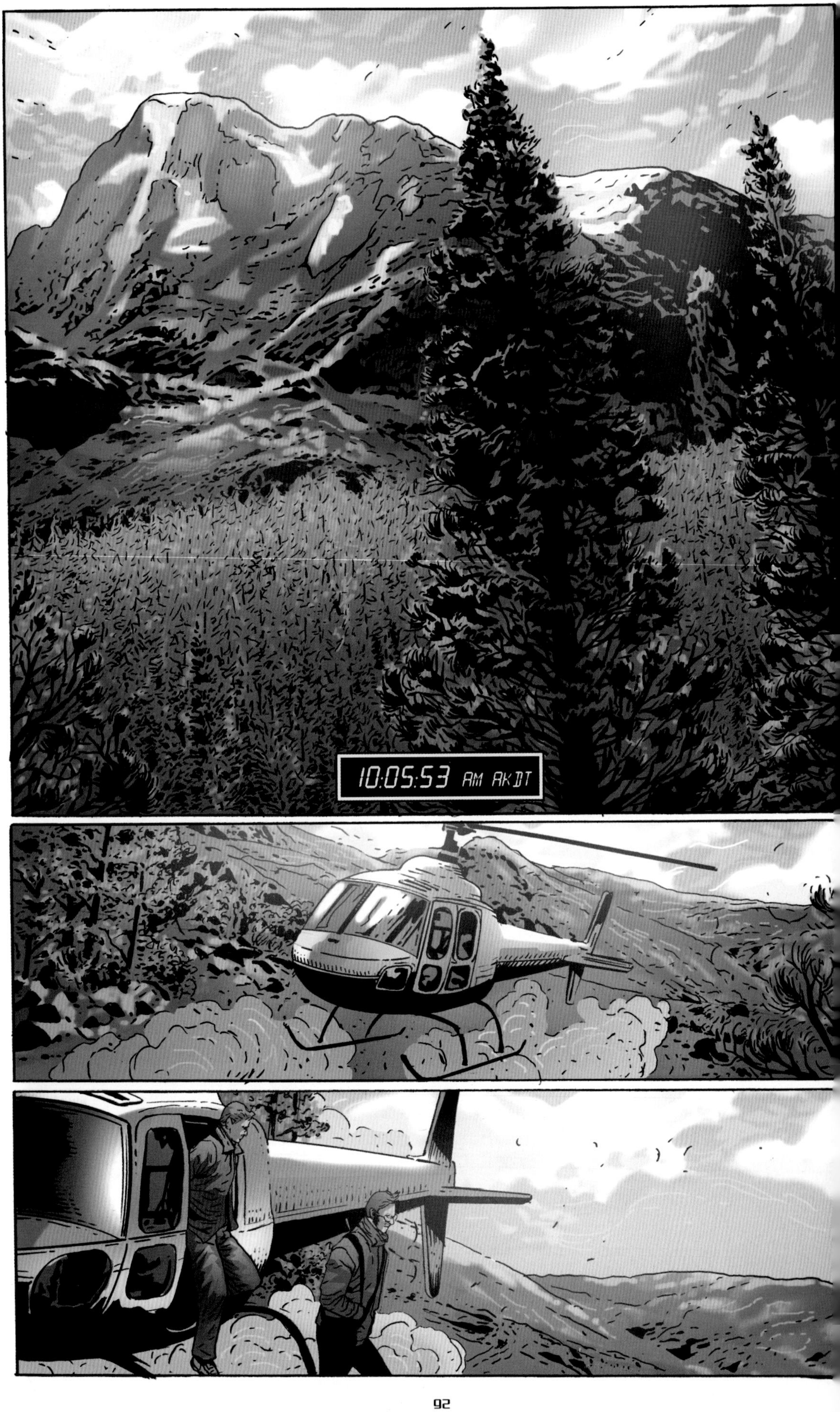
10:05:53 AM AKDT

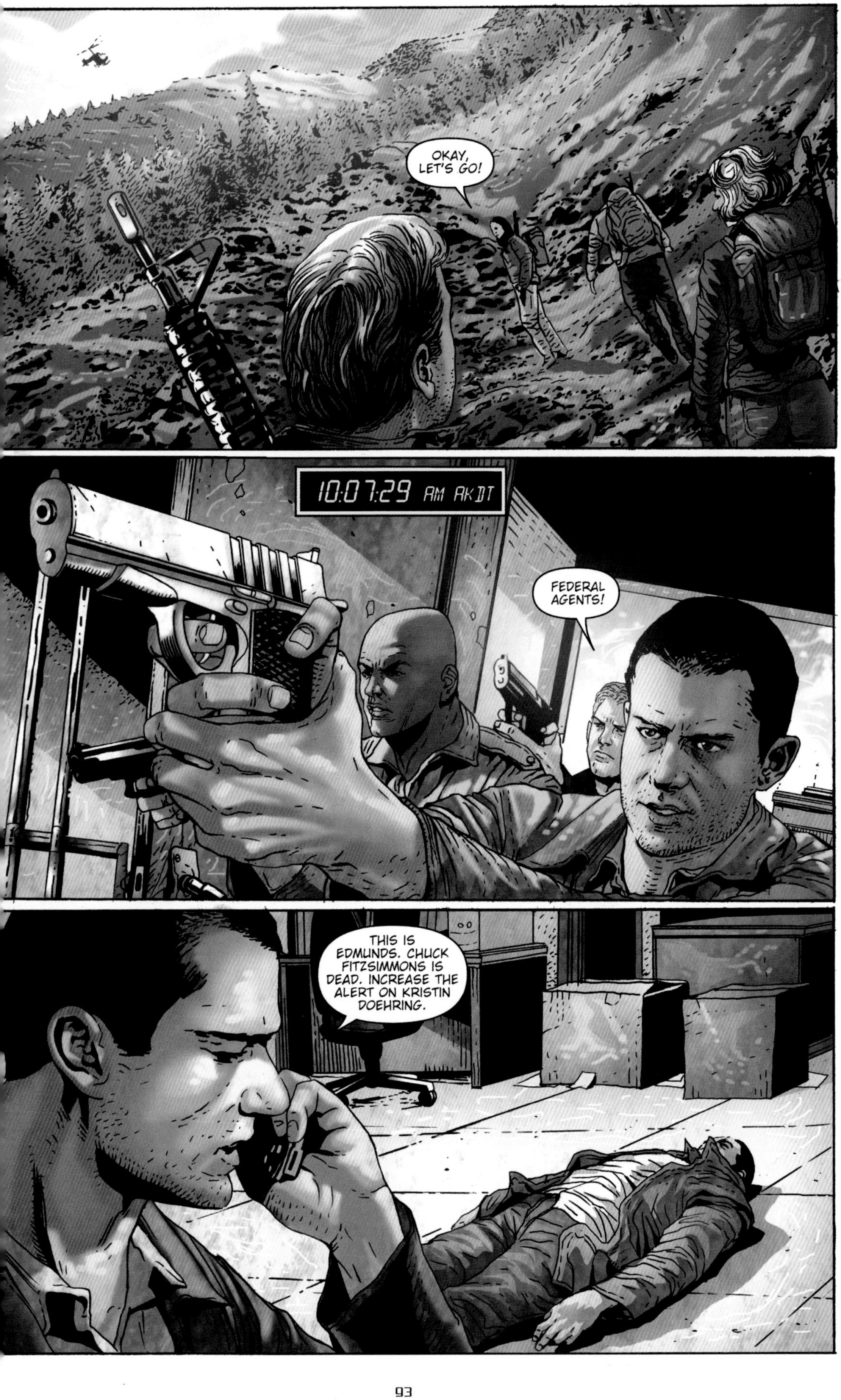
OKAY, LET'S GO!
10:07:29 AM AKDT
FEDERAL AGENTS!
THIS IS EDMUNDS. CHUCK FITZSIMMONS IS DEAD. INCREASE THE ALERT ON KRISTIN DOEHRING.

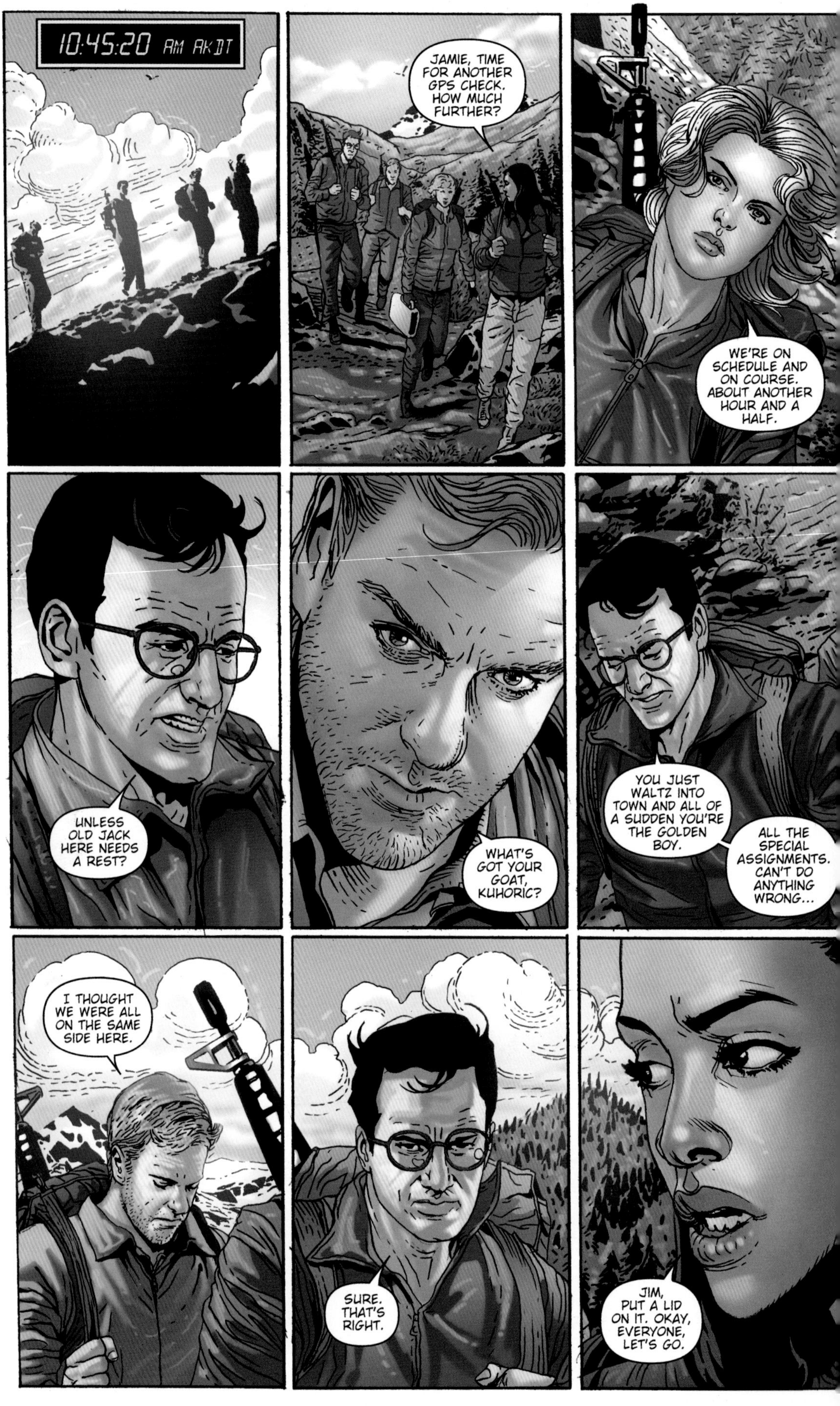
10:45:20 AM AKDT
JAMIE, TIME FOR ANOTHER GPS CHECK. HOW MUCH FURTHER?
WE'RE ON SCHEDULE AND ON COURSE. ABOUT ANOTHER HOUR AND A HALF.
UNLESS OLD JACK HERE NEEDS A REST?
WHAT'S GOT YOUR GOAT, KUHORIC?
YOU JUST WALTZ INTO TOWN AND ALL OF A SUDDEN YOU'RE THE GOLDEN BOY.
ALL THE SPECIAL ASSIGNMENTS. CAN'T DO ANYTHING WRONG...
I THOUGHT WE WERE ALL ON THE SAME SIDE HERE.
SURE. THAT'S RIGHT.
JIM, PUT A LID ON IT. OKAY, EVERYONE, LET'S GO.

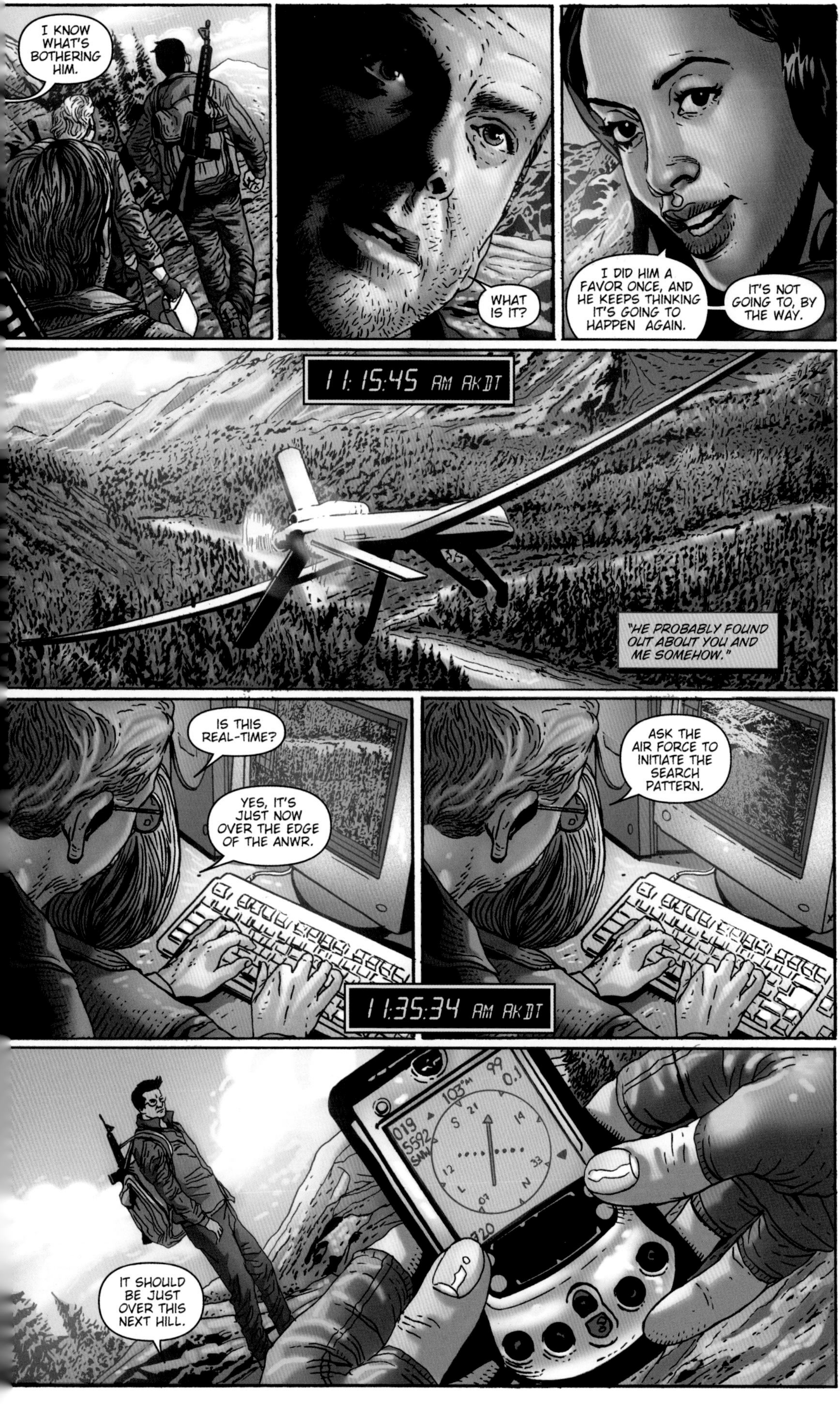
I KNOW WHAT'S BOTHERING HIM.
WHAT IS IT?
I DID HIM A FAVOR ONCE, AND HE KEEPS THINKING IT'S GOING TO HAPPEN AGAIN.
IT'S NOT GOING TO, BY THE WAY.
11:15:45 AM AKDT
"HE PROBABLY FOUND OUT ABOUT YOU AND ME SOMEHOW."
IS THIS REAL-TIME?
YES, IT'S JUST NOW OVER THE EDGE OF THE ANWR.
ASK THE AIR FORCE TO INITIATE THE SEARCH PATTERN.
11:35:34 AM AKDT
IT SHOULD BE JUST OVER THIS NEXT HILL.

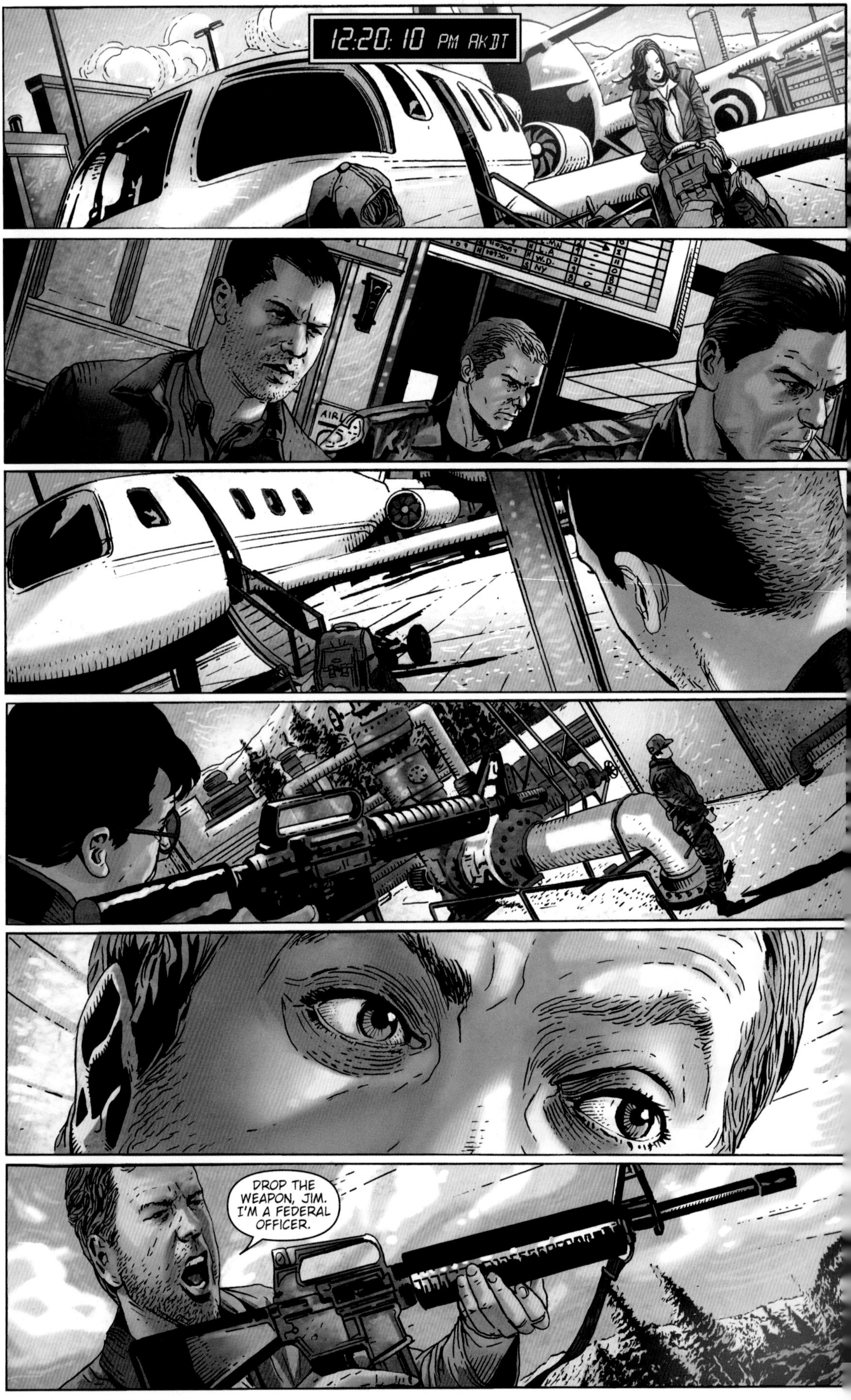
12:20:10 PM AKDT
DROP THE WEAPON, JIM. I'M A FEDERAL OFFICER.

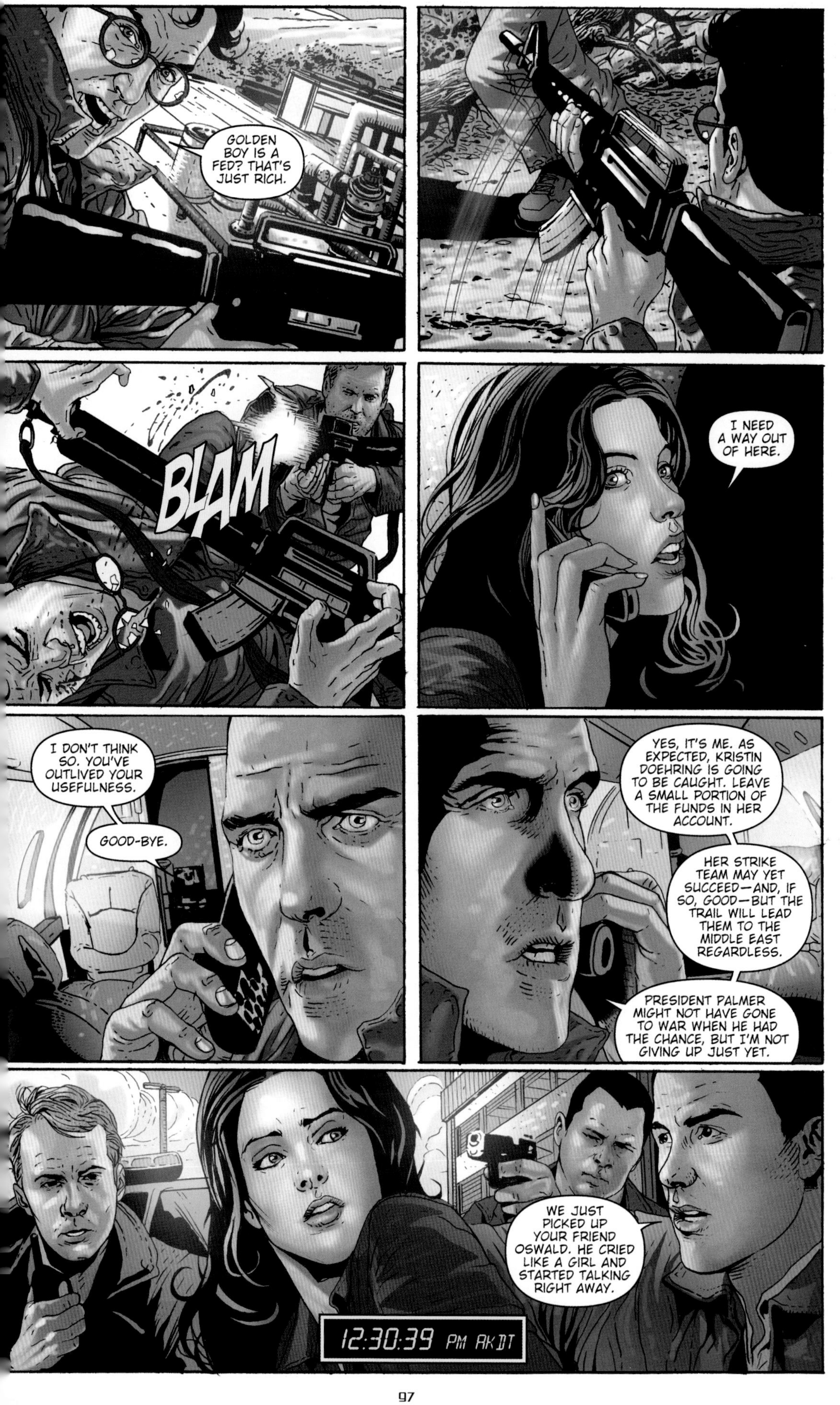

GOLDEN BOY IS A FED? THAT'S JUST RICH.
BLAM
I NEED A WAY OUT OF HERE.
I DON'T THINK SO. YOU'VE OUTLIVED YOUR USEFULNESS.
GOOD-BYE.
YES, IT'S ME. AS EXPECTED, KRISTIN DOEHRING IS GOING TO BE CAUGHT. LEAVE A SMALL PORTION OF THE FUNDS IN HER ACCOUNT.
HER STRIKE TEAM MAY YET SUCCEED—AND, IF SO, GOOD—BUT THE TRAIL WILL LEAD THEM TO THE MIDDLE EAST REGARDLESS.
PRESIDENT PALMER MIGHT NOT HAVE GONE TO WAR WHEN HE HAD THE CHANCE, BUT I'M NOT GIVING UP JUST YET.
WE JUST PICKED UP YOUR FRIEND OSWALD. HE CRIED LIKE A GIRL AND STARTED TALKING RIGHT AWAY.
12:30:39 PM AKDT

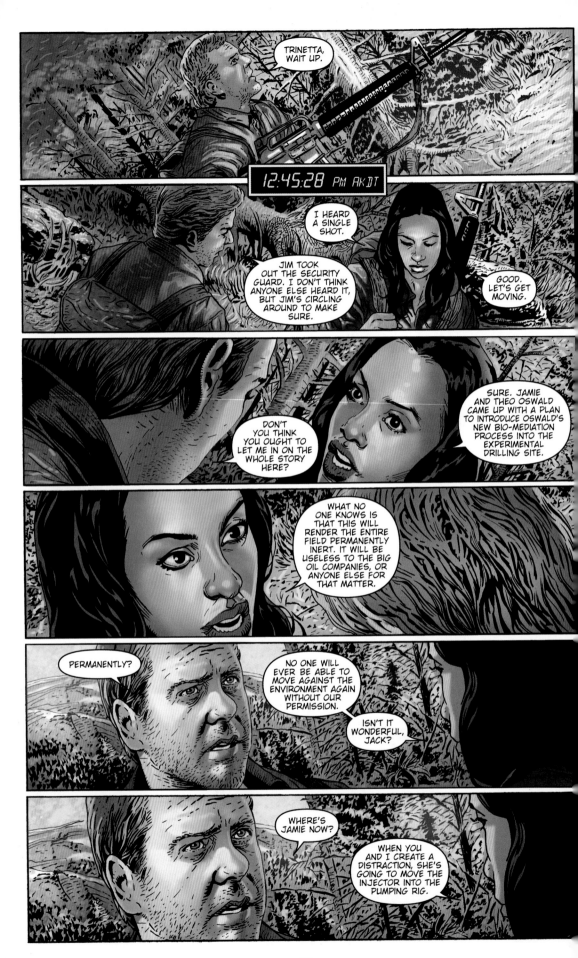

TRINETTA, WAIT UP.

12:45:28 PM AKDT

I HEARD A SINGLE SHOT.

JIM TOOK OUT THE SECURITY GUARD. I DON'T THINK ANYONE ELSE HEARD IT, BUT JIM'S CIRCLING AROUND TO MAKE SURE.

GOOD. LET'S GET MOVING.

DON'T YOU THINK YOU OUGHT TO LET ME IN ON THE WHOLE STORY HERE?

SURE. JAMIE AND THEO OSWALD CAME UP WITH A PLAN TO INTRODUCE OSWALD'S NEW BIO-MEDIATION PROCESS INTO THE EXPERIMENTAL DRILLING SITE.

WHAT NO ONE KNOWS IS THAT THIS WILL RENDER THE ENTIRE FIELD PERMANENTLY INERT. IT WILL BE USELESS TO THE BIG OIL COMPANIES, OR ANYONE ELSE FOR THAT MATTER.

PERMANENTLY?

NO ONE WILL EVER BE ABLE TO MOVE AGAINST THE ENVIRONMENT AGAIN WITHOUT OUR PERMISSION.

ISN'T IT WONDERFUL, JACK?

WHERE'S JAMIE NOW?

WHEN YOU AND I CREATE A DISTRACTION, SHE'S GOING TO MOVE THE INJECTOR INTO THE PUMPING RIG.

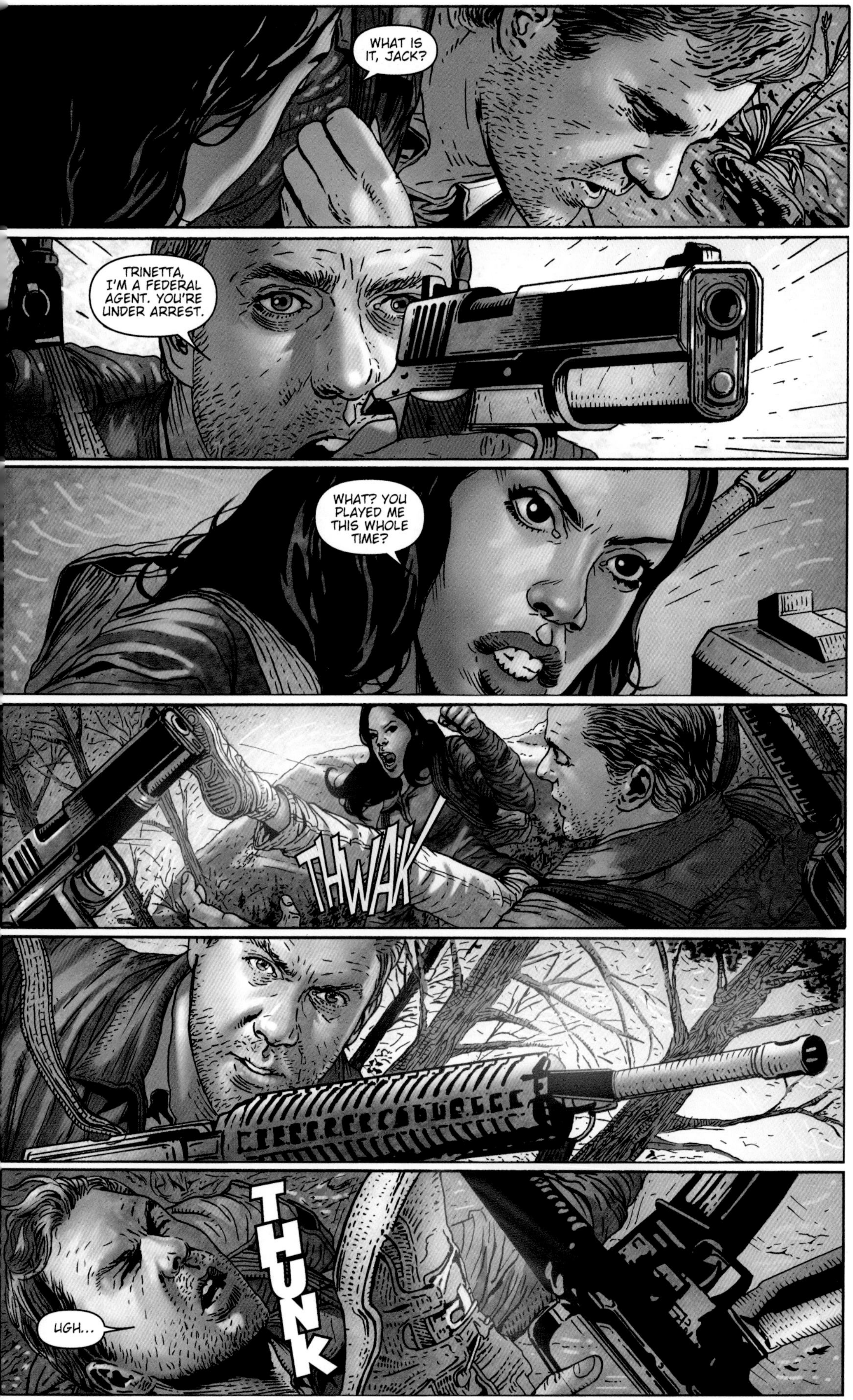

WHAT IS IT, JACK?
TRINETTA, I'M A FEDERAL AGENT. YOU'RE UNDER ARREST.
WHAT? YOU PLAYED ME THIS WHOLE TIME?
THWAK
THUNK
UGH...

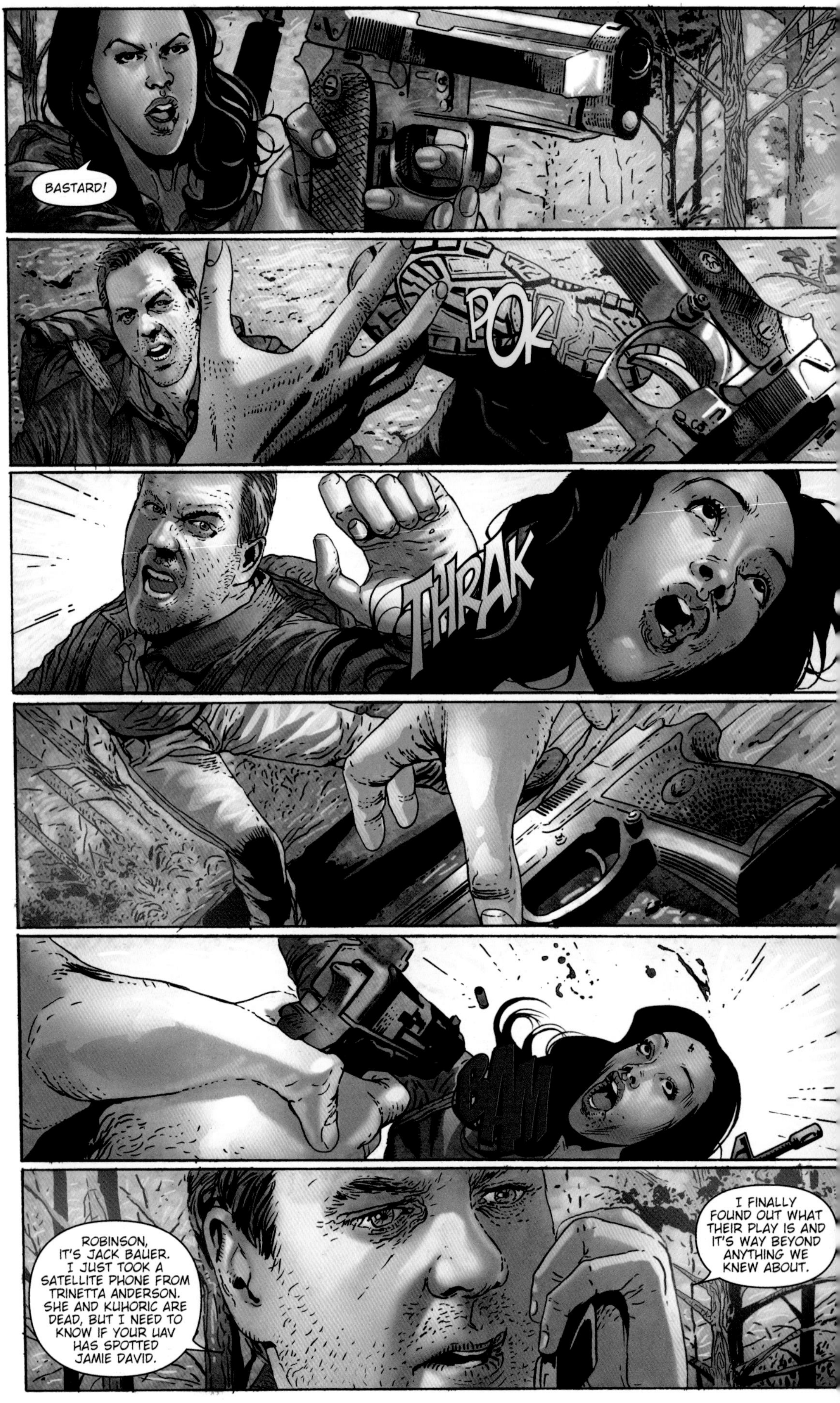
BASTARD!
POK
THRAK
ROBINSON, IT'S JACK BAUER. I JUST TOOK A SATELLITE PHONE FROM TRINETTA ANDERSON. SHE AND KUHORIC ARE DEAD, BUT I NEED TO KNOW IF YOUR UAV HAS SPOTTED JAMIE DAVID.
I FINALLY FOUND OUT WHAT THEIR PLAY IS AND IT'S WAY BEYOND ANYTHING WE KNEW ABOUT.

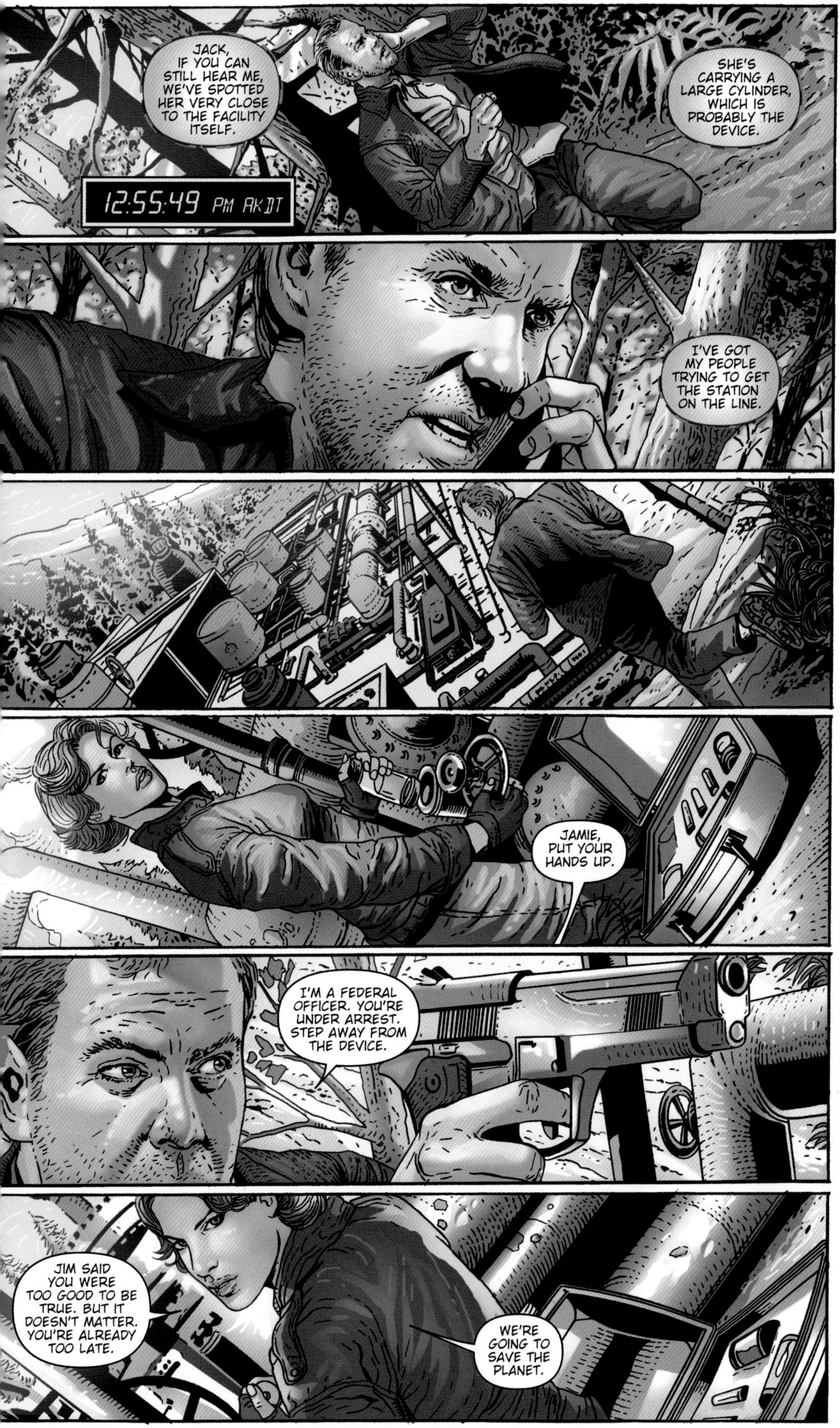
JACK, IF YOU CAN STILL HEAR ME, WE'VE SPOTTED HER VERY CLOSE TO THE FACILITY ITSELF.
SHE'S CARRYING A LARGE CYLINDER, WHICH IS PROBABLY THE DEVICE.
12:55:49 PM AKDT
I'VE GOT MY PEOPLE TRYING TO GET THE STATION ON THE LINE.
JAMIE, PUT YOUR HANDS UP.
I'M A FEDERAL OFFICER. YOU'RE UNDER ARREST. STEP AWAY FROM THE DEVICE.
JIM SAID YOU WERE TOO GOOD TO BE TRUE. BUT IT DOESN'T MATTER. YOU'RE ALREADY TOO LATE.
WE'RE GOING TO SAVE THE PLANET.

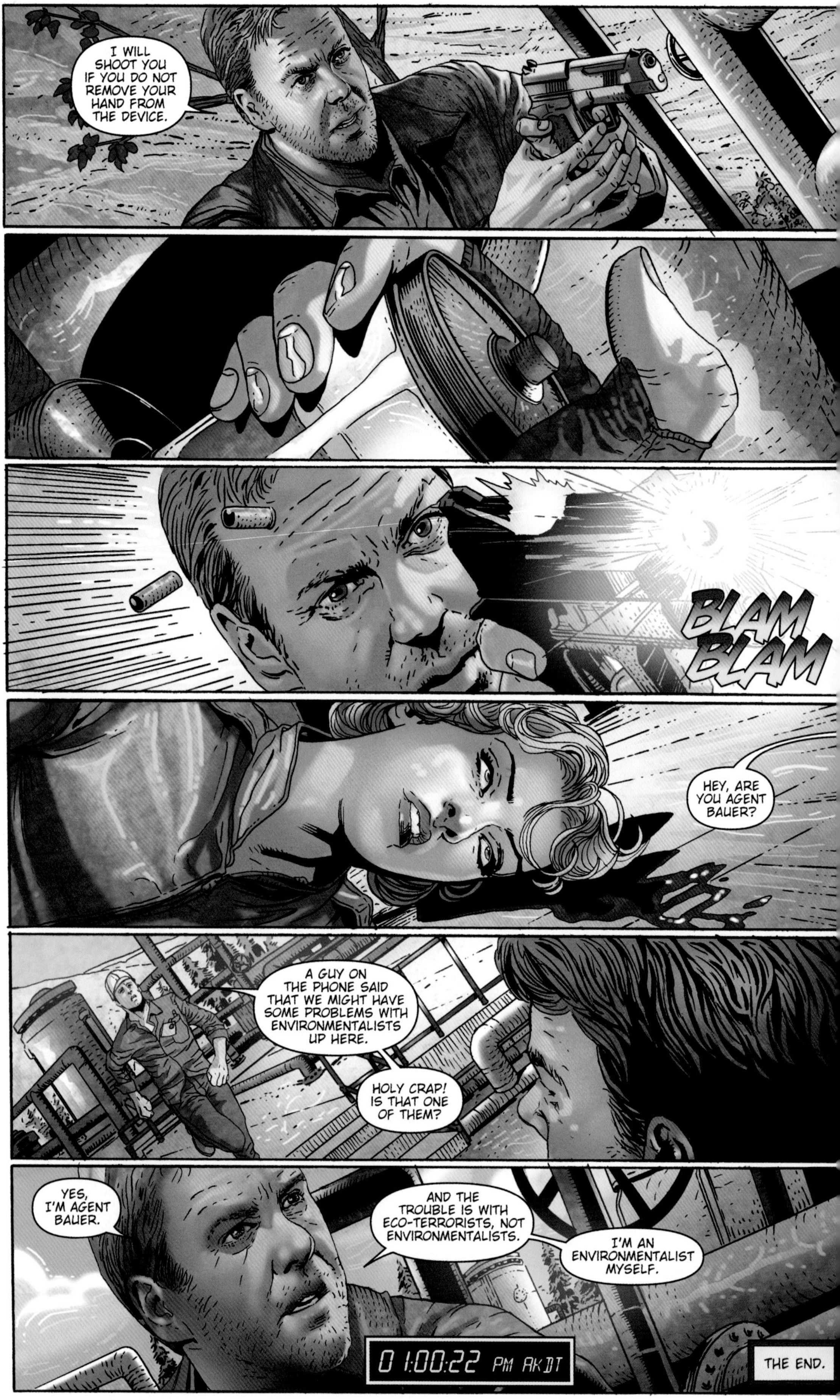
I WILL SHOOT YOU IF YOU DO NOT REMOVE YOUR HAND FROM THE DEVICE.
BLAM BLAM
HEY, ARE YOU AGENT BAUER?
A GUY ON THE PHONE SAID THAT WE MIGHT HAVE SOME PROBLEMS WITH ENVIRONMENTALISTS UP HERE.
HOLY CRAP! IS THAT ONE OF THEM?
YES, I'M AGENT BAUER.
AND THE TROUBLE IS WITH ECO-TERRORISTS, NOT ENVIRONMENTALISTS.
I'M AN ENVIRONMENTALIST MYSELF.
0 1:00:22 PM AKDT
THE END.

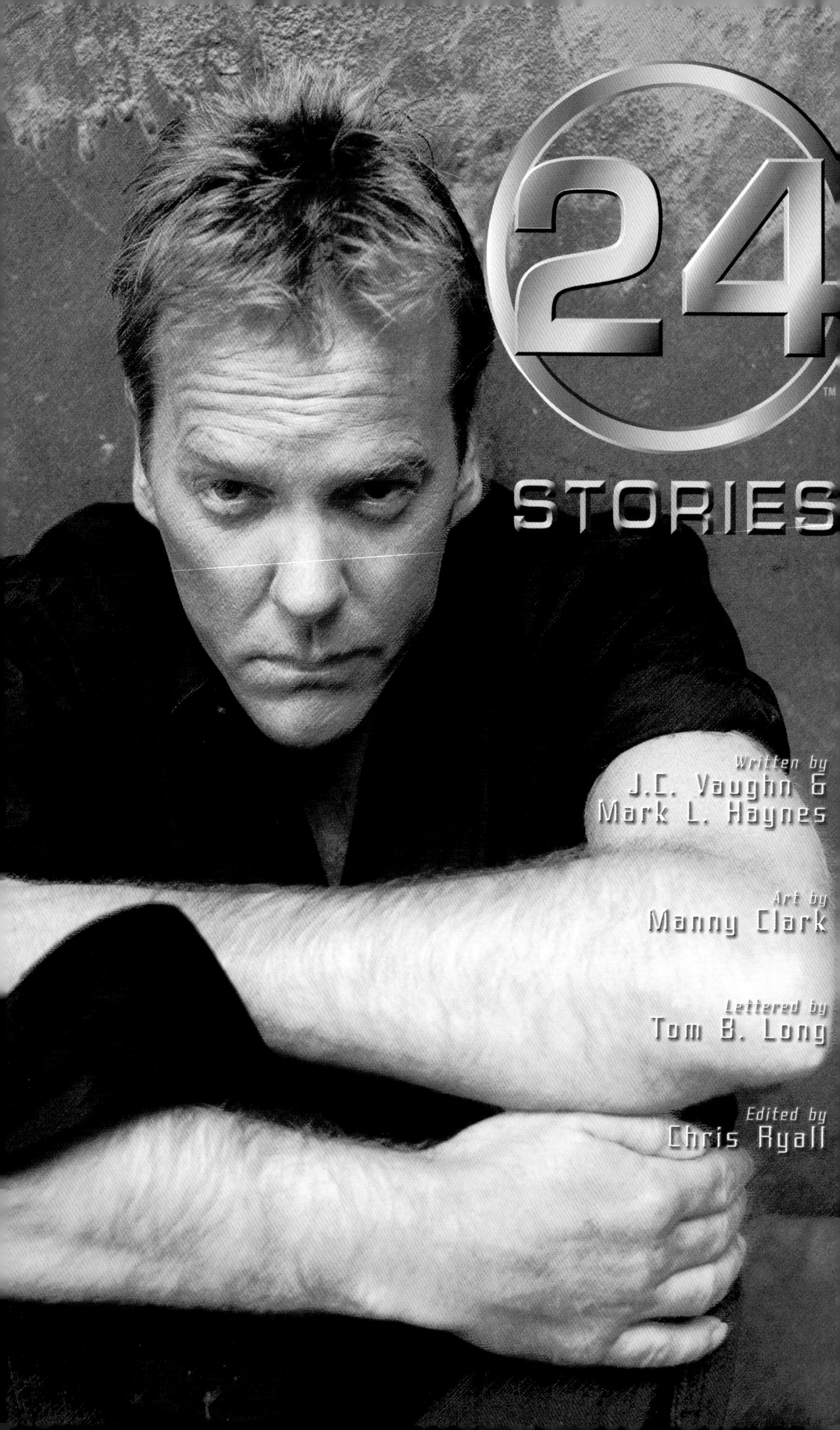
24
STORIES
Written by
J.C. Vaughn &
Mark L. Haynes
Art by
Manny Clark
Lettered by
Tom B. Long
Edited by
Chris Ryall

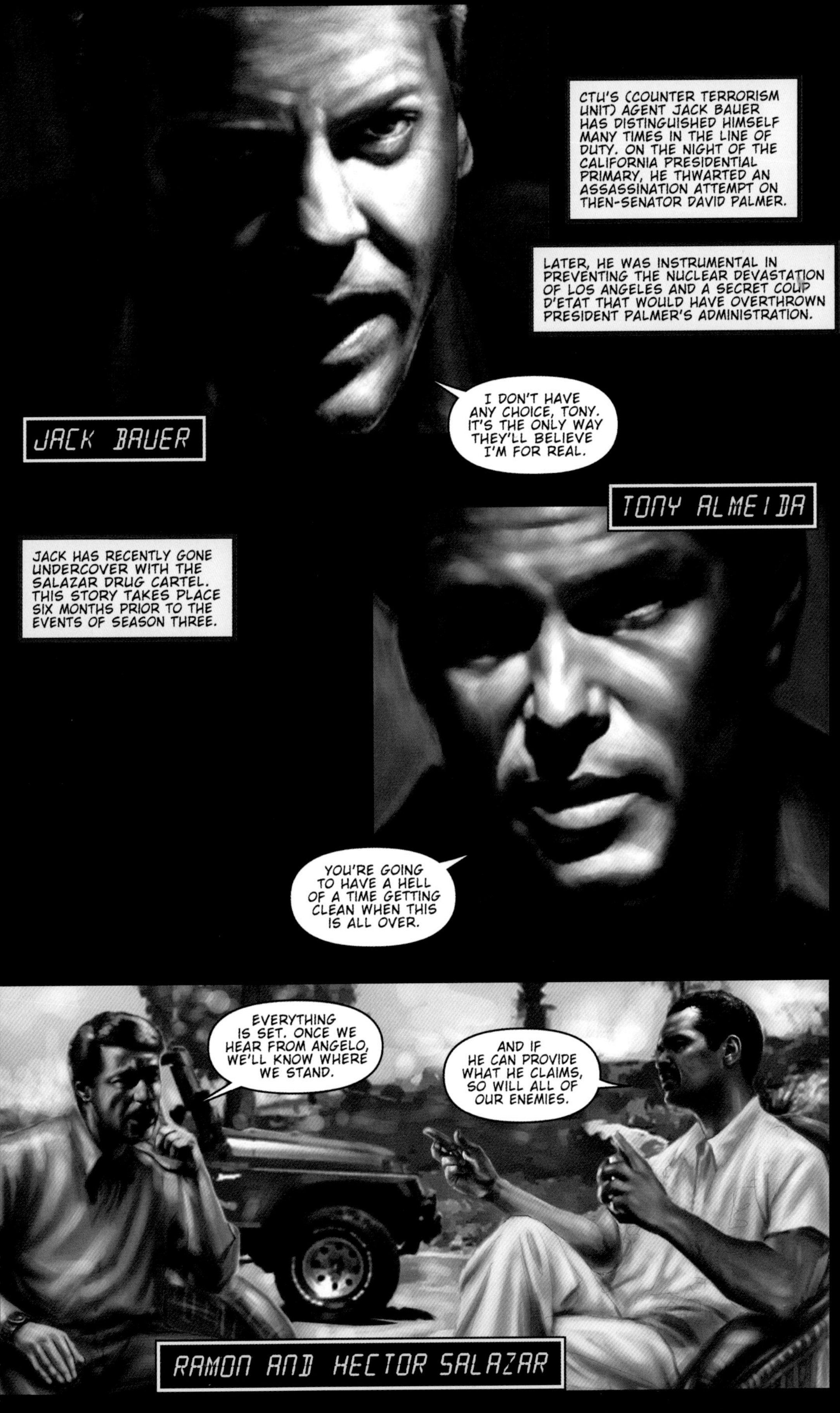
CTU'S (COUNTER TERRORISM UNIT) AGENT JACK BAUER HAS DISTINGUISHED HIMSELF MANY TIMES IN THE LINE OF DUTY. ON THE NIGHT OF THE CALIFORNIA PRESIDENTIAL PRIMARY, HE THWARTED AN ASSASSINATION ATTEMPT ON THEN-SENATOR DAVID PALMER.
LATER, HE WAS INSTRUMENTAL IN PREVENTING THE NUCLEAR DEVASTATION OF LOS ANGELES AND A SECRET COUP D'ETAT THAT WOULD HAVE OVERTHROWN PRESIDENT PALMER'S ADMINISTRATION.
JACK BAUER
I DON'T HAVE ANY CHOICE, TONY. IT'S THE ONLY WAY THEY'LL BELIEVE I'M FOR REAL.
TONY ALMEIDA
JACK HAS RECENTLY GONE UNDERCOVER WITH THE SALAZAR DRUG CARTEL. THIS STORY TAKES PLACE SIX MONTHS PRIOR TO THE EVENTS OF SEASON THREE.
YOU'RE GOING TO HAVE A HELL OF A TIME GETTING CLEAN WHEN THIS IS ALL OVER.
EVERYTHING IS SET. ONCE WE HEAR FROM ANGELO, WE'LL KNOW WHERE WE STAND.
AND IF HE CAN PROVIDE WHAT HE CLAIMS, SO WILL ALL OF OUR ENEMIES.
RAMON AND HECTOR SALAZAR

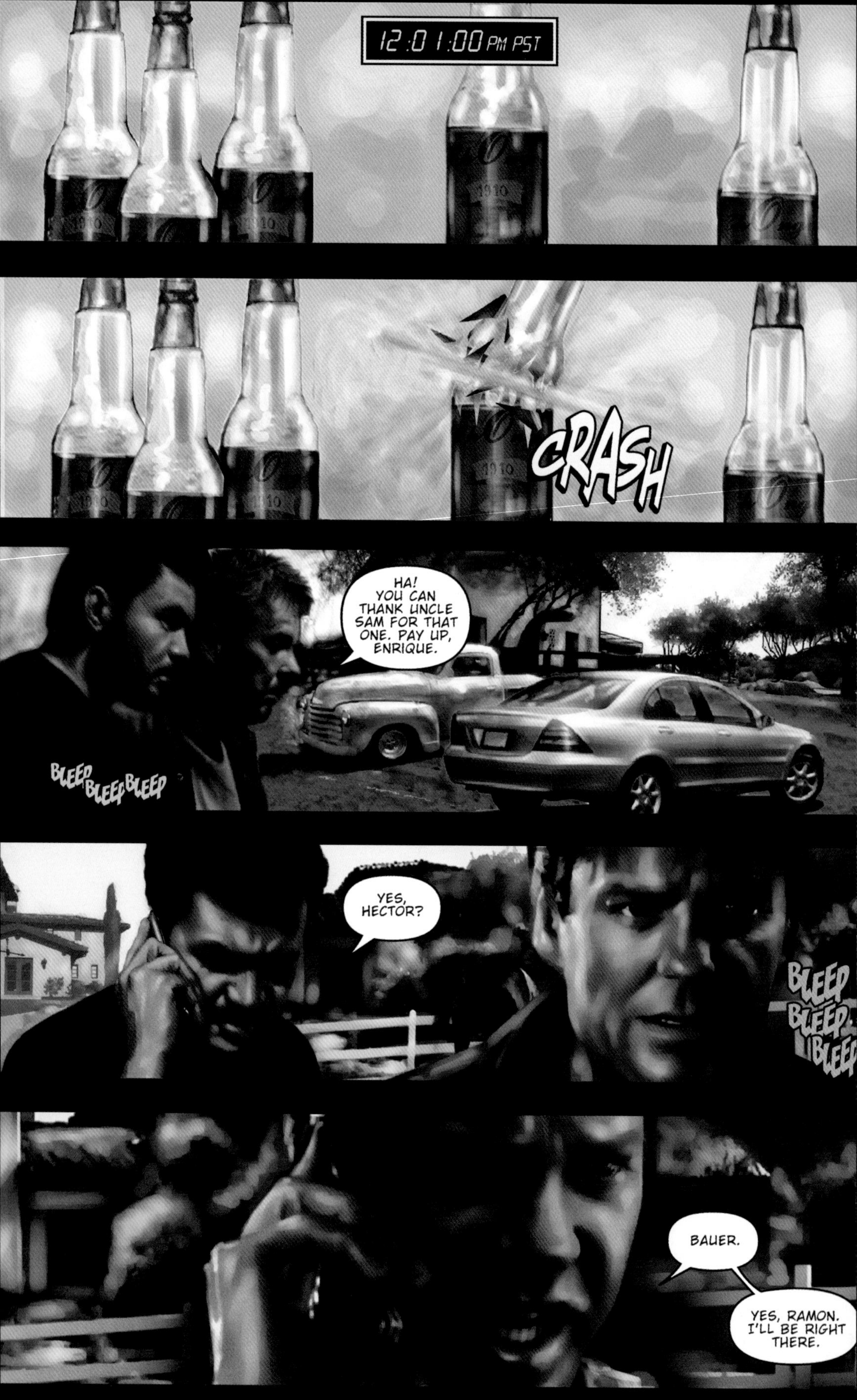
12:01:00 PM PST
CRASH
HA! YOU CAN THANK UNCLE SAM FOR THAT ONE. PAY UP, ENRIQUE.
BLEEP BLEEP BLEEP
YES, HECTOR?
BLEEP BLEEP BLEEP
BAUER.
YES, RAMON. I'LL BE RIGHT THERE.

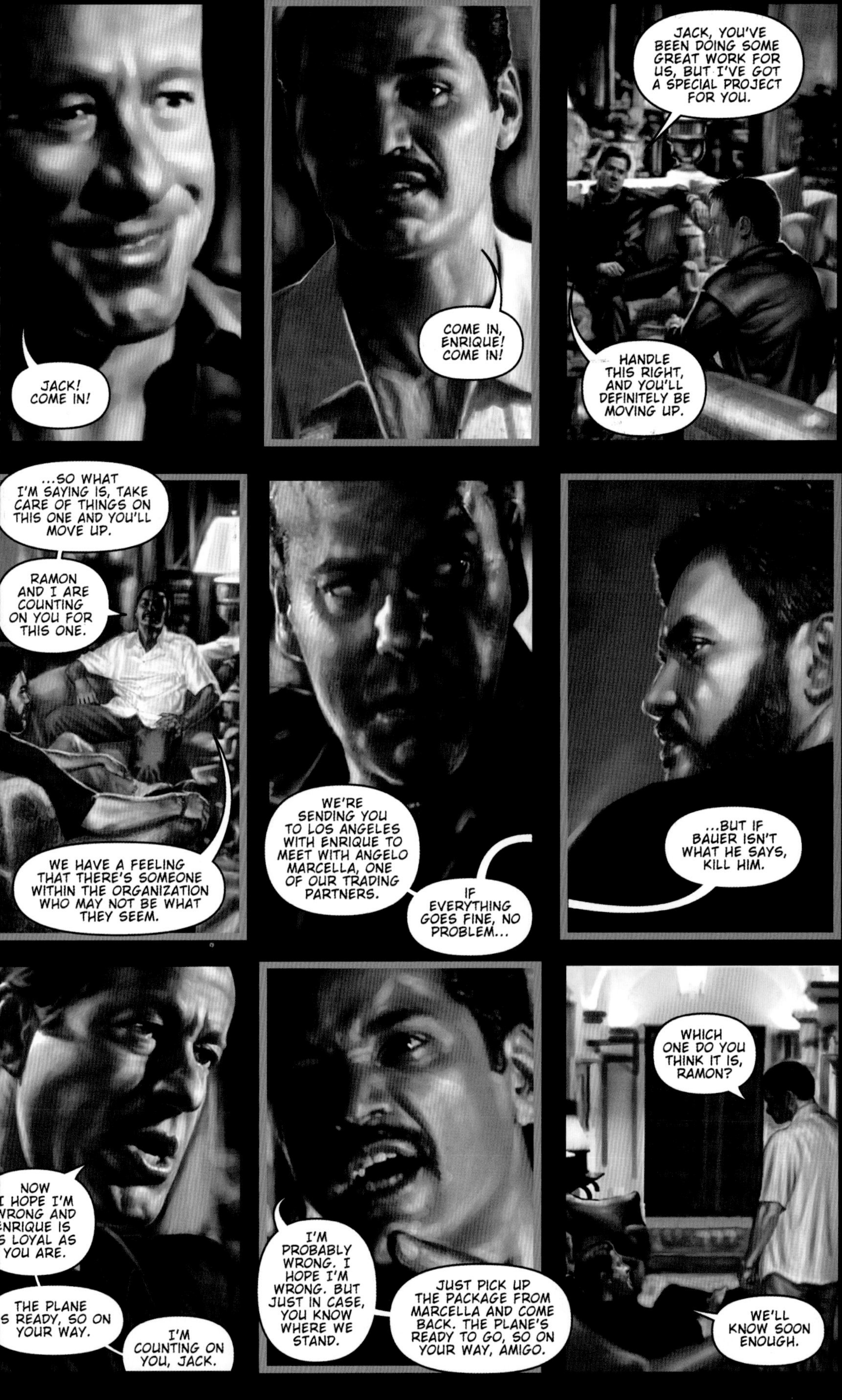
JACK! COME IN!
COME IN, ENRIQUE! COME IN!
JACK, YOU'VE BEEN DOING SOME GREAT WORK FOR US, BUT I'VE GOT A SPECIAL PROJECT FOR YOU.
HANDLE THIS RIGHT, AND YOU'LL DEFINITELY BE MOVING UP.
...SO WHAT I'M SAYING IS, TAKE CARE OF THINGS ON THIS ONE AND YOU'LL MOVE UP.
RAMON AND I ARE COUNTING ON YOU FOR THIS ONE.
WE HAVE A FEELING THAT THERE'S SOMEONE WITHIN THE ORGANIZATION WHO MAY NOT BE WHAT THEY SEEM.
WE'RE SENDING YOU TO LOS ANGELES WITH ENRIQUE TO MEET WITH ANGELO MARCELLA, ONE OF OUR TRADING PARTNERS.
IF EVERYTHING GOES FINE, NO PROBLEM...
...BUT IF BAUER ISN'T WHAT HE SAYS, KILL HIM.
NOW I HOPE I'M WRONG AND ENRIQUE IS S LOYAL AS YOU ARE.
THE PLANE S READY, SO ON YOUR WAY.
I'M COUNTING ON YOU, JACK.
I'M PROBABLY WRONG. I HOPE I'M WRONG. BUT JUST IN CASE, YOU KNOW WHERE WE STAND.
JUST PICK UP THE PACKAGE FROM MARCELLA AND COME BACK. THE PLANE'S READY TO GO, SO ON YOUR WAY, AMIGO.
WHICH ONE DO YOU THINK IT IS, RAMON?
WE'LL KNOW SOON ENOUGH.

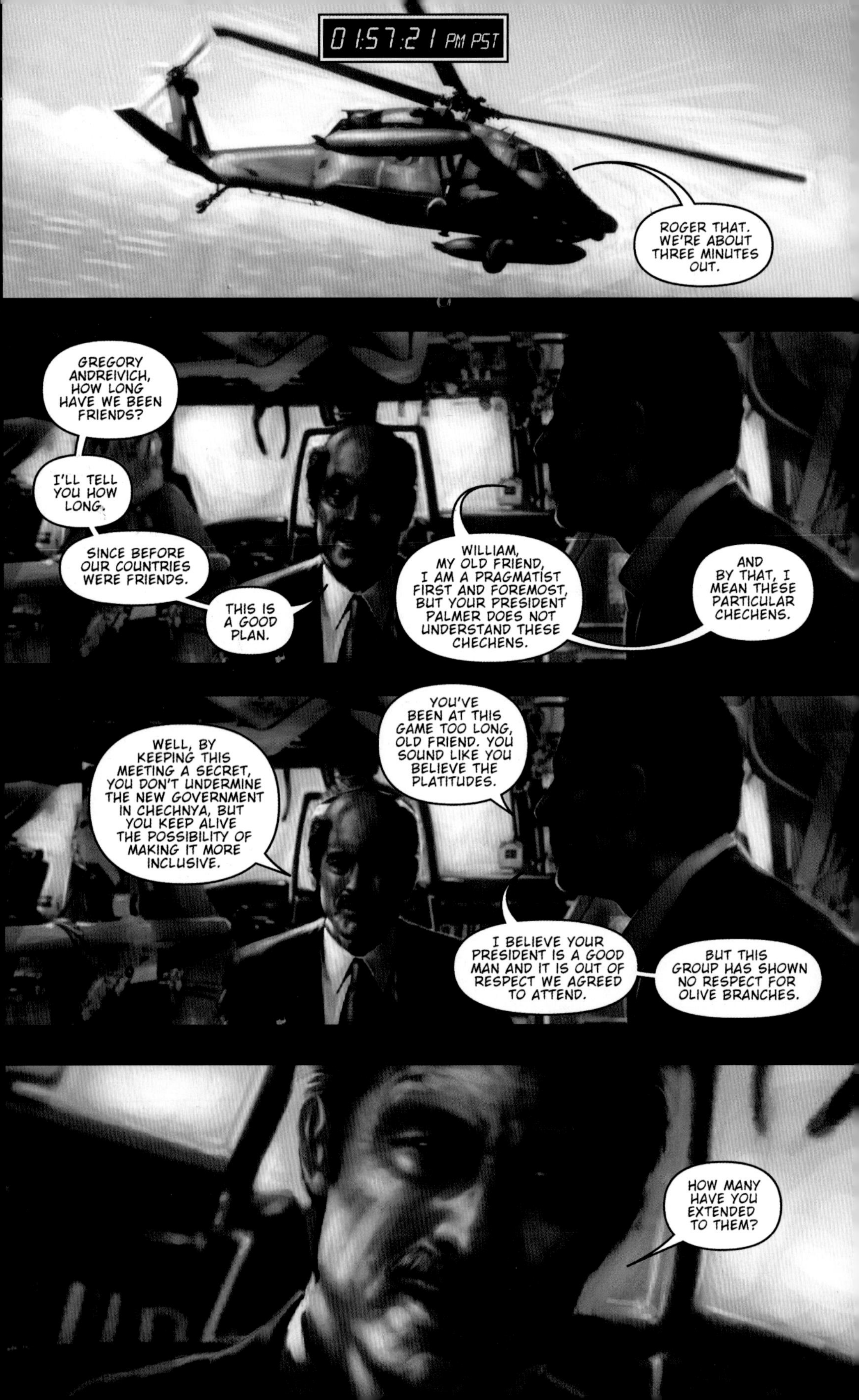
01:57:21 PM PST
ROGER THAT. WE'RE ABOUT THREE MINUTES OUT.
GREGORY ANDREIVICH, HOW LONG HAVE WE BEEN FRIENDS?
I'LL TELL YOU HOW LONG.
SINCE BEFORE OUR COUNTRIES WERE FRIENDS.
THIS IS A GOOD PLAN.
WILLIAM, MY OLD FRIEND, I AM A PRAGMATIST FIRST AND FOREMOST, BUT YOUR PRESIDENT PALMER DOES NOT UNDERSTAND THESE CHECHENS.
AND BY THAT, I MEAN THESE PARTICULAR CHECHENS.
WELL, BY KEEPING THIS MEETING A SECRET, YOU DON'T UNDERMINE THE NEW GOVERNMENT IN CHECHNYA, BUT YOU KEEP ALIVE THE POSSIBILITY OF MAKING IT MORE INCLUSIVE.
YOU'VE BEEN AT THIS GAME TOO LONG, OLD FRIEND. YOU SOUND LIKE YOU BELIEVE THE PLATITUDES.
I BELIEVE YOUR PRESIDENT IS A GOOD MAN AND IT IS OUT OF RESPECT WE AGREED TO ATTEND.
BUT THIS GROUP HAS SHOWN NO RESPECT FOR OLIVE BRANCHES.
HOW MANY HAVE YOU EXTENDED TO THEM?

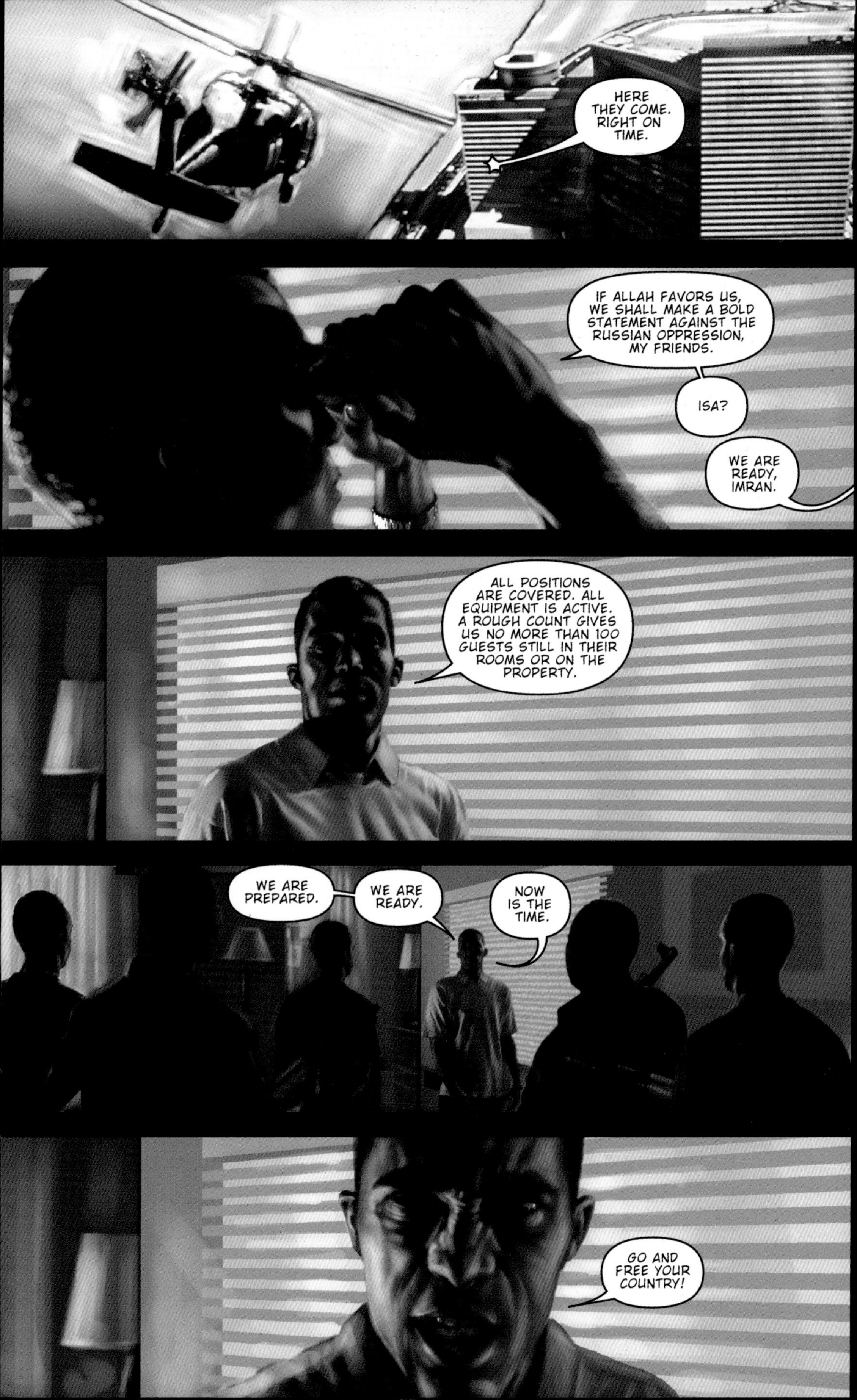
HERE THEY COME. RIGHT ON TIME.
IF ALLAH FAVORS US, WE SHALL MAKE A BOLD STATEMENT AGAINST THE RUSSIAN OPPRESSION, MY FRIENDS.
ISA?
WE ARE READY, IMRAN.
ALL POSITIONS ARE COVERED. ALL EQUIPMENT IS ACTIVE. A ROUGH COUNT GIVES US NO MORE THAN 100 GUESTS STILL IN THEIR ROOMS OR ON THE PROPERTY.
WE ARE PREPARED.
WE ARE READY.
NOW IS THE TIME.
GO AND FREE YOUR COUNTRY!

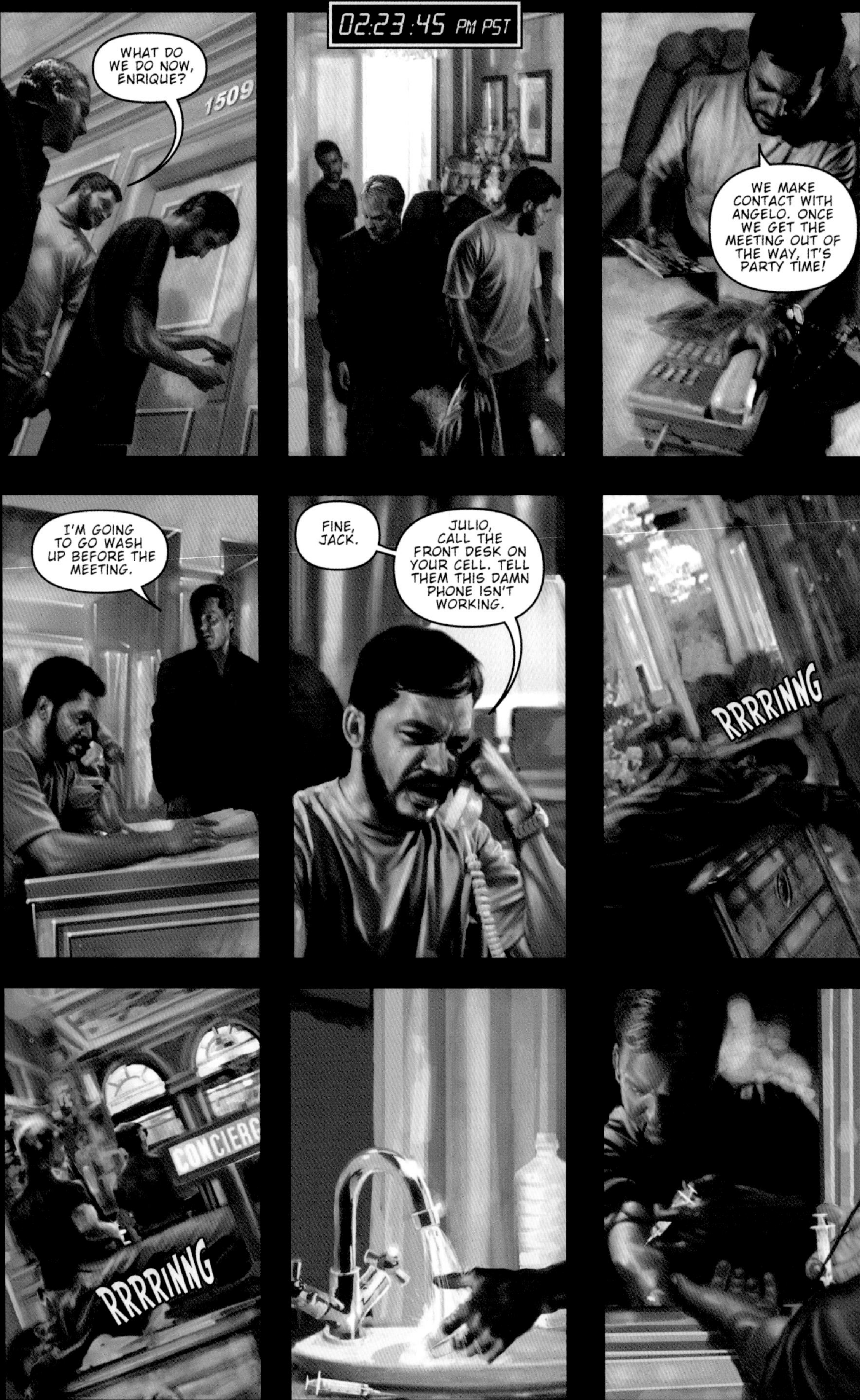
02:23:45 PM PST
WHAT DO WE DO NOW, ENRIQUE?
1509
WE MAKE CONTACT WITH ANGELO. ONCE WE GET THE MEETING OUT OF THE WAY, IT'S PARTY TIME!
I'M GOING TO GO WASH UP BEFORE THE MEETING.
FINE, JACK.
JULIO, CALL THE FRONT DESK ON YOUR CELL. TELL THEM THIS DAMN PHONE ISN'T WORKING.
RRRRINNG
CONCIERG
RRRRINNG

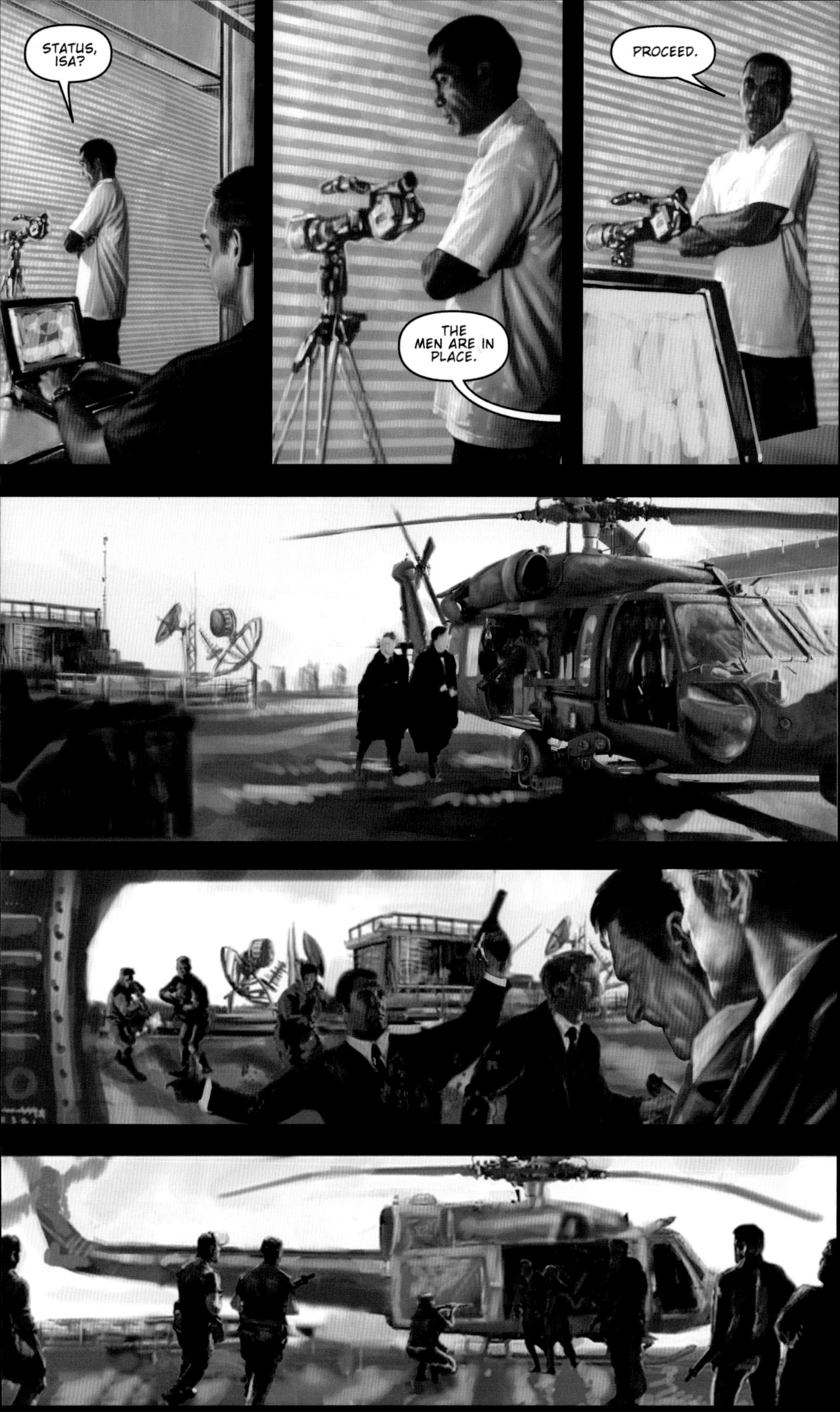
STATUS, ISA?
THE MEN ARE IN PLACE.
PROCEED.

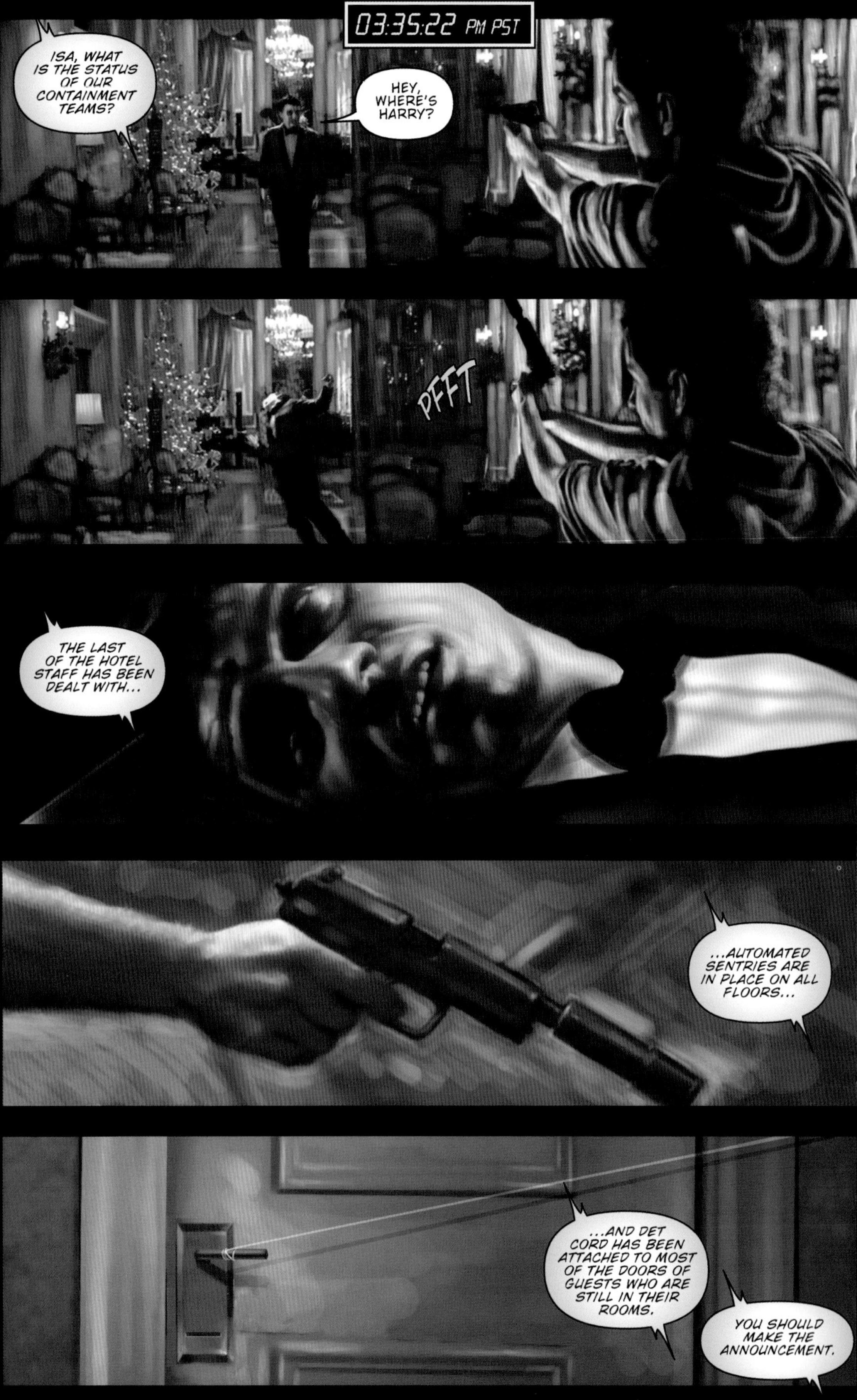
03:35:22 PM PST
ISA, WHAT IS THE STATUS OF OUR CONTAINMENT TEAMS?
HEY, WHERE'S HARRY?
PFFT
THE LAST OF THE HOTEL STAFF HAS BEEN DEALT WITH...
...AUTOMATED SENTRIES ARE IN PLACE ON ALL FLOORS...
...AND DET CORD HAS BEEN ATTACHED TO MOST OF THE DOORS OF GUESTS WHO ARE STILL IN THEIR ROOMS.
YOU SHOULD MAKE THE ANNOUNCEMENT.

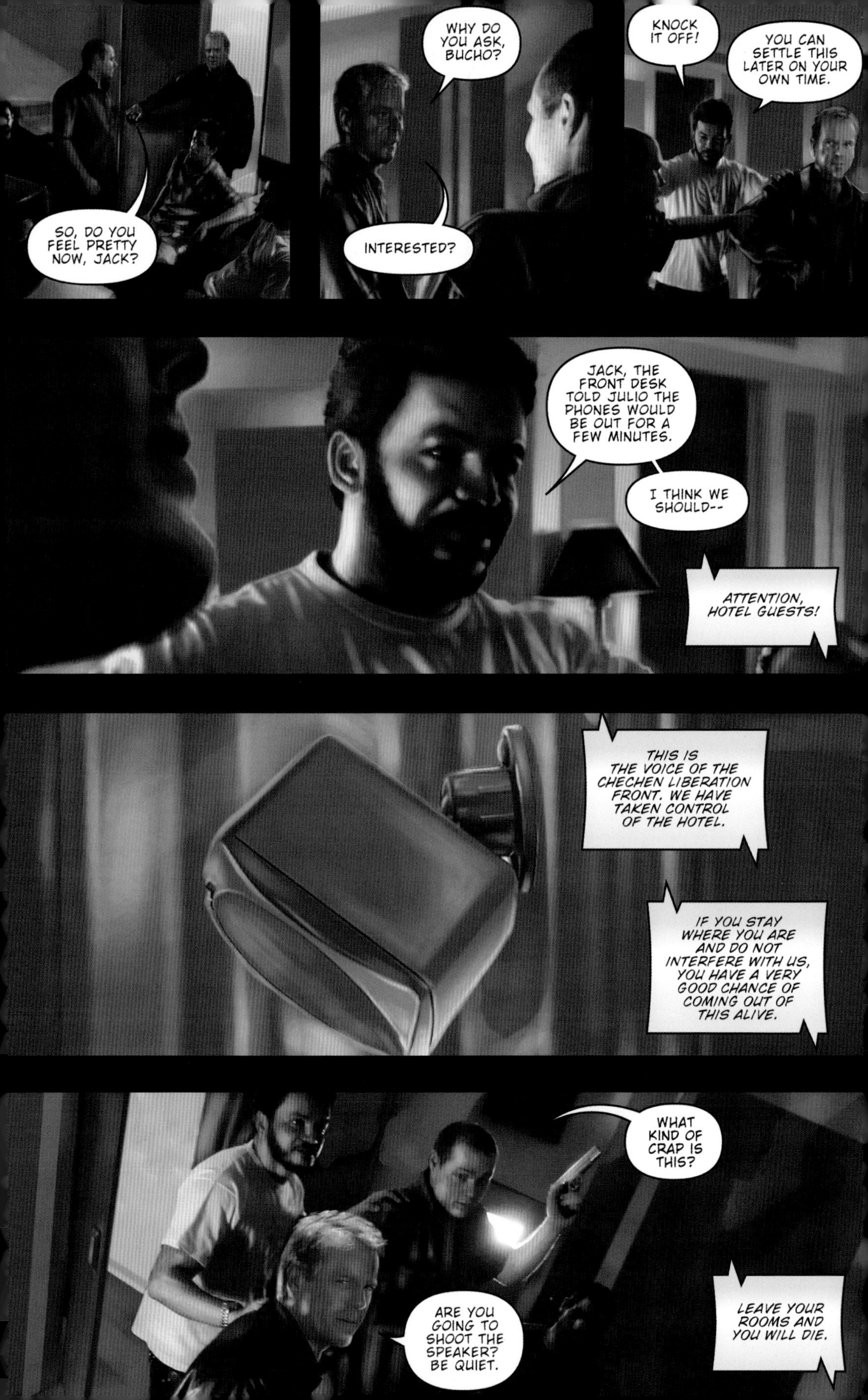
SO, DO YOU FEEL PRETTY NOW, JACK?
WHY DO YOU ASK, BUCHO?
INTERESTED?
KNOCK IT OFF!
YOU CAN SETTLE THIS LATER ON YOUR OWN TIME.
JACK, THE FRONT DESK TOLD JULIO THE PHONES WOULD BE OUT FOR A FEW MINUTES.
I THINK WE SHOULD--
ATTENTION, HOTEL GUESTS!
THIS IS THE VOICE OF THE CHECHEN LIBERATION FRONT. WE HAVE TAKEN CONTROL OF THE HOTEL.
IF YOU STAY WHERE YOU ARE AND DO NOT INTERFERE WITH US, YOU HAVE A VERY GOOD CHANCE OF COMING OUT OF THIS ALIVE.
WHAT KIND OF CRAP IS THIS?
ARE YOU GOING TO SHOOT THE SPEAKER? BE QUIET.
LEAVE YOUR ROOMS AND YOU WILL DIE.

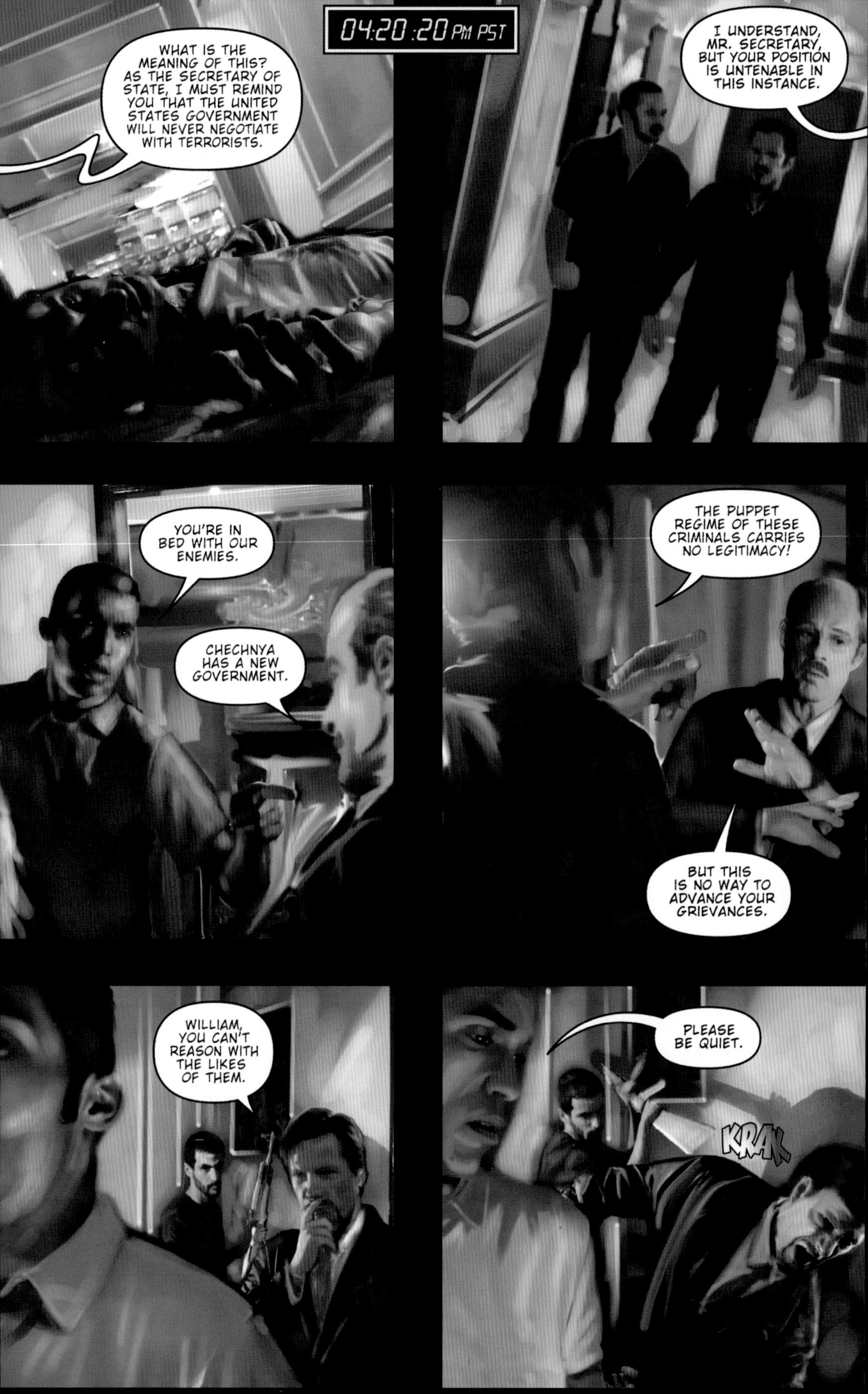
04:20:20 PM PST
WHAT IS THE MEANING OF THIS? AS THE SECRETARY OF STATE, I MUST REMIND YOU THAT THE UNITED STATES GOVERNMENT WILL NEVER NEGOTIATE WITH TERRORISTS.
I UNDERSTAND, MR. SECRETARY, BUT YOUR POSITION IS UNTENABLE IN THIS INSTANCE.
YOU'RE IN BED WITH OUR ENEMIES.
CHECHNYA HAS A NEW GOVERNMENT.
THE PUPPET REGIME OF THESE CRIMINALS CARRIES NO LEGITIMACY!
BUT THIS IS NO WAY TO ADVANCE YOUR GRIEVANCES.
WILLIAM, YOU CAN'T REASON WITH THE LIKES OF THEM.
PLEASE BE QUIET.
KRAK

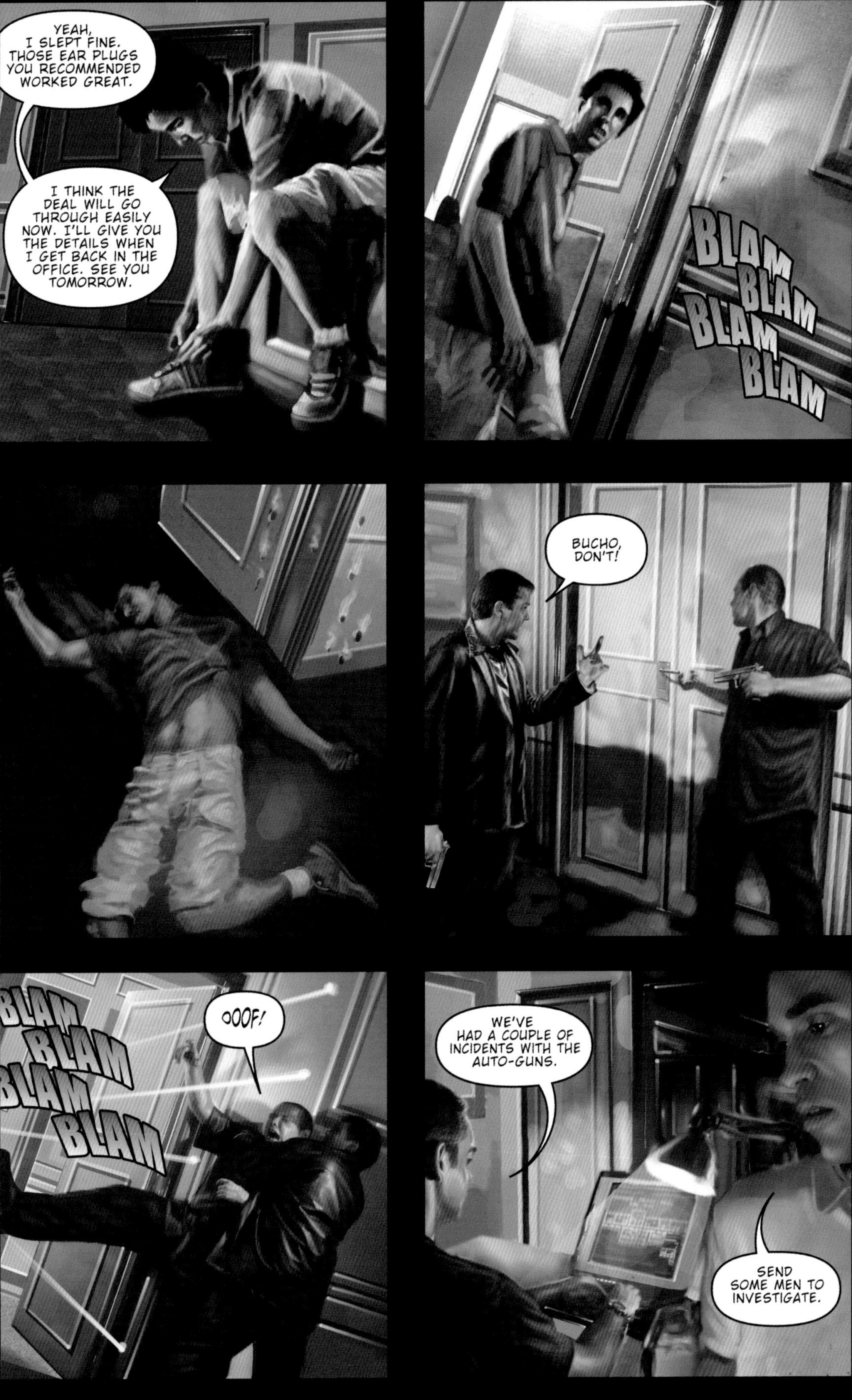
YEAH, I SLEPT FINE. THOSE EAR PLUGS YOU RECOMMENDED WORKED GREAT.
I THINK THE DEAL WILL GO THROUGH EASILY NOW. I'LL GIVE YOU THE DETAILS WHEN I GET BACK IN THE OFFICE. SEE YOU TOMORROW.
BLAM BLAM BLAM BLAM
BUCHO, DON'T!
BLAM BLAM BLAM BLAM
OOOF!
WE'VE HAD A COUPLE OF INCIDENTS WITH THE AUTO-GUNS.
SEND SOME MEN TO INVESTIGATE.

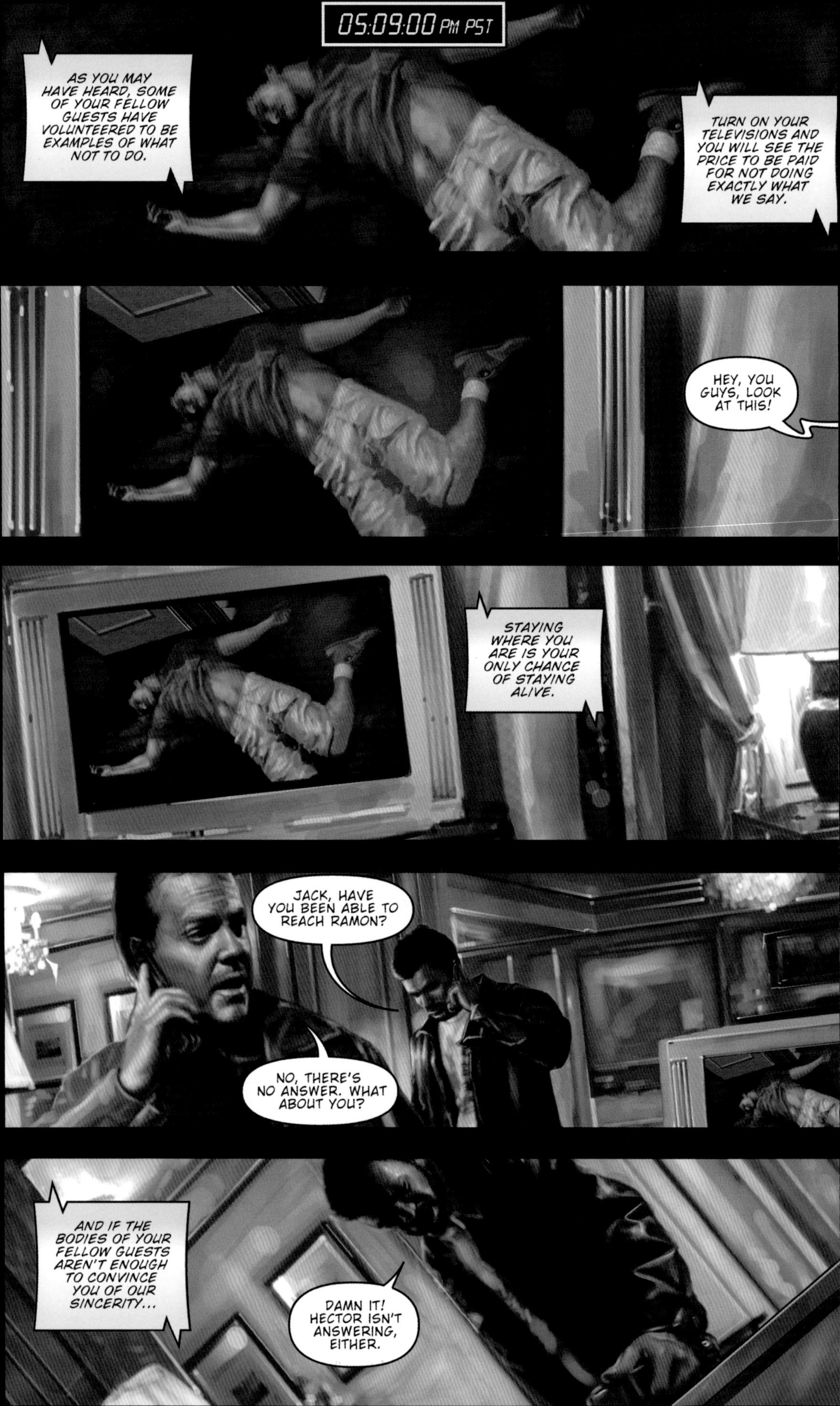
05:09:00 PM PST
AS YOU MAY HAVE HEARD, SOME OF YOUR FELLOW GUESTS HAVE VOLUNTEERED TO BE EXAMPLES OF WHAT NOT TO DO.
TURN ON YOUR TELEVISIONS AND YOU WILL SEE THE PRICE TO BE PAID FOR NOT DOING EXACTLY WHAT WE SAY.
HEY, YOU GUYS, LOOK AT THIS!
STAYING WHERE YOU ARE IS YOUR ONLY CHANCE OF STAYING ALIVE.
JACK, HAVE YOU BEEN ABLE TO REACH RAMON?
NO, THERE'S NO ANSWER. WHAT ABOUT YOU?
AND IF THE BODIES OF YOUR FELLOW GUESTS AREN'T ENOUGH TO CONVINCE YOU OF OUR SINCERITY...
DAMN IT! HECTOR ISN'T ANSWERING, EITHER.

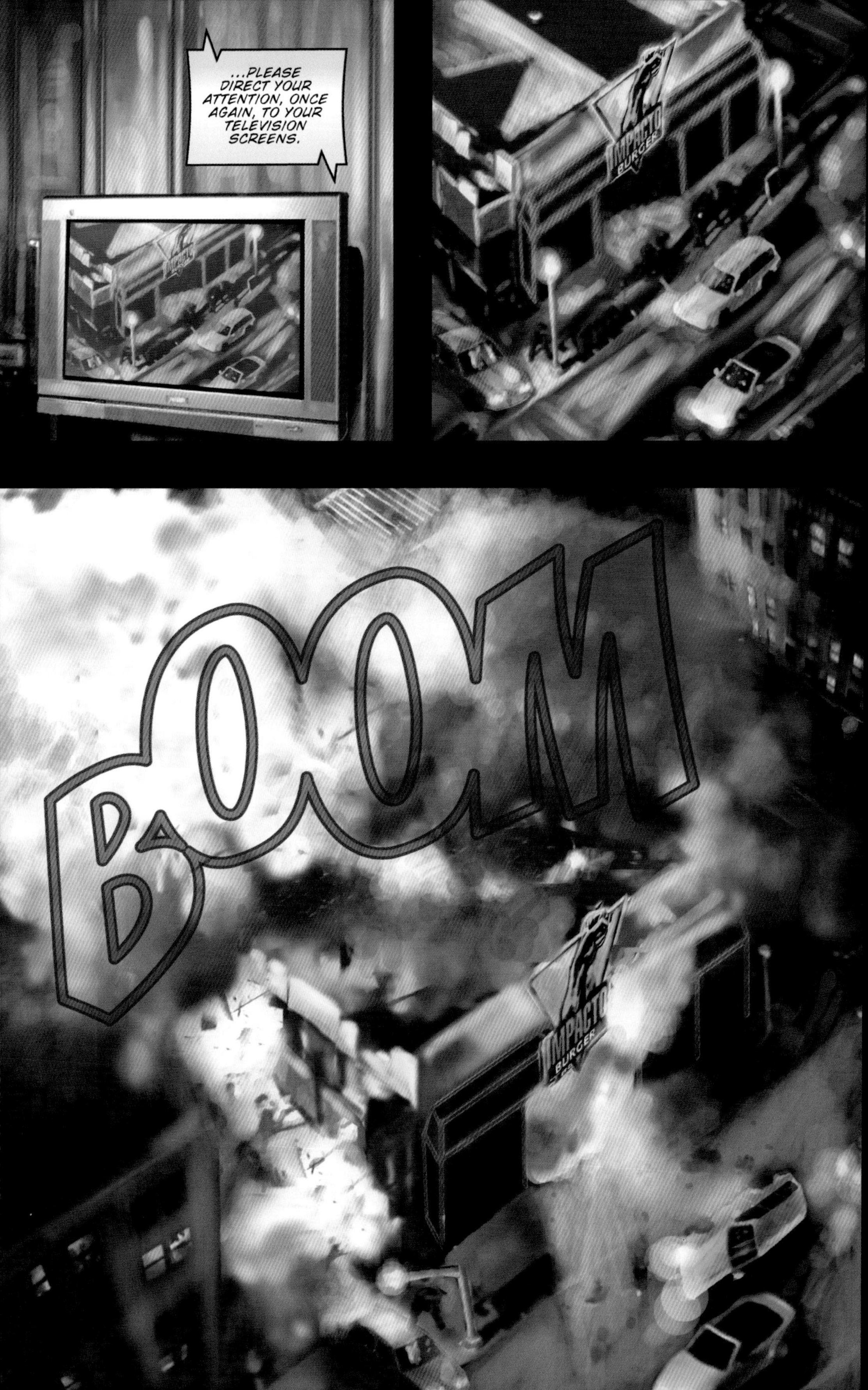
...PLEASE DIRECT YOUR ATTENTION, ONCE AGAIN, TO YOUR TELEVISION SCREENS.
IMPACTO BURGER
BOOM
IMPACTO BURGER

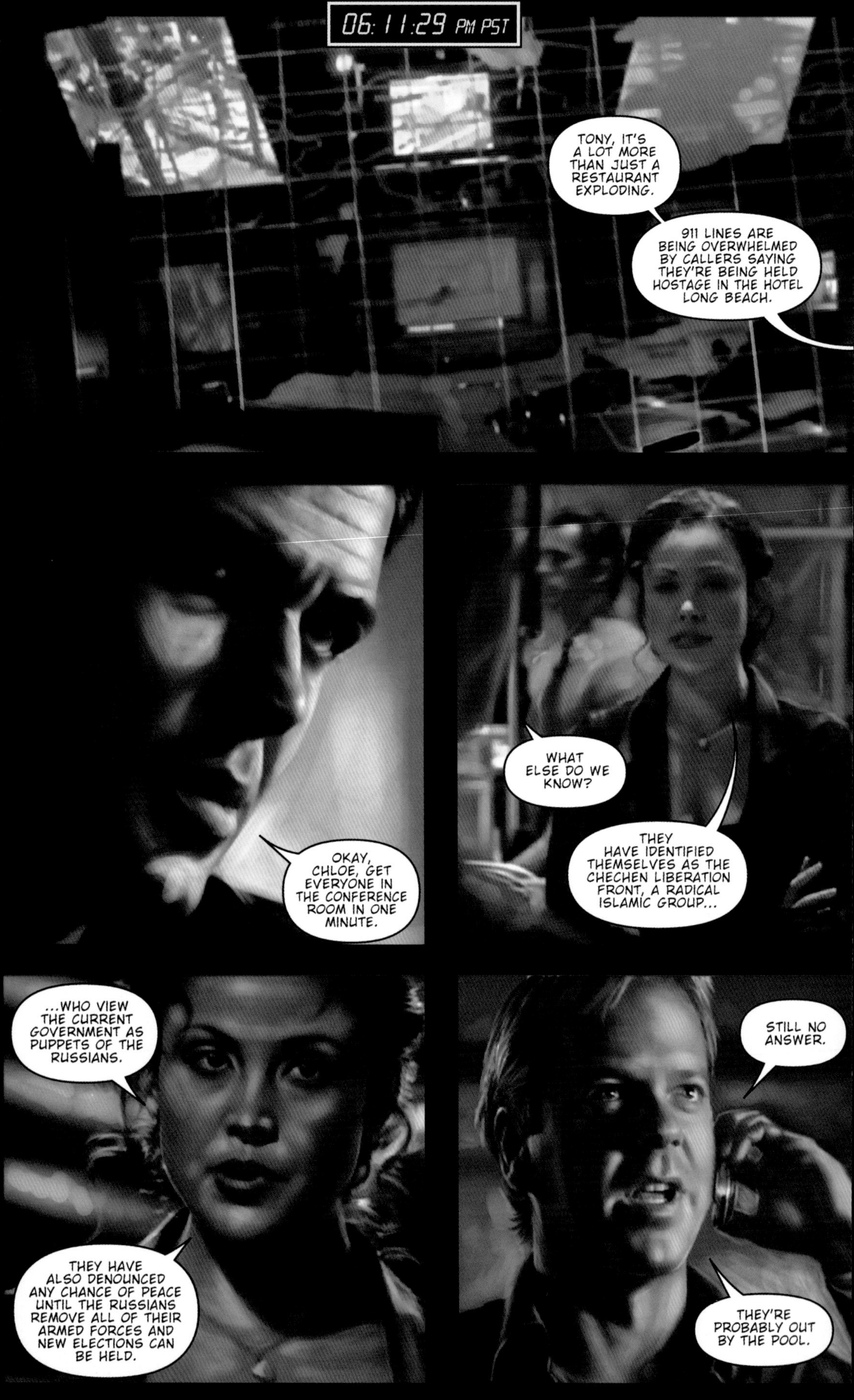
06:11:29 PM PST
TONY, IT'S A LOT MORE THAN JUST A RESTAURANT EXPLODING.
911 LINES ARE BEING OVERWHELMED BY CALLERS SAYING THEY'RE BEING HELD HOSTAGE IN THE HOTEL LONG BEACH.
OKAY, CHLOE, GET EVERYONE IN THE CONFERENCE ROOM IN ONE MINUTE.
WHAT ELSE DO WE KNOW?
THEY HAVE IDENTIFIED THEMSELVES AS THE CHECHEN LIBERATION FRONT, A RADICAL ISLAMIC GROUP...
...WHO VIEW THE CURRENT GOVERNMENT AS PUPPETS OF THE RUSSIANS.
THEY HAVE ALSO DENOUNCED ANY CHANCE OF PEACE UNTIL THE RUSSIANS REMOVE ALL OF THEIR ARMED FORCES AND NEW ELECTIONS CAN BE HELD.
STILL NO ANSWER.
THEY'RE PROBABLY OUT BY THE POOL.

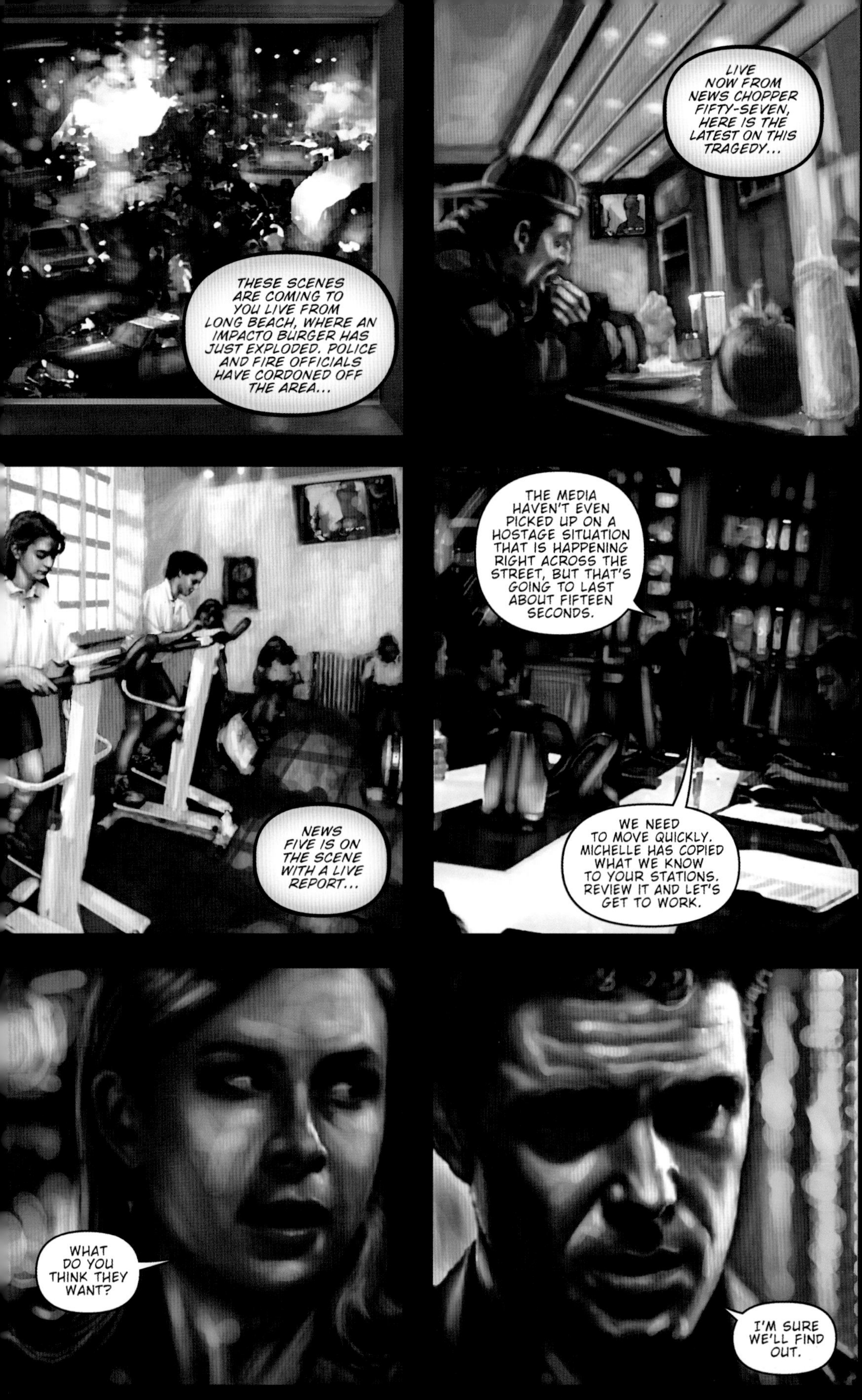
THESE SCENES ARE COMING TO YOU LIVE FROM LONG BEACH, WHERE AN IMPACTO BURGER HAS JUST EXPLODED. POLICE AND FIRE OFFICIALS HAVE CORDONED OFF THE AREA...
LIVE NOW FROM NEWS CHOPPER FIFTY-SEVEN, HERE IS THE LATEST ON THIS TRAGEDY...
NEWS FIVE IS ON THE SCENE WITH A LIVE REPORT...
THE MEDIA HAVEN'T EVEN PICKED UP ON A HOSTAGE SITUATION THAT IS HAPPENING RIGHT ACROSS THE STREET, BUT THAT'S GOING TO LAST ABOUT FIFTEEN SECONDS.
WE NEED TO MOVE QUICKLY. MICHELLE HAS COPIED WHAT WE KNOW TO YOUR STATIONS. REVIEW IT AND LET'S GET TO WORK.
WHAT DO YOU THINK THEY WANT?
I'M SURE WE'LL FIND OUT.

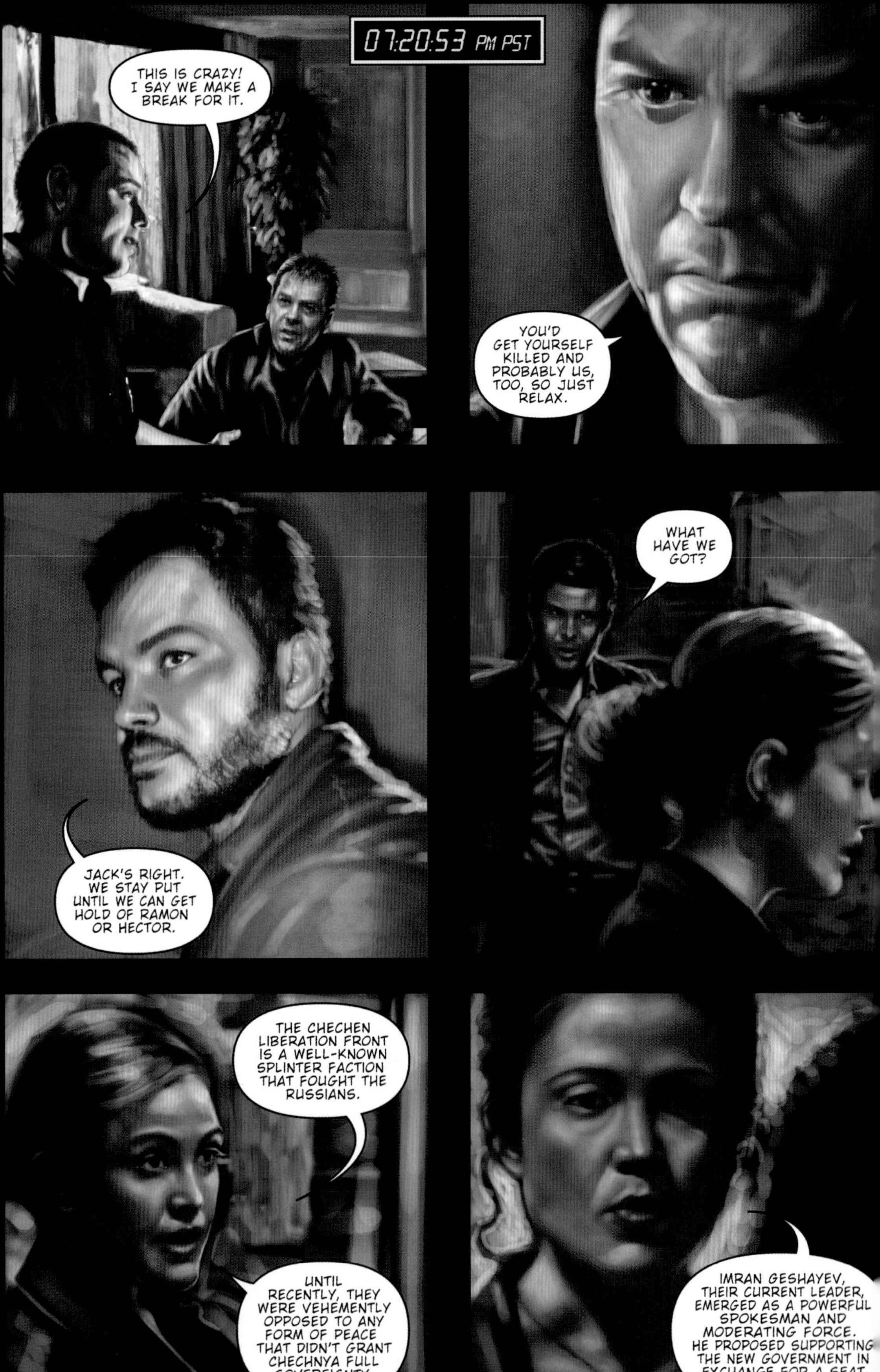
07:20:53 PM PST
THIS IS CRAZY! I SAY WE MAKE A BREAK FOR IT.
YOU'D GET YOURSELF KILLED AND PROBABLY US, TOO, SO JUST RELAX.
JACK'S RIGHT. WE STAY PUT UNTIL WE CAN GET HOLD OF RAMON OR HECTOR.
WHAT HAVE WE GOT?
THE CHECHEN LIBERATION FRONT IS A WELL-KNOWN SPLINTER FACTION THAT FOUGHT THE RUSSIANS.
UNTIL RECENTLY, THEY WERE VEHEMENTLY OPPOSED TO ANY FORM OF PEACE THAT DIDN'T GRANT CHECHNYA FULL SOVEREIGNTY.
IMRAN GESHAYEV, THEIR CURRENT LEADER, EMERGED AS A POWERFUL SPOKESMAN AND MODERATING FORCE. HE PROPOSED SUPPORTING THE NEW GOVERNMENT IN EXCHANGE FOR A SEAT AT THE TABLE.

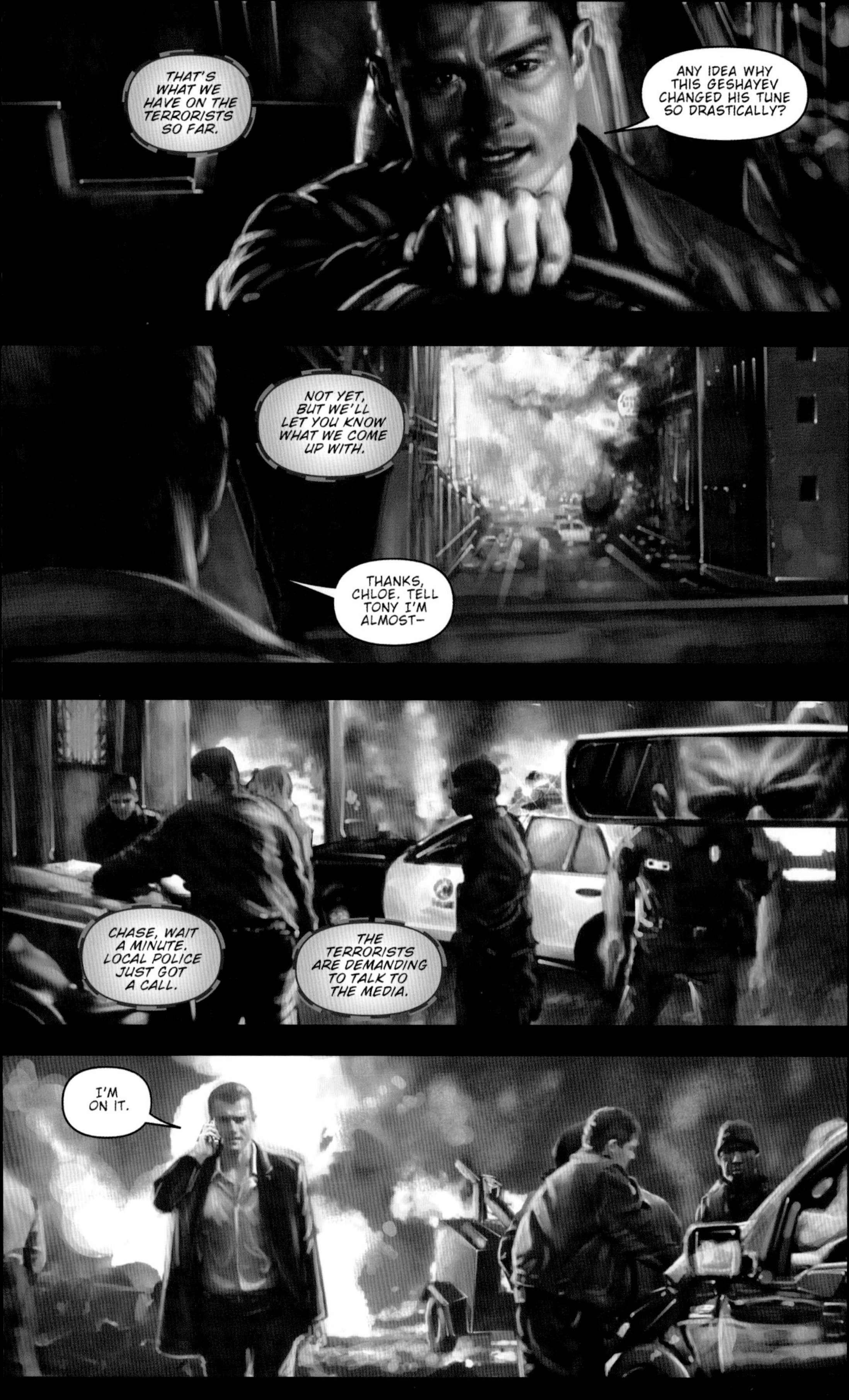
THAT'S WHAT WE HAVE ON THE TERRORISTS SO FAR.
ANY IDEA WHY THIS GESHAYEV CHANGED HIS TUNE SO DRASTICALLY?
NOT YET, BUT WE'LL LET YOU KNOW WHAT WE COME UP WITH.
THANKS, CHLOE. TELL TONY I'M ALMOST–
CHASE, WAIT A MINUTE. LOCAL POLICE JUST GOT A CALL.
THE TERRORISTS ARE DEMANDING TO TALK TO THE MEDIA.
I'M ON IT.

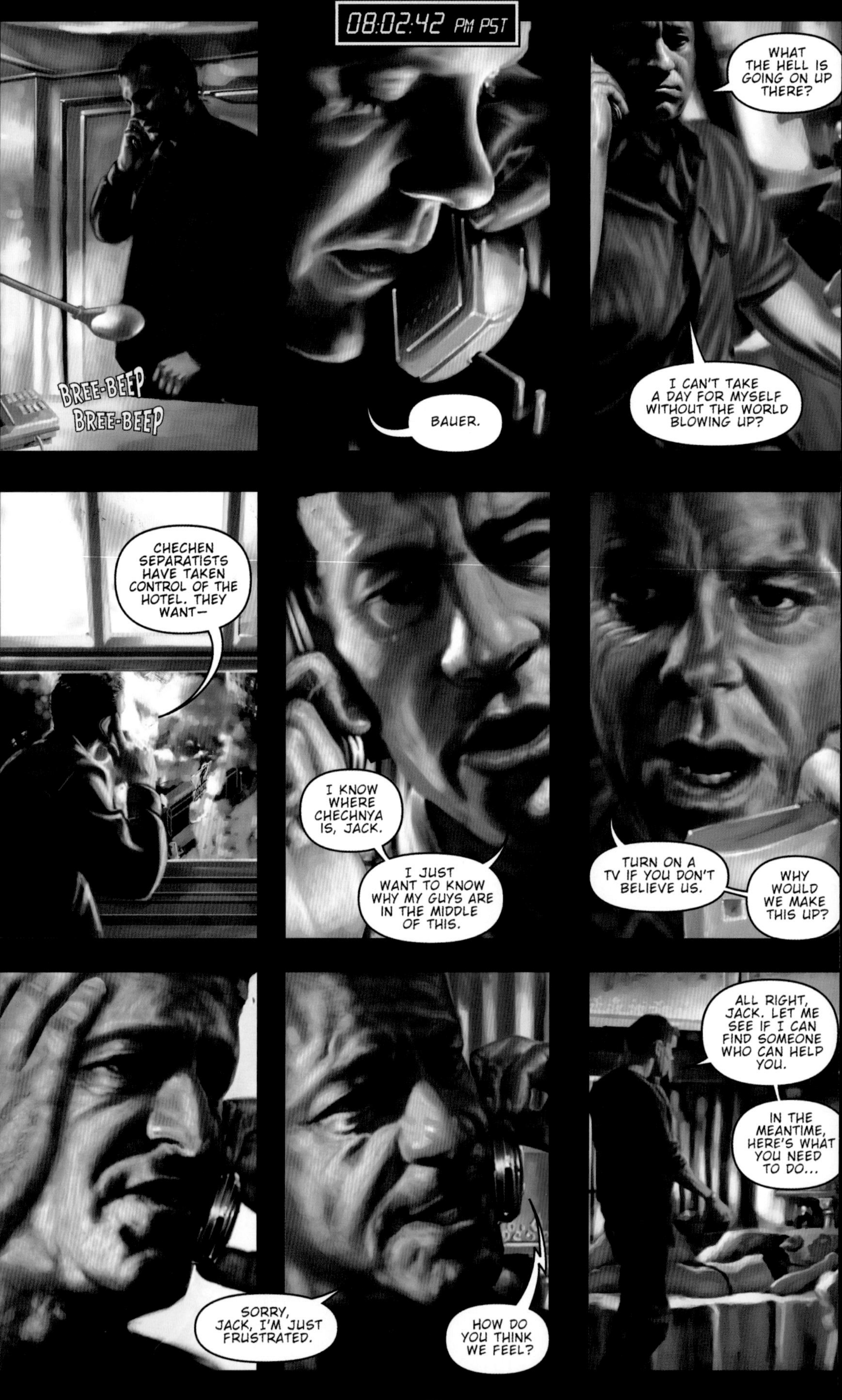
08:02:42 PM PST
BREE-BEEP
BREE-BEEP
BAUER.
WHAT THE HELL IS GOING ON UP THERE?
I CAN'T TAKE A DAY FOR MYSELF WITHOUT THE WORLD BLOWING UP?
CHECHEN SEPARATISTS HAVE TAKEN CONTROL OF THE HOTEL. THEY WANT—
I KNOW WHERE CHECHNYA IS, JACK.
I JUST WANT TO KNOW WHY MY GUYS ARE IN THE MIDDLE OF THIS.
TURN ON A TV IF YOU DON'T BELIEVE US.
WHY WOULD WE MAKE THIS UP?
SORRY, JACK, I'M JUST FRUSTRATED.
HOW DO YOU THINK WE FEEL?
ALL RIGHT, JACK. LET ME SEE IF I CAN FIND SOMEONE WHO CAN HELP YOU.
IN THE MEANTIME, HERE'S WHAT YOU NEED TO DO...

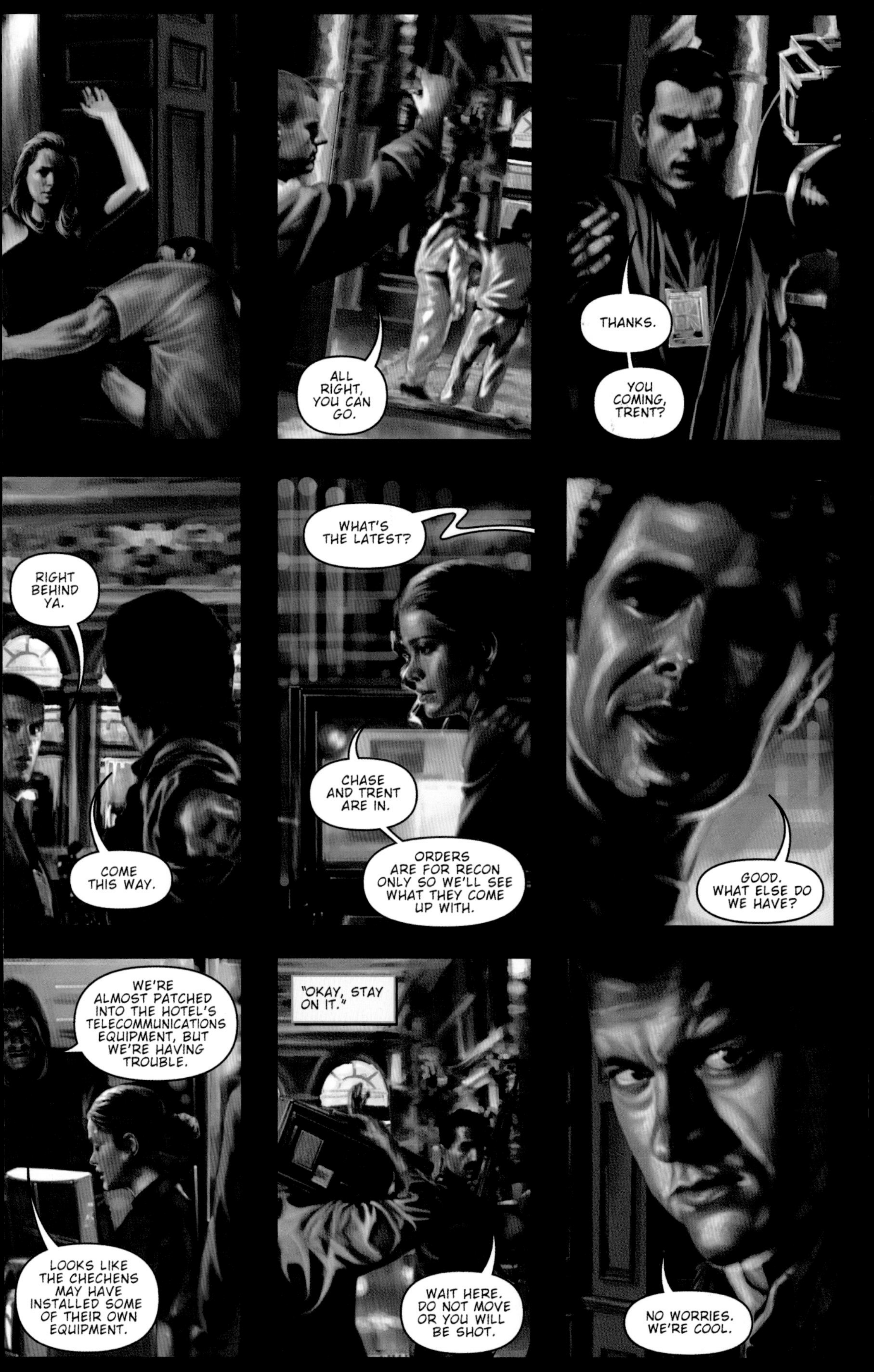
ALL RIGHT, YOU CAN GO.
THANKS.
YOU COMING, TRENT?
RIGHT BEHIND YA.
COME THIS WAY.
WHAT'S THE LATEST?
CHASE AND TRENT ARE IN.
ORDERS ARE FOR RECON ONLY SO WE'LL SEE WHAT THEY COME UP WITH.
GOOD. WHAT ELSE DO WE HAVE?
WE'RE ALMOST PATCHED INTO THE HOTEL'S TELECOMMUNICATIONS EQUIPMENT, BUT WE'RE HAVING TROUBLE.
LOOKS LIKE THE CHECHENS MAY HAVE INSTALLED SOME OF THEIR OWN EQUIPMENT.
"OKAY, STAY ON IT."
WAIT HERE. DO NOT MOVE OR YOU WILL BE SHOT.
NO WORRIES. WE'RE COOL.

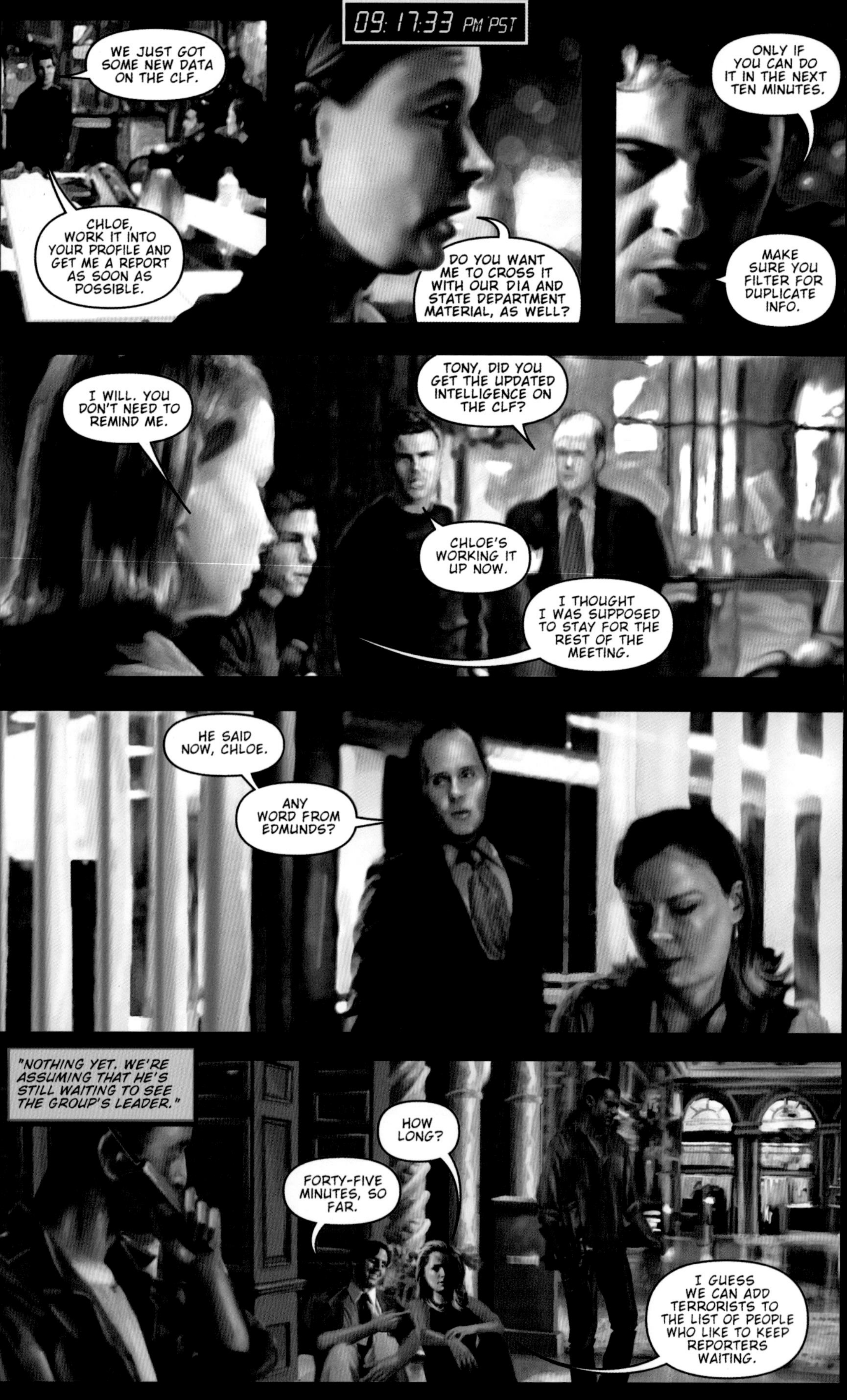
09:17:33 PM PST
WE JUST GOT SOME NEW DATA ON THE CLF.
CHLOE, WORK IT INTO YOUR PROFILE AND GET ME A REPORT AS SOON AS POSSIBLE.
DO YOU WANT ME TO CROSS IT WITH OUR DIA AND STATE DEPARTMENT MATERIAL, AS WELL?
ONLY IF YOU CAN DO IT IN THE NEXT TEN MINUTES.
MAKE SURE YOU FILTER FOR DUPLICATE INFO.
I WILL. YOU DON'T NEED TO REMIND ME.
TONY, DID YOU GET THE UPDATED INTELLIGENCE ON THE CLF?
CHLOE'S WORKING IT UP NOW.
I THOUGHT I WAS SUPPOSED TO STAY FOR THE REST OF THE MEETING.
HE SAID NOW, CHLOE.
ANY WORD FROM EDMUNDS?
"NOTHING YET. WE'RE ASSUMING THAT HE'S STILL WAITING TO SEE THE GROUP'S LEADER."
HOW LONG?
FORTY-FIVE MINUTES, SO FAR.
I GUESS WE CAN ADD TERRORISTS TO THE LIST OF PEOPLE WHO LIKE TO KEEP REPORTERS WAITING.

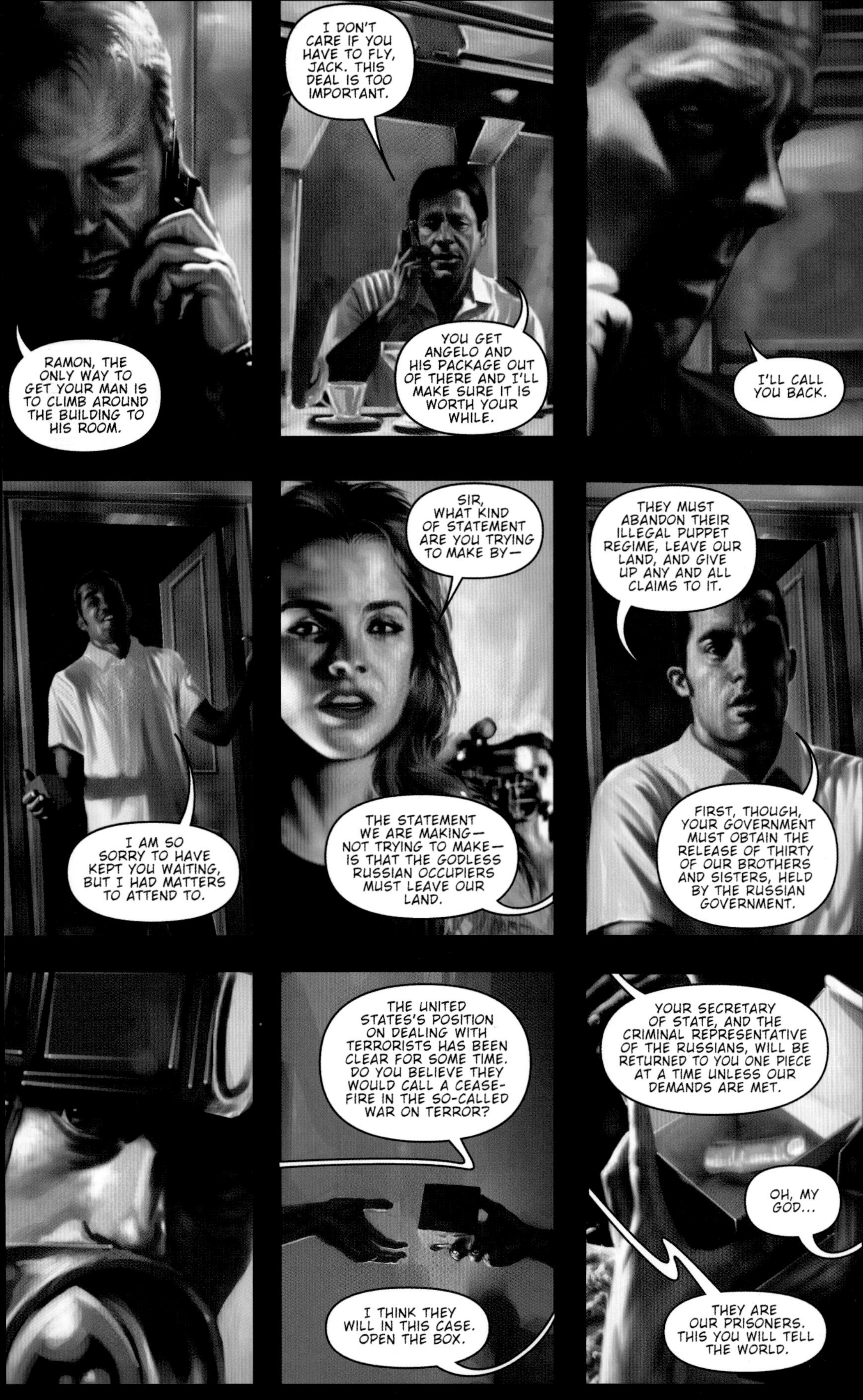
RAMON, THE ONLY WAY TO GET YOUR MAN IS TO CLIMB AROUND THE BUILDING TO HIS ROOM.
I DON'T CARE IF YOU HAVE TO FLY, JACK. THIS DEAL IS TOO IMPORTANT.
YOU GET ANGELO AND HIS PACKAGE OUT OF THERE AND I'LL MAKE SURE IT IS WORTH YOUR WHILE.
I'LL CALL YOU BACK.
I AM SO SORRY TO HAVE KEPT YOU WAITING, BUT I HAD MATTERS TO ATTEND TO.
SIR, WHAT KIND OF STATEMENT ARE YOU TRYING TO MAKE BY—
THE STATEMENT WE ARE MAKING— NOT TRYING TO MAKE— IS THAT THE GODLESS RUSSIAN OCCUPIERS MUST LEAVE OUR LAND.
THEY MUST ABANDON THEIR ILLEGAL PUPPET REGIME, LEAVE OUR LAND, AND GIVE UP ANY AND ALL CLAIMS TO IT.
FIRST, THOUGH, YOUR GOVERNMENT MUST OBTAIN THE RELEASE OF THIRTY OF OUR BROTHERS AND SISTERS, HELD BY THE RUSSIAN GOVERNMENT.
THE UNITED STATES'S POSITION ON DEALING WITH TERRORISTS HAS BEEN CLEAR FOR SOME TIME. DO YOU BELIEVE THEY WOULD CALL A CEASE-FIRE IN THE SO-CALLED WAR ON TERROR?
I THINK THEY WILL IN THIS CASE. OPEN THE BOX.
YOUR SECRETARY OF STATE, AND THE CRIMINAL REPRESENTATIVE OF THE RUSSIANS, WILL BE RETURNED TO YOU ONE PIECE AT A TIME UNLESS OUR DEMANDS ARE MET.
OH, MY GOD...
THEY ARE OUR PRISONERS. THIS YOU WILL TELL THE WORLD.

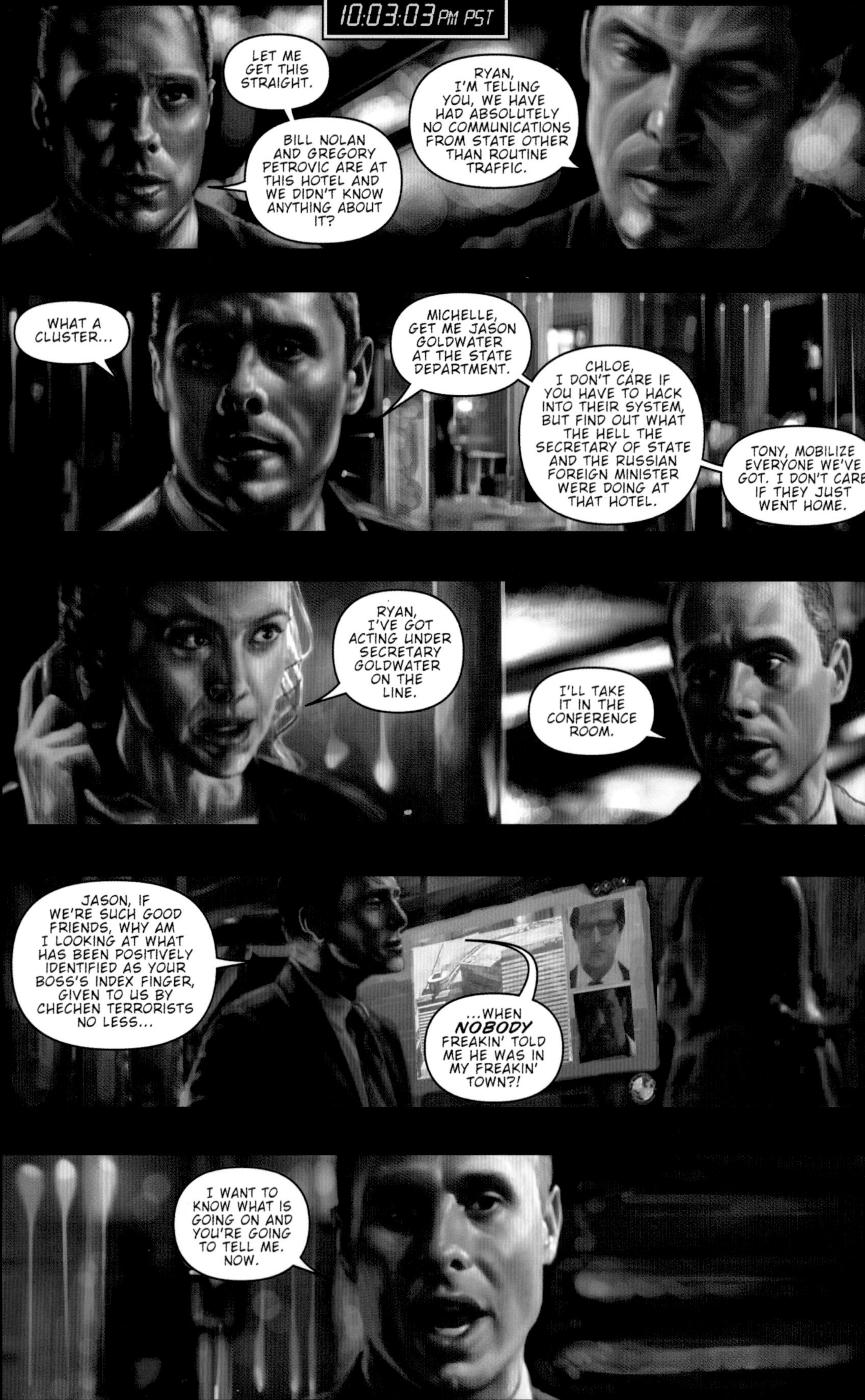
10:03:03 PM PST
LET ME GET THIS STRAIGHT.
BILL NOLAN AND GREGORY PETROVIC ARE AT THIS HOTEL AND WE DIDN'T KNOW ANYTHING ABOUT IT?
RYAN, I'M TELLING YOU, WE HAVE HAD ABSOLUTELY NO COMMUNICATIONS FROM STATE OTHER THAN ROUTINE TRAFFIC.
WHAT A CLUSTER...
MICHELLE, GET ME JASON GOLDWATER AT THE STATE DEPARTMENT.
CHLOE, I DON'T CARE IF YOU HAVE TO HACK INTO THEIR SYSTEM, BUT FIND OUT WHAT THE HELL THE SECRETARY OF STATE AND THE RUSSIAN FOREIGN MINISTER WERE DOING AT THAT HOTEL.
TONY, MOBILIZE EVERYONE WE'VE GOT. I DON'T CARE IF THEY JUST WENT HOME.
RYAN, I'VE GOT ACTING UNDER SECRETARY GOLDWATER ON THE LINE.
I'LL TAKE IT IN THE CONFERENCE ROOM.
JASON, IF WE'RE SUCH GOOD FRIENDS, WHY AM I LOOKING AT WHAT HAS BEEN POSITIVELY IDENTIFIED AS YOUR BOSS'S INDEX FINGER, GIVEN TO US BY CHECHEN TERRORISTS NO LESS...
...WHEN ***NOBODY*** FREAKIN' TOLD ME HE WAS IN MY FREAKIN' TOWN?!
I WANT TO KNOW WHAT IS GOING ON AND YOU'RE GOING TO TELL ME. NOW.

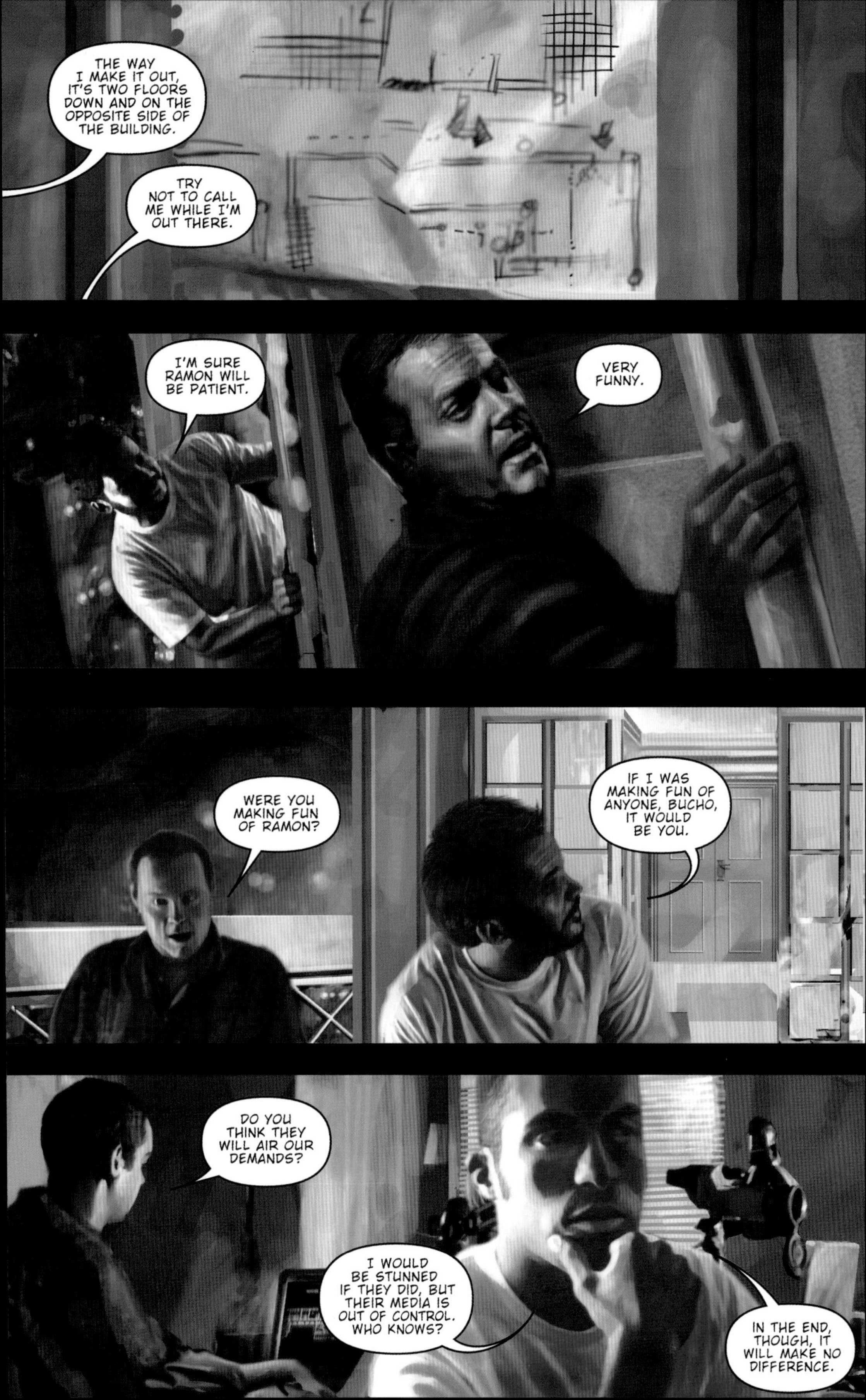
THE WAY I MAKE IT OUT, IT'S TWO FLOORS DOWN AND ON THE OPPOSITE SIDE OF THE BUILDING.
TRY NOT TO CALL ME WHILE I'M OUT THERE.
I'M SURE RAMON WILL BE PATIENT.
VERY FUNNY.
WERE YOU MAKING FUN OF RAMON?
IF I WAS MAKING FUN OF ANYONE, BUCHO, IT WOULD BE YOU.
DO YOU THINK THEY WILL AIR OUR DEMANDS?
I WOULD BE STUNNED IF THEY DID, BUT THEIR MEDIA IS OUT OF CONTROL. WHO KNOWS?
IN THE END, THOUGH, IT WILL MAKE NO DIFFERENCE.

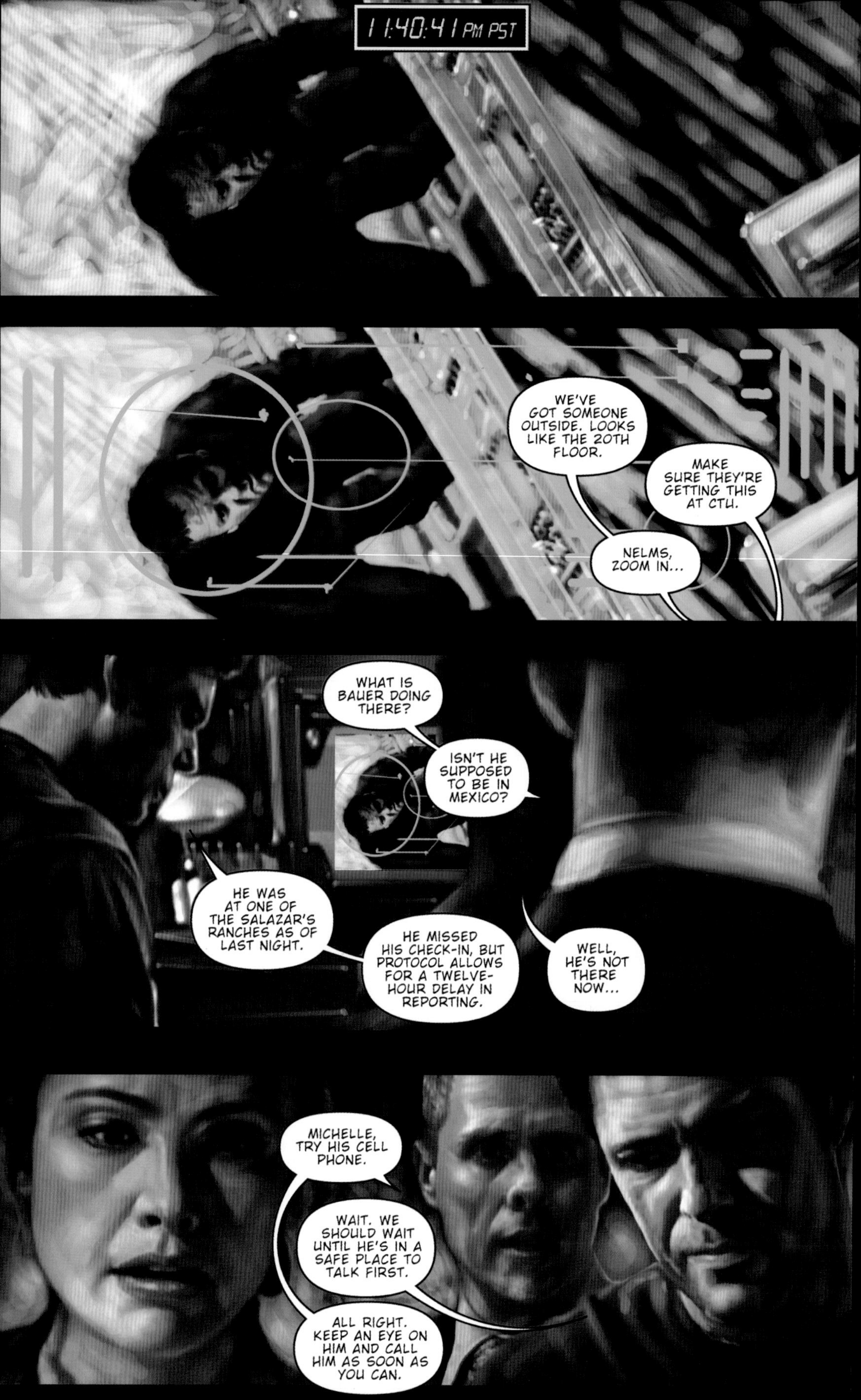
11:40:41 PM PST
WE'VE GOT SOMEONE OUTSIDE. LOOKS LIKE THE 20TH FLOOR.
MAKE SURE THEY'RE GETTING THIS AT CTU.
NELMS, ZOOM IN...
WHAT IS BAUER DOING THERE?
ISN'T HE SUPPOSED TO BE IN MEXICO?
HE WAS AT ONE OF THE SALAZAR'S RANCHES AS OF LAST NIGHT.
HE MISSED HIS CHECK-IN, BUT PROTOCOL ALLOWS FOR A TWELVE-HOUR DELAY IN REPORTING.
WELL, HE'S NOT THERE NOW...
MICHELLE, TRY HIS CELL PHONE.
WAIT. WE SHOULD WAIT UNTIL HE'S IN A SAFE PLACE TO TALK FIRST.
ALL RIGHT. KEEP AN EYE ON HIM AND CALL HIM AS SOON AS YOU CAN.

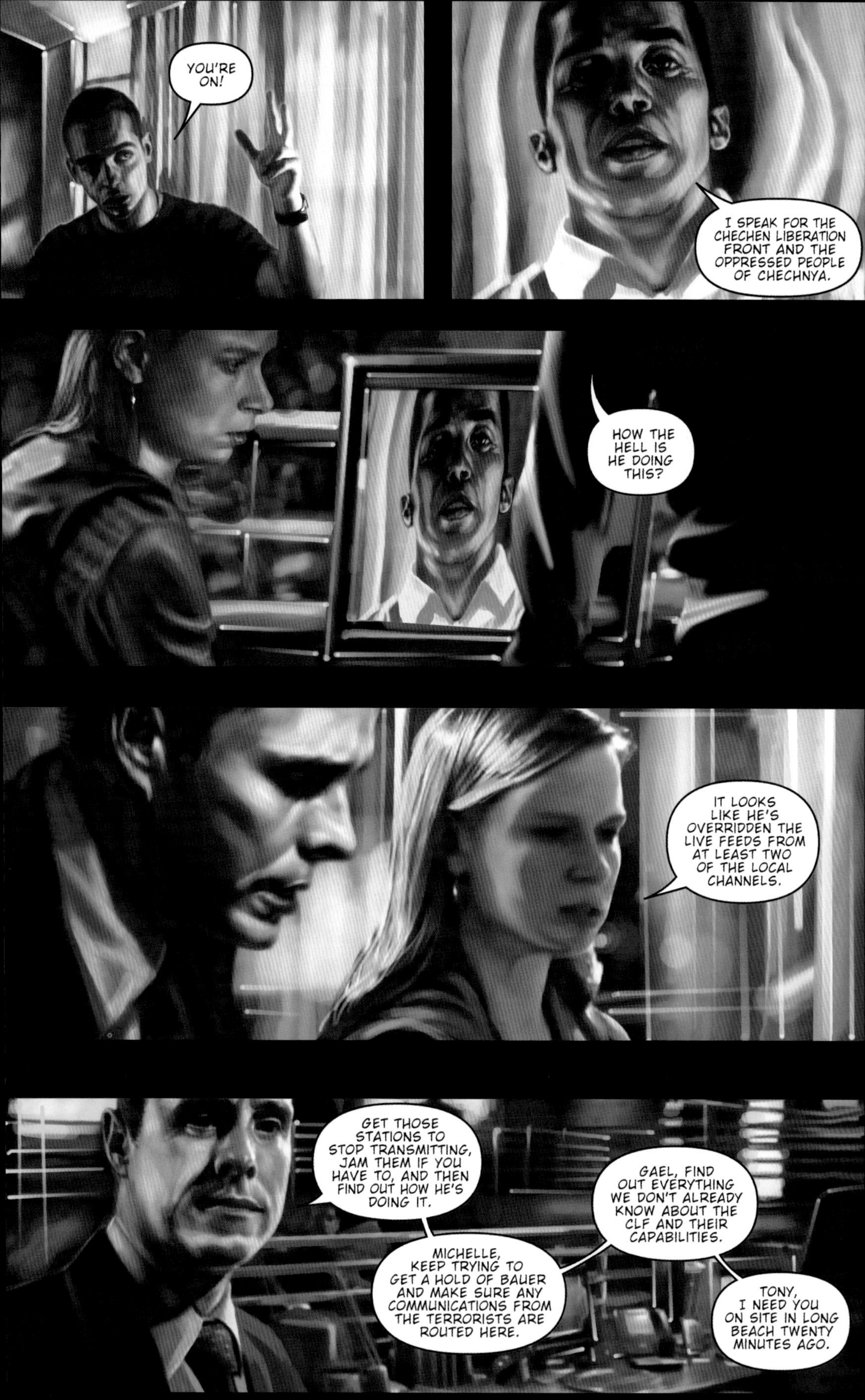
YOU'RE ON!
I SPEAK FOR THE CHECHEN LIBERATION FRONT AND THE OPPRESSED PEOPLE OF CHECHNYA.
HOW THE HELL IS HE DOING THIS?
IT LOOKS LIKE HE'S OVERRIDDEN THE LIVE FEEDS FROM AT LEAST TWO OF THE LOCAL CHANNELS.
GET THOSE STATIONS TO STOP TRANSMITTING, JAM THEM IF YOU HAVE TO, AND THEN FIND OUT HOW HE'S DOING IT.
MICHELLE, KEEP TRYING TO GET A HOLD OF BAUER AND MAKE SURE ANY COMMUNICATIONS FROM THE TERRORISTS ARE ROUTED HERE.
GAEL, FIND OUT EVERYTHING WE DON'T ALREADY KNOW ABOUT THE CLF AND THEIR CAPABILITIES.
TONY, I NEED YOU ON SITE IN LONG BEACH TWENTY MINUTES AGO.

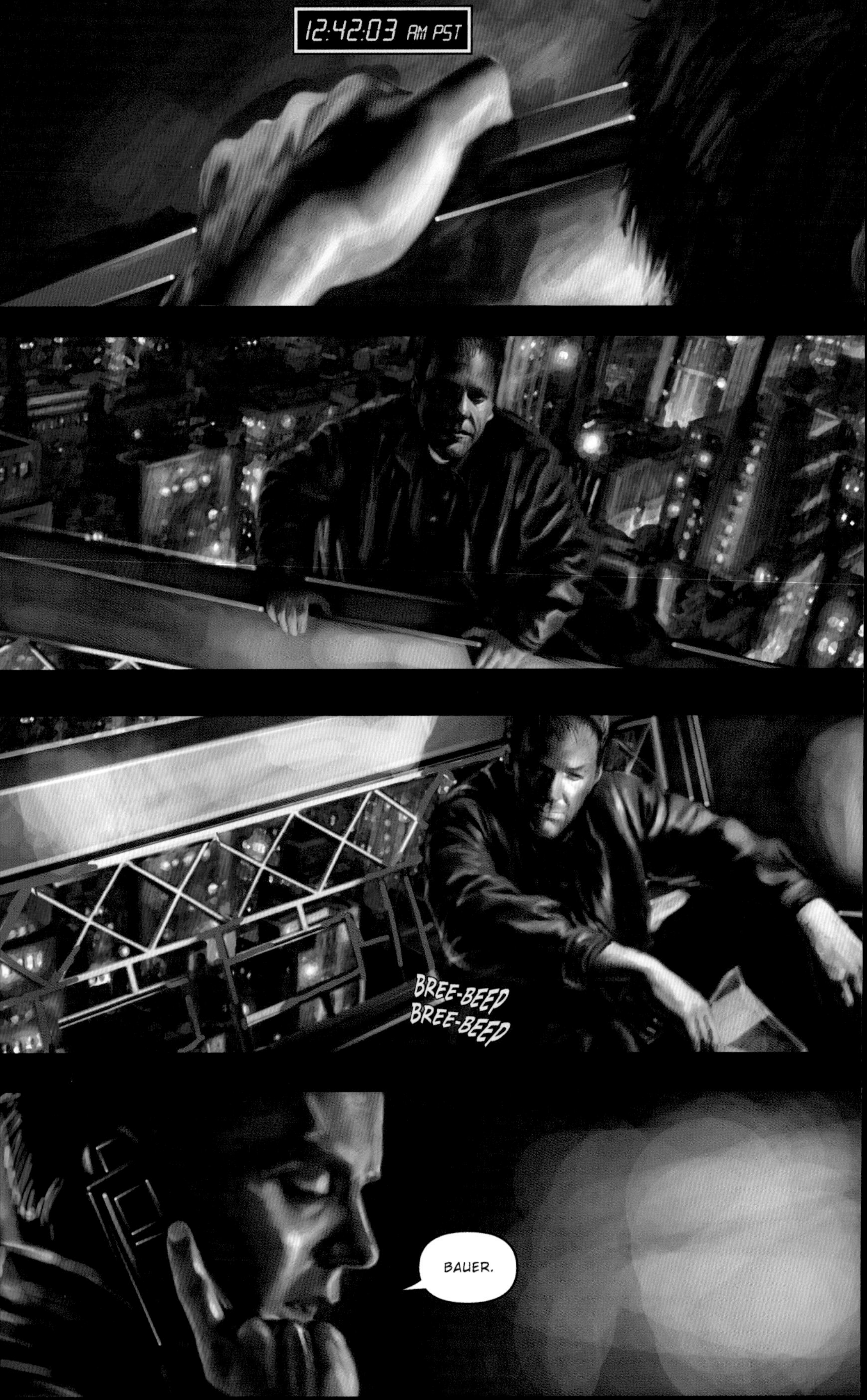
12:42:03 AM PST
BREE-BEEP
BREE-BEEP
BAUER.

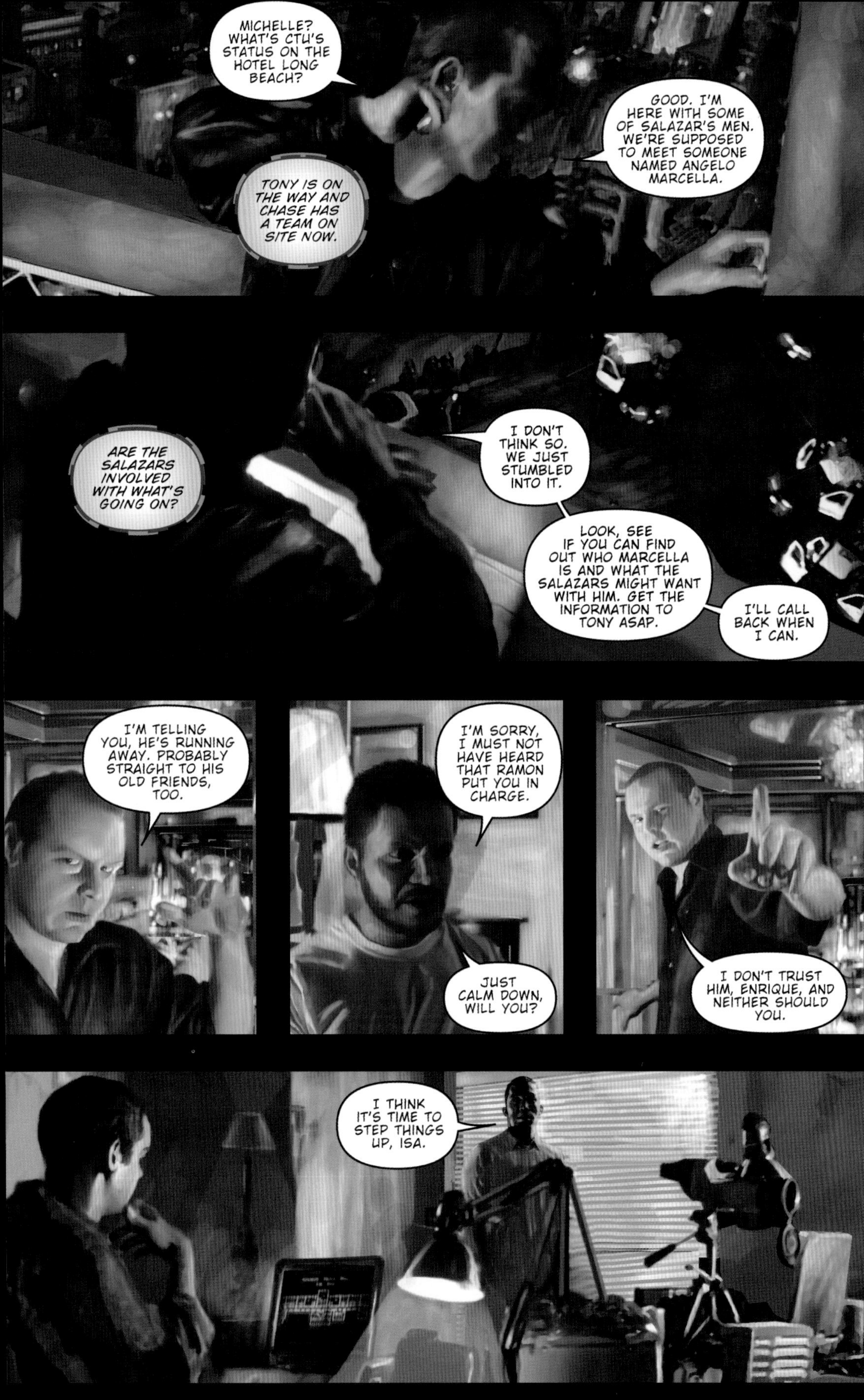
MICHELLE? WHAT'S CTU'S STATUS ON THE HOTEL LONG BEACH?
TONY IS ON THE WAY AND CHASE HAS A TEAM ON SITE NOW.
GOOD. I'M HERE WITH SOME OF SALAZAR'S MEN. WE'RE SUPPOSED TO MEET SOMEONE NAMED ANGELO MARCELLA.
ARE THE SALAZARS INVOLVED WITH WHAT'S GOING ON?
I DON'T THINK SO. WE JUST STUMBLED INTO IT.
LOOK, SEE IF YOU CAN FIND OUT WHO MARCELLA IS AND WHAT THE SALAZARS MIGHT WANT WITH HIM. GET THE INFORMATION TO TONY ASAP.
I'LL CALL BACK WHEN I CAN.
I'M TELLING YOU, HE'S RUNNING AWAY. PROBABLY STRAIGHT TO HIS OLD FRIENDS, TOO.
I'M SORRY, I MUST NOT HAVE HEARD THAT RAMON PUT YOU IN CHARGE.
JUST CALM DOWN, WILL YOU?
I DON'T TRUST HIM, ENRIQUE, AND NEITHER SHOULD YOU.
I THINK IT'S TIME TO STEP THINGS UP, ISA.

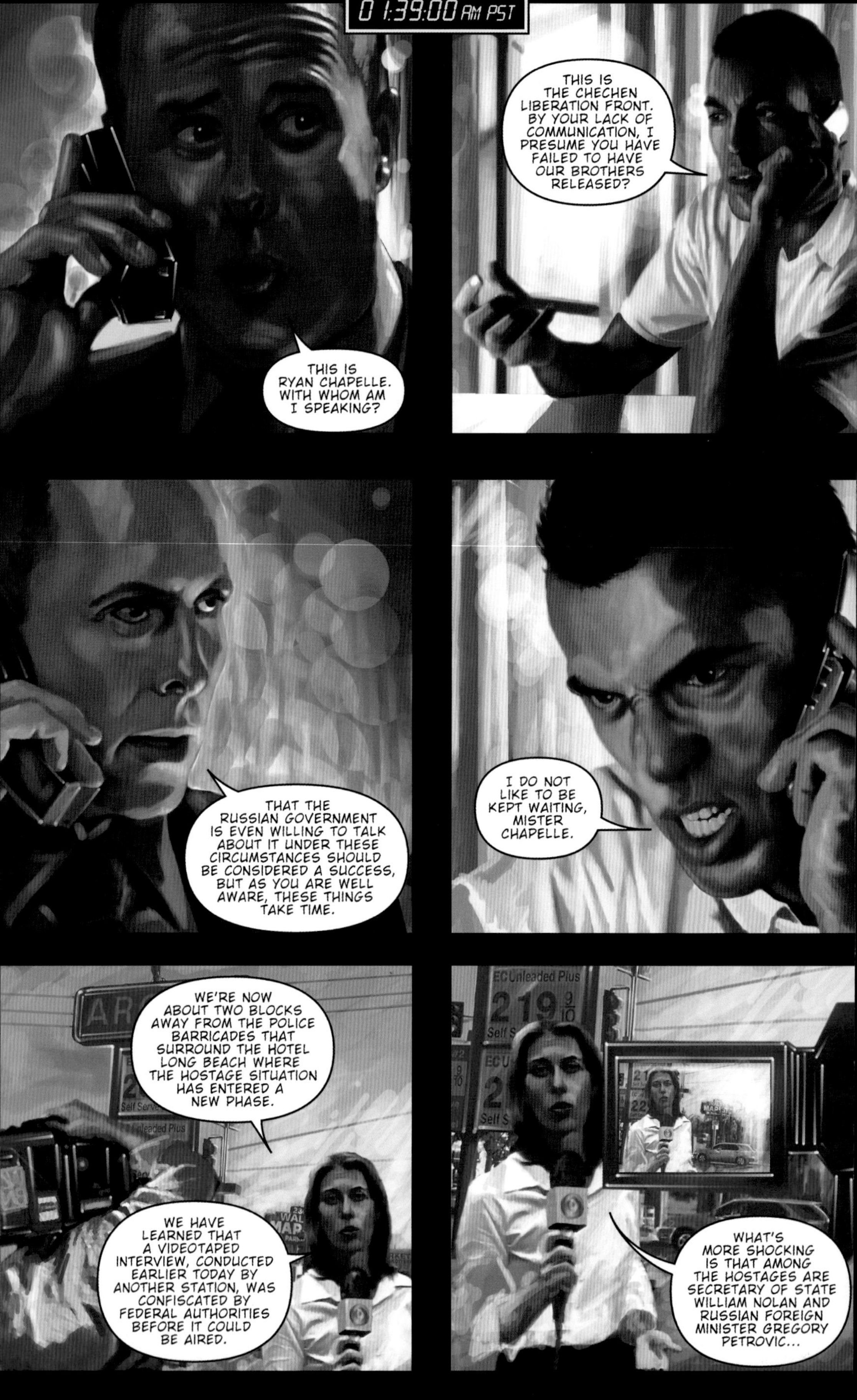
THIS IS RYAN CHAPELLE. WITH WHOM AM I SPEAKING?
THIS IS THE CHECHEN LIBERATION FRONT. BY YOUR LACK OF COMMUNICATION, I PRESUME YOU HAVE FAILED TO HAVE OUR BROTHERS RELEASED?
THAT THE RUSSIAN GOVERNMENT IS EVEN WILLING TO TALK ABOUT IT UNDER THESE CIRCUMSTANCES SHOULD BE CONSIDERED A SUCCESS, BUT AS YOU ARE WELL AWARE, THESE THINGS TAKE TIME.
I DO NOT LIKE TO BE KEPT WAITING, MISTER CHAPELLE.
WE'RE NOW ABOUT TWO BLOCKS AWAY FROM THE POLICE BARRICADES THAT SURROUND THE HOTEL LONG BEACH WHERE THE HOSTAGE SITUATION HAS ENTERED A NEW PHASE.
WE HAVE LEARNED THAT A VIDEOTAPED INTERVIEW, CONDUCTED EARLIER TODAY BY ANOTHER STATION, WAS CONFISCATED BY FEDERAL AUTHORITIES BEFORE IT COULD BE AIRED.
WHAT'S MORE SHOCKING IS THAT AMONG THE HOSTAGES ARE SECRETARY OF STATE WILLIAM NOLAN AND RUSSIAN FOREIGN MINISTER GREGORY PETROVIC...

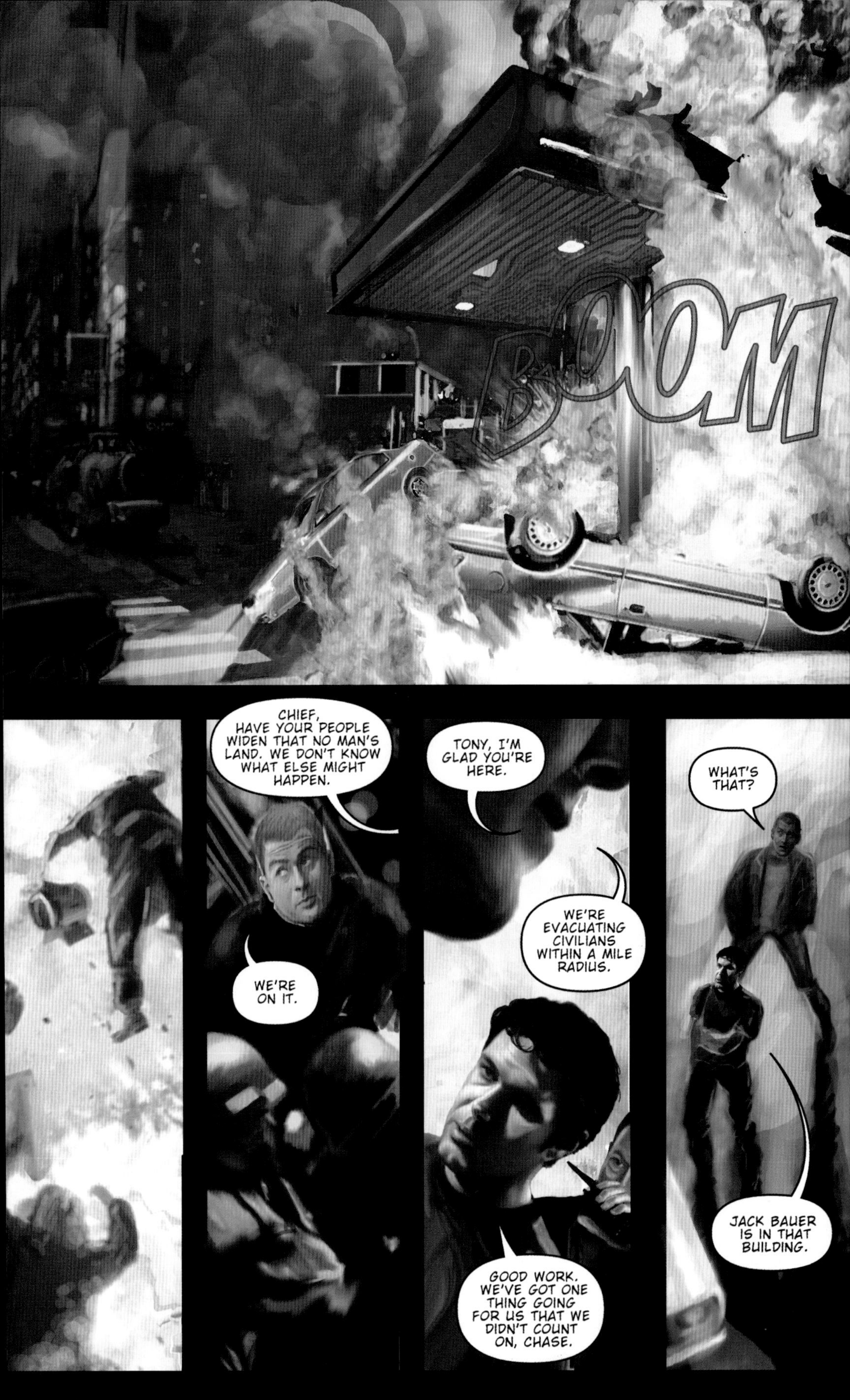
BOOM
CHIEF, HAVE YOUR PEOPLE WIDEN THAT NO MAN'S LAND. WE DON'T KNOW WHAT ELSE MIGHT HAPPEN.
WE'RE ON IT.
TONY, I'M GLAD YOU'RE HERE.
WE'RE EVACUATING CIVILIANS WITHIN A MILE RADIUS.
GOOD WORK. WE'VE GOT ONE THING GOING FOR US THAT WE DIDN'T COUNT ON, CHASE.
WHAT'S THAT?
JACK BAUER IS IN THAT BUILDING.

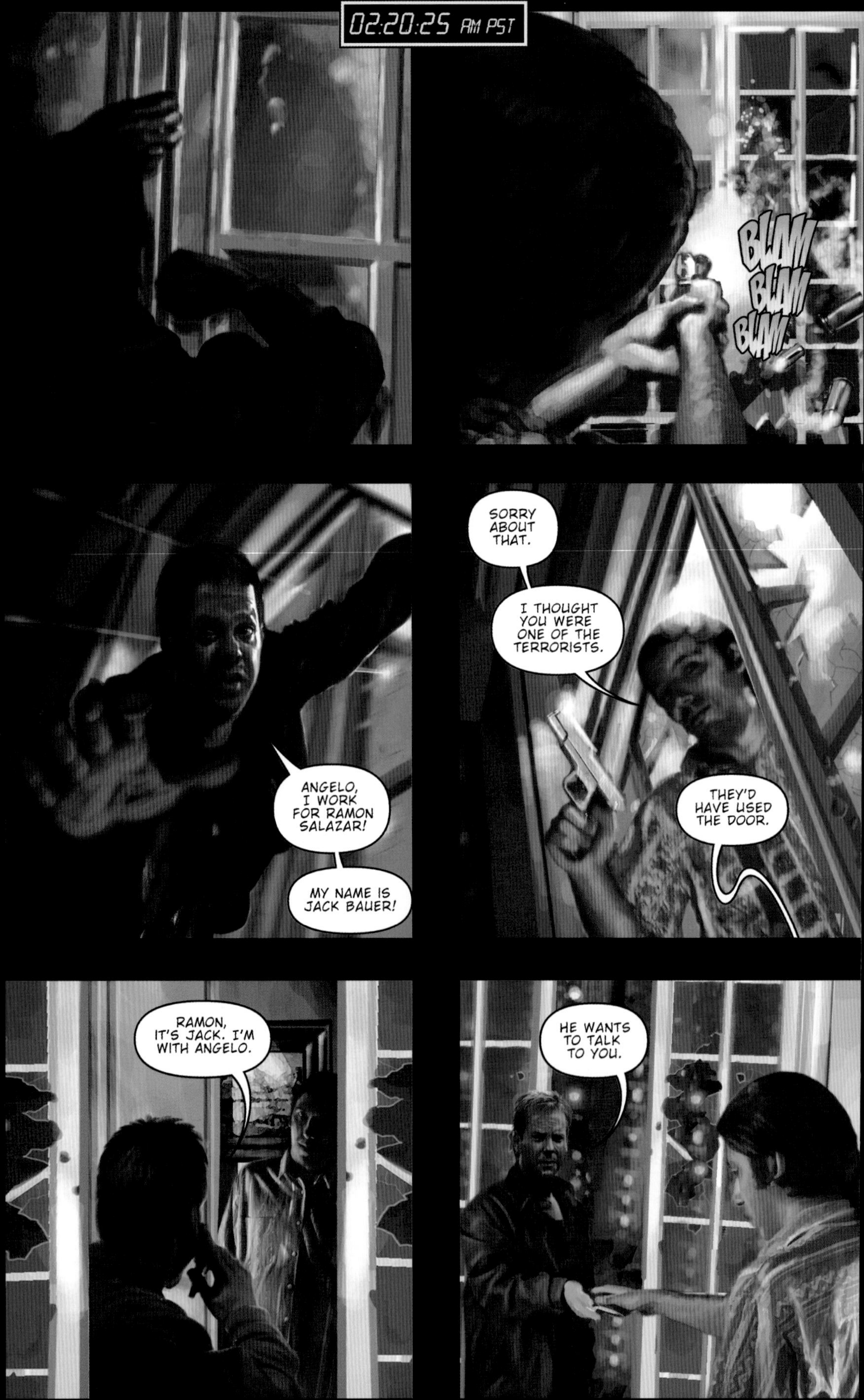
02:20:25 AM PST
BLAM
BLAM
BLAM
ANGELO, I WORK FOR RAMON SALAZAR!
MY NAME IS JACK BAUER!
SORRY ABOUT THAT.
I THOUGHT YOU WERE ONE OF THE TERRORISTS.
THEY'D HAVE USED THE DOOR.
RAMON, IT'S JACK. I'M WITH ANGELO.
HE WANTS TO TALK TO YOU.

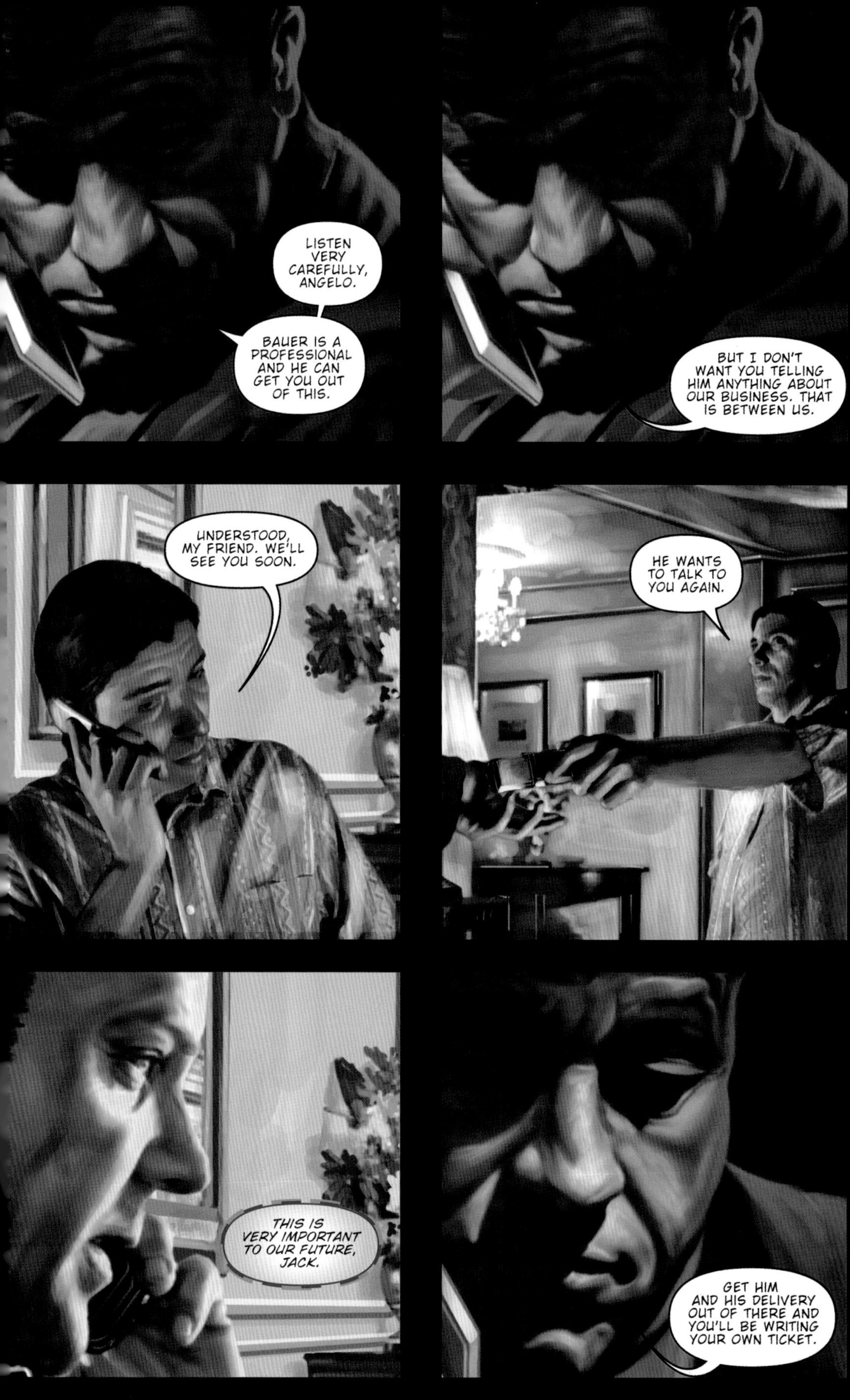
LISTEN VERY CAREFULLY, ANGELO.
BAUER IS A PROFESSIONAL AND HE CAN GET YOU OUT OF THIS.
BUT I DON'T WANT YOU TELLING HIM ANYTHING ABOUT OUR BUSINESS. THAT IS BETWEEN US.
UNDERSTOOD, MY FRIEND. WE'LL SEE YOU SOON.
HE WANTS TO TALK TO YOU AGAIN.
THIS IS VERY IMPORTANT TO OUR FUTURE, JACK.
GET HIM AND HIS DELIVERY OUT OF THERE AND YOU'LL BE WRITING YOUR OWN TICKET.

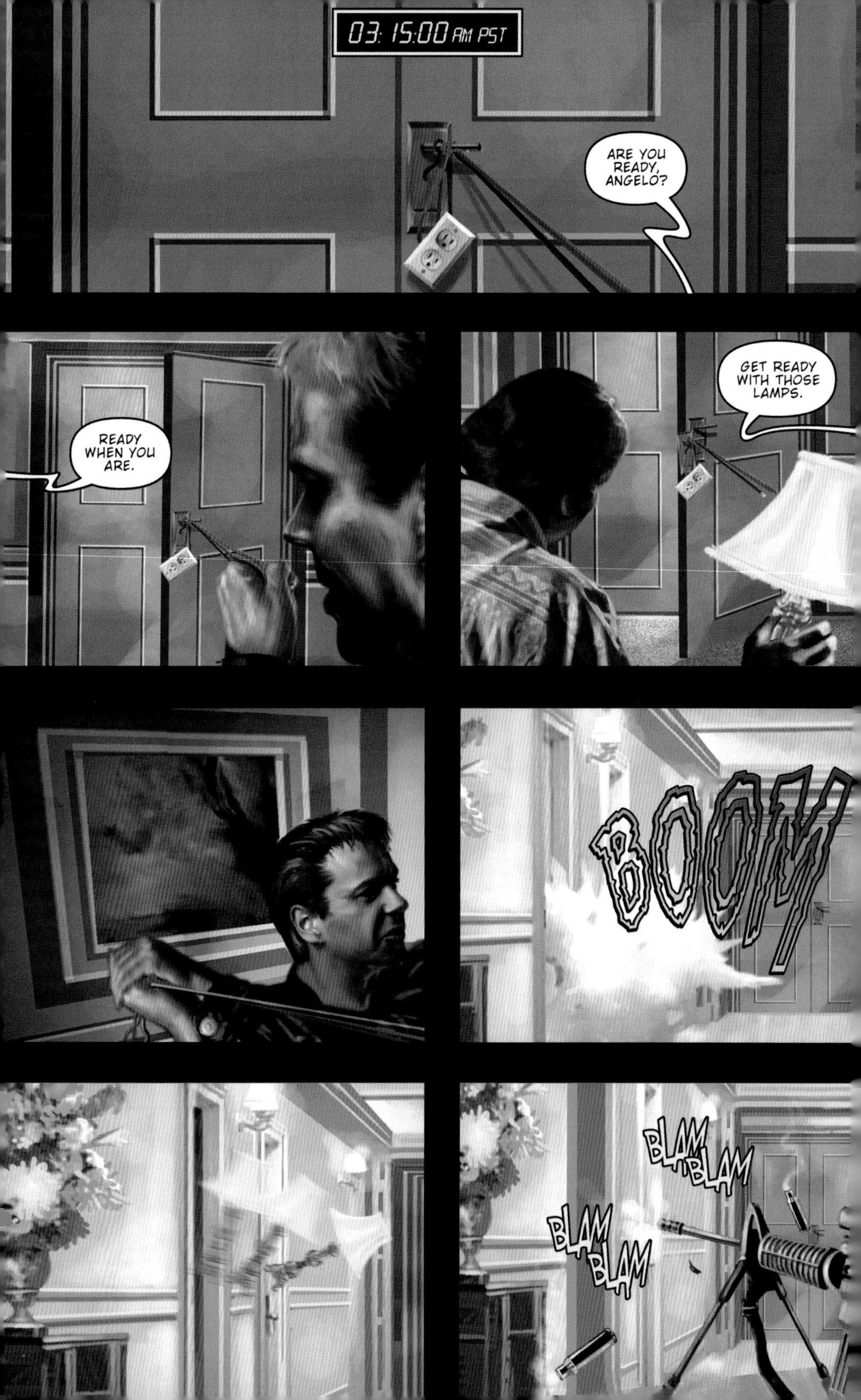
03: 15:00 AM PST
ARE YOU READY, ANGELO?
READY WHEN YOU ARE.
GET READY WITH THOSE LAMPS.
BOOM
BLAM BLAM
BLAM BLAM

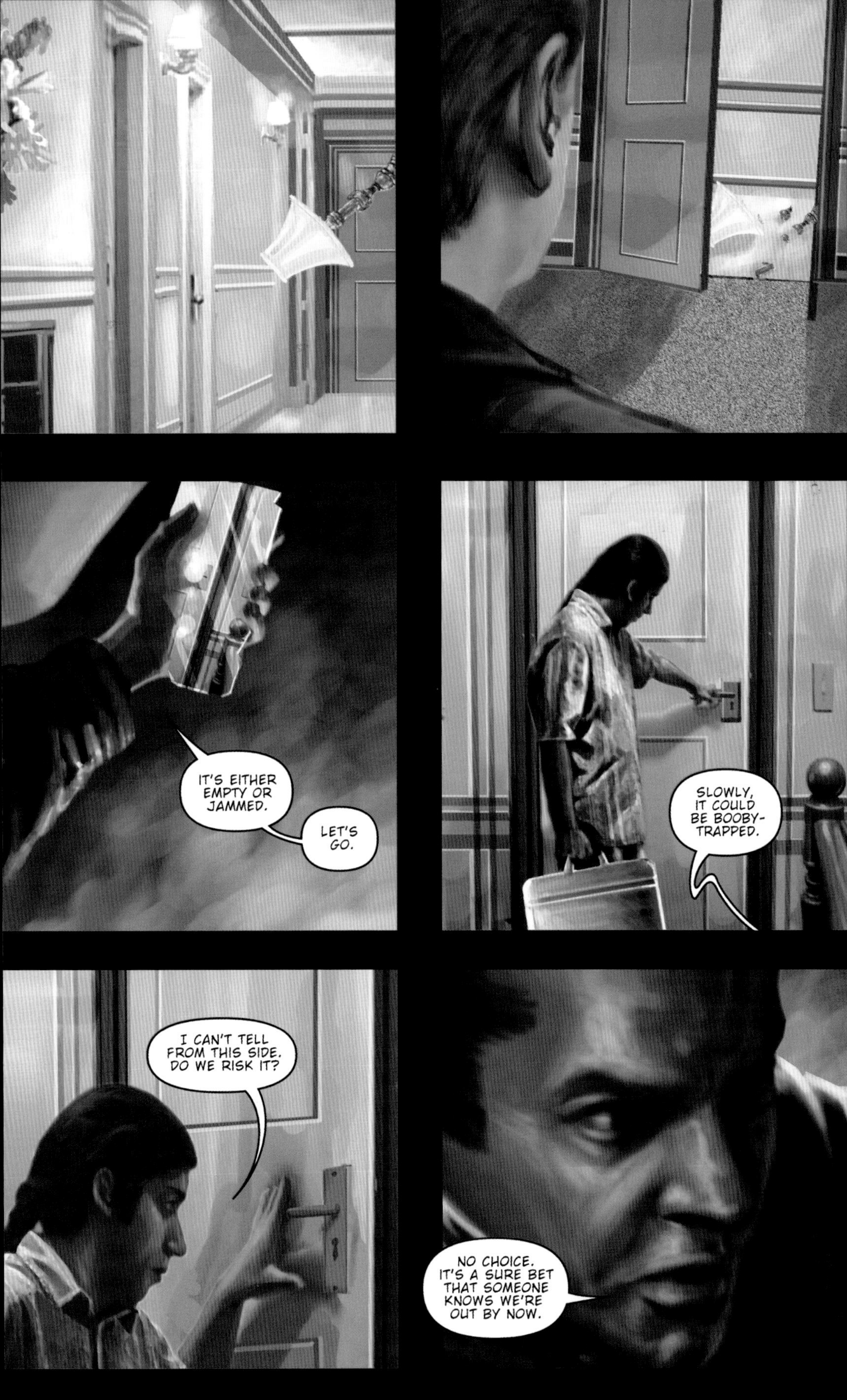
IT'S EITHER EMPTY OR JAMMED.
LET'S GO.
SLOWLY, IT COULD BE BOOBY-TRAPPED.
I CAN'T TELL FROM THIS SIDE. DO WE RISK IT?
NO CHOICE. IT'S A SURE BET THAT SOMEONE KNOWS WE'RE OUT BY NOW.

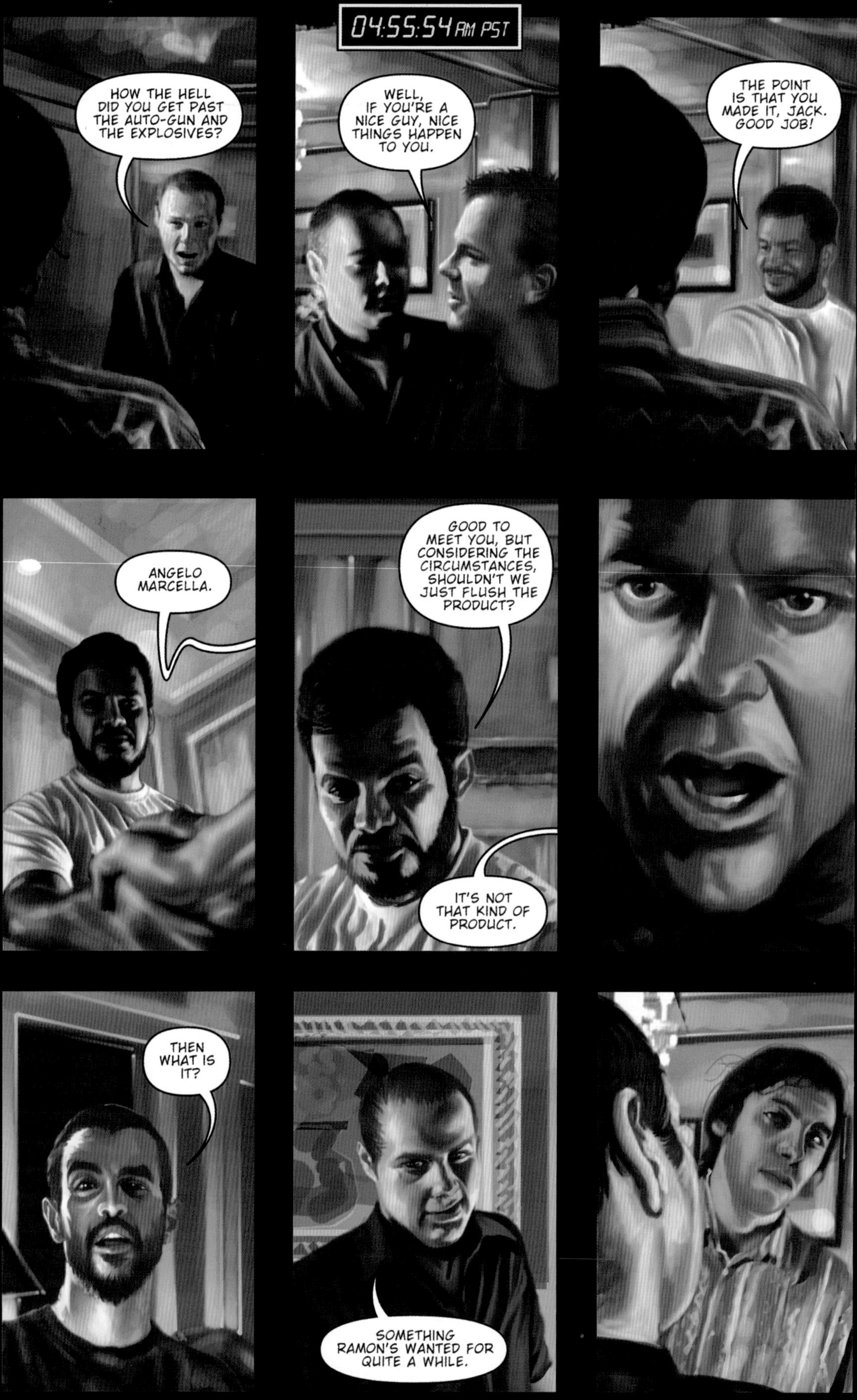
04:55:54 AM PST
HOW THE HELL DID YOU GET PAST THE AUTO-GUN AND THE EXPLOSIVES?
WELL, IF YOU'RE A NICE GUY, NICE THINGS HAPPEN TO YOU.
THE POINT IS THAT YOU MADE IT, JACK. GOOD JOB!
ANGELO MARCELLA.
GOOD TO MEET YOU, BUT CONSIDERING THE CIRCUMSTANCES, SHOULDN'T WE JUST FLUSH THE PRODUCT?
IT'S NOT THAT KIND OF PRODUCT.
THEN WHAT IS IT?
SOMETHING RAMON'S WANTED FOR QUITE A WHILE.

WHATEVER IT IS, IT CAN WAIT UNTIL RAMON WANTS TO TELL US ABOUT IT.

SMART MAN, JACK. RAMON WILL APPRECIATE THAT KIND OF LOYALTY.

HE'S LOYAL, ALL RIGHT. SO LONG AS THE "H" KEEPS COMING, EH, JACK?

I'M GOING TO CALL RAMON AND GET INSTRUCTIONS.

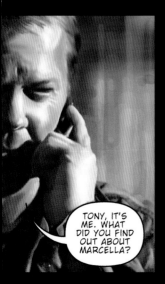

TONY, IT'S ME. WHAT DID YOU FIND OUT ABOUT MARCELLA?

HE'S WANTED BY THE BRITISH, THE PORTUGUESE, AND EVEN THE FRENCH. THEY HAVE LINKED HIM TO FIVE SEPARATE THEFTS OF ADVANCED WEAPONS TECHNOLOGY.

IF HE'S CONNECTED WITH THE SALAZARS, EVERYTHING YOU SUSPECTED ABOUT THEM COULD BE TRUE.

I KNEW I SMELLED A RAT!

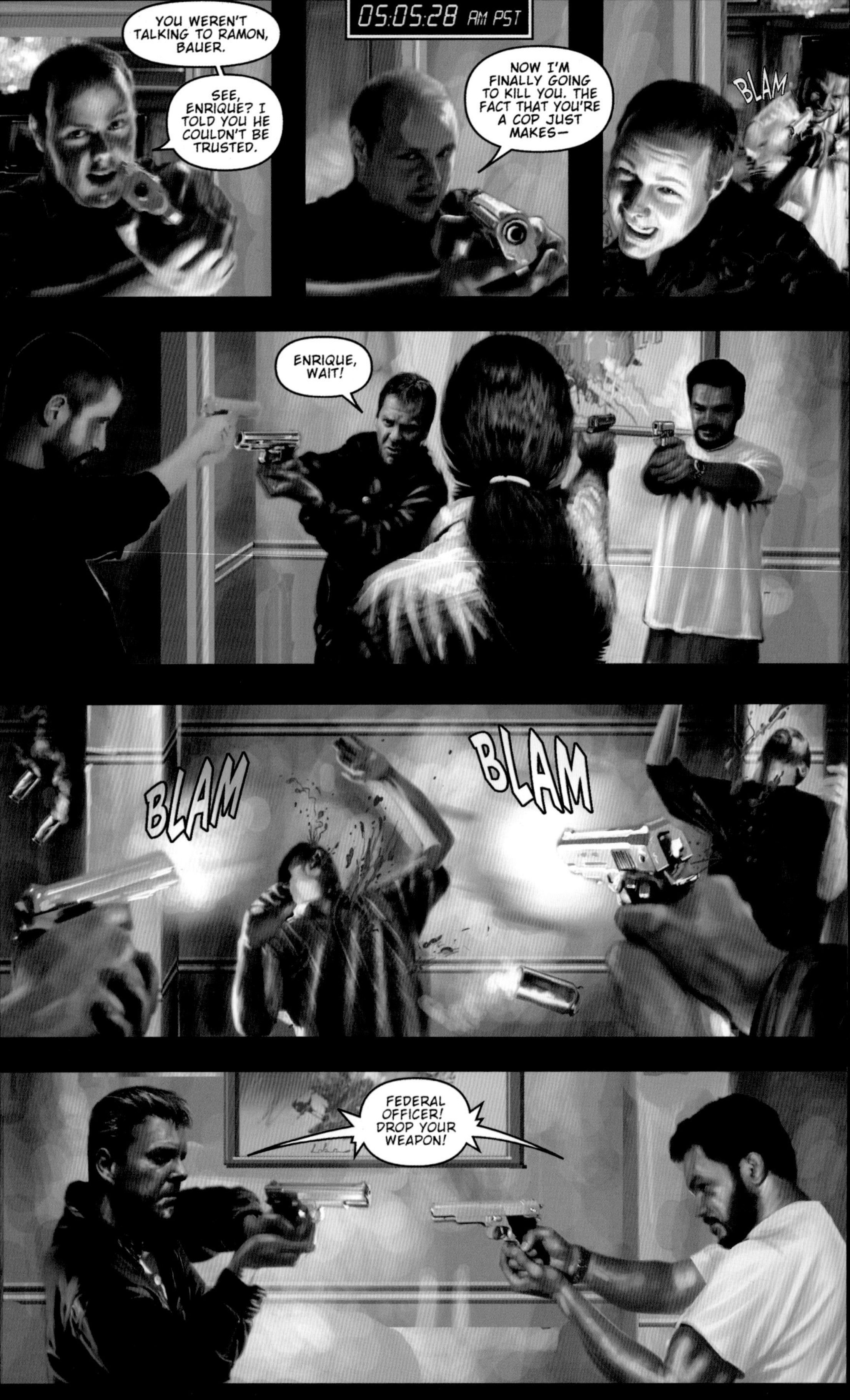
05:05:28 AM PST
YOU WEREN'T TALKING TO RAMON, BAUER.
SEE, ENRIQUE? I TOLD YOU HE COULDN'T BE TRUSTED.
NOW I'M FINALLY GOING TO KILL YOU. THE FACT THAT YOU'RE A COP JUST MAKES—
BLAM
ENRIQUE, WAIT!
BLAM
BLAM
FEDERAL OFFICER! DROP YOUR WEAPON!

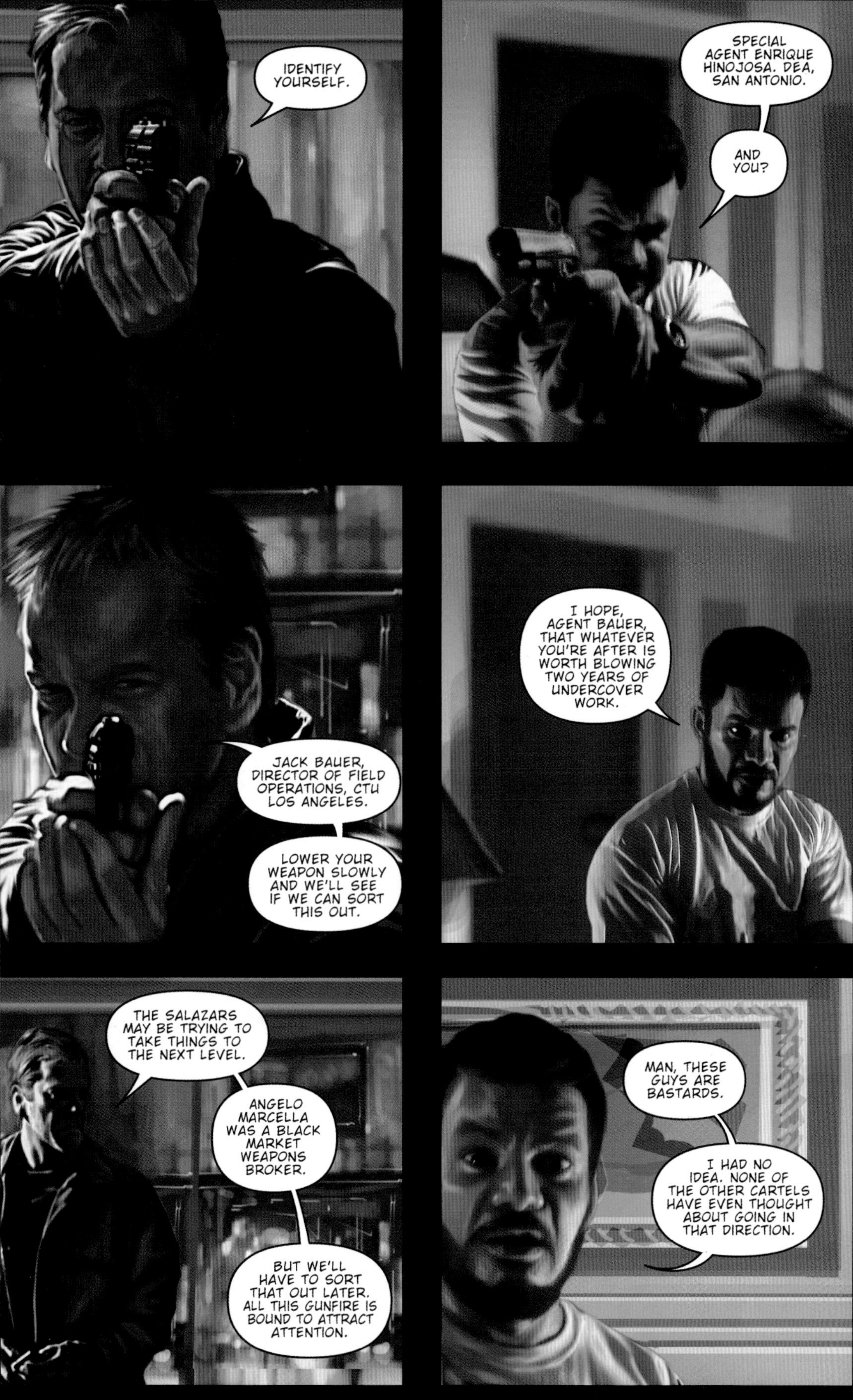
IDENTIFY YOURSELF.
SPECIAL AGENT ENRIQUE HINOJOSA. DEA, SAN ANTONIO.
AND YOU?
JACK BAUER, DIRECTOR OF FIELD OPERATIONS, CTU LOS ANGELES.
LOWER YOUR WEAPON SLOWLY AND WE'LL SEE IF WE CAN SORT THIS OUT.
I HOPE, AGENT BAUER, THAT WHATEVER YOU'RE AFTER IS WORTH BLOWING TWO YEARS OF UNDERCOVER WORK.
THE SALAZARS MAY BE TRYING TO TAKE THINGS TO THE NEXT LEVEL.
ANGELO MARCELLA WAS A BLACK MARKET WEAPONS BROKER.
BUT WE'LL HAVE TO SORT THAT OUT LATER. ALL THIS GUNFIRE IS BOUND TO ATTRACT ATTENTION.
MAN, THESE GUYS ARE BASTARDS.
I HAD NO IDEA. NONE OF THE OTHER CARTELS HAVE EVEN THOUGHT ABOUT GOING IN THAT DIRECTION.

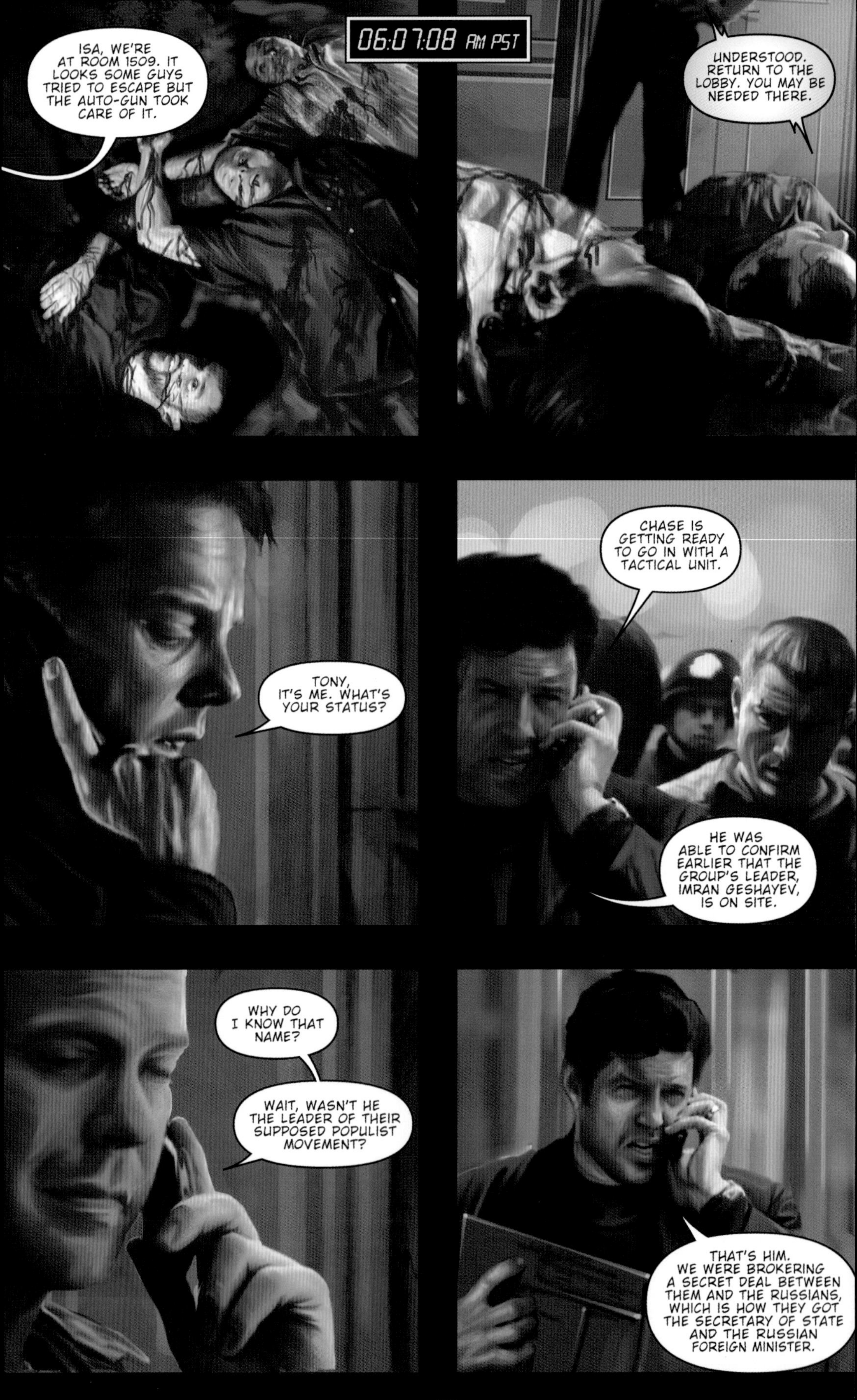

06:07:08 AM PST
ISA, WE'RE AT ROOM 1509. IT LOOKS SOME GUYS TRIED TO ESCAPE BUT THE AUTO-GUN TOOK CARE OF IT.
UNDERSTOOD. RETURN TO THE LOBBY. YOU MAY BE NEEDED THERE.
TONY, IT'S ME. WHAT'S YOUR STATUS?
CHASE IS GETTING READY TO GO IN WITH A TACTICAL UNIT.
HE WAS ABLE TO CONFIRM EARLIER THAT THE GROUP'S LEADER, IMRAN GESHAYEV, IS ON SITE.
WHY DO I KNOW THAT NAME?
WAIT, WASN'T HE THE LEADER OF THEIR SUPPOSED POPULIST MOVEMENT?
THAT'S HIM. WE WERE BROKERING A SECRET DEAL BETWEEN THEM AND THE RUSSIANS, WHICH IS HOW THEY GOT THE SECRETARY OF STATE AND THE RUSSIAN FOREIGN MINISTER.

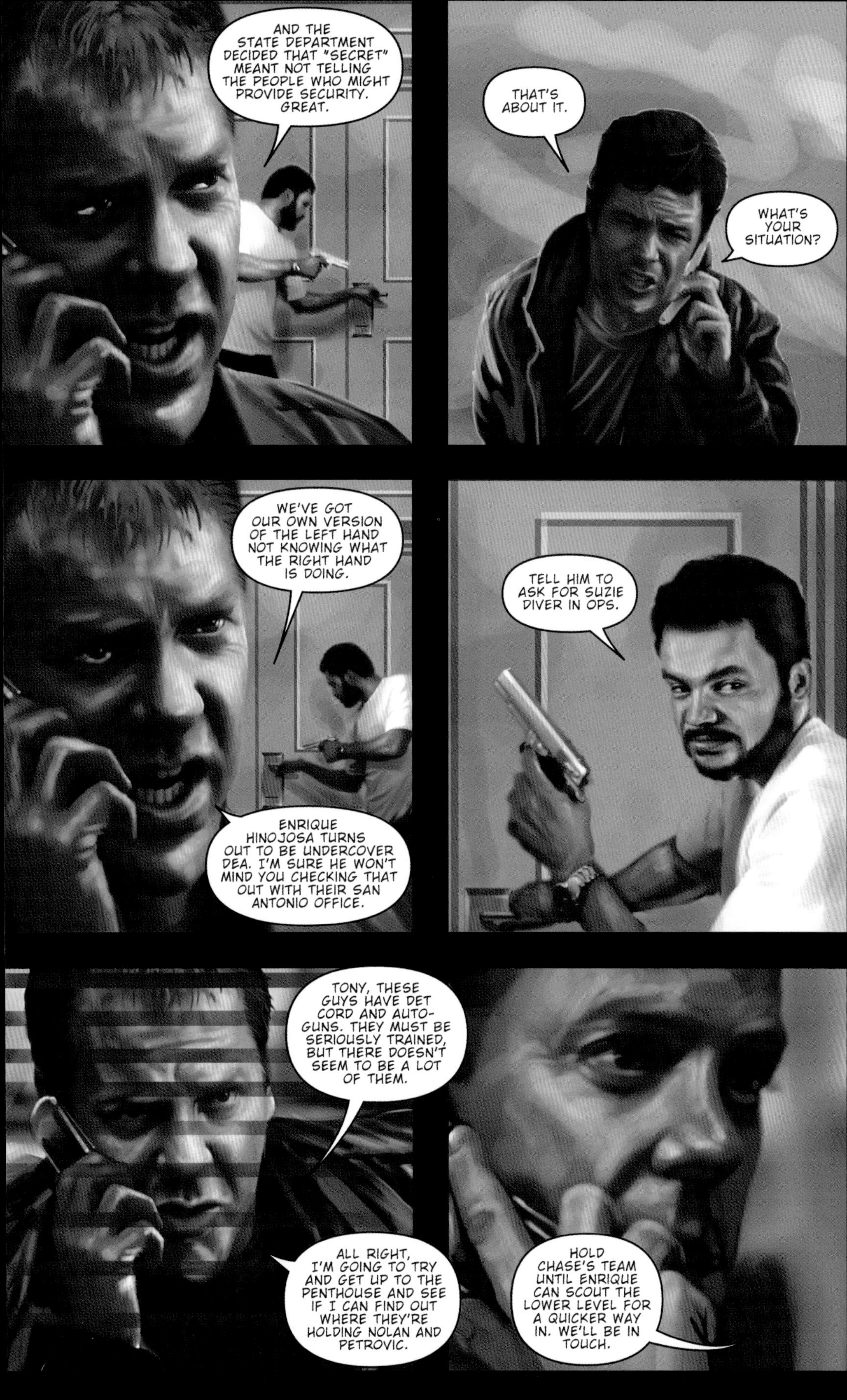
AND THE STATE DEPARTMENT DECIDED THAT "SECRET" MEANT NOT TELLING THE PEOPLE WHO MIGHT PROVIDE SECURITY. GREAT.
THAT'S ABOUT IT.
WHAT'S YOUR SITUATION?
WE'VE GOT OUR OWN VERSION OF THE LEFT HAND NOT KNOWING WHAT THE RIGHT HAND IS DOING.
ENRIQUE HINOJOSA TURNS OUT TO BE UNDERCOVER DEA. I'M SURE HE WON'T MIND YOU CHECKING THAT OUT WITH THEIR SAN ANTONIO OFFICE.
TELL HIM TO ASK FOR SUZIE DIVER IN OPS.
TONY, THESE GUYS HAVE DET CORD AND AUTO-GUNS. THEY MUST BE SERIOUSLY TRAINED, BUT THERE DOESN'T SEEM TO BE A LOT OF THEM.
ALL RIGHT, I'M GOING TO TRY AND GET UP TO THE PENTHOUSE AND SEE IF I CAN FIND OUT WHERE THEY'RE HOLDING NOLAN AND PETROVIC.
HOLD CHASE'S TEAM UNTIL ENRIQUE CAN SCOUT THE LOWER LEVEL FOR A QUICKER WAY IN. WE'LL BE IN TOUCH.

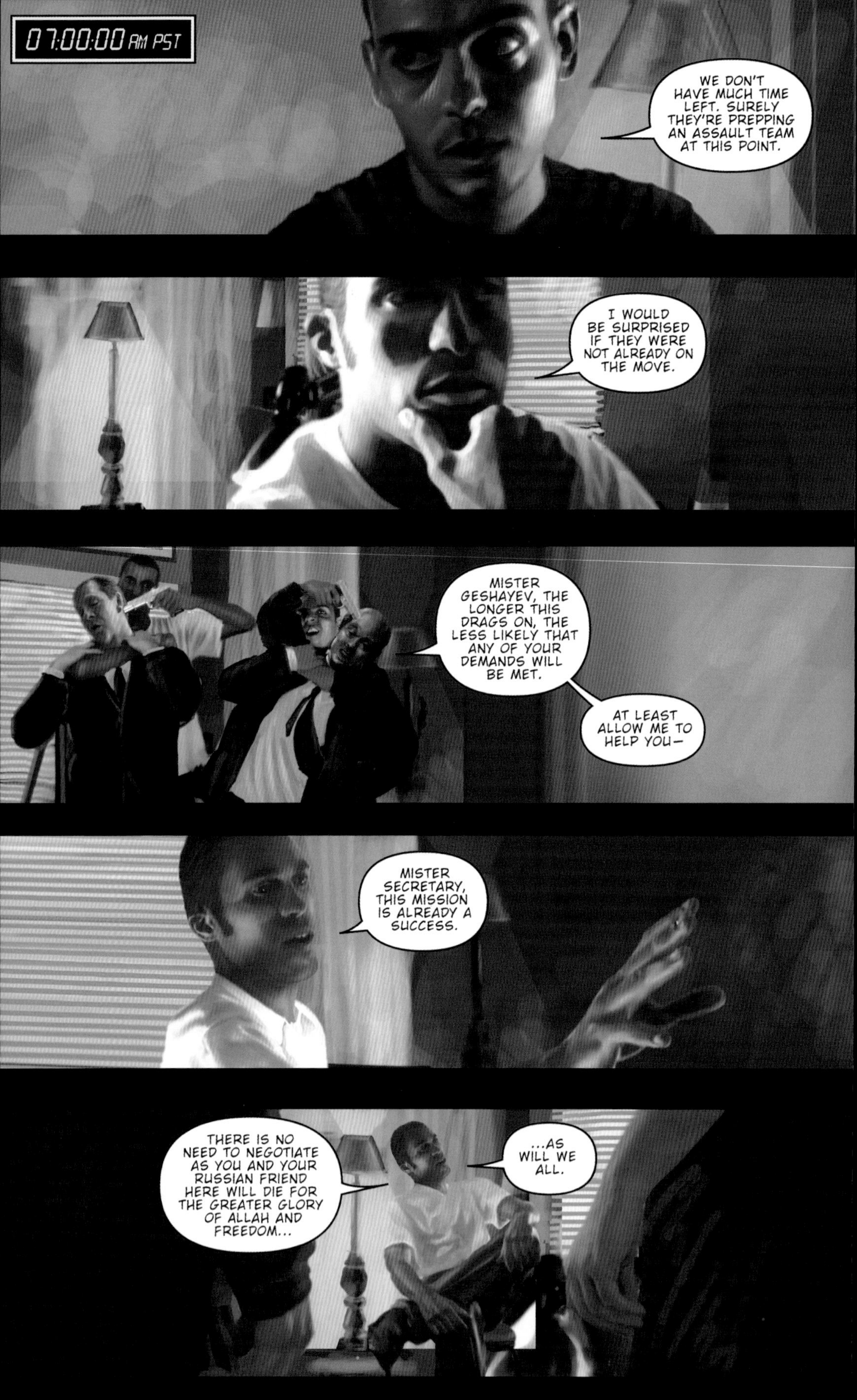
07:00:00 AM PST
WE DON'T HAVE MUCH TIME LEFT. SURELY THEY'RE PREPPING AN ASSAULT TEAM AT THIS POINT.
I WOULD BE SURPRISED IF THEY WERE NOT ALREADY ON THE MOVE.
MISTER GESHAYEV, THE LONGER THIS DRAGS ON, THE LESS LIKELY THAT ANY OF YOUR DEMANDS WILL BE MET.
AT LEAST ALLOW ME TO HELP YOU—
MISTER SECRETARY, THIS MISSION IS ALREADY A SUCCESS.
THERE IS NO NEED TO NEGOTIATE AS YOU AND YOUR RUSSIAN FRIEND HERE WILL DIE FOR THE GREATER GLORY OF ALLAH AND FREEDOM...
...AS WILL WE ALL.

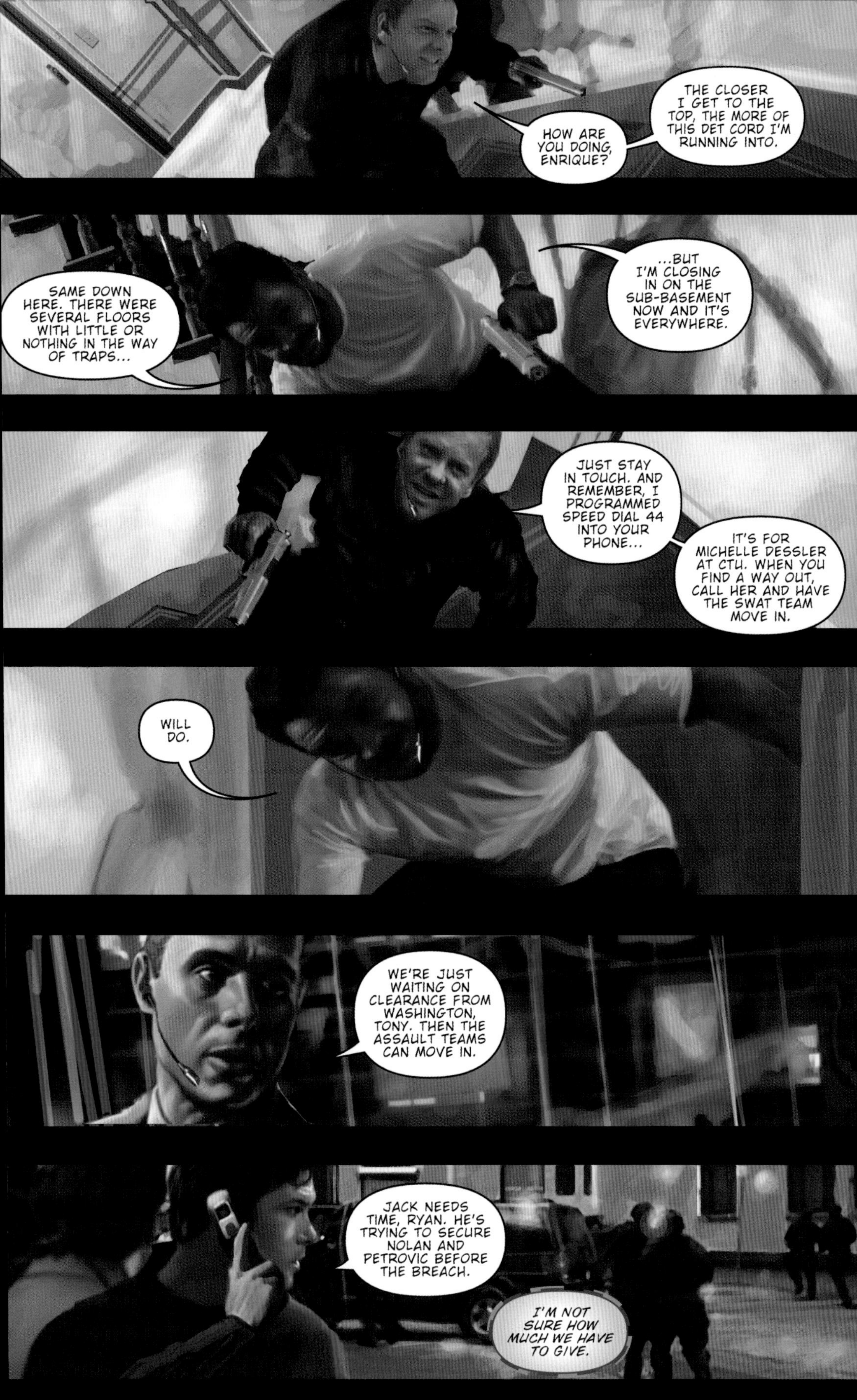
HOW ARE YOU DOING, ENRIQUE?
THE CLOSER I GET TO THE TOP, THE MORE OF THIS DET CORD I'M RUNNING INTO.
SAME DOWN HERE. THERE WERE SEVERAL FLOORS WITH LITTLE OR NOTHING IN THE WAY OF TRAPS...
...BUT I'M CLOSING IN ON THE SUB-BASEMENT NOW AND IT'S EVERYWHERE.
JUST STAY IN TOUCH. AND REMEMBER, I PROGRAMMED SPEED DIAL 44 INTO YOUR PHONE...
IT'S FOR MICHELLE DESSLER AT CTU. WHEN YOU FIND A WAY OUT, CALL HER AND HAVE THE SWAT TEAM MOVE IN.
WILL DO.
WE'RE JUST WAITING ON CLEARANCE FROM WASHINGTON, TONY. THEN THE ASSAULT TEAMS CAN MOVE IN.
JACK NEEDS TIME, RYAN. HE'S TRYING TO SECURE NOLAN AND PETROVIC BEFORE THE BREACH.
I'M NOT SURE HOW MUCH WE HAVE TO GIVE.

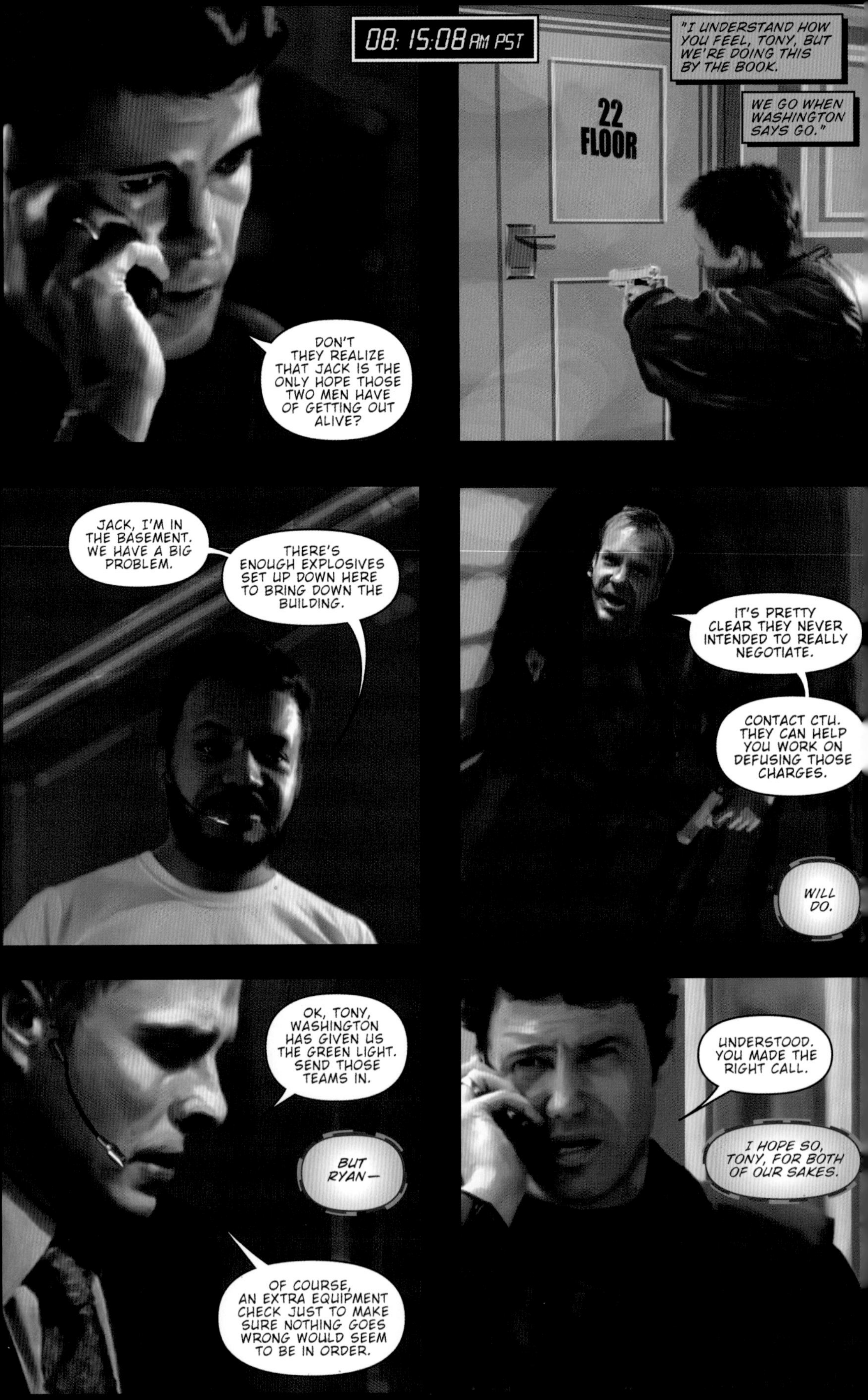
08: 15:08 AM PST
DON'T THEY REALIZE THAT JACK IS THE ONLY HOPE THOSE TWO MEN HAVE OF GETTING OUT ALIVE?
22 FLOOR
"I UNDERSTAND HOW YOU FEEL, TONY, BUT WE'RE DOING THIS BY THE BOOK.
WE GO WHEN WASHINGTON SAYS GO."
JACK, I'M IN THE BASEMENT. WE HAVE A BIG PROBLEM.
THERE'S ENOUGH EXPLOSIVES SET UP DOWN HERE TO BRING DOWN THE BUILDING.
IT'S PRETTY CLEAR THEY NEVER INTENDED TO REALLY NEGOTIATE.
CONTACT CTU. THEY CAN HELP YOU WORK ON DEFUSING THOSE CHARGES.
WILL DO.
OK, TONY, WASHINGTON HAS GIVEN US THE GREEN LIGHT. SEND THOSE TEAMS IN.
BUT RYAN—
OF COURSE, AN EXTRA EQUIPMENT CHECK JUST TO MAKE SURE NOTHING GOES WRONG WOULD SEEM TO BE IN ORDER.
UNDERSTOOD. YOU MADE THE RIGHT CALL.
I HOPE SO, TONY, FOR BOTH OF OUR SAKES.

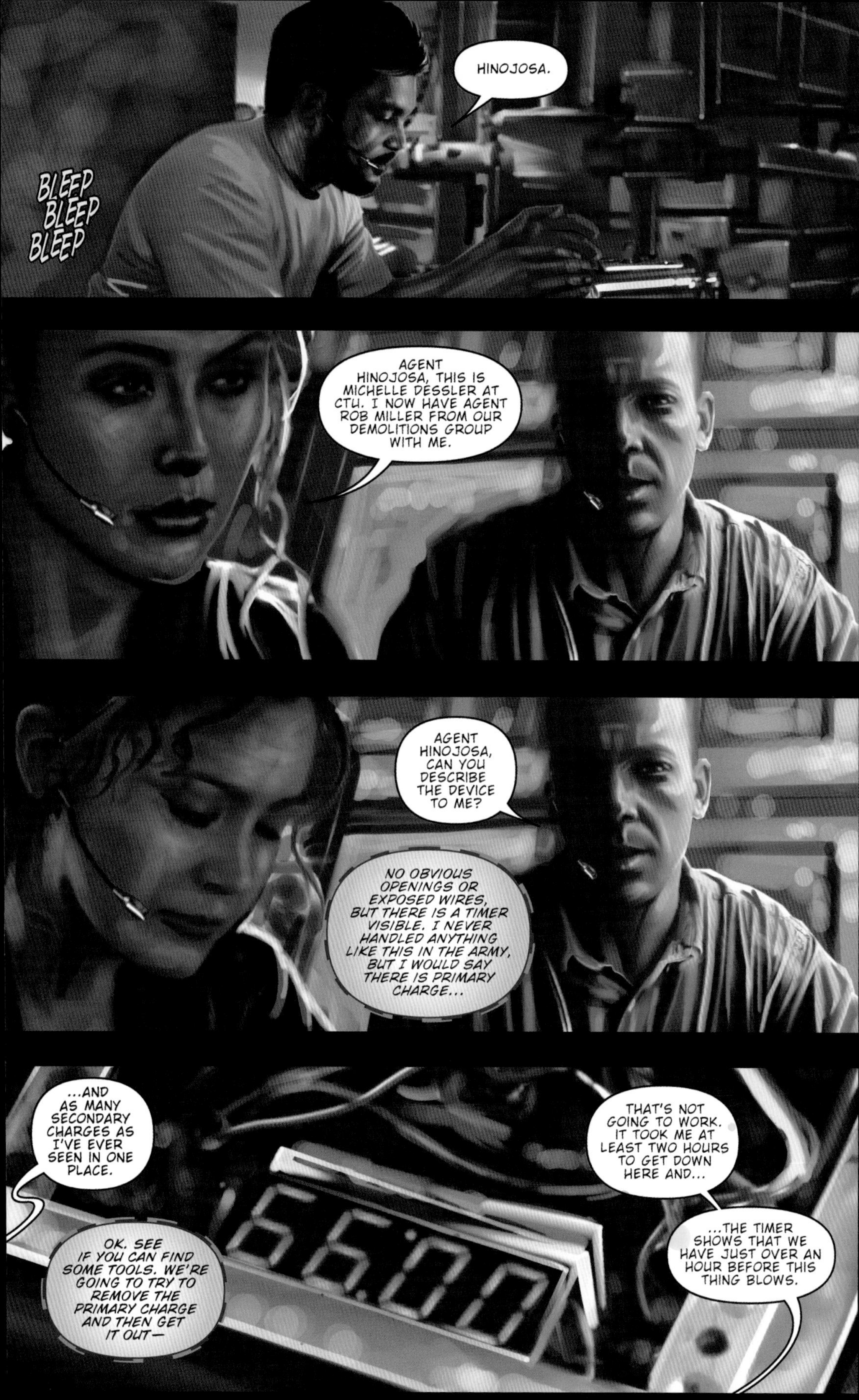
BLEEP
BLEEP
BLEEP
HINOJOSA.
AGENT HINOJOSA, THIS IS MICHELLE DESSLER AT CTU. I NOW HAVE AGENT ROB MILLER FROM OUR DEMOLITIONS GROUP WITH ME.
AGENT HINOJOSA, CAN YOU DESCRIBE THE DEVICE TO ME?
NO OBVIOUS OPENINGS OR EXPOSED WIRES, BUT THERE IS A TIMER VISIBLE. I NEVER HANDLED ANYTHING LIKE THIS IN THE ARMY, BUT I WOULD SAY THERE IS PRIMARY CHARGE...
...AND AS MANY SECONDARY CHARGES AS I'VE EVER SEEN IN ONE PLACE.
OK. SEE IF YOU CAN FIND SOME TOOLS. WE'RE GOING TO TRY TO REMOVE THE PRIMARY CHARGE AND THEN GET IT OUT—
THAT'S NOT GOING TO WORK. IT TOOK ME AT LEAST TWO HOURS TO GET DOWN HERE AND...
...THE TIMER SHOWS THAT WE HAVE JUST OVER AN HOUR BEFORE THIS THING BLOWS.
66:00

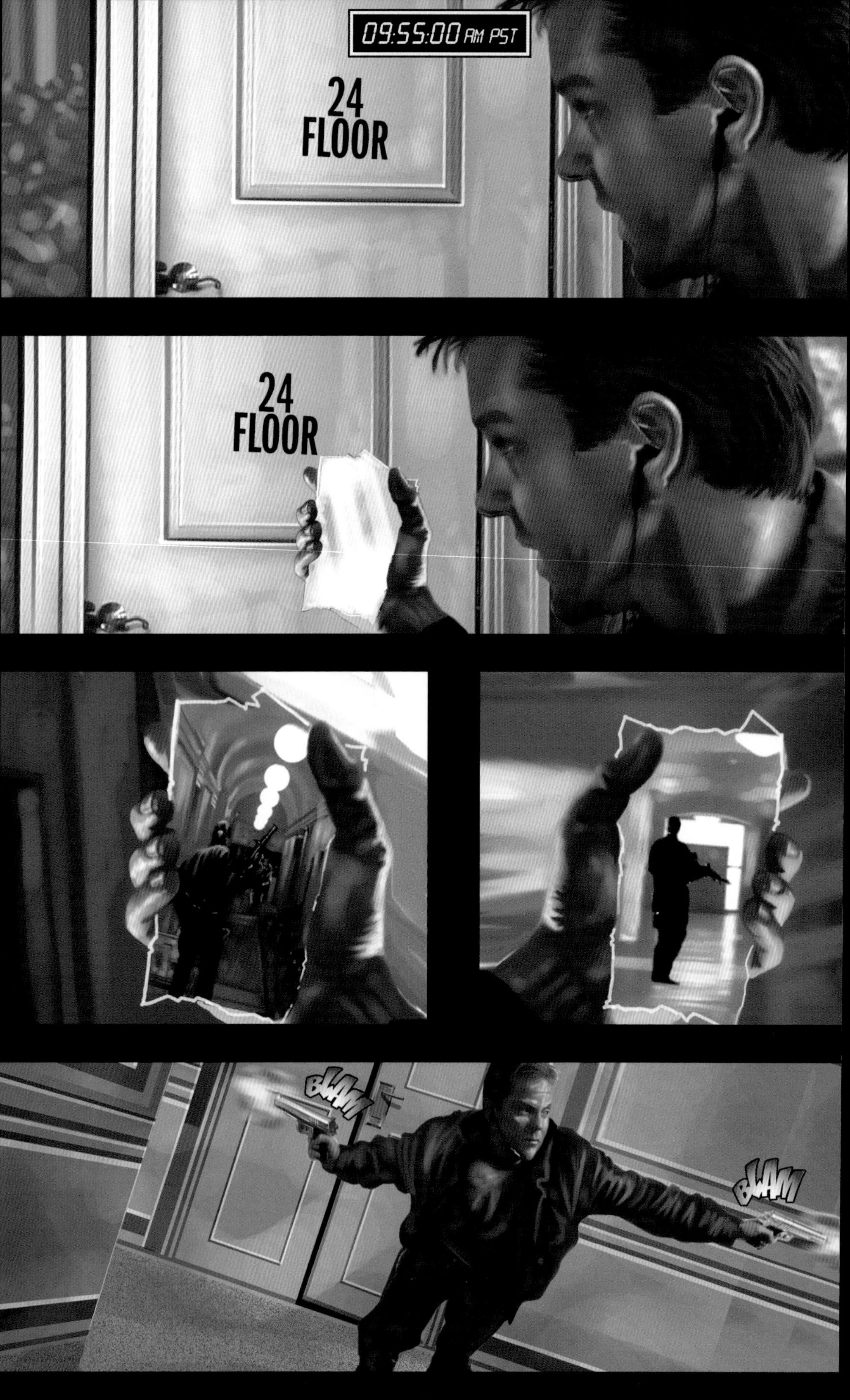
09:55:00 AM PST
24 FLOOR
24 FLOOR
BLAM
BLAM

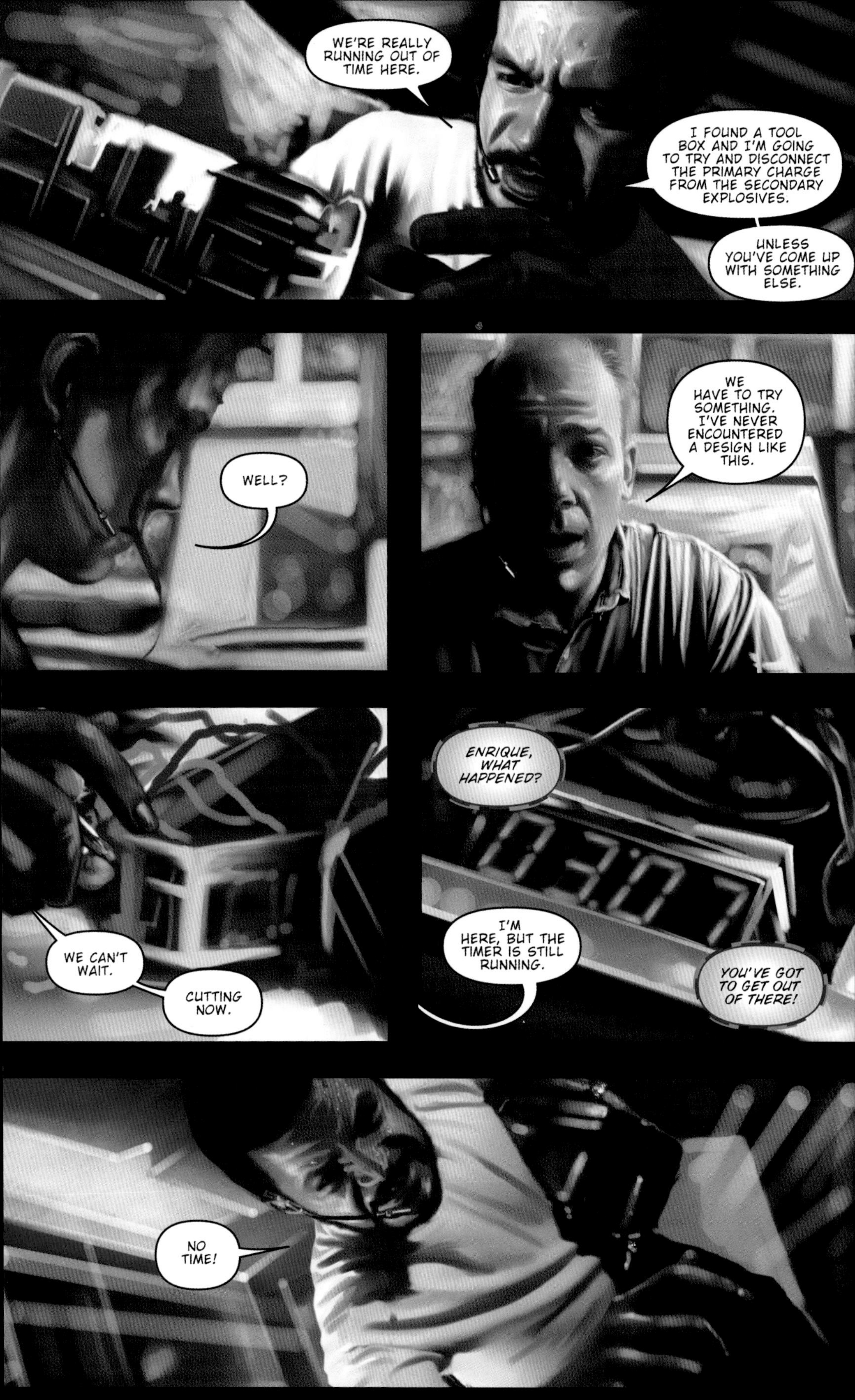
WE'RE REALLY RUNNING OUT OF TIME HERE.
I FOUND A TOOL BOX AND I'M GOING TO TRY AND DISCONNECT THE PRIMARY CHARGE FROM THE SECONDARY EXPLOSIVES.
UNLESS YOU'VE COME UP WITH SOMETHING ELSE.
WELL?
WE HAVE TO TRY SOMETHING. I'VE NEVER ENCOUNTERED A DESIGN LIKE THIS.
WE CAN'T WAIT.
CUTTING NOW.
ENRIQUE, WHAT HAPPENED?
I'M HERE, BUT THE TIMER IS STILL RUNNING.
YOU'VE GOT TO GET OUT OF THERE!
NO TIME!

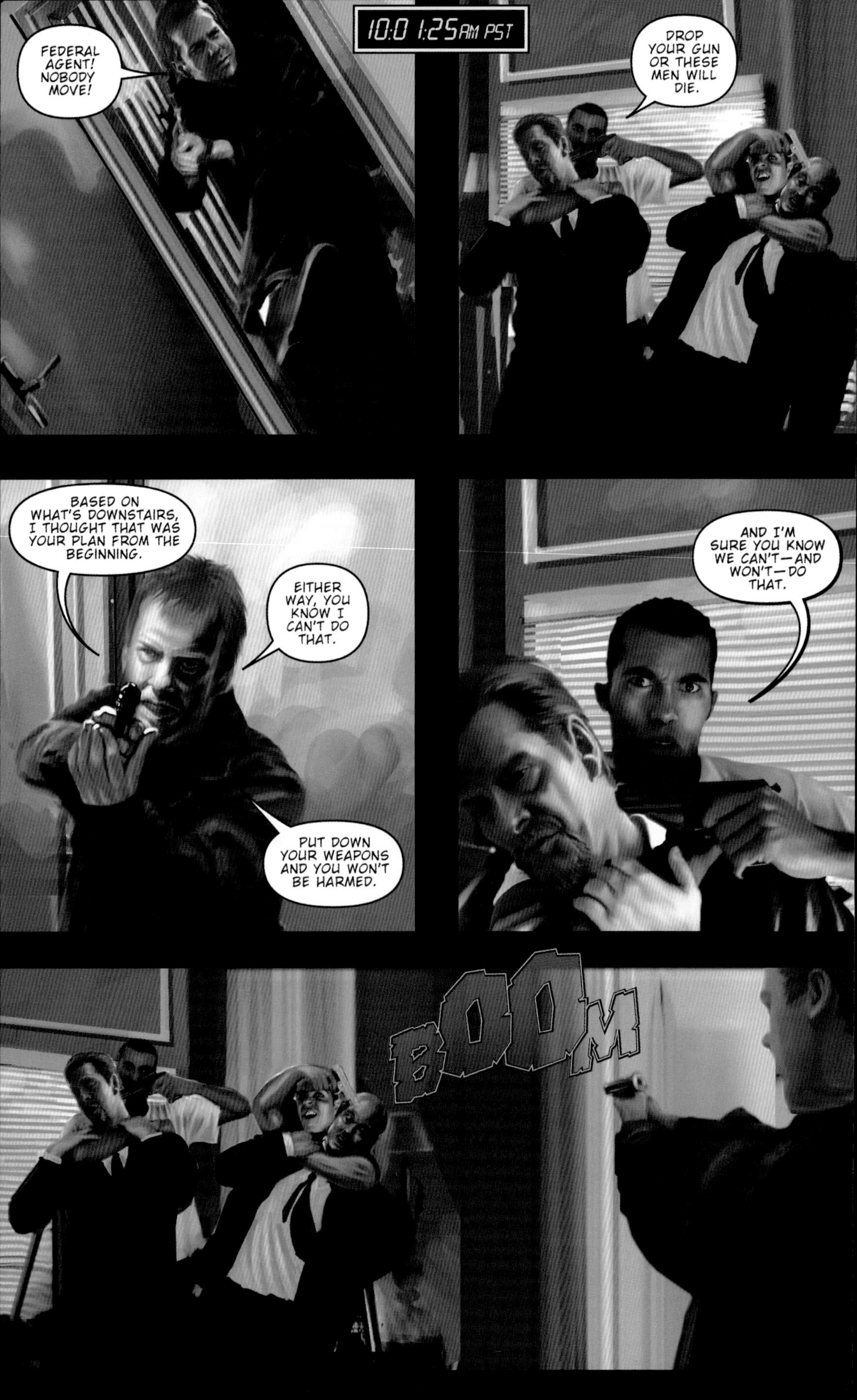
10:01:25 AM PST
FEDERAL AGENT! NOBODY MOVE!
DROP YOUR GUN OR THESE MEN WILL DIE.
BASED ON WHAT'S DOWNSTAIRS, I THOUGHT THAT WAS YOUR PLAN FROM THE BEGINNING.
EITHER WAY, YOU KNOW I CAN'T DO THAT.
PUT DOWN YOUR WEAPONS AND YOU WON'T BE HARMED.
AND I'M SURE YOU KNOW WE CAN'T—AND WON'T—DO THAT.
BOOM

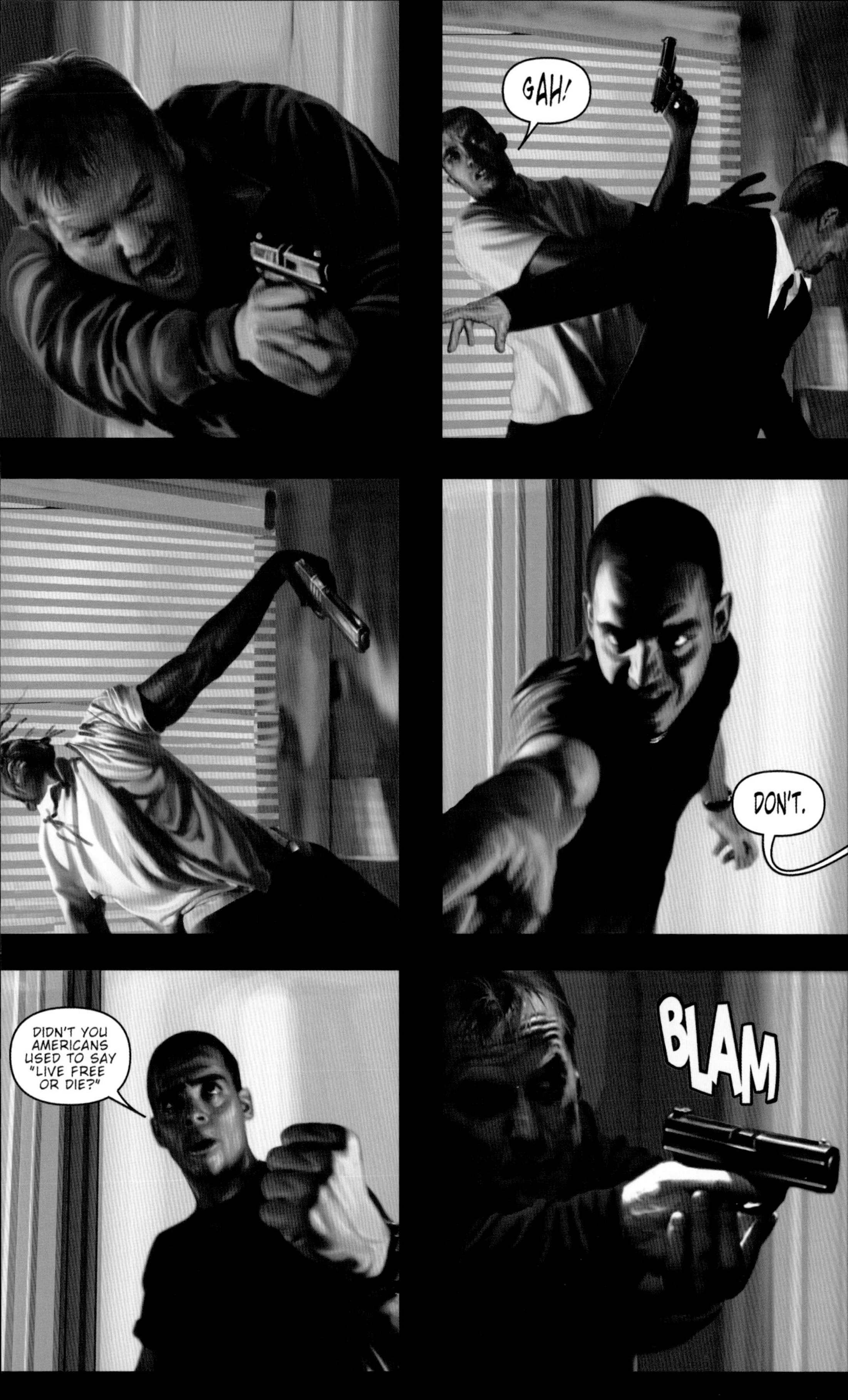
GAH!
DON'T.
DIDN'T YOU AMERICANS USED TO SAY "LIVE FREE OR DIE?"
BLAM

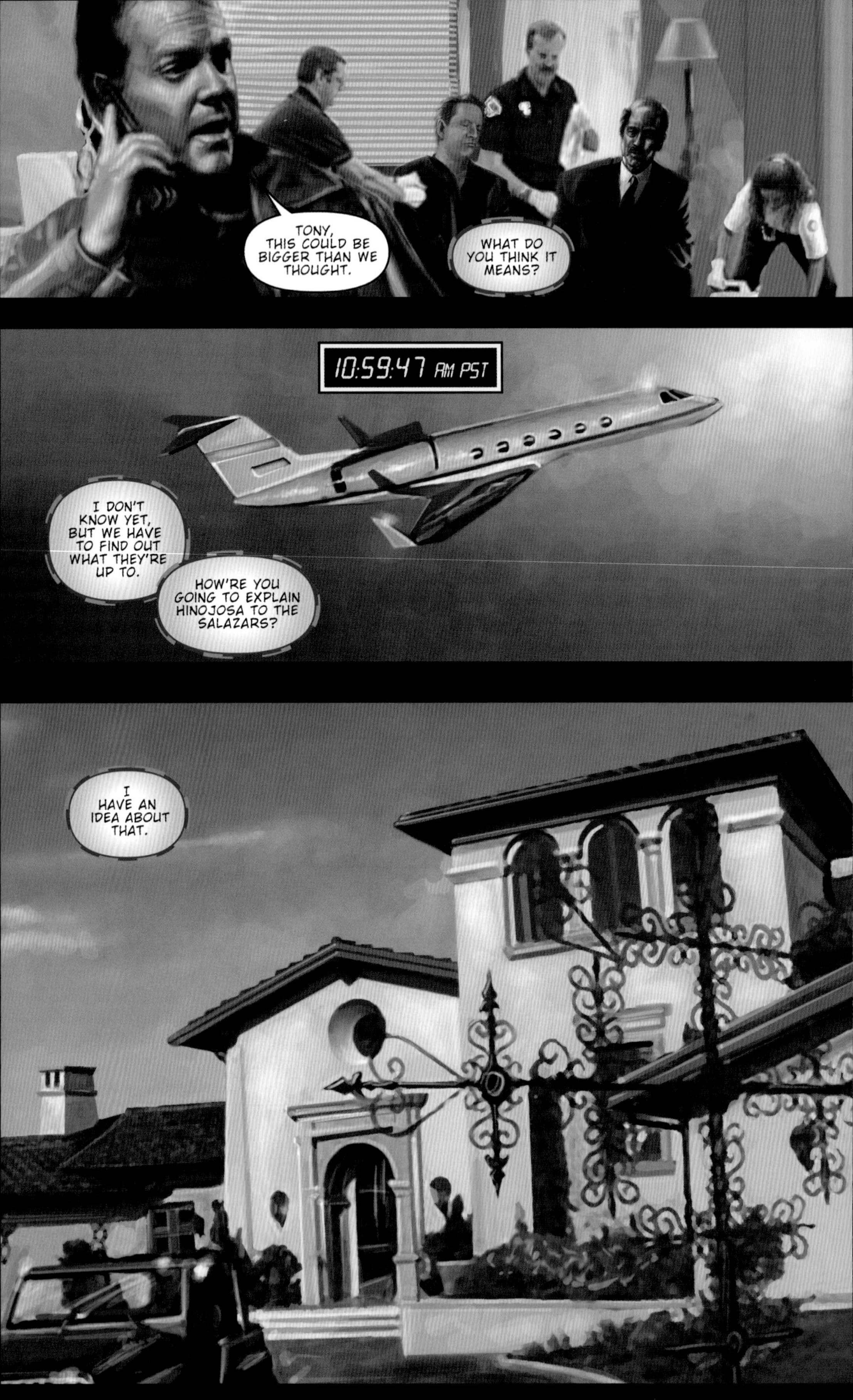
TONY, THIS COULD BE BIGGER THAN WE THOUGHT.
WHAT DO YOU THINK IT MEANS?
10:59:47 AM PST
I DON'T KNOW YET, BUT WE HAVE TO FIND OUT WHAT THEY'RE UP TO.
HOW'RE YOU GOING TO EXPLAIN HINOJOSA TO THE SALAZARS?
I HAVE AN IDEA ABOUT THAT.

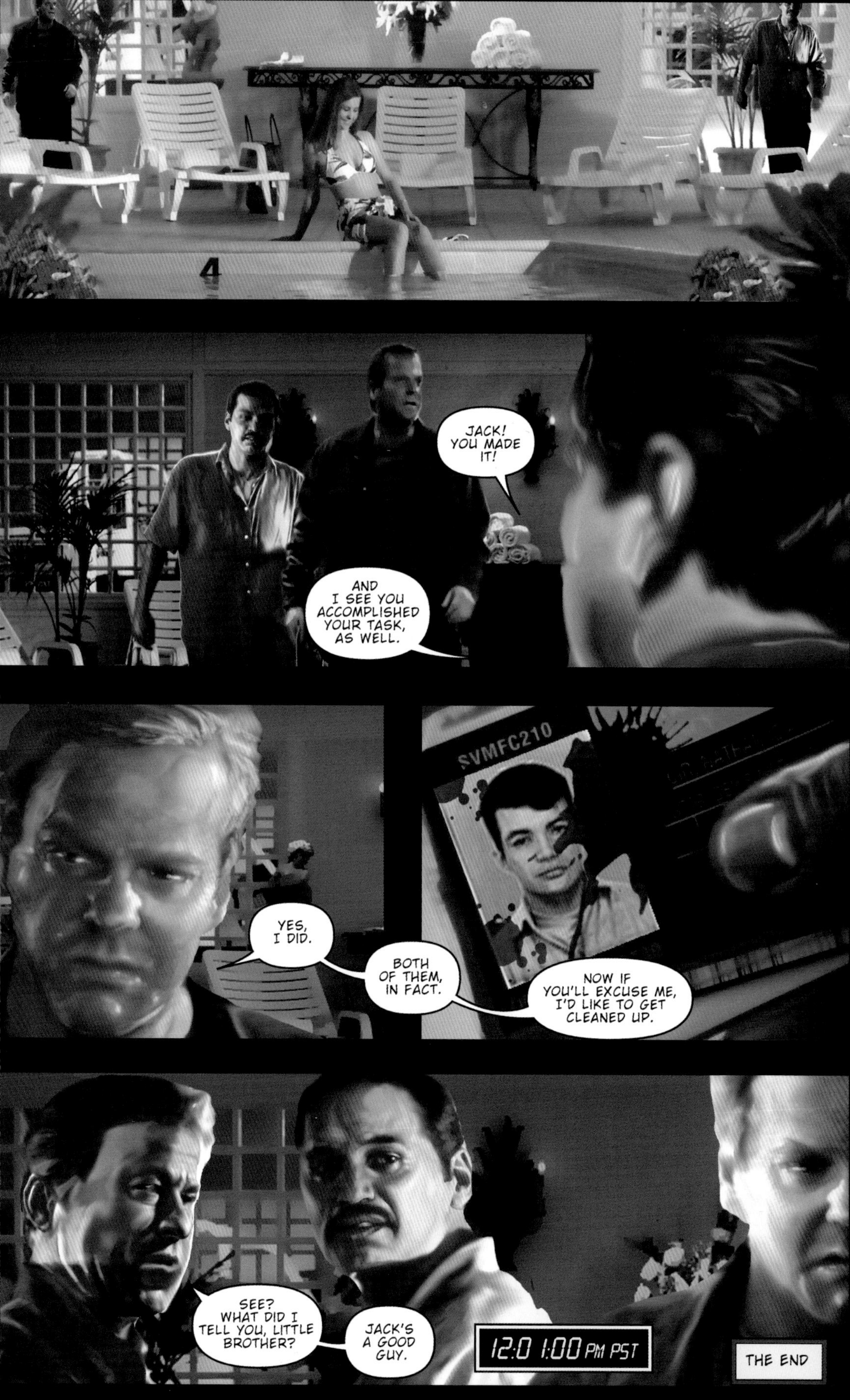
JACK! YOU MADE IT!
AND I SEE YOU ACCOMPLISHED YOUR TASK, AS WELL.
SVMFC210
YES, I DID.
BOTH OF THEM, IN FACT.
NOW IF YOU'LL EXCUSE ME, I'D LIKE TO GET CLEANED UP.
SEE? WHAT DID I TELL YOU, LITTLE BROTHER?
JACK'S A GOOD GUY.
12:01:00 PM PST
THE END

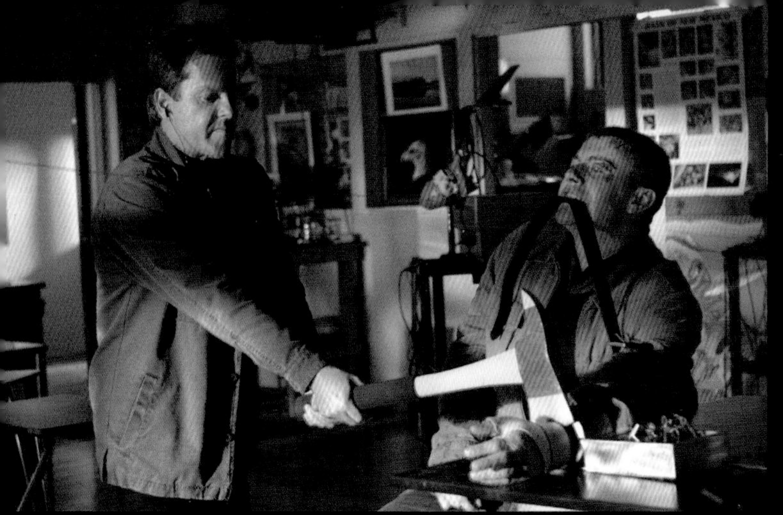

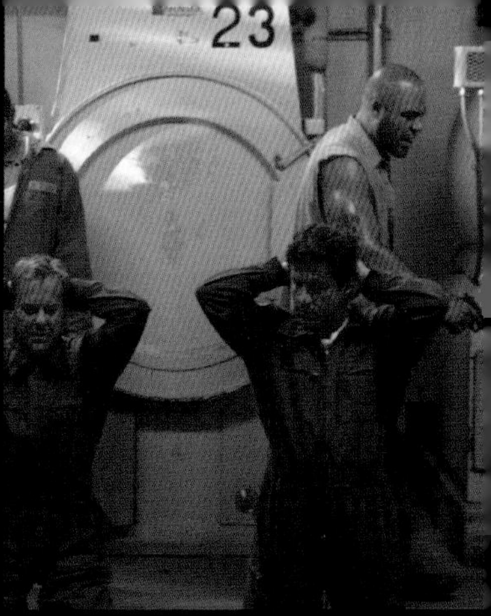
23

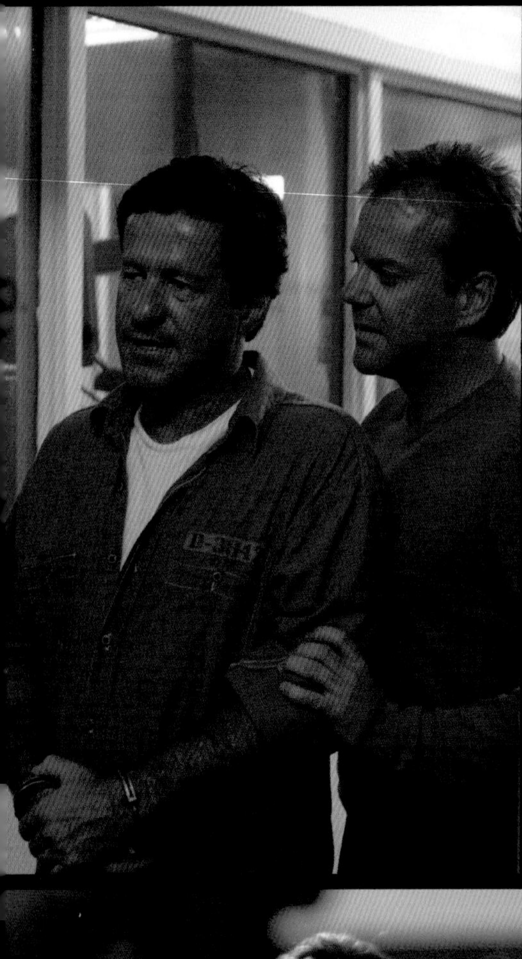

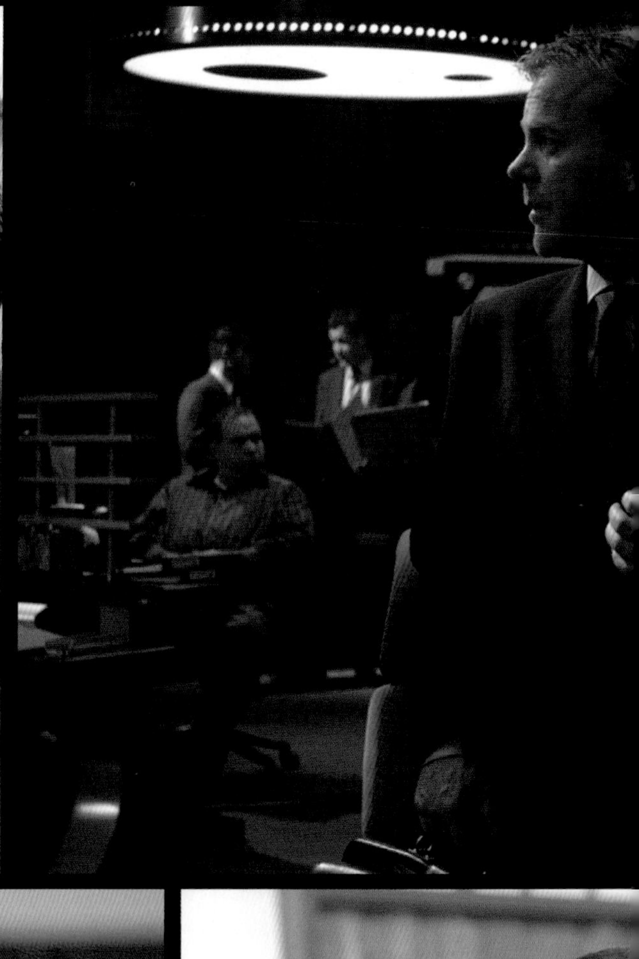

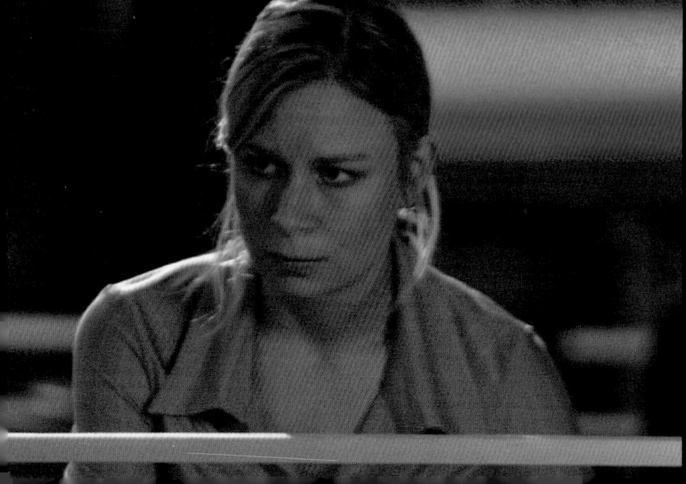

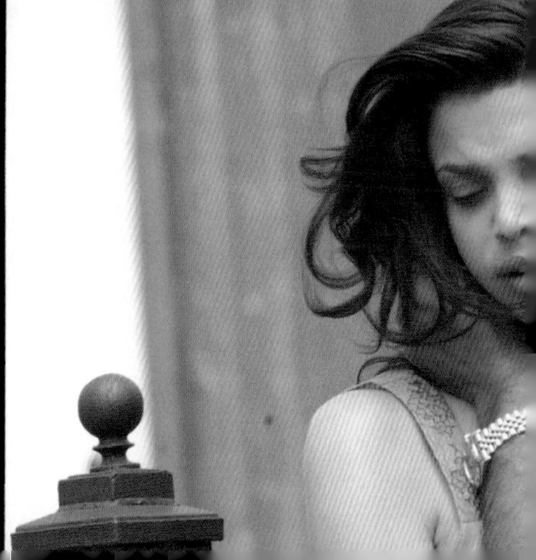

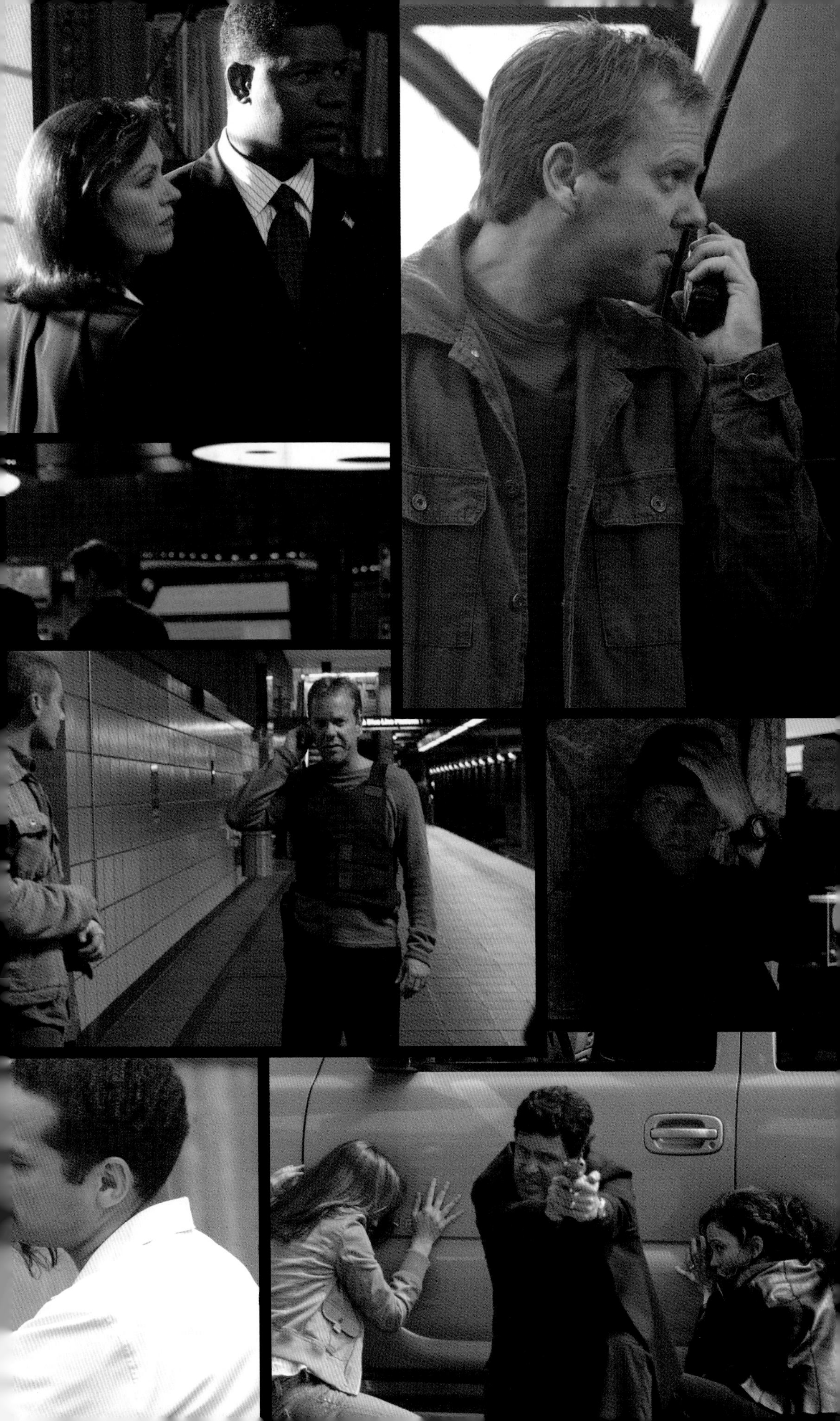

Books of interest from IDW Publishing

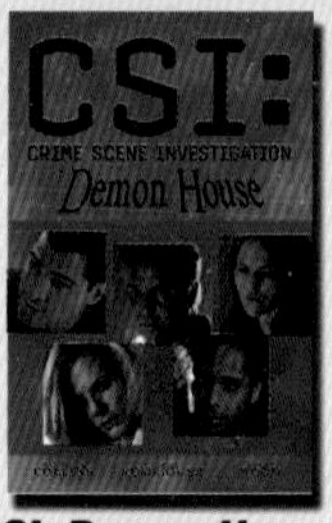
CSI:
CRIME SCENE INVESTIGATION
Demon House

CSI: Demon House
Max Allan Collins
Gabriel Rodriguez/Ashley Wood
124 pages • $19.99
ISBN: 1-932382-34-8

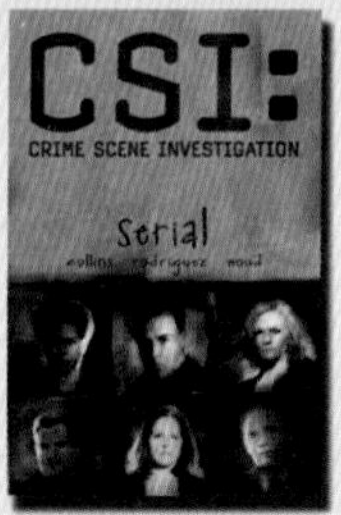
CSI:
CRIME SCENE INVESTIGATION
Serial
collins rodriguez wood

CSI: Serial
Max Allan Collins
Gabriel Rodriguez/Ashley Wood
144 pages • $19.99
ISBN: 1-932382-02-X

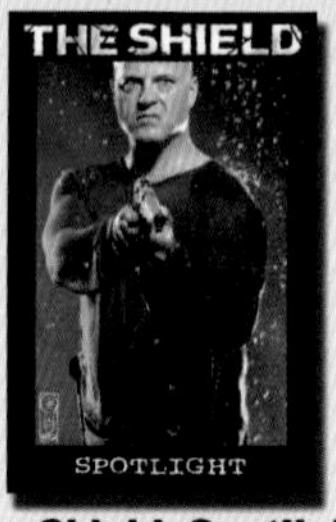
THE SHIELD
SPOTLIGHT

The Shield: Spotlight
Jeff Mariotte
Jean Diaz/Tommy Lee Edwards
128 pages • $19.99
ISBN: 1-932382-23-2

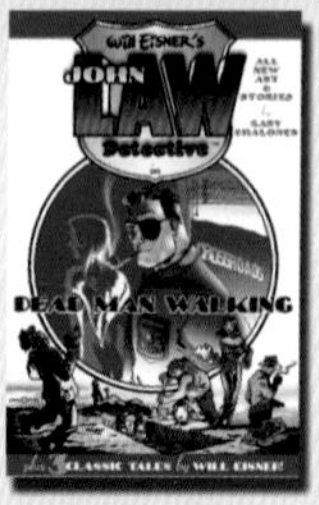
JOHN LAW
Detective
DEAD MAN WALKING

Will Eisner's John Law
Will Eisner/Gary Chaloner
80 pages • $14.99
ISBN: 1-932382-27-5

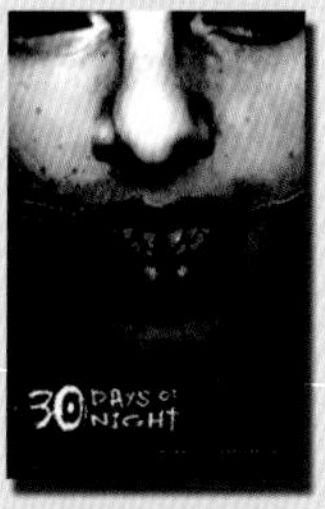
30 DAYS OF NIGHT

30 Days of Night
Steve Niles/Ben Templesmith
104 pages • $17.99
ISBN: 0-9719775-5-0

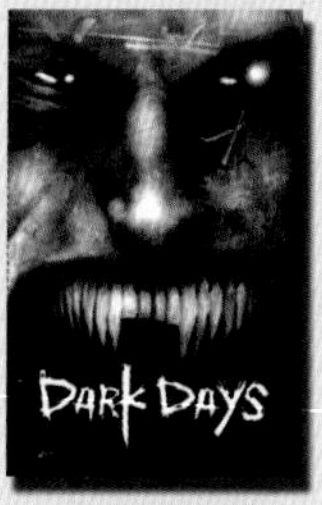
DARK DAYS

Dark Days
Steve Niles/Ben Templesmith
144 pages • $19.99
ISBN: 1-932382-16-X

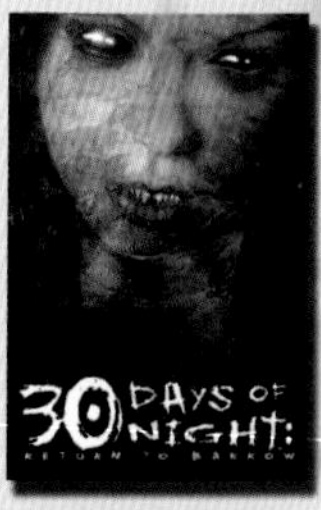
30 DAYS OF NIGHT:
RETURN TO BARROW

30 Days of Night:
Return to Barrow
Steve Niles/Ben Templesmith
144 pages • $19.99
ISBN: 1-932382-36-4

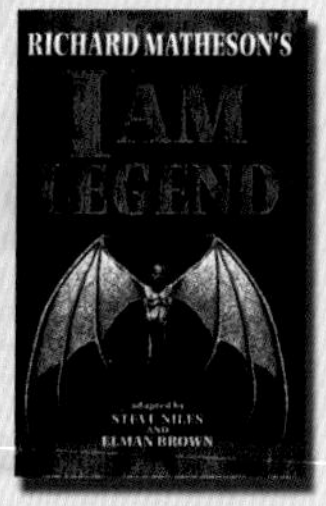
RICHARD MATHESON'S
I AM LEGEND

Richard Matheson's
I Am Legend
adapted by Steve Niles/Elman Bro
248 pages • HC • $35.00
ISBN: 1-932382-08-9

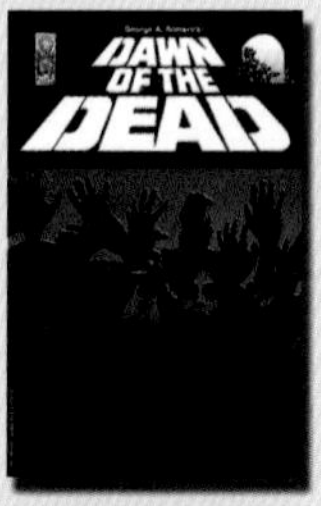
DAWN OF THE DEAD

George A. Romero's
Dawn of the Dead
Steve Niles/Chee
104 pages • $17.99
ISBN: 1-932382-32-1

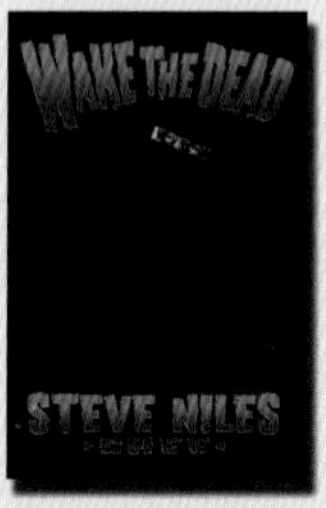
WAKE THE DEAD
STEVE NILES

Wake the Dead
Steve Niles/Chee
128 pages • $19.99
ISBN: 1-932382-22-4

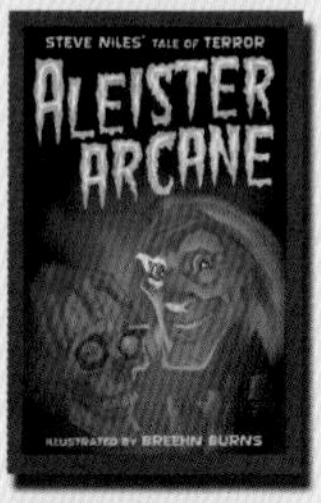
STEVE NILES' TALE OF TERROR
ALEISTER ARCANE
ILLUSTRATED BY BREEHN BURNS

Aleister Arcane
Steve Niles/Breehn Burns
104 pages • $17.99
ISBN: 1-932382-33-X

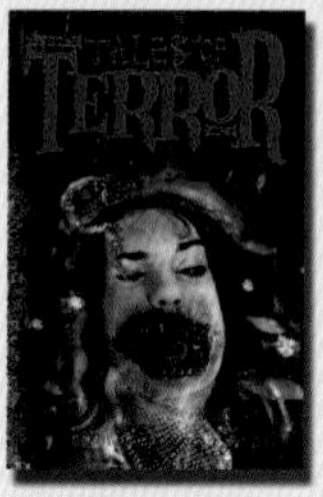
TALES OF TERROR

IDW's Tales of Terror
Various
96 pages • HC • $16.99
ISBN: 1-932382-31-3

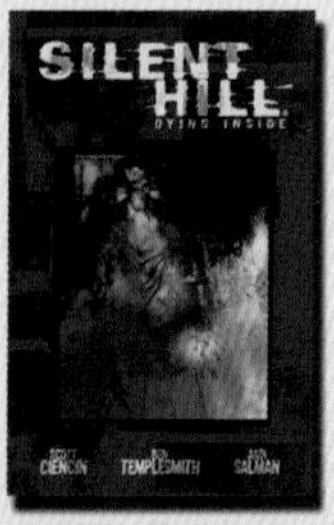
SILENT HILL
DYING INSIDE
CIENCIN TEMPLESMITH SALMAN

Silent Hill: Dying Inside
Scott Ciencin/Ben Templesmith
Aadi Salman/Ashley Wood
128 pages • $19.99
ISBN: 1-932382-24-0

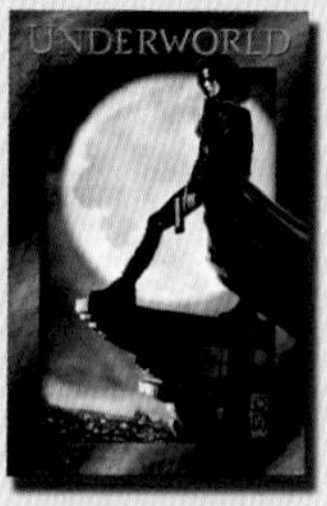
UNDERWORLD

Underworld
Kris Oprisko/Danny McBride
Nick Postic/Nick Marinkovich
144 pages • $19.99
ISBN: 1-932382-26-7

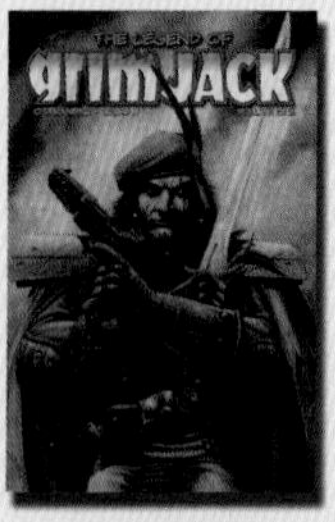
GRIMJACK

The Legend of GrimJack
Volume One
John Ostrander/Timothy Truman
128 pages • $19.99
ISBN: 1-932382-51-8

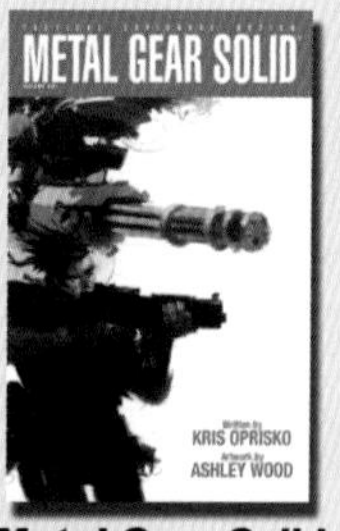
METAL GEAR SOLID
KRIS OPRISKO
ASHLEY WOOD

Metal Gear Solid
Volume 1
Kris Oprisko • Ashley Wood
152 pages • $19.99
ISBN: 1-932382-81-X

www.**idwpublishing**.com